ANGLING
& THE LAW

PETER CARTY & SIMON PAYNE

MERLIN UNWIN BOOKS

First published in Britain by Merlin Unwin Books, 1998
ISBN 1873674309

Published by
Merlin Unwin Books
Palmers House
7 Corve Street, Ludlow
Shropshire SY8 1DB

British Library Cataloguing-in-Publication Data:
A catalogue record for this book is available from the British Library.

Designed and typeset in Times by Merlin Unwin Books.
Printed in Great Britain by Redwood Books.

CONTENTS

GLOSSARY OF TERMS & ABBREVIATIONS

Common Law	Judge made law based on the concept of precedent
Corporeal fishery:	Fishery owned together with the land
CGT:	Capital Gains Tax
CJ:	Chief Justice
Comm Reg Dec	Commons Registration Decision
CRA:	Commons Registration Act 1965
Crib:	A wicker work fish trap usually used for trapping salmon
Cross line:	A fixed line (ie. fixed to the bank in some way) normally with a number of baited hooks or lures which passes from one side of a river or lake to another
Cruive:	A wickerwork or, occasionally, wooden enclosure placed in tidal waters or on weirs mainly used for trapping salmon or sea trout
DAO:	Designation area order
DETR:	Department of the Environment, Transport and the Regions
DFA:	Diseases of Fish Acts 1937 & 1983
Draft net:	See Seine net
Exclusive fishery:	A fishery in the ownership of one or more persons from which they may exclude others
EIA:	Environmental Impact Assessment
EPA:	Environmental Protection Act 1990
Fishing mill dam:	A dam used partly for the purpose of taking fish or allowing fish to be taken (eg. in traps on the weir) and partly to supply water for other purposes (eg milling)
Fishing weir:	Any obstruction fixed to the banks or bed of a river across part or all of the river (whether temporary or permanent) and used exclusively for taking fish (eg. by trap) or to help them to be taken (by the fish coming into a place from which they may be easily removed)
Gaff:	Barbed fishing spear
IDB:	Internal Drainage Board
Incorporeal fishery:	Fishing rights owner separately from the land
Injunction:	Court order ordering the defendant to refrain from or to do an act
Keep net:	A net for keeping live fish in, normally with a view to release. These are commonly used in coarse fishing especially match fishing to allow a precise tally (and weight) of fish caught to be determined
Keep sack:	A sack for keeping live fish in, normally with a view to release. These are typically used for keeping large or specimen fish in (eg. carp)
Kelt:	Salmon which have recently spawned
LA:	Larceny Act 1861
LCJ:	Lord Chief Justice
LDA:	Land Drainage Act 1991
LGFA:	Local Government Finance Act 1988
LGRA:	Local Government and Rating Act 1997
LFDC:	Local Flood Drainage Committee
LJ:	Lord Justice
LNR:	Local Nature Reserve
LRA:	Land Registration Act 1925
LTA:	Landlord and Tenant Act 1954

MAFF:	Ministry of Agriculture Fisheries and Food
Medium filum:	Imaginary boundary line running down the middle of a watercourse
Main river:	River under control of Environment Agency for land drainage purposes
Members' club:	A Society of persons who join together to form an unincorporated (ie. not a company) association (see Chapter 9)
NFA:	National Federation of Anglers
NFSA:	National Federation of Sea Anglers
Non-main river:	River not in control of Environment Agency for land drainage purposes
NLO:	Net Limitation Order
NRA:	National Rivers Authority
Otter lath or jack:	A combination of running out lures or bait by hand line or rod and line, but using something (eg. a pole or floating piece of wood or even a small boat or vessel according to s.1 Salmon and Freshwater Fisheries Act 1975) between the bait or lure allowing fishing in a place or way which could not be achieved without the presence of the otter lath or jack. The classic example of 'otter fishing' according to *Alton v Parker* (1891) is fishing from a boat with a hook attached to a free floating piece of wood about eighteen inches long (the 'otter').
PA:	Prescription Act 1832
PACE:	Police and Criminal Evidence Act 1984
PPG:	Planning Policy Guidance Note
Prescription:	Acquired ownership of fishing rights through long use and enjoyment (see 4.1, Chapter 5)
Profit à prendre:	See incorporeal fishery above
Putt/putcher/ putt nets:	Fish traps made of baskets of wickerwork, erected upon stages, typically firmly fixed in the shore by stakes about 13 or 14 feet high and bound together by cross bars, on which rests the putts placed one above the other with the side mouth up or down stream, as they are intended to take fish on the ebb or flow of the tide. The putts themselves are long conical baskets, typically with a mouth from three to five feet wide, and end in a narrow point that will prevent a fish of moderate size passing through.
QC:	Queen's Counsel
RFAC:	Regional fisheries advisory committee
RFDC:	Regional flood defence committee
Riparian owner:	The owner of land touching a lake or river (see Chapter 6)
Riparian rights:	Rights deriving from riparian ownership (see Chapter 6)
SA:	Salmon Act 1986
SAFFA:	Salmon and Freshwater Fisheries Act 1975
Salmon coop:	A device for trapping salmon and sea trout which will normally be paced on a weir and will trap the fish as they migrate upstream. A coop consists of two wooden frames set at about 45° to each other with a gap at the apex (which is at the downstream end). When the coop is being used, the passage of the fish out of the top of the apex is obstructed by further frames and the fish trapped in the coop can be netted out.
SATA:	Salmon and Trout Association
Seine net:	Seine nets are long nets with a weighted bottom edge and floats on the top edge to keep this at, or near, the waters surface. They are stretched out into a river, lake or estuary (normally by a boat) and then

	drawn in to the shore trapping the fish in the area of water enclosed.
Set line:	Any unattended line (normally fixed to the bank but potentially simply an abandoned rod) with one or more baited hooks or lures attached to it. Similar to a cross line but not attached to both banks
Several fishery:	Same as exclusive fishery above
SFC:	Sea fisheries committee
SFRA:	Sea Fisheries Regulation Act 1966
SI:	Statutory instrument
Snatches:	This is an illegal fishing line used with a view to foul hooking a fish
SSSI:	Site of special scientific interest
Stake nets:	This is a fixed vertical net normally located in shallow or inter-tidal waters and fixed in place with stakes. It is normally arranged so that there is only a small entrance to the net and therefore as the tide recedes, fish are trapped.
Stroke hauls:	This is a contraption consisting of three hooks fixed together back to back and weighted with lead, and used to attempt to foul hook fish
TA:	Theft Act 1968
TCPA:	Town and Country Planning Act 1990
Trunk:	Perforated floating box in which fish are kept
TSA:	Territorial Sea Act 1987
Water keeper:	Non Environment Agency water bailiff
WA:	Water Act 1989
WCA:	Wildlife and Countryside Act 1981
WRA:	Water Resources Act 1991
Unclean fish:	Fish that is spawning or has just spawned
UNCLOS:	United Nations Convention on the Law of the Sea 1982
VAT:	Value Added Tax

List of Cases

LIST OF STATUTES

LIST OF STATUTORY INSTRUMENTS

LIST OF EC DIRECTIVES

FOREWORD

It is over 20 years since Michael Gregory's classic text *Angling and the Law* was published. We are both grateful for Michael's support in writing a new book on the subject. His work set a high standard to follow. We have done our best. Many important legal changes have taken place in angling law over the intervening years - the growth of a comprehensive law of environmental protection, the Salmon and Freshwater Fisheries Act 1975 and Salmon Act 1986 being the main highlights.

Writing any legal textbook is like shooting at a moving target. The law is constantly evolving, and periodically goes through periods of revolutionary change. With a comprehensive review of fisheries legislation being undertaken by the present Government and proposals for major changes (improvements from the anglers' point of view) to the law relating to water abstraction in the pipeline, the extent of our problem may be appreciated. We have stated the law as at 1 January 1998, but where possible have incorporated more recent developments.

There are a number of people whose help we would wish to acknowledge. Simon Jackson for reading draft chapters and offering constructive criticism, and whose practical experience of acting for anglers and clubs is second to none. Peter's mother Audrey for her hard work and patience in typing the text, amending it and amending it again. Merlin Unwin for taking on the project and his patient good humour in dealing with us. We have received help from various sources but the final text is ours and so, therefore, are any errors.

We have written this book with the angler, riparian owner and angling club in mind. As anglers ourselves and with our legal experience, we have tried to identify the ways in which the law impacts on angling, how it may be used to protect fishing interests, and how legal pitfalls may be avoided. We hope it is of interest and use.

Peter Carty, London
Simon Payne, Plymouth

July 1998

CHAPTER 1

FRAMEWORK OF ANGLING LAW

This chapter is concerned with the various sources of law relating to fishing from modern day statutes and regulations to ancient rights based on established case law principles. In addition, it explains the organisation, powers and duties of those involved in regulating fishing. Finally, it introduces to those not familiar with the law some of the basic legal concepts which are encountered elsewhere within the book.

1. SOURCES OF ANGLING LAW

In general terms, law in England and Wales may be derived from a variety of diverse sources. Angling law is no different. In broad terms, the sources may be from statutory sources passed by Parliament (also called legislation), or what are called common law sources: law based on case law built up over many years. These sources and some other less significant origins of angling law are considered in more detail.

1.1 Statutes and statutory instruments

Acts of Parliament which have been passed by both the House of Commons and House of Lords called statutes are an important source. These Acts are divided in sections and sub-sections referred to by number and letter and may frequently include details in Schedules which are rather like an appendix or annex to the key text but in the case of statutes are part of the law which is passed. Statutes frequently include powers for the appropriate minister in the government (normally in the case of angling law the Minister for Agriculture Food and Fisheries, Secretary of State for the Environment, Transport and Regions (formerly the Secretary of State for the Environment but since May 1997 reorganised and expanded by the new Labour Government) or Secretary of State for Wales), to make regulations or orders (also called delegated legislation). These regulations or orders are often called statutory instruments. They have to be passed by Parliament but can be approved on very much faster procedures than a statute. Where a statute may take many months to become law regulations often take only a few weeks. In the case of statutory instruments the passing of the enabling section in the statute (which enables or gives power to the minister to make the regulations) establishes the principle and the detail of how the principle is to be implemented is left to the regulations. Thus statutes and statutory instruments are inevitably bound together.

1.1.1 Examples of statutes and statutory instruments in angling law

Perhaps the single most important statute on freshwater fishing whether coarse or game is the Salmon and Freshwater Fisheries Act 1975 (SAFFA). Throughout this book you will find numerous references to it. For example it contains laws on how you may fish, what alterations may be made to fisheries to avoid obstructions to fish, fishing licences and powers of water bailiffs. As to statutory instruments, under s.28 SAFFA the Minister for Agriculture Fisheries and Food can make an order for the general regulation of fisheries within an area. In 1977, statutory instrument number 1586 was made prohibiting the use of a gaff on the River Thames (this has now been superseded by national byelaws banning the use of gaffs throughout England and Wales). There is some concern when important issues of law are left to be dealt with by statutory instrument. This arises because of the ease with which a statutory instrument can be made by Parliament compared with the relatively entrenched position of a statute or primary legislation as it is called. This issue arose for anglers for example during the passage of the Environment Bill (now Environment Act 1995) through Parliament. Angling groups were concerned that the obligation on the National Rivers Authority (as it then was) to advertise applications for consent to discharge pollutants into rivers and streams was being eroded by being left to subsidiary (ie. statutory instrument) legislation rather than, as it had been, in primary legislation (Schedule 10 of the Water Resources Act 1991). For specific detail on this issue see Chapter 9.

1.1.2 Interpretation of statutes and statutory instruments

The words used in any statute seek to be as precise as possible. Indeed most statutes include a section devoted entirely to definitions usually called the 'Interpretation' section. However, inevitably there are ambiguities over what precisely any particular section of a statute may mean. In these cases it is left to the courts (if necessary the appeal courts) to interpret the statute. When they do so they develop what is called common (or judge made) law. The common law system in England and Wales is not completely hit or miss and unpredictable, the interpretation does not just depend on the particular judge or how he or she is feeling. Although the details of the system are beyond the needs of anglers interested in the law, the common law is based on the doctrine of precedent. This in broad terms requires that recognition is given to previous decided cases and in the case of decision by the higher courts of appeal (the Court of Appeal and House of Lords) that previous decisions must be followed by lower courts. Court decisions are very often (and in the case of appeal decisions invariably) reported in a variety of law reports so that they can be accessed by lawyers and judges anxious to properly apply the common law. Thus, a body of case law builds up providing greater detail on how a particular statute or statutory instrument should be applied. An example of these principles in operation is the case of *R v Dovermoss* (1995) which concerned the meaning of 'poisonous noxious or polluting matter'. Section 85 of the 1991 Water Resources Act prohibits the entry of such matter into 'controlled waters' which includes freshwater streams and rivers. The Court of Appeal had to decide whether the slurry which was washed off a farmer's fields by rainfall was 'poisonous noxious or polluting' given that all it had done was cause local drinking water to taste and smell unpleasant. The Court of Appeal interpreted s 85 as preventing the entry of matter which was likely to make water physically impure, foul, filthy, dirtied, tainted, stained or befouled. The effect of the slurry therefore made it polluting matter. The statement of these principles will now be binding on any future judge (except if the matter were to be considered by our highest court of appeal, the House of Lords) who has to decide the same sort of issue.

1.2 Common law

The common law is not only about interpreting or putting 'the meat on the bones' of statutes. It also concerns, perhaps more importantly, the contribution of the judges to developing certain principles independently of Parliament and statute. Whereas statutes and regulations and their interpretation tend to concentrate on public law issues, the regulation of fishing by public bodies in what is perceived to be the public interest is concerned with private law rights. That is the rights which exist between two or more private individuals and do not involve public regulation by the police, Environment Agency or water bailiffs. So for example common law has developed the law of tort. In broad terms a tort is a duty owed by one person to another without the need to prove any pre-existing contractual or other relationship between the persons involved. This includes ancient rights of landowners to take action if someone trespasses on their land. The action will normally result in an award of damages to the landowner against the trespasser or in some cases where the trespass is still going on or is likely to be repeated a court order (or injunction) preventing this from taking place. As trespass is (without more for example malicious damage or theft) in most cases a civil matter (but bear in mind the Criminal Justice and Public Order Act 1994) the much quoted 'Trespassers will be prosecuted' rarely has any truth behind the threat. Similarly in the case of the owners of fishing rights they may be able to bring an action based on the law of tort , in fact the tort of private nuisance, where the flow or water quality of their stretch of river has been adversely affected. Damages might be sought for lost fish and injunctions to prevent future harm (see Chapter 10). The common law is flexible in how it applies the general principles to any particular case although this does result in a degree of uncertainty as to how a particular case may be dealt with. For example, in *Rawson v Peters* (1972) the court, in applying the general principle that the owner of fishing rights can bring an action in nuisance for disturbance, held that canoeists passing up and down a non-navigable river were liable in nuisance (see Chapter 16). The common law, besides developing principles in the law of tort, has also developed in numerous other areas but of particular relevance to angling is the law of contract. This is important in terms of running fishing clubs and acquiring fishing rights and fish for stocking.

1.3 Civil and criminal law and public and private law

In considering any of the sources of law it is important to bear in mind whether the law which is being considered is *civil* or *criminal* in nature. This affects which courts have to be used, who is involved in any court action and what the consequences are. To make matters more confusing the same facts may give rise to consequences in civil or private law and public law. An example will illustrate this. Suppose that a farmer has a failure with his silage clamp and a large quantity of highly polluting raw silage enters a local river. The matter is reported promptly to the local office of the Environment Agency (who as will be seen are responsible for regulating water pollution) who immediately send out a team who spend time and money trying to contain the incident. Regrettably the pollution results in the death of over 1,000 trout on the river. A local fishing club own the fishing rights. In terms of public law both the SAFFA and Water Resources Act 1991 apply. These allow the Environment Agency to prosecute the farmer for having committed crimes under both Acts. The prosecution will be brought in magistrates court in first instance but might (although in most cases will not) be finally dealt with in the Crown Court. If the Environment Agency do not bring a prosecution it is possible but very unusual for a private prosecution to be brought by someone who has an interest in what happened. Perhaps the fishing club might do this. In any event if a prosecution is brought and the farmer convicted (after either pleading guilty or after a trial having pleaded not guilty) he will be punished. This will normally be by way of a fine. The maximum fine in the magistrates court is £20,000 and in the Crown Court it is unlimited. In theory the farmer could be imprisoned for up to two years. In reality the likely fine in a case like this is a few thousand pounds. That money does not go to the Environment Agency. Nor does it go to the fishing club. It will go into government coffers.

At the same time in public law under s.161 of the Water Resources Act 1991 the Environment Agency may seek to recover the costs of the works they undertook to try to limit the incident. If the farmer will not agree to pay up this will go to the civil courts County or High Court depending on the amount involved and complexity of the dispute.

Finally, in private law the fishing club might sue the farmer (who may well have insurers who deal with the case for him) for the damages they have suffered on the basis that the pollution of their fishery amounted to a private nuisance under the law of tort. This will be undertaken in the civil courts where the fishing club will be the plaintiff and the farmer the defendant. If successful the fishing club will obtain judgement against the defendant for a sum of money to represent their loss. If the pollution was continuing or thought to be likely to recur an injunction might be obtained as well requiring the farmer to take steps to prevent this. All of these principles are explored in much more detail in the rest of the book but it is essential to understand the underlying classifications of the law.

1.4 Byelaws

In practice an important source of angling law are byelaws. Although over the years the public bodies responsible for fisheries have changed (now the principal body responsible is the Environment Agency) there have long been powers for byelaws to be made concerning fishing. This is another type of delegated legislation (like statutory instruments) only in this case instead of the power to make laws being delegated to a government minister it is placed in the hands of a public body. The current law is contained in section 210 and Schedule 25 of the Water Resources Act 1991 which allows the Environment Agency to make byelaws both specifically for fisheries purposes and in respect of certain navigable waters to regulate fishing. Existing byelaws made by the National Rivers Authority or water authorities before water privatisation in 1989 remain valid although the Agency could review, update or abolish them if it wishes. SAFFA is the principal statute under which fishing byelaws have, in the past, been made.

In addition to the powers of the Agency to make byelaws statutory water undertakers, basically the privatised water companies, may also make byelaws regulating fishing owned or managed by it under the Water Industry Act 1991.

The byelaw making powers of the Environment Agency and specific fishery byelaws are considered below.

1.5 Other sources of law

In addition to the basic sources of law outlined above one or two other matters need to be borne in mind.

1.5.1 European law

As a member of the European Union some of the law relating to fishing and to water is derived from European law. The European Union has got specific power to pass laws on the environment inserted into the amended 1957 Treaty of Rome in 1986 by a subsequent Treaty called the Single European Act. Although European law may take the form of decisions, regulations or directives in the sphere of the environment and recreational fishing, it is directives which are the only source of significance. Directives require that the members of the European Union (for example the United Kingdom) implement laws and other necessary measures to comply with what the Directive says within a time period specified in the Directive. Thus, a Directive will lead to some form of UK law if it is implemented. Typically that will be a statute or statutory instrument. An example of European law in the angling area is the Freshwater Fish Directive (Directive No 78/659) passed in 1978. Member states under the Directive must achieve minimum water quality standards for salmon, trout or grayling or salmonoid waters and coarse or cyprinid waters which are so designated by the Member State. As the Directive does not actually require any particular waters to be designated by a member state it is of limited practical effect. No specific UK law has been passed in respect of the Directive but its quality standards can be achieved through the Water Resources Act 1991 *(*see Chapter 9).

1.5.2 Customary law

Law may also be derived through very long standing customs or practices. Customary law forms the basis for some law which affects fishing. For example, the rules on foreshore fishing rights lie in ancient custom (see Chapter 8).

1.5.3 Guidance notes and codes of practice

In many cases, particularly concerning environmental protection, the Government may issue guidance notes or Codes of Practice. Sometimes these are specifically provided for in a statute and may have to be laid before Parliament. In other cases they are entirely non-statutory but may be an important indicator of how the law should be applied or interpreted by a particular public body. Strictly these guidance notes are not 'law' but they are very important and persuasive in practice.

An example of this type of 'law' are the Codes of Practice which the Department of the Environment, Transport and the Regions (formerly just the Department of the Environment before the new Labour Government's reorganisation in May 1997) can issue to the Environment Agency on how it should fulfil its environmental and recreational duties under the Environment Act. These are considered later in this chapter. Another important example is the Code of Good Agricultural Practice for the Protection of Water, considered in Chapter 9.

2. BASIC FRAMEWORK OF LEGISLATION ON ANGLING

Legislation on angling may be divided into that concerned with recreational fishing in freshwaters (be it game or coarse) and that about sea angling. In addition, legislation is concerned with establishing the public law framework and the various bodies responsible for angling. Then there is a category of legislation concerned with water flows, quality and pollution. Finally, there are some pieces of legislation concerned with a variety of peripheral matters which anglers or angling clubs may come across.

This section merely sets out the framework of the legislation to give a general overview of how the law fits together. Other parts of the book then deal with the law in much more detail.

2.1 Salmon and Freshwater Fisheries Act 1975 (SAFFA)

There have already been numerous references to this Act in this chapter. For the law on freshwater fishing this is the single most important piece of legislation. It has been periodically amended and updated and continues to be altered. For example, the 1995 Environment Act is changing the 1975 Act to improve the protection of native fish stocks from the risk of swimming into a place from which water is being abstracted by, for example, a farmer or fish farm, and the risk of captive fish in a fish farm escaping.

SAFFA sets out the basic framework of law on:
   (a) Close seasons (see Chapter 14);
   (b) Fishing licences (both for rod and line and commercial netting) (see Chapter 12);
   (c) Banning certain fishing methods (for example the use of explosives!) - (see Chapter 13);
   (d) Protection of fish from water abstraction points by gratings or screens (see Chapter 11);

(e) Anti-pollution criminal offences although the main legislation on this is contained in the Water Resources Act 1991 (see Chapter 9);

(f) Controls over the creation of obstructions to the passage of fish particularly salmon and migratory trout. For example regulations over creating dams and weirs and duties to create and maintain fish passes or ladders (see Chapter 19);

(g) Licensing controls over the introduction of live fish into inland waters (see Chapter 15);

(h) Rules protecting spawning and young fish, for example prohibiting the taking of unclean fish (see Chapter 13).

As the Act sets out this fairly comprehensive range of controls over fishing it is of course important that the rules are backed with 'teeth'. Most of the laws are backed with criminal sanctions if they are breached. SAFFA makes special adaptations to the rules of criminal law to make them fit to the special position of anglers, for example allowing a court to ban someone from holding a fishing licence or requiring their fishing tackle to be forfeited (Schedule 4 SAFFA). Finally, the Act requires a 'police' force to enforce it. These are the Environment Agency water bailiffs who are considered in a little more detail below.

2.2 Salmon Act 1986 (SA)

This Act is concerned with trading in salmon and sea trout. It arose out of concern that 'poached' fish was easily making its way into legitimate shops and markets. The Act therefore sets up a system of dealer licensing and also made it a crime to handle salmon in suspicious circumstances.

2.3 Diseases of Fish Acts 1937 and 1983 (DFA 1937 and 1983)

These Acts are concerned with the control of certain fish diseases, for example furunculosis or fungus. The legislation is aimed at the prompt reporting of disease, the prevention of any further spread of the infection and the monitoring of fish in identified infected waters. There is a specific chapter on fish disease (see Chapter 18).

2.4 Water Resources Act 1991 (WRA)

This Act contains important Agency powers and duties relating to water quality, water pollution control and prevention (see Chapter 9), abstraction and water flows (see Chapter 11). In addition, the Act includes details of a number of the Agency powers, for example on fishery byelaws (Schedule 25). This Act also includes some provisions for the Agency to set up a scheme to improve fisheries and obtain contributions to the costs of such a scheme from the riparian owners (see Chapter 15). Finally, the Act includes restrictions on the works which may be carried out to rivers and lakes without first obtaining Agency consent.

2.5 Land Drainage Act 1991 (LDA)

Steps to control flooding can, particularly when large engineering works are undertaken, have a drastic effect on angling quality. The 1991 Act sets up the framework for authorising flood control measures and includes some checks and balances to protect the interests of those affected including anglers (see Chapter 20). In addition the Act has provisions for permitting in river works and alterations and bridges (see Chapters 15 and 20).

2.6 Sea Fish Regulation Act 1986

This Act is the principal piece of legislation concerned solely with sea fisheries. It is important to bear in mind (see below) that the Environment Agency in many cases is able to regulate activities affecting fishing on estuaries and within coastal waters under the legislation described above. The 1986 Act is not aimed mainly at angling interests. Its focus is on commercial fishing. However, there are overlaps and potential conflicts. The 1986 Act provides for the setting up of local fisheries committees. These committees may make byelaws regulating sea fishing. These may be relevant to anglers for example by banning fishing for or the taking of certain species at particular times. The Salmon Act 1986 extended the byelaw-making powers by allowing the making of byelaws to protect migratory trout and salmon. However, the consent of the Environment Agency is needed before the local fisheries committee can pass any such byelaws.

Breach of any fisheries committee byelaws is a criminal offence with a maximum fine of £5000. The local fisheries committee can appoint fishery officers to ensure the byelaws are being obeyed.

Finally the 1986 Act tries to deal with the issue of overlapping powers and duties especially in respect of estuaries and rivers between a local fisheries committee, the Environment Agency and any harbour authority. This is considered below.

2.7 Miscellaneous legislation

The book aims to cover the law applicable to not only fishing itself but the other matters which anglers or angling clubs may come across through their sport. Because of this there are a wide range of miscellaneous pieces of legislation which may be relevant.

2.7.1 Lead weights

In relation to fishing itself the Control of Pollution (Anglers' Lead Weights) Order 1986 (SI 1986/1992) bans the supply of smaller lead weights.

2.7.2 *Predator control and Wildlife and Countryside Act 1981*

If a fishing club or fisherman wishes to control predators they may find themselves in conflict with wildlife protection legislation under the Wildlife and Countryside Act 1981 (see Chapter 16). In addition the same Act controls the introduction of non-native species to waters in this country (eg. catfish) - (see Chapter 15).

2.7.3 *Miscellaneous legislation on fish stocking*

If a club becomes involved in fish stocking then in addition to the rules concerning the introduction of fish into inland waters under the 1975 Act mentioned above, the law on transportation of live fish (Fish Health Regulations 1992 (SI 1992/3300)) or importation of live fish (Importation of Live Fish (England and Wales) Act 1980 and Animal Health Act 1981) may be relevant.

2.7.4 *Major fishery works and miscellaneous legislation*

If a person or club owns fishing rights but wants to carry out some major works to alter the fishery various pieces of legislation may come into play. First if the works are substantial enough they may require planning consent under the 1990 Town and Country Planning Act (see Chapter 15). If a fish farm is proposed various rules must be complied with including registration under the Diseases of Fish Act 1983 and complying with the Fisheries Act 1981 (see Chapter 18). If (in river) works are required Environment Agency or Drainage Board consent may be needed under WRA or LDA (see Chapter 15).

2.7.5 *Miscellaneous legislation on poaching*

When the issue of poaching arises not only may the 1975 Act and Salmon Act 1986 be relevant but critically in many cases the police will be able to bring a prosecution for theft or attempted theft under the Theft Act 1968. Theft will only be possible to prove as a charge if the fish are in a private pond *R v Steer* (1704). This is the case because wild fish at liberty in a river are not the property of anyone until captured. However to deal with this problem the Theft Act creates criminal offences of unlawfully taking or destroying fish from a private fishery or attempting to do so. A genuine belief by the 'poacher' that they had the right to fish (ie. the consent of the owner) is a good defence (*Halse v Alder* (1874)). This is important for the angler who for example makes a genuine mistake about the boundaries of the water he is allowed to fish. The Theft Act draws a distinction between offences committed at night and those committed during the daytime. These rules are considered in more detail in Chapter 17. In particular the issue of making citizen's arrests of poachers is considered.

2.7.6 Shellfishery legislation

The relevant legislation for shell fisheries the Shellfish Acts 1967 and 1973 (see Chapter 8).

2.7.7 Miscellaneous environmental legislation

It is possible that other legislation concerning the environment generally may be relevant to the angler. For example if an area where he fishes is a designated nature habitat under the Wildlife and Countryside Act 1981 or if there is a problem with littering (by anglers or others) under the Litter Act 1983 (see Chapter 16).

3. ORGANISATION OF FISHERY REGULATION

This section briefly describes the main bodies that an angler may encounter in dealing with a legal issue. Chapter 1 explains the history of fishery regulation. This Chapter considers the current position as it has developed since 1989.

3.1 Water Act 1989 and its aftermath

In 1989 following the Water Act that year, fisheries, and indeed the regulation of water generally, underwent a revolution. The supply and sewerage functions were privatised and the regulatory matters including those relating to fisheries and flood and land drainage were given to a new national independent body, the National Rivers Authority (NRA). Although a national body, the NRA was organised on a regional basis which broadly followed the boundaries of previous regional water authorities. These boundaries are still in many cases used for the regional organisation of the water and fisheries functions of the NRA's successor the Environment Agency.

The NRA became responsible for fisheries legislation including SAFFA under the supervision of national government and via local and regional fisheries committees. The NRA was also crucially responsible for water quality and pollution control.

The NRA was abolished on 1 April 1996 being replaced by another independent national body for England and Wales, the Environment Agency.

This took over all NRA functions relevant to anglers as well as being responsible for a range of other environmental protection issues such as the disposal of waste and pollution from the most environmentally significant processes.

3.2 The Functions of central government in fishery regulation

Responsibilities in central government for matters affecting anglers are shared between the Department of the Environment, Transport and the Regions (DETR) - this was formerly just the Department of the Environment but was reorganised in May 1997 to incorporate transport and regional matters -, the Ministry of Agriculture, Food and Fisheries (MAFF), and the Welsh Office.

3.2.1 Fishery functions of central government

As regards fisheries policy under the SAFFA, Diseases of Fish Acts and Fisheries Act 1981 (on fish farms) the Minister for Agriculture, Food and Fisheries, or in Wales, the Secretary of State for Wales, are responsible. Many, but not all, of the regulatory functions have been delegated to the Environment Agency. For example, if unlicensed fishing takes place or illegal methods are used, the Environment Agency will deal with this matter. That said MAFF retain the ability to appoint their own 'authorised officers' who have the same powers as water bailiffs under s.41 SAFFA. On the other hand some issues are still to be dealt with only by central government at MAFF. An example of this is designation of waters that are being diseased. The fisheries' functions and division between MAFF and the Department of the Environment (DoE) as it then was, was altered slightly by the Water Act 1989 (Schedule 17 of Paragraph 1) which now provides for most fisheries functions of central government to be exercisable concurrently by the Minister for Agriculture, Fisheries and Food and the Secretary of State for the Environment, Transport and the Regions increasing the amount of power of the DoE (now DETR) over pure fisheries matters.

3.2.2 Non-fishery functions of central government

The DETR oversees a number of critical non-fisheries functions which are important to anglers such as water abstraction and river flows and pollution control. Besides having overall policy control for fisheries, central government retains significant powers over the operation of fishing at a local level. A number of the Agency powers are only able to be used with the approval of central government for example. The making of net limitation orders, increasing of licence fees for angling or commercial fishing or the making of fishery byelaws are all examples of this.

Throughout the book it is indicated what the specific roles are in relation to particular pieces of legislation.

3.3.3 Duties on central government

There are a number of important duties to promote conservation and recreation imposed on the Environment Agency described below. The key duties in s.7 Environment Act 1995 apply to central government ministers as well as the Agency in most cases and may be used in the same way in arguments and challenges to central government action or inaction on fishery issues.

3.3.4 Fishery powers of central government

Central government has important powers to involve itself with fishery regulation on a local level through what is now s.115 Water Resources Act 1991. This allows the Secretary of State for Environment, Transport and the Regions or Minister for Agriculture, Fisheries and Food to make an order for the modification of certain applicable fishing legislation for a particular area. Any order made under this section may modify the provisions of:

(a) SAFFA;

(b) Section 142 (which concerns contributions from fisheries owners for fisheries improvements (see Chapter 15) and s.156 Water Resources Act 1991 (which grants powers to the Agency to acquire land or other rights for fisheries purposes);

(c) Any local Act of Parliament which affects fisheries in a particular area.

These are major powers because the main legislation regulating commercial and recreational fishing in inland and estuarine waters is the SAFFA. Any Order made under s.115 has to pass through a procedure of advertisement and consultation (particularly between central government and the Agency) and has to be laid before Parliament. The procedures are fully set out in s.115 (3) (6).

An example of the use of the predecessor to s.115 (s.28 SAFFA which was worded almost identically) is shown by the case of *R v Minister for Agriculture, Fisheries and Food ex p Wear Valley District Council* (1988). In this case the Minister had made an order allowing the use of commercial nets called 'T' nets in the Wear estuary area even though these were fixed engines under the 1975 Act and therefore (except in one or two unusual cases which did not apply here) illegal under the Act. The Order overrode this part of SAFFA in the area specified. A local authority successfully challenged the making of the Order by a judicial review in the High Court on the grounds that the wrong procedure for making the Order had been followed.

Section 115 orders may therefore be used in a way which is damaging to angling interests, or a way that is positive for their protection by for example extending Environment Agency powers.

4. ENVIRONMENT AGENCY

The principal responsible body for freshwater and coastal fishing is (since 1 April 1996) the Environment Agency. The Agency was established under the Environment Act 1995. It took over from a range of other regulatory organisations on that day. It has superseded Her Majesty's Inspectorate of Pollution, the waste regulation authorities and most importantly from a fisheries point of view the National Rivers Authority. The NRA was set up in 1989 and ceased to exist on 1 April 1996. The Agency is independent of Government, but the non executive governing board of the Agency is made up of between eight and fifteen members appointed by the Secretary of State for the Environment, Transport and the Regions and the Minister of Agriculture, Fisheries and Food. The current Chairman is Lord de Ramsay. The running of the Agency lies with Agency staff lead by the Chief Executive. The Agency is organised through a series of regional offices and internally runs its water management functions on a river catchment basis, but its pollution control role on the political boundaries of the local authorities whose waste functions the Agency took over. From a legal point of view the Agency is subject to a range of important statutory duties and obligations. Some are specific to fisheries. Others, although more general, may have relevance to the fishery functions.

4.1 Fisheries duty of the Environment Agency

4.1.1 General duty with regard to fisheries
The Agency is under a duty to maintain, improve and develop salmon fisheries, trout fisheries, freshwater fisheries and eel fisheries (s.6 (6) Environment Act 1995). This reproduces and replaces the identical duty under which the NRA operated (s.114 Water Resources Act 1991). The Agency's fishery functions cover waters within the whole of England and Wales and coastal waters (up to six miles from established tidal baselines). Two problem rivers are the Rivers Esk and Tweed as these form the border between England and Scotland. The applicable law and organisation of fishery regulation in Scotland is in many cases different from England and Wales. The scope of this book is limited to England and Wales. As regards the two border rivers, the fisheries functions (but not pollution or land

drainage) for the Esk (and its tributaries up to source) are a matter for the Environment Agency even if they are located in Scotland. However, the River Tweed as defined (in the Tweed Fisheries (Amendment) Act 1859 and byelaws) is excluded from the jurisdiction of the Agency.

4.1.2 Other fishery functions

Other fishery functions of the Agency are principally under the Diseases of Fish Acts 1937 and 1983, the Salmon and Freshwater Fisheries Act 1975 and the fisheries parts of the Water Resources Act 1991. The legislation which is described in this book covers a range of matters from poaching to fishing methods, close seasons to commercial netting, rod licensing to fisheries improvements.

4.1.3 Non-fishery functions

The Agency is also responsible for some non-fishing matters which are very important to anglers. For example, it is responsible for controlling pollution to inland and coastal waters (see Chapter 9) and oversees and in some cases is responsible for flood protection and land drainage (see Chapter 20). The general duties described below operate on both the pure fisheries' matters and the broader range of issues affecting fishing interests.

4.1 General duties of the Environment Agency

4.1.1 Sustainable development

The Agency is subject to a number of duties which, although not directed simply at fisheries' matters, are relevant to angling interests. Under s.4 Environment Act 1995 the principal aim of the Agency is to discharge its functions so as to protect or enhance the environment as a whole and to make a contribution to sustainable development. Sustainable development is the rather grand idea developed in the 1970s and 1980s that any development by the current generation should not compromise the ability of future generations to meet their needs. The Act provides for the issuing of specific guidance to the Agency by the Secretary of State to explain how this aim may be translated into specific aims for each part of the Agency's functions. With regard to fisheries, the guidance issued (*The Environment Agency and Sustainable Development: Statutory Guidance* (1996)) offers the following advice:

(a) That the Agency is to continue to build upon the work of its predecessors;

(b) The Agency should monitor fish stocks and take action to restrict exploitation where this is necessary for the conservation of stocks;

(c) It should seek to develop sustainable fisheries by: (i) Controls on exploitation; (ii)Anti-poaching measures; (iii) Scrutiny of planning applications; (iv) Flood defence schemes (v) The way it deals with water abstraction licence applications and discharge consent applications (vi) Habitat restoration and stocking.

(d) In exercising its fisheries functions it should have regard to the views of those representing fisheries interests and fishery managers;

(e) Fisheries objectives will be furthered by achieving its broader objectives of a sustainable water environment in terms of both quality and supply.

4.1.2 Conservation and recreation duties

The Agency is under a duty, to such extent as it considers desirable, to promote the conservation and enhancement of the natural beauty of inland and coastal waters and land associated with such waters, the conservation of flora and fauna which are dependent on an aquatic environment and the use of such waters for recreational purposes (s.6 Environment Act 1995). In considering how to fulfil the recreational duty the Agency must take into account the needs of the chronically sick or disabled. These duties are taken further by s.7 Environment Act 1995. This requires that central government and the Agency should when formulating any proposals or exercising any power seek to further the conservation and enhancement of natural beauty and the conservation of flora, fauna and geological and physiographical features of special interest. In relation to exercising its pollution control functions the Agency must fulfil a more 'watered down' version of the duty to 'have regard' to those matters.

The Agency's conservation duties are not limited to natural features. Under s.7 they extend to having regard to the desirability of protecting and conserving buildings, sites and objects of archaeological, architectural, engineering or historic interest as well as considering the effects of any proposals on the economic or social well being of local communities in rural areas.

With regard to recreation, the Agency is under a duty to consider the desirability of maintaining public access to open areas and places of natural beauty and buildings of historic interest.

The Agency is also under specific duties in relation to notified sites of special scientific interest (SSSIs) under s.28 Wildlife and Countryside Act 1981 under s.8 Environment Act 1995. This provides for consultation between English Nature or the Countryside Council for Wales and the

Agency over any proposals which may adversely affect the SSSI. The Secretary of State has power to issue a Code of Practice detailing how the Agency should interpret and apply its duties with respect to conservation, recreation and access. No Code has yet been issued, but the Agency is being advised in the meantime to rely on the Code issued to the National Rivers Authority Code of Practice on Conservation, Access and Recreation (1989).

4.1.3 Costs and benefits duty

Where the Agency is considering exercising a power, as opposed to a duty, it is under a duty in s.39 Environment Act 1995 to take into account the costs and benefits (both financial and non-financial) in deciding whether to, and if so how to, exercise the power. The duty does not apply if it is unreasonable for such a balancing costs and benefits to be undertaken.

4.1.4 Significance of duties and judicial review

These duties may seem very broad and general, and therefore difficult to enforce. However, they are significant to angling interests in a number of ways. First, when the Agency is developing proposals it is important that they take the duties into account. They must be able to justify how these matters have been considered. In correspondence over a contentious matter, an angling club might for example draw attention to the duty concerned and ask for confirmation that it has been considered in respect of a number of specific conservation concerns.

4.1.4.1 Judicial review

If the duty is not fulfilled, then any decision of the Agency is likely to be flawed and might be challenged by a process called judicial review (under Rules of the Supreme Court Order 53). In such a process the High Court can consider whether a decision has been taken lawfully. If it has not normally, it will quash the decision and require the authority to take it again. The role of the courts is not to review the decisions themselves (unless they are so unreasonable or perverse that no authority could have made them). Rather, the purpose is to ensure that in taking any decision all relevant matters are weighed up and no irrelevant matters are taken into account.

4.1.4.2 Judicial review and angling

An example of these judicial review principles in an angling context is the Court of Appeal decision in *Cutts v Southern Water and Wessex Water* (1990). In this case Mr Cutts brought a judicial review of two water authorities' failure to take adequate action in respect of pollution from fish farms and obstructions to the passage of migratory fish. Lord Justice Mustill set out the principles on which any judicial review is to be based: 'The first principle is that the court is concerned to review, not the decision, but the process by which it is reached. The court will only intervene if persuaded that something has gone wrong with the process of deciding.'

Mr Cutts alleged that the water authorities were failing to exercise available powers under SAFFA and that this breached their general duty under s.28 SAFFA to maintain, improve and develop salmon and trout fisheries. Since water privatisation, this duty is now imposed on the Environment Agency (see above). The court decided that the water authorities were acting rationally in the decision they took with regard to a number of specific pollution and obstruction problems and therefore the court would not intervene.

4.1.4.3 Environment Agency duties and accountability

The Agency is making itself accountable over the conservation, access and recreation duties by annual reporting on these matters. For example, in the *Conservation, Access and Recreation Annual Report* 1995/96 the Agency revealed that it had that year been involved in 192 recreation projects, for example creating new paths and platforms for disabled anglers. It had also undertaken an information campaign with young canoeists promoting good practice and respect for other river users. Under the conservation duty, it reported a range of projects relating to otters, bats and crayfish, as well as scrutinising planning applications and undertaking river restoration.

4.1.4.4 Anglers and the Agency

The range of duties and powers described above explain the legal framework which governs the relationship between anglers and the Agency. In practical terms, the Agency has set out how it sees its relationship with angling in its free publication *Anglers and the Agency* (1997). This says that the Agency's vision for fisheries is that: 'All waters in England and Wales will be capable of sustaining healthy and thriving fish populations and everyone will have an opportunity to experience a diverse range of quality fishing.'

Then the document sets out how the Agency will attempt to achieve this through the exercise of its functions. It has identified four key areas for action. First, the Agency will work to protect and improve existing fish stocks (by monitoring existing fish populations and undertaking fish rescues from drought or pollution affected waters) and develop new fish stocks by stocking. Secondly, the Agency will work to protect and improve the environment for fish. This can be achieved by protecting water quality (through pollution controls), safeguarding river flows (particularly through abstraction licensing) and by enhancing fish habitats (by carrying out works to, for example, create pools and fish passes or improve spawning grounds). Thirdly, the Agency will use fishery regulation to pursue its overall vision for fisheries. The powers over the regulation of fisheries include the control of poaching, fish introductions and Agency byelaws. Finally, the Agency will seek to improve the environment for anglers by providing information and services to anglers (for example phoneline information on river levels, responding promptly via a 24-hour hotline to reports of pollution or fish in distress, etc.), protecting wildlife which adds to the pleasure of angling and by promoting fisheries restoration and development.

The Agency fulfils most of these fisheries' functions by means of funding from licence fees.

4.2 Conservation, recreation and access duties - Water companies and land drainage boards

Similar duties to those described above are imposed on the statutory water plcs appointed under the Water Industry Act 1991 and on land drainage boards under the Land Drainage Act 1991 (as amended) - (see Chapter 20). These may be of use to anglers in dealing with those bodies.

4.3 Environment Agency structure

The Environment Agency itself is a body corporate separate from Government and made up of a board of appointees of the Secretary of State for the Environment, Transport and the Regions, Wales and the Minister of Agriculture, Fisheries and Food. This Board oversees the work of the Agency but, in practice, it is its employed officers from Chief Executive downwards who run the Agency. They do so with the assistance and advice of a number of advisory committees. There are regional Environmental Protection Advisory Committees, as well as an Advisory Committee for Wales. Of particular importance to anglers are the fisheries advisory committees.

4.3.1 Regional Fisheries Advisory Committees (RFACs)

The Agency must establish regional Fisheries Advisory Committees and may also establish local advisory committees, covering much smaller areas (s.13 Environment Act 1995). In all cases, the members may not also be members of the Agency and must be persons interested in fisheries which often includes representatives of anglers. This committee structure is similar to that which was operated by the National Rivers Authority. There are one or two changes to the fisheries' committees under the Environment Act 1995. First, it is now clear that the committees' remit includes recreation, conservation and navigation issues as well as purely fisheries' concerns. Secondly, the Chair (who holds a paid post, unlike other committee members who are just paid expenses) is appointed by central government. The Government's policy of advertising such posts and committee appointments hopefully will continue to give anglers the opportunity to be part of policy making within the Agency. The Agency is bound to consult its fisheries' committees about fulfilling its various duties with regard to fisheries. Meetings are generally open to the public (Water Consolidation (Consequential Provisions) Act 1991 Schedule 1).

4.3.1.1 Practical importance of RFACs

RFACs are important as a means of achieving accountability for Environment Agency action and inaction. It is often worth finding out who are the members of the local RFAC (or even trying to become a member) so that they can be lobbied about what the Agency is doing. RFACs have a broad range of responsibility and might deal with the Agency response to a particular incident, or a matter of Agency policy more generally.

4.4 Byelaw making powers of the Environment Agency

Fisheries and angling matters have always been regulated by byelaws as well as by national legislation. The power to make byelaws on fisheries' seasons and methods has been passed down from the River Boards to the water authorities and the National Rivers Authority and now to the Environment Agency. Byelaws are able to be made by the Agency under a delegated power from Parliament (now contained in the Water Resources Act 1991 Schedule 25), but are subject to confirmation by the Secretary of State for the Environment, Transport and the Regions/Wales, or the Minister for Agriculture, Fisheries and Food. Although they are subject to confirmation by central government, they must be put forward in the first place by the Agency. The nature of most byelaws is that they are local laws applying to only one area or river catchment. However, in recent times the NRA and the Agency have created national byelaws which cover the whole of England and Wales.

4.4.1 Matters which may be regulated by fishery byelaws

In legal terms, the important powers to create byelaws for the Agency are contained in paragraph 6 and 6A (inserted by the Environment Act 1995) of Schedule 25 of the Water Resources Act 1991.

These paragraphs allow byelaws to be made on a range of issues including:

(a) Close seasons (including dispensing with the close season for freshwater fish or rainbow trout);

(b) Catch returns;

(c) Fishing methods (covering both rod and line and other methods, for example netting);

(d) Size of fish that may be taken;

(e) Fishing within specified distances of obstructions such as dams or weirs;

(f) Allowing the placing of so called fixed engines (see Chapter 13) basically fixed nets at particular times or places;

(g) Requiring the marking of licensed nets and boats or coracles;

(h) Prohibiting the carrying of nets in boats of any unlicensed net or unmarked net (where marking is needed);

(i) Authorising angling for eels during the close season for freshwater fish;

(j) Regulating angling at night;

(k) Regulating discharges or deposits detrimental to fish;

(l) Promoting marine or aquatic environmental purposes which includes the conservation or enhancement of the natural beauty or amenity of marine or aquatic or waterside areas, or of any features of archaeological or historic interest in such areas, or the conservation of flora or fauna associated with such areas (New power inserted by the Environment Act 1995).

4.4.2 Breach of byelaws

Where byelaws are created, breaching them will be a criminal offence which may be punished by a fine of up to £2,500. The Agency will normally bring any prosecution for breach of byelaws.

4.4.3 Byelaw making procedure

The procedure for making byelaws is set out in Schedule 26 to the Water Resources Act 1991. The byelaws are prepared in draft by the Agency and are then put out to public consultation, which will include formal advertisement in the *London Gazette* (see Chapter 11) and such other places as the Agency thinks fit (in fact, the Agency widely advertises any byelaw changes in practice). They are then sent to the Secretary of State/Minister for Agriculture, Fisheries and Food for confirmation. If there are formal objections to the byelaws, the Secretary of State then he may hold a public local inquiry. In respect of byelaws concerning discharges detrimental to fish (see *(k)* above), generally an inquiry must be held if anyone affected objects. In any event, with or without an inquiry, the Secretary of State/Minister may then confirm the byelaws with or without modifications or *refuse* to confirm the byelaws. A date is normally fixed for the byelaws to come into effect (if no date is fixed, they are deemed to come into force one month after confirmation). The Secretary of State/Minister has the power to revoke existing byelaws.

Confirmed byelaws are held by Environment Agency offices where they are available for public inspection and copies can be obtained.

4.4.4 Environment Agency and national byelaws

The first national byelaws were introduced to abolish the coarse close season on still waters. This has lead to a general review of fishery byelaws in a series of phases which will lead to simplification and greater consistency in byelaws over the country. The Environment Agency introduced the first phase of the national byelaws review which applies to a number of angling issues throughout England and Wales. This first phase has been confirmed in two batches, in December 1996 and March 1997 (with one exception which still awaits confirmation). The byelaws are considered in detail at the appropriate point in the text. However, in broad terms, they:

(a) regulate the maximum numbers of rods which may be used by an angler;

(b) dispense with the annual close season for rainbow trout on all lakes, ponds and reservoirs;

(c) retain the annual close season for brown trout (which vary locally according to local byelaws);

(d) remove the annual close season for coarse fishing on lakes, ponds and reservoirs (which had already been done in many cases) but extends this lifting to many fisheries within sites of special scientific interest;

(e) prohibit the use of gaffs altogether;

(f) requirements for landing nets, keep nets and keep sacks regulating size and construction and use (these byelaws have yet to be confirmed). The second phase is underway and will lead to a second set of national byelaws in 1998.

Phase 2 of the National Byelaws address a range of issues including:

(a) use of crayfish as bait;

(b) otter guards on eel nets;

(c) removal of fish;

(d) return of foul hooked fish;

(e) live bait fishing;

(f) eel net returns;

(g) trolling;
(h) rod length;
(i) attending rods.

4.4.5 Compensation and fishery byelaws

It seems that byelaws are a useful mechanism for controlling a wide range of fishery matters. However, there are compensation provisions in s.212 Water Resources Act 1991 which will apply to byelaws which affect certain types of commercial fishing. Byelaws prohibiting the use of any instrument, or specifying or controlling the use of nets for the taking of salmon, trout or freshwater fish are subject to these rules. They do not apply to so called fixed engines (see Chapter 19). Compensation is payable by the Agency to the owner or occupier of any fishery adversely affected by the byelaws. This is most likely to involve compensation to commercial netsmen who find that they are restricted in their netting under rigorous byelaws. It is conceivable that compensation could be payable to angling interests if the byelaws relaxed the general law and made commercial fishing easier, to the detriment of angling.

4.5 Environment Agency bailiffs

The Environment Agency has the power under s.32 SAFFA to appoint water bailiffs to enforce the provisions of the Act. An Environment Agency bailiff is for the purposes of the 1975 Act treated as if they were a police constable with the same powers of arrest, search and seizure under the Police Acts and Police and Criminal Evidence Act 1984 (s.36 SAFFA). These bailiffs are important for the enforcement of fishery regulation and their powers are considered in Chapter 17.

4.6 Environment Agency prosecution

The key regulatory tool for the Environment Agency in fishery matters is the bringing of criminal prosecutions. For example, prosecution for angling, without a licence, in breach of byelaws, or poaching. The remainder of this work has a large number of references to numerous criminal offences relevant to angling particularly under SAFFA and WRA. This section sets out some of the basic principles applicable to the bringing of any prosecution. To place this in context, the Agency's predecessor, the National Rivers Authority, brought some 5,000 prosecutions each year for fishery related criminal offences. The Agency is given statutory authority to bring criminal proceedings under s.37 Environment Act 1995.

However minor or technical the offence, the general criminal burden of proof applies. This requires that the prosecution (the Agency in this case) proves each and every element of the offence by means of admissible evidence (*Woolmington v Director of Public Prosecutions* (1935)). The evidence may range from admissions made by the defendant, to eye witnesses, or physical evidence (for example a dead fish). Not only does the prosecution have to prove each element of the offence, but it must do so to a high standard of proof so that the magistrates (or, exceptionally for fishery matters, jury) are satisfied beyond reasonable doubt of guilt (*Ferguson v The Queen* (1979)). If there is an exception to the criminal offence, then the defendant bears the burden of proving he falls within the exception, but has a lower standard of proof than the balance of probabilities (s.101 Magistrates Courts Act 1980 and *R v Edwards* (1975)). For example, if in a prosecution for unlicensed fishing the defendant alleges he had a licence, he must prove this on the balance of probabilities. In general all prosecutions begin in the magistrates court for the petty sessional division (although as a matter of law the jurisdiction is County based (s.2 Magistrates Courts Act 1980) in which the offence was committed. Most fishery offences will be dealt with by the magistrates' court, either by means of a guilty plea and sentencing, or by not guilty plea and trial and, of course, sentence if this results in a conviction. Some fishery offences are, however, triable. Either way this means they may be dealt with either in the magistrates' court or Crown Court (by judge and jury). These offences will generally only be committed to the Crown Court if they are so serious that the magistrates consider their sentencing powers are inadequate, or because the defendant is pleading not guilty and decides to opt for trial by jury. Finally, the courts' powers of forfeiture are greater in the Crown Court (see below) and for this reason the Agency may want a case to be disposed of there.

There are a couple of procedural peculiarities to fishery prosecutions. First, where the offence is alleged to be committed at sea, then the magistrates' court at any place abutting the sea coast in that area has jurisdiction to deal with the case (s.37 and Schedule 4, Paragraph 2 SAFFA). Secondly, magistrates must obviously be, and be seen to be, impartial. However, membership of a society for the protection of fish shall not disqualify a magistrate from dealing with a fishery case, but obviously if an offence is alleged to have been committed on land belonging to a magistrate, or in relation to a fishery which the magistrate owns or occupies, then they will be ineligible to hear the case (Schedule 4, Paragraph 4 SAFFA). When a prosecution is brought for a fishery offence, guilt is often clear but the matter may be fairly minor (for example a first time failure to fish without a rod licence). The magistrates' court system allows for defendants to plead guilty by post for offences. Under s.12 Magistrates Courts Act 1980, any adult can plead guilty by post to a summary only offence (ie. one that cannot be tried in the Crown Court) providing the maximum penalty does not exceed three months imprisonment. In these cases it is often advisable to write a covering letter explaining the circumstances of the offence and offering any possible mitigation (see below).

4.6.1 Fishery fixed penalty offences

The Environment Act 1995 introduced new powers to create a fixed penalty system for dealing with breaches of fishery law (s.104 Environment Act 1995). This section inserts a new s.37A into the SAFFA which will allow a person accused of a fishery offence to discharge their liability, without conviction, by paying a fixed sum within a specified period. If they do not pay the fixed penalty within the time period, they may be prosecuted in the normal way. Whether the chance to deal with a criminal offence in this way is open to the accused is at the discretion of the Agency official. The fixed penalty system may cover offences under the SAFFA, the Salmon Act 1986, byelaw offences and certain miscellaneous offences relating to orders made under s.115, s.116 and s.142 WRA.

The details of the system (the specific offences to be covered, the amount of the penalty and the time period) are to be set out in regulations. No regulations have yet been made, or even drafted.

4.6.2 Sentencing for fishery offences

Sentencing for any criminal offence is driven by a number of factors. First, the maximum applicable penalties under the statute concerned. Secondly, the range of aggravating or mitigating circumstances which make the offence, more or less serious. For example, an aggravating feature of an offence of poaching might be that it was at night and involved using poison and nets to kill large numbers of salmon for commercial sale. Mitigation, on the other hand, might be where only one salmon was taken for the poacher's own table. Thirdly, the circumstances of the accused will be very important. In particular, the previous convictions of the defendant or any cautions and the personal circumstances - especially financial means - are critical. The Magistrates Association *Sentencing Guidelines* (1997) have recently been updated to stress the importance of taking into account the accused's means in setting fines.

For most fishery offences the appropriate sentence will be a fine, but in some cases imprisonment is both appropriate and likely. For example, in *R v Smith* (1982) two accused were prosecuted for unlicensed fishing under s.27 SAFFA. Both had previous convictions one for a range of offences including burglary, theft, assault, and poaching offences and the other had three previous poaching convictions. Sentences of nine and six months were imposed.

Although strictly not a matter of sentence, one should bear in mind the power of the court to make two additional types of financial order against a person on conviction. First, an award of costs may be made to the Environment Agency under the Prosecution of Offences Act 1985. Secondly, where a person has suffered a loss as a result of the offence an award of compensation may be made under s 35 Powers of Criminal Courts Act 1973. For example, a club which lost fish to a poacher might seek an award of compensation.

4.6.3 Sentencing - forfeiture of tackle, etc.

A peculiarity of prosecutions under the SAFFA or the Salmon Act 1986 is the power of the court to impose orders of forfeiture and to disqualify persons from holding a licence. These powers are contained in Schedule 4 SAFFA. There are separate powers of forfeiture under the Theft Act 1968 (see Chapter 17).

The forfeiture powers of the magistrates extend to:

(a) Any fish taken by the defendant or in his possession at the time of the offence;

(b) Any instrument (for example fishing tackle), bait or other thing used in the commission of the offence;

(c) Any substance or device unlawfully possessed under s.5 SAFFA (see Chapter 13), eg. explosives or poisons.

An Environment Agency water bailiff has the power to seize anything which may be forfeited by the court and then this will be held pending the outcome of the prosecution, although perishable items (particularly fish) may be sold, in which case the proceeds may then be forfeited. Where seized fish form part of the prosecution evidence, care should be taken before they are disposed of to consider the case of *Anderson v Loverack* (1976) (see Chapter 13). A number of ambiguities exist in relation to the powers of forfeiture. Does the power to size fish only relate to fish illegally in the accused's possession? This may well be the interpretation intended but the wording is far from clear.

There is also some uncertainty of the breadth of the word 'instrument'. This issue arose in the case of *Gibson v Ryan* (1968) when the court had to decide whether an inflatable rubber dinghy and a fish basket amounted to instruments under Scottish legislation. The court held that neither amounted to instruments, as there was a distinction between instruments used to *take* fish and things which *assist* in the commission of the offence (but note, there are specific powers to forfeit boats and vehicles in limited cases described below). The words used in Schedule 4 link the power of seizure of an item to its use in the offence. This means that the particular offence has to be considered to decide what the extent of the powers actually are. In relation to angling it is unclear the extent of the power to seize keep nets or a fishing basket in relation to unlicensed fishing. Whereas, for the same offence, it is surely clear that a power of forfeiture and seizure exists over the rod, reel, line and landing net.

Where a prosecution is dealt with by the Crown Court, there are powers to forfeit any vessel or vehicle (Schedule 4, Paragraph 5 SAFFA) used in or in connection with the offence, or in which any unlawfully possessed substance or device was contained when the offence was committed. Environment Agency bailiffs may seize a vessel or vehicle where it is liable to be forfeited. This means that in order to do so they must suspect an offence triable by the Crown Court has been committed.

In *R v Williams* (1991) the Court of Appeal decided that the powers of forfeiture under the SAFFA (in this case of a boat, engine and nets) extended to matters not owned by the accused. The court said that caution should be exercised before forfeiting matters belonging to someone other than the accused or a member of his immediate family.

4.6.4 Sentencing - licence disqualification

Following conviction for an offence under the SAFFA or the Salmon Act 1986, the court has power to forfeit an existing fishing licence (whether rod or net or other, and whether individual or general - see Chapter 12) and to disqualify the accused from holding a licence for up to five years (Schedule 4, Paragraph 9 SAFFA). The SAFFA requires that anyone who is a licence holder and is prosecuted shall either deliver it, send it or bring it with him to the court hearing. If the accused fails to do this and is ordered to surrender the licence to the court and fails to do so, he will commit a further offence (Schedule 4, Paragraph 10 SAFFA). Any licence forfeited is then sent to the Environment Agency and, if the Agency did not bring the prosecution, notification of any disqualification will be sent to the Agency by the court.

4.7 Private prosecution

In general, criminal prosecutions may be brought by any person not just by a prosecuting authority such as the Crown Prosecution Service or the Environment Agency (s.6 Prosecution of Offences Act 1985). There are exceptional cases: for example the offence of damaging of protected habitat under s.28 Wildlife and Countryside Act 1981 does not allow private prose-cutions. Anglers or clubs or associations, such as the Anglers' Conservation

Association, are able to mount private prosecutions for fishery related offences. Clearly this may be time consuming and expensive and therefore should be seen as a last resort if the Agency cannot be persuaded to act. Private prosecutions are considered in a little more detail in relation to water pollution in Chapter 9.

4.8 Other Environment Agency powers

The Environment Agency has a wide range of powers to fulfil its diverse functions. Some of these are particularly important to fisheries. It has extensive powers of investigation in respect of pollution (s.108 Environment Act 1995). It has powers to compulsorily acquire land (with central government approval) s.155 WRA, or to acquire rights over land (s.168 WRA). There are specific powers to acquire land or other rights for fishery purposes (s.156 WRA considered in detail in Chapter 19), for example creating a fish pass by a weir or dam. Paragraph 39 of Schedule 3 SAFFA authorises the Agency in purchasing or leasing by agreement any fishery or fishing rights or any fish farm.

In respect of main rivers (see Chapter 20) it has powers to carry out flood defence and land drainage works and maintain and improve any such works already in existence (s.165 WRA). These powers also extend to providing and operating flood warning systems (s.166 WRA).

5. OTHER BODIES AFFECTING ANGLING AND THE LAW

5.1 Local authorities and National Parks

Local authorities are organised in fairly diverse ways in England and Wales. In some areas there is 'two tier' local government with responsibilities split between county and district or city councils. In others, there is 'unitary' local government with one council responsible for all matters. Anglers may come across local authorities in various ways. First, local authorities are responsible for certain pollution legislation. For example, litter control, public health and statutory nuisances are matters for local authorities (see Chapter 16). Local authorities are responsible for the planning system (see Chapter 15) and for granting planning permission and enforcing the rules on planning.

On a more specific level, local authorities have the power to provide and charge for fishing in inland and coastal waters (under the Local Government (Miscellaneous Provisions) Act 1976). So, certain local authority owned lakes or ponds or stretches of river may offer angling. National parks are subject to their own developing system of administration. In the past they have been operated through the relevant county council (via a National Parks' Committee, having a fairly high degree of autonomy), or in a couple of cases via a joint board (where otherwise the Park would by covered by more than one county council). Following the Environment Act 1995 Part III, the plan is to set up autonomous National Park Authorities' separate from the local authorities in the area, which will take over the main local authority functions for the National Park, including planning controls.

5.2 Internal drainage boards

Internal drainage boards have responsibility for land drainage and flood defence in respect of 'non main rivers' (see Chapter 20 for the distinction between main and non main rivers). They are created and operate under the Land Drainage Act 1991. They are considered in detail in Chapter 20.

5.3 British Waterways Board

The British Waterways Board owns or manages well over 2000 miles of inland waterways and canals. The Board operates under the Transport Act 1962, which classifies the waters it is responsible for (listed in Schedule 12 to the 1962 Act) into commercial waterways (which are to be operated primarily for the commercial carriage of freight), cruising waterways (which are to be principally available for cruising, fishing and other recreational purposes) and the remainder not falling into either category.

The Board is under duties to maintain its cruising and commercial waterways in navigable state (s.104 Transport Act 1962). The Board has power to make byelaws (subject to ministerial approval) in relation to the waterway. There are also various powers for the Board and local authorities to improve access for amenity or recreation to Board waters (s.111 and s.114 Transport Act 1962).

Clearly, anglers will be concerned to see that their interests are adequately recognised by the Board in the way it manages its waterways and the byelaws created. The Inland Waterways Amenity Advisory Council is a forum for the discussion of such issues. Section 110 Transport Act 1962 requires that the Council shall include persons who have knowledge and interest in a range of matters, including fishing. The Council members are central government appointees. The Council may also create regional committees. The Council may advise and make recommendations to the Board and central government. The British Waterways Board is under a special duty with regard to the River Severn. The dams on the Severn have been constructed under the Severn Navigation Acts 1842 and 1853 and, as such, are exempt from the duties in s.9 SAFFA concerning fish passes (see Chapter 19). Section 40 SAFFA requires that any fish passes on the Severn shall be maintained in an efficient state by the Board.

5.4 Nature Conservation bodies

Where angling is in a nature reserve, anglers may come across the various public bodies involved with nature conservation. Following reforms in the Environmental Protection Act 1990, the key bodies are: English Nature, in England, and the Countryside Council for Wales, in Wales. They are responsible for sites of special scientific interest, under the Wildlife and Countryside Act 1981 and for national nature reserves designated under the National Parks and Access to the Countryside Act 1949. Local authorities may also have nature reserve powers in respect of local nature reserves, also created under the 1949 Act. In all cases, nature reserves may create restrictions via byelaws or other means on what may be done within the reserve. These are considered in Chapter 16.

5.5 Police

The Police may be involved with angling if a public order situation develops over protests against fishing (see Chapter 16), or in connection with certain criminal offences such as theft of fish or poaching (see Chapter 17). The Environment Agency has power under Paragraph 39 of Schedule 3 SAFFA to obtain the services of the police to assist it and, if this takes place, a police constable then has the same powers as an Environment Agency water bailiff (s.36 (3) SAFFA).

5.6 Non-governmental organisations

Some non-governmental organisations may be very influential in angling matters. The Anglers' Conservation Association and Salmon and Trout Association have both had important impacts for anglers by their campaigns and legal actions brought (see Chapters 7, 9 and 10). When angling interests are threatened by pollution, a wider range of non-governmental organisations concerned with the broader environment may well be influential in bringing about environmental improvements. Not all non-governmental organisations will be working for, or even in sympathy with, angling interests. The League against Cruel Sports and Royal Society for the Protection of Birds have both had their disagreements with the angling fraternity in recent years.

6. Getting Information from Public Bodies

Information is critical to any campaign or scrutiny of the action or inaction of a public body and, often, data is vital to the bringing of any sort of legal proceedings. When trying to obtain information from a public body, cooperation and tact are likely to be more productive than being overly assertive of rights. However, where this fails to produce results,there exist certain rights to access information held by certain bodies. First of all, the Environmental Information Regulations 1992 (implementing EC Directive 90/313/EEC) (SI 1992/3240) are designed to ensure free access to information concerning the environment held by public bodies. There are various important exceptions to what information is available (eg. reports in draft, or information concerning legal proceedings). There is also ambiguity over which bodies are covered by the obligation to reveal information concerning the environment to the public. Although it is clear that local authorities and the Environment Agency, as well as central government, are covered, it is uncertain whether bodies such as privatised utilities are within the Regulations. The Department of the Environment (as it then was) has published *Freedom of Access to Information on the Environment* (1992) and *Green Rights and Responsibilities: A Citizens Guide to the Environment* (1992) which provide further information. The Environment Agency also maintains public registers of information on environmental matters. There is a water register under s.190 WRA and the Control of Pollution (Applications, Appeals and Registers) Regulations 1996 (SI 1996/2971). This register includes a range of information including details of discharge consents permitting pollution of water and prosecutions for pollution.

7. REVIEW OF SALMON AND FRESHWATER FISHERIES LEGISLATION

On 7 July 1997, the Agriculture Minister announced a comprehensive review of salmon and freshwater fisheries legislation. It is to review all aspects of law and policy on fisheries. It is to be expected that this review will lead to changes to the law probably taking effect early in the new millenium.

CHAPTER 2

THE LEGAL HISTORY OF ANGLING

The history of angling is inextricably linked to the development of the law on the ownership of fisheries, pollution and the administrative bodies having fishery responsibilities. References to fisheries appear in the Domesday Book and many cases have been heard which have clarified the law on the classification of fisheries. Magna Carta was fundamental in establishing the public right to fish. Nevertheless, it was not until the middle of the nineteenth century that people began to realise that with the Industrial Revolution came pollution and its effects on fisheries. This was recognised by the Commissioners who enquired into the causes of dwindling salmon stocks in 1861. The conflict between manufacturing and agriculture on the one hand and fishery interests on the other is one that continues to the present day. The recent case, *Broderick v Gale and Ainslie* (1992) serves to show how a modern industry, fish farming, can damage angling interests (see Chapter 15).

1. 1066 AND THE DOMESDAY BOOK

The Domesday Book refers to many fisheries in existence at the date of the survey. Eels at that time were considered the choice fish and it is a feature that rent for fisheries was paid in eels. A fishery at Hemel Hampstead in Hertfordshire paid rent of '*iiij molendinae de 37s. 4d. Et 300 eels, less 25*'. In Haiforde in Dorset the rent was '*ij piscatores de 900 anguillis*'. There are also entries for the payment of rent in salmon for fisheries in Chester, Devon and Hereford and one in Petersham, Surrey, of eels and lampreys.

The fisheries mentioned in the Domesday Book were not used for pleasure. They were commercial. No mention is made of the number of rods allowed on the water! The King was surveying England and wanted to know how much the fisheries were worth. It would be many years before fisheries would be valued according to their sporting value. William I had just conquered England and he wanted to know the value of his new kingdom.

Fisheries existed in almost every part of the Kingdom, not only in inland waters, but also in tidal waters. Fisheries were located at Clackton and Thurrock in Essex, at Chepstow and Tewkesbury in Gloucestershire, at Norton on the Mersey, in Devon at Bideford and Cornworthy on the Dart, in Kent at Stoke and Hoo on the Medway, among many others. Fishing weirs are mentioned at Fulham and Isleworth in Middlesex. Many of the names are difficult to place because of the changes in the country's coastline, but fisheries obviously existed in all waters, still, flowing and coastal.

2. KING JOHN AND THE BARONS

One of the major sources of conflict over the years has been between the public and the private right to fish. 'Putting in defence' is the ancient phrase used to describe the creation of a private fishery which entitles the owner to exclude the public. Before Magna Carta, the King could exclude the public and keep the fishery to himself, or grant the fishery to a subject as part of a manor. He could also grant it in gross, which means that the fishery was granted separately from the land. How this was done is not known, since no records exist. However, the presumption nowadays is that the King had the right to bar public fishing in a fishery. With the upheaval in the land as a result of King John's abuse of his position, the barons rebelled and forced the King to sign Magna Carta, protecting what we now call basic human rights. By Chapter 16 of Magna Carta, the King was prevented from barring the public right to fish:

> No banks (rivers) shall be defended from henceforth but such as were in defence at the time of King Henry our grandfather, by the same places and the same bounds as they were wont to be in his time.

However, even after Magna Carta, records show that the King was still issuing writs putting rivers in defence. In 1238, Henry III sent writs to the Sheriff of Worcester to put the Avon in defence between Pershore and Evesham. It appears that Henry III issued many such writs ordering the construction of bridges to help him to enjoy his sport. This is called the right of riviation. It seems that if the King wanted to enjoy a day's sport in any region he would send a writ to the local sheriff ordering him to carry out works such as building bridges and also forbidding the local population from going near the water whilst he was there. After 1247 there is no further reference in the records to any such writs. It is presumed that the right fell into disuse because of its unpopularity - the construction of bridges would have been costly and time consuming.

The question remains, nevertheless, that surely this right of riviation contravened the terms of Magna Carta? By way of an answer, Moore in *The History and Law of Fisheries* (1903) argues that Magna Carta merely enshrined in law what had been going on for many years. He maintains that by 1215 most fisheries had become either public or private. King John could no longer grant a private fishery where a public fishery had previously existed, since the ownership of fisheries in his kingdom had been established long before he came to the throne. He further argues that these writs issued by the King merely allowed him to enjoy other sports, not fishing.

Further doubt has been expressed by Lord Blackburn in *Neill v Duke of Devonshire* (1882) that the right of riviation related to fishing. Most probably, it had more to do with the King enjoying the sport of fowling and falconry.

> And there seems to me considerable doubt whether the 16th chapter of Magna Carta did more than restrain the writ de defensione ripariae when the King was about to come into a county all persons might be forbidden from approaching the banks of the river, whether tidal or not, that the King might have his pleasure in fowling and fishing therein ...

To all intents and purposes, whilst this is an interesting historical argument, the right of the public to fish in tidal waters cannot be taken away and Magna Carta is today taken as the source of that law. As Lord Blackburn remarked, 'But in *Malcomson v O'Dea* (1865) it was laid down that since Magna Carta no new exclusive fishery could be created by the Crown. This must be held to settle what the law now is ...'

3. FISHERIES

In Chapter 4 the various kinds of fisheries are explained. The terminology used is interchangeable and confusing. To all intents and purposes, the modern distinction is between exclusive and non-exclusive fisheries. However, legal argument has raged over the classification of fisheries.

Woolrych in his *Law of Waters* lists for four types of fishery: several, free, common of fishery and fishery in gross. The major dispute centred around whether there was a distinction between a several and free fishery. Earlier cases and title deeds showing title to land used the Latin phrases '*libera piscaria*' and '*separalis piscaria*' - free and several fisheries respectively - without differentiating them. Woolrych argued that whilst a several fishery is 'an exclusive property' a free fishery is 'no other than an unlimited common of fishery.' By the latter he means that it was a public fishery.

However, by the start of this century when Moore wrote *The History and Law of Fisheries* he dismisses this distinction stating that several and free are synonymous and that the only difference is between exclusive and non-exclusive fisheries.

4. POLLUTION AND FISHERIES ADMINISTRATION

Much of the early anti-pollution legislation was introduced to protect public health. If fisheries were also protected, this was purely incidental to the purpose of the Act. For example, The Gas Works Clauses Act 1847 provides that if any gas company causes any gas washings or substances to flow into any stream, or do any act connected with the making of gas whereby any stream is fouled, the company is liable to a fine of £200. No mention is made of the protection of fish.

The latter half of the nineteenth century saw the enactment of The Rivers Prevention of Pollution Acts 1876-1893 which were aimed more at the protection of fisheries but were really anti-pollution legislation. A range of offences was created which could be enforced by a sanitary authority, or a person affected by the pollution. However, to a large extent, these were ineffective since they safeguarded industrial interests and placed insurmountable obstacles in the way of a successful prosecution. If pollution was caused by a mine or manufacturing processes, first, only the sanitary authority could bring proceedings, secondly, the permission of the Minister of Health was required and then, finally, only if the Minister was satisfied that the means of rendering the polluting matter harmless are reasonably practical and that no material injury will be inflicted by such proceedings to the interests of industry could the prosecution proceed. As an attempt at environmental protection, it was heavily weighted in the industrialist's favour.

This period also saw growing governmental concern over the decline in salmon populations. In 1860, Commissioners were appointed to inquire into salmon fisheries. Their report resulted in the Salmon Fishery Act 1861. For the first time, prescribed methods of taking fish were set down, close seasons clarified and offences enacted for taking immature and spawning fish. The Freshwater Fisheries Act 1878 followed and was the first major piece of legislation governing coarse fishing. However, as time passed, inadequacies in the legislation became apparent and a plethora of statutes were passed to fill these gaps. The lack of effective protection for fisheries from pollution remained.

It was not until after The First World War, with the enactment of the Salmon and Freshwater Fisheries Act 1923, that the protection of fisheries become a primary concern. This Act consolidated and amended legislation relating to salmon and freshwater fisheries. It repealed a total of eighteen acts of Parliament and codified what had been a confusing array of legislation into one act. Under s.55, power was given to the Fishery Boards, established under The Salmon and Freshwater Fisheries Act 1907, to institute proceedings - under the Rivers Pollution Prevention Acts 1876 to 1893 - that a sanitary authority could take. For the first time, this gave effective powers to a body likely to be much more vigilant in fighting the pollution of fisheries. The section specifically states that a board may take a prosecution for the protection of fisheries in their district. Under s.59 (l)(p), the Boards were also given the power by byelaws to regulate the deposit of any matter detrimental to salmon, trout or freshwater fish.

Previously, under s.5 of the Salmon Fishery Act 1861, any person who caused or knowingly permitted to flow into any waters containing salmon any liquid or solid matter poisonous to fish, or which killed fish, was guilty of an offence. However, the prosecution had to show that the waters contained salmon and that the polluting matter had poisoned or killed fish. This does not sound too onerous but they also had to combat the defence available to the polluter that it had used the best practical means within a reasonable cost to render the matter harmless - again not such a difficult obstacle. But the defendant could escape prosecution if he could show that a permanent remedy cost more than £100. This is a range of obstacles enough to deter any would be prosecutor.

Section 8 of the 1923 Act improved the position by providing that the prosecution only needed to prove the waters contained fish and that the polluting matter had caused the waters to be injurious to fish. The defence of best practical means was still available but the £100 limit on a permanent remedy was dispensed with. However, the consent of the Minister was still required for a prosecution by a fishing board of a mining or manufacturing pollution. With all the pressure that could be applied on the Minister, no doubt many prosecutions were quietly filed away. More generally, this Act also saw protection given to the spawning grounds, spawn and food of fish. The 1923 Act was a major step in the right direction. It marked the recognition by central government that fisheries had to be protected.

It is perhaps misleading to say that no legislation to protect fisheries had been passed before the 1923 Act. The Malicious Damage Act 1873 made it an offence to put lime or other noxious substances into private fisheries or salmon rivers with the intent to destroy fish, as did the Fisheries (Dynamite) Act 1877 to use dynamite or other explosive substances to catch or destroy fish in a public fishery. However, before the 1923 Act, legislation protecting fisheries was piecemeal, littered with obstacles and weighted in favour of industry.

4.1 To the present day

The next major development occurred after the Second World War. Many of the fishery boards experienced problems as a result of inadequate income (some had as little as £200 per year). Some had amalgamated. Eventually, the 45 remaining fishery boards were replaced by 32 river boards under the River Boards Act 1948. These boards were given the duties of administering the Salmon and Freshwater Fisheries Acts and land drainage and also took on the function of pollution prevention. Soon after, the Rivers (Prevention of Pollution) Act 1951 was passed making it an offence to discharge into any stream any poisonous, noxious or polluting matter. However, in this Act there was still a provision that the consent of the Minister of Housing and Local Government was needed for such a prosecution of a local authority from sewage disposal or sewerage works.

A review of fishery law was undertaken by the Bledisloe Committee in 1961. It stated that the 'present fishery code is 38 years old and is largely a re-enactment of earlier salmon fishery legislation.' It recommended that there was still a need for fishery powers since the Rivers (Prevention of Pollution) Act dealt with the long continued discharge of normal waste waters from industry or houses. It felt that section 8 of the 1923 Act was still required to deal with sporadic pollution.

The Water Resources Act 1963 followed this report and the river boards were replaced by area river authorities which were granted water resource as well as fishery and pollution functions. To a large extent these river authorities were the forerunners of the National Rivers Authority with all these functions combined.

Moving into more recent times, 1973 saw the creation of the water authorities. However, their crucial weakness was the combination of pollution prevention and provision of sewage services in one organisation. Essentially, they were self policing in relation to sewage pollution. With the privatisation of the water supply industry in 1989, these gamekeeper and poacher functions were separated between the National Rivers Authority and the water companies. In April 1995, the NRA was replaced with the Environment Agency (see Chapter 1), incorporating within it Her Majesty's Inspectorate of Pollution and the Waste Regulation Authorities and this brings us to the present day.

CHAPTER 3

THE FISH

For the angler's purposes, fish can be divided into four categories: salmon, trout, freshwater or coarse fish and sea fish. Sea fish are considered in the chapter on sea angling. The statutory definition of each fish is found in s. 41 of the Salmon and Freshwater Fisheries Act 1975 (SAFFA). Salmon means 'all fish of the salmon species and includes part of a salmon'. Trout means 'any fish of the salmon family commonly known as trout including migratory trout and char'. Freshwater fish means 'any fish living in fresh water exclusive of salmon and trout and of any kinds of fish which migrate to and from tidal waters'. Eels 'includes elvers and the fry of eels.' These definitions are important because they apply to the various parts of SAFFA which regulate illegal methods of fishing, close seasons and obstructions, (see Chapters 13, 14 and 19 respectively). In addition, if fish are killed and fall within these definitions then they have the protection of s.4 SAFFA (see Chapter 9).

A final and somewhat anomalous category is royal fish. A statute passed during the reign of Edward II, the *Prerogativa Regis* (*17 Ed. II st. 1, c. II* (1324)) laid down that whales and sturgeons taken within the King's dominion shall belong to the King. Sir Matthew Hale in *De Jure Maris* found that royal fish were 'sturgeon, grampuses or great fish' and that royal fish 'taken in the wide sea' belong to the taker. In practical terms, this category has little relevance nowadays although there was an interesting case heard in the early part of the last century. In *Lord Warden and Admiral of the Cinque Ports v R (in his office of Admiralty)* (1831) the crews of seven oyster smacks, having discovered a whale three miles from the shore, towed it to Whitstable beach. The Judge confirmed that a whale found on the shore or caught near the coasts of Great Britain is the property of the Crown. The fishermen received salvage for their services. The dispute was not with the Crown but, as the title of the case suggests, between the Lord High Admiral and the Admiral of the Cinque Ports. To whom did the whale belong, or to put it another way, to whom had the Crown granted the right to take whales? Looking through the records, the Judge found that the Crown had granted the right to whales and other royal fish to the Admirals of the Cinque Ports earlier than any such right was granted to the Lord High Admirals. The whale was therefore the property of the Admirals of the Cinque Port.

1. WHO OWNS FISH?

This is becoming an increasingly important question for anglers. Clubs and fishery owners spend large sums each year in stocking their waters to provide sport for their members or their clients. What, for instance, does a club do if it is thrown off its water by the owner of the fishery who then turns the fishery into a day ticket water and benefits from all the stocking carried out by the club? In addition, there are obvious implications for the crime of theft which are discussed in Chapter 13.

The general rule regarding wild animals is that they are *ferae naturae* and that there is no absolute property in them whilst living. Therefore, nobody owns fish. However, as with most legal rules, this must be qualified: 'The Heire shall have the Deer in the Park, and by the same reason, the Fish.' This is the judgment of Mr Justice Popham in *Greye's Case* (1594). A man had bought fish of different species and stocked them into his pond. He then died. The Plaintiff ('the Heire' mentioned in Mr Justice Popham judgment) had brought an action in trespass against the Defendant (the executor of his estate) who had netted the fish in the pond which were, he claimed, his property by inheritance. The Defendant was found guilty of theft.

The judgement confirms that it is a 'felony' to steal fish out of a 'trunk [a perforated floating box in which fish are kept] or some narrow place where they are put to be taken at will and pleasure'. The judgment, however, due to its age is confusing and the word 'chattels' is used to describe the fish which only suggests that the fish were the Plaintiff's property.

Any difficulties are resolved by the later case of *R v Steer* (1704). A quantity of carp were stolen from a private pond. The Judge held that the fish were the property of the owner of the pond. The reasoning behind this decision lies in the fact that the fish cannot swim away from an enclosed pond and, thereby, be lost.

The law makes the distinction between rivers or lakes in multiple ownership and those waters in single ownership. It is absurd to try to retain ownership of a fish that may swim up or downstream into a part of the river in another's ownership. However, fish in a lake in one individual's owner-ship belong to the owner. It is only when fish are located in rivers or lakes in multiple ownership that they become absolute *ferae naturae*. The principle was expressed in the American case of *People v Truckee Lumber Co* (1897). Justice Van Fleet stated:

> While the right of fishing in his own land is exclusively in the riparian owner, this does not imply or carry the right to destroy what he does not take. He does not own the fish in the stream. His right of property attaches only to those he reduces to actual

possession, and he cannot lawfully kill or obstruct the free passage of those not taken.

(It should be noted that American cases are only persuasive in English and Welsh courts and do not create a precedent as such).

A word of warning must be sounded. Ownership of fish in lakes will depend on the circumstances. At one extreme, no one will seek to argue that goldfish in an ornamental pond are not owned by the householder. At the other, a lake may have several feeder streams, several riparian owners and outlets into other rivers and lakes. The fish swimming in such a lake would be *ferae naturae*. In between these two examples there is a large grey area. There have been no useful decided cases and it remains to be seen where the courts will draw the line.

The *ferae naturae* principle has led to some unusual judicial decisions. In *Snape v Dobbs* (1823) the parties had separate interests in two pieces of land over which a reservoir was created. The local Act creating the fishery allowed 'the owner or owners of land on which the reservoir is made to let all the water out of such reservoir once every seven years to take fish therein'. A dispute arose between the two owners over the ownership of the fish in the reservoir. It was decided that, when water was drawn off under the terms of the Act, they were entitled to such fish as came to rest on their soil. This appears entirely consistent with the *ferae naturae* doctrine. However, it has to be said that the downstream owner stood to benefit the most since more fish would inevitably have settled on his land as the water passed over it.

Watson v Goldsbrough (1986) is an interesting case. The Middlesbrough Angling Club spent substantial sums of money in stocking a fishing pond. Despite the fact that a draft lease was drawn up between the club and the owner of the pond (a farmer), it was never legally completed. The club carried out the restocking on the basis it would be granted a ten year lease. The farmer was made aware of this. Nevertheless, he tried to sell the ponds and the club brought an action to stop him doing so. The club argued that they had a binding agreement with the farmer on the basis of the doctrine of a proprietary estoppel. The Judge explained this concept:

> An owner of land cannot stand by and watch somebody else expend money on his land in the knowledge that the person expending the money either mistakenly thinks he already has an interest in the land or has an expectation encouraged or known to the owner that he will obtain such an interest from the owner.

The Judge found in favour of the club granting it a lease of one year and allowing it to take the fish from the pond as long as a 'proper and sufficient stock of fish' was maintained in the ponds. The fish were, therefore, the club's since it had stocked the water in the expectation, encouraged by the farmer, that it would be granted a lease.

This principle of estoppel gives a fishery owner another basis to argue that he owns the fish in his fishery as well as the argument that the fish are not wild and therefore belong to him.

2. WHEN IS A FISH CAUGHT?

It is not only the ownership of fish that has caused dispute but also the point during the process of capture when they become the property of an individual. The facts of *Young v Hitchens* (1844) are most instructive. A trawler had virtually encircled a shoal of pilchards when an enterprising competitor rowed his boat into the net and prevented the trawlerman from securing the fish. It was held by Lord Chief Justice Denham that the trawlerman had not secured the fish and his action in trespass failed. This case decided that it was the act of seizing which induced ownership and not the attempt to do so. The trawlerman had not actually seized the fish in the sense that he left a gap in his net allowing another fisherman to interfere. The fish were not in his control.

Several whaling cases heard in the nineteenth century shed further light on this. In *Aberdeen Arctic Co. v Salter* (1862), a whaler harpooned a whale but was unable to retain possession. When the whale died, it was recovered by another whaler. It was held that the whale belonged to the first whaler since he had caught it first. It would appear that seizing need only be temporary. Can this apply to a fish that survives the attempt to catch it? The earlier case of *Hogarth v Jackson* (1827) found that the whale belongs to the whaler who harpoons it first, despite the fact that the harpoon does not stay in the body of the whale. If the whale (or fish) is lost then it remains the property of the whaler (fisherman) whether it dies or not. This was confirmed by *Skinner v Chapman* (1827) where the whale broke free from the harpoon yet remained the property of the first striker.

This could lead to the unusual situation where a fisherman hooks a fish only to lose it whilst reeling it in. The fish could then swim to another fishery either up or downstream where it is caught by another riparian owner. Is it open to the first fisherman to argue that the fish is his on the basis that, like the harpoon, the hook became dislodged from the fish? Theoretically, the answer is yes. However, the question is somewhat mischievous. It is improbable that the angler, disgruntled at losing his quarry, will confront his companion, in the belief that the fish he has just caught was the one which threw his hook earlier in the day!

QUESTION

My club has rented a lake on a farmer's land for nearly twenty years. This has not been recorded in writing. When we took it over it was little better than a hole in the ground. Since then we have cleared it of all litter, including an old car, constructed pegs with facilities for disabled anglers, planted trees, constructed a footpath to the lake and, most important, stocked it with fish. In fact, the carp that we stocked in the first years have now grown on to specimen size and must now each be worth a considerable sum of money. The farmer has just told us that this will be our last season fishing the lake. We have another lake that we actually own. Are the fish ours and can we restock them into that lake? We have also heard the farmer is going to turn the lake into a commercial fishery and will be benefitting from our fish.

Answer

The answer to this question cannot be a definite 'yes' or 'no'. These facts whilst not unusual have never been tested in Court. The big problem is that there is nothing in writing. Your club only has a licence to fish the lake. If a clause had been inserted in the licence (see Chapter 5 for the difference between a lease and a licence) like that in paragraph 7 of the second schedule of the lease in the Appendix then the fish would have been yours. Technically, the lake is owned by the farmer and following *R v Steer* the fish belong to the farmer. Fish in a lake in the ownership of one individual belong to that person. It may be that your club can rely on the doctrine of proprietary estoppel as in *Watson v Goldsbrough*, but it will have to prove that it stocked the fish in the expectation the lease would continue and the farmer knew that. You could also rely on the doctrine of unjust enrichment, whereby the law provides a remedy to prevent an individual or company from retaining the money of, or some benefit from, another which is against conscience that he should keep. In the case of *Greenwood v Bennett* (1972), the defendant was not permitted to enrich himself unjustly at the Plaintiff's expense. This is untested in this kind of case, but it could be used by a club in these circumstances.

CHAPTER 4

THE LEGAL NATURE
OF FISHERIES

Angling may take place in a variety of arenas - dry fly fishing on a clear chalk stream, for specimen carp in a lake, for salmon on a fast-flowing Scottish river, for roach and bream in a canal, or at sea for any number of species. This chapter will focus on three aspects of the fishery: the general distinctions between still and flowing waters and between natural and artificial waters, the fishery's components and how they are classified legally.

1. THE FISHERY

Fisheries can be found in any water - rivers, streams, tributaries, estuaries, canals, lakes and ponds. Everyday language provides only very loose categories - one angler's river will be another's stream and one's angler's lake will be another's pond. There are no universally accepted definitions. However, a general distinction can be made between watercourses in the sense of flowing waters and still waters. For the angler, the former may be a very slow flowing canal or the upper reaches of a river with pools and riffles. A good example of the latter is a day ticket lake run on a commercial basis.

The distinction between artificial and natural watercourses is important because riparian rights do not automatically attach to the former (see Chapter 6). Artificial watercourses are canals, drainage ditches, aqueducts or flumes (an artificial channel for water to be applied to an industrial use). It may well be that the origin of a watercourse is unknown such that it does not easily fall into either category. An individual owning property next to a watercourse may claim the fishery in a watercourse but this may be disputed on the basis that it is artificial. There are no hard and fast rules that can be applied to resolve such a dispute and each case will be decided on its facts.

In *Roberts v Richards* (1881), the watercourse in question was partly natural and partly artificial. However, neither section could be distinguished from the other. It was held that even if the watercourse was artificial it was constructed to allow riparian rights to attach to the owners of the banks. Similarly, in *Baily & Co v Clark, Son and Morland* (1902), the Plaintiff millowners took water from an artificial channel which had existed for some centuries and was supplied with water from a natural channel. An argument arose over the Plaintiff's right to abstract water. The Court held that it should be inferred that the channel had been constructed on the basis that all riparian proprietors should have the same rights.

However, the law does make the distinction between temporary and permanent artificial watercourses. Riparian rights will only be acquired as long as it was constructed for lasting purposes. In *Arkwright v Gell* (1839) the channel was an artificial stream which drained certain mines and that was its sole purpose. Due to its temporary nature, the Court found that the owners of the banks of the stream could not force the mine owners to continue the discharge.

1.1 The Watercourse

Section 221(1) of the Water Resources Act 1991 (WRA), the statute which regulates water resources and pollution, states that a watercourse includes 'all rivers, streams, ditches, drains, cuts, culverts, dykes, sluices, sewers and passages through which water flows, but excludes mains and other pipes' which belong to the Environment Agency or a water company. This definition is only used when interpreting the WRA and is not generally applicable.

However, all watercourses have three components which are common to any description applied to it: the bed, the banks and the water contained within it. The common law sheds more light on the definition of watercourse.

1.1.1 The bed

The bed is that part of the river which forms the channel between the banks. In *Goolden v Thames Conservators* (1897) the bed of a non-tidal river was defined as the soil underneath the waters of the river between its banks. The American case of *State of Alabama v State of Georgia* (64 U.S. 5150) gave a more explicit definition:

> The bed of a river is that portion of its soil which is alternatively covered and left bare as there may be an increase or diminution in the supply of water, and which is adequate to contain it at its average and mean stage during the entire year without reference to the extraordinary freshets [a flood or overflowing of a river caused by heavy rains or melted snow] of the winter or spring, or the extreme droughts of the summer or autumn.

This definition was approved in the case of *Hindson v Ashby* (1896) where Lord Justice Smith stated it 'in apt language, conveys what I mean to express as to what constitutes a bed of a river'.

The more recent case of *Electronic Leasing v Jackson* (1993) also referred to *Hindson v Ashby*. That case involved a dispute over mooring rights. The Plaintiff owned land next to a river. On the basis that the then National Rivers Authority owned the bed of the River Thames by virtue of the Thames Conservancy Act 1857, the Defendant argued that the bank formed part of the bed. The Court rejected this stating that '... the Plaintiff's registered title extends down to the water's edge (i.e. the ordinary high water mark of the river) and includes the bank from the towpath down to the water's edge'. The situation was complicated by this towpath which ran by the river.

The Judge found that, whilst the towpath was in public ownership, the section of the bank from the edge of the path to the water was owned by the Plaintiff. Therefore, each time the boat owners crossed this part of the land to reach their boats they were trespassing.

1.1.2 The banks

The definition of the banks of a river has proved more problematic. In *Jones v Mersey River Board* (1957) the definition turned upon the interpretation of the former Land Drainage Act 1930 which allowed the drainage board to deposit matter removed during dredging on the banks of the river. The Court found that strict rules could not be laid down but that each case depends on its facts. In doing so, it found that the word 'bank' included not only the vertical face of the bank but also so much of the land adjoining the river which helped to contain it. This definition was borne out in the American case of *Howard v Ingersoll* (1851) which found that the banks were 'those elevations of land which confine the waters when they rise out of the bed'.

The extent of the banks may have implications for the angler. Many leases or licences (see for example Paragraph 6 of the First Schedule of the specimen licence in the Appendix) will contain obligations and liabilities concerning banks and maintenance.

1.1.3 The water

The water in the fishery cannot be owned. The owner of the fishery has certain rights over the water in terms of purity and quantity (see Chapter 6). However, the water is not his and his use of it is governed by the rights and duties of a riparian owner. The law regarding the abstraction of water is dealt with in detail in Chapter 11. Riparian owners are entitled, at common law, to abstract water for ordinary purposes. It is only when the water is abstracted that it becomes their property.

1.2 Still Waters

The case law regarding the beds, banks and water of flowing waters also applies to lakes and ponds. Statute makes specific provision for still waters.

Section 104 (1) (c) WRA includes most lakes and ponds as 'inland freshwaters' in the definition of 'controlled waters'. If a fishery is a 'controlled water' then it will have the protection of the criminal law in that a polluter may be fined and prosecuted if found guilty. If it falls outside the definition, then a polluter cannot be prosecuted (see Chapter 9). A lake that does *not* discharge into other rivers or waters is not a controlled water.

For the purposes of water abstraction (see Chapter 11), still waters fall into the category of 'discrete waters'. Discrete waters are defined as inland waters comprising:

(a) a lake, pond or reservoir which does not discharge into any other inland water; or

(b) one of a group of two or more lakes, ponds or reservoirs and watersconnecting them, where none of the inland waters in the group discharges to any inland waters outside the group; ...' (s.221 (1) WRA).

If a water falls outside this definition then it will also fall outside the licensing system. However, the common law rules governing the use of the water will still apply.

Most of the case law applies to the ownership of lakes rather than their definition. In *MacKenzie v Bankes* (1878), two lakes were joined by a narrow shallow channel which was not a river and was divided by a causeway of loose stones. The Plaintiff tried to claim that he owned both lakes since that would give him the right of fishing and boating on both. The Court decided they were separate lakes. It found that the waters of the lakes did not mix and the fact that the channel could not be called a river was immaterial. It formed a barrier between the lakes.

To find a definition one must turn to American law again. In *Wood v Maitland*, a lake was seen to have two basic meanings as either 'a body of water of considerable size surrounded by land' or 'a widened portion of a river or lagoon'.

2. THE FISHERY IN ITS LEGAL CONTEXT

Fundamental to the angler is the legal nature of his fishery. It is significant for him in terms of the rights that it confers and, thereby, how he can develop and protect it. Chapter 1 referred to the nineteenth century argument over the distinction between a free and several fishery. The ownership of fisheries is a complex subject, with the law over the years making numerous distinctions. Practically speaking for the angler, there are two distinctions that form the basis of an understanding of the ownership of fisheries. The first is between public and private fishery and the second is between a corporeal and incorporeal fishery.

2.1. Private and public fisheries

2.1.1 Public fisheries

Although doubt has been cast upon the origin of the rule, it is now generally accepted that the public right to fish was preserved when the barons forced King John to sign Magna Carta in 1215 (see Chapter 1). Seen as an abuse of its rights, this prohibited the Crown from granting a private fishery to the exclusion of the public in tidal watercourses and the foreshore. Prior to Magna Carta, the Crown had frequently exercised its right to exclude the right of the public to fish and grant a private fishery. Nowadays, the public right to fish can only be excluded by an Act of Parliament. A prime example is the Sea Fisheries (Shellfish) Act 1967, which allows the Minister of Agriculture, Fisheries and Food to create a private shellfishery.

The principal feature of public fisheries is that generally they only exist in waters that are tidal. The public has no general right to fish in non-tidal waters. It may well be that a private owner allows the public to fish in his fishery because he is happy for them to do so, or he is ignorant of his rights, but the public cannot acquire a right to fish in his water. Even if the public has been fishing a section of a river for tens of years, this does not prevent the owner from excluding them if he wishes to do so. The legal rationale behind this rule is that the public is a vague and fluctuating body and cannot acquire a right to fish. In *Pearce v Schotcher* (1882), the Defendant was charged with fishing in a private fishery on the Dee. He argued that as the public had fished the spot 'during the whole period of living witnesses', a public right had been acquired. This was emphatically rejected by the Judge. No public right to fish can be acquired by the public where the tide does not ebb and flow.

2.1.1.1 The boundary between public and private fishing

The obvious question to ask is: How does an angler judge where the public right to fish ends and the private right starts? There is no absolute rule and enquiries would have to be made with the Environment Agency or local landowners. Past cases have suggested that the tidal limit is where freshwater prevails. In *Horne v MacKenzie* (1839), the Judge rejected this, arguing that it would not solve the problem because the rights of the parties would be changed with the ebb and flow of the water. Salinity may be the factor in some cases, such that the tidal limit is reached where the water is not salty. In *Reece v Miller* (1882), the Defendant maintained there was a public right to fish because the water was salty. Mr Justice Grove said it was not necessary that the water should be salty but 'the spot must be one where the tide in the ordinary and regular course of things flows and reflows'. Generally, this is a question to be decided according to each river and will turn upon whether there is sufficient evidence to describe the water as tidal at any one particular point.

2.1.1.2 Permitted methods of angling

The public right of fishing does not mean that any method may be adopted. Fishing devices, for example fixed engines, cannot be fixed to the soil (see Chapter 19). In *Malcomson v O'Dea* (1863), Mr Justice Willes said that 'The soil of "navigable waters"... is prima facie in the Crown.' Therefore, the use of engines would mean an exercise of the right on soil not owned by the public. The right extends only to fishing by rod and line, drawing nets or any other ordinary method.

A final important point must be made that rights of navigation and fishing are not interconnected. Simply because the public has a right to fish in a fishery does not mean that it also has the right to navigate in that stretch and vice versa. This question is explored more fully in Chapter 16.

2.1.2 Private fisheries

The terminology relating to private fisheries is confusing. A myriad of terms is used without proper distinction. It is, therefore, essential at the outset to define all the relevant terms:

* *exclusive fishery* - as its name reveals, this allows the owner to exclude anyone he desires from the fishery
* *several fishery* - same as exclusive fishery
* *free fishery* - same as exclusive and several fishery
* *common of fishery* - also known as a common of piscary, this right arises where the owner grants the right to fish to a number of people.

A 'several fishery' may be divided between the right to take floating fish and the right to take oysters. Two several fisheries can therefore exist within one person's ownership. In *Seymour v Courtenay* (1771), Lord Clifford granted a fishery to the Plaintiffs, but reserved to himself the right to take the oysters together with 'a right of taking fish for the supply of his own table'. The Plaintiffs took an action against the Defendants for trespass to the fishery. The Defendants who interfered with the Plaintiffs fishing argued that because Lord Clifford had reserved the oystery and a right to fish himself the Plaintiffs could not have an exclusive fishery and, therefore, could not sue in trespass. The Judge rejected this argument stating that two different types of fishery could exist in the same piece of land.

3. CORPOREAL OR INCORPOREAL

The second distinction is between a corporeal and an incorporeal fishery. A landowner may want to sell the right to fish and not the land to which the right attaches. When he does so he sells the incorporeal fishery - so called because it is without body, merely being a right to do something. If he sells the land on which the fishery is located then he is selling the corporeal fishery. Whilst this may seem a somewhat artificial distinction in that the purchaser buys what he wants (the fishery), it is important for the rights that he derives, especially if his fishery is polluted.

Another term for an incorporeal fishery is a *profit à prendre*. This is the right to take something from another's land. In this instance, it is the fish that are taken away from the owner's land. For practical purposes, a *profit à prendre* and incorporeal fishery are one and the same.

4. PRESUMPTIONS ON THE OWNERSHIP OF FISHERIES

If there is a dispute about the ownership of a fishery, there are two important presumptions that help to decide the issue. First, it is presumed that the owner of the soil is also the owner of the right of fishing over it. The law assumes that the fishery is corporeal unless it can be shown that the right to fish has been separated from the land by a lease or conveyance. Confusingly, the second presumes the owner of the right to fish is the owner of the soil beneath it. In *Hanbury v Jenkins* (1901), Mr Justice Buckley said, '... it must be taken as settled that when a several fishery is proved to exist, the owner of the fishery is presumed to be the owner of soil unless there is evidence to the contrary'. He went on to say, 'you can scarcely enjoy one without the other'.

A situation may develop where two parties claim the fishery with one owning the soil. Both parties have the benefit of each presumption. Such a dispute could only be decided on the evidence that each can produce. However, this conflict does have important implications if the fishery owner wanted to improve the fishery by making weirs, groynes or creating pools (see Chapter 15). He would have to show that he owns the soil, otherwise he would be trespassing.

These presumptions do not apply to artificial waters where the right of fishery will be controlled by the statute authorising its construction. In the *Grand Union Canal Company v Ashby* (1861), the question of who owned the fishery turned upon the interpretation of the Act giving the company power to construct the canal. The Court found that the Plaintiff not only owned the fishery under the terms of the Act but also, by presumption, the soil.

5. THE *MEDIUM FILUM* RULE

5.1 Non-tidal rivers

The rule regarding the extent of the ownership of the bed of the river is that the riparian owners are entitled to the soil *usque ad medium filum aquae*. This means that there is an imaginary line running down the centre of the river or stream, called the *medium filum*, and each owner is entitled to the soil up to but not beyond that line. It follows from this that if both banks are owned by the same person, then all the soil of the watercourse belongs to him.

This rule is only a presumption. As such, it can be rebutted by contrary evidence. In the title deeds to the land there may be a clause which specifically excludes the bed of a river which forms the boundary with its neighbour. If a dispute arose over the boundary between their lands, then surrounding circumstances such as who owns the fishing rights or whether the river is navigable could be used to decide the issue.

This then raises the important question of where can the angler fish from? If the fishery owner only owns the right of fishing can he cast his line to fish in the water above the soil owned by his neighbour? In the Scottish case of *Fotheringham v Kerr* (1984), the question of whether, as a general rule, each proprietor of land on opposite banks of a river had a right to fish by rod and line for fish from his own bank as far as the medium filum, or was entitled to fish beyond the *medium filum*, was answered. The Court found that the true principle was that each proprietor was entitled to stand on his own bank or to wade out to the limit of his property, the *medium filum*, and to fish as far across the river as he could reach by normal casting or spinning.

5.2 Tidal rivers

The *medium filum* rule is relatively simple to apply to non-tidal rivers, but its application is more problematic in tidal rivers. Should the line be drawn according to the level of water at high or low tide? Both approaches could lead to different results but, as yet, a case has not been taken to the Courts to decide the issue. However, the question may be of little significance since it is the Crown that owns the soil of tidal waters unless a private right of fishing exists.

5.3 Changes to the course of a river

Another problem is caused by the natural changes to the course of rivers and streams. This can take place imperceptibly over a period of time (known as accretion) or suddenly (avulsion). With the former the boundary follows the natural change in the course of the river. With the latter, the boundaries remain as before thus depriving the owner of one parcel of land of the right to fish.

Importantly, the rule does not apply to canals or tidal rivers. Ownership of the bed will depend upon the Act of Parliament creating the canal and will probably rest with the company which constructed the canal or the owner of the land over which the canal passes.

5.4 Still waters

In contrast, it is generally accepted that the *medium filum* rule does apply to still waters. The case of *Bristow v Cormican* (1878) decided that the Crown has no legal right to the fishery in an inland non-tidal lake. It follows that the public has no right to fish in such still waters. For example, in *Bourke v Davis* (1889) a private lake bordered a public road but this did not entitle the general public to launch boats from that point on to the lake to fish.

Interesting questions on the extent of ownership will arise where a lake is bordered by many properties. Lakes are not uniform in shape. A perfect circle or rectangle would be easy to divide up. The ownership of the soil will depend on its facts and no further conclusions can be applied other than the medium filum rule applies.

QUESTIONS

Question 1

My club fishes a stretch of river near the estuary. It borders onto the area where the public can fish. We find that the public sometimes comes onto our land and we have to ask them to leave. Where exactly does the public right to fish end?

Answer

A definite answer cannot be given to your question. It will take much time and research to resolve where your private fishery starts and the public right of fishing ends. The law leaves each case to be decided on its facts. Evidence, such as your club's title deeds or, if you lease, your landlord's deeds must be read carefully (see Chapter 5). Also, statements from older members of the club and locals will help to establish the point. Scientific evidence on salinity and the flow of the tide will be very useful. For the present, a sign erected at the point where you think your fishery starts will go some way to protecting your club's fishing rights from trespass by members of the public.

Question 2

We want to carry out improvements to our fishery. When we spoke to the Environment Agency to ask for consent to put boulders in the river to create pools and increase the flow, its fishery officer said we might need the permission of the landowner. We own the fishing rights on a ninety-nine year lease. We asked our solicitor if we owned the bed. He looked at our lease and said it was inconclusive because clause 1 said the landlord let the fishing rights 'and so much of the bed and banks' as he was able. Our landlord can be difficult about these sorts of things and we want to be certain of our ground.

Answer

There are two issues here. First are you the owners of the corporeal or incorporeal fishery? If the former then you do not need the landlord's permission. If the latter, then you do. Much will depend on how the lease is interpreted. Does it lease the bed and banks as well as the fishery? This is the crux. Second, there may be a battle of the presumptions. If the landlord cannot show that he owns the bed and banks and if no one else can show ownership, then the law presumes that your club will be the owner of the soil. Again, only the permission of the Agency is needed. However, if your landlord shows that he owns the bed and banks, then he is also presumed to own the fishery which he has let to you. His permission will be needed.

If you cannot resolve the problem, the best tack might be to approach the landlord and stress that such work can only increase the value of his asset.

One final qualification must be made in that the works may involve planning considerations - see Chapter 15 in this respect.

CHAPTER 5

THE OWNERSHIP AND PROTECTION OF FISHERIES

Anglers frequently have a false sense of security that simply because a loose arrangement has existed for many years between itself and the landowner - for example, the gift of a bottle of whisky at Christmas - that it will always own the fishery. Often, a club spends much money in providing platforms, cutting weeds, planting trees and especially restocking only to be told by the landowner to vacate the fishery with little or no notice. Justifiably aggrieved upon being given notice to quit, this sense of grievance is only made worse when the club finds out that there is no avenue to claim compensation.

There are several ways in which a fishery may be owned and it will be a matter for negotiation between the owner of the fishery whether he wants to sell, lease or licence. The following only relates to private fisheries. It was firmly held in *Smith v Andrews* (1891) that the public, as a fluctuating and uncertain body, cannot own a several fishery.

1. How is a Fishery Owned?

1.1 Freehold

The purchaser of a fishery may either buy the land upon which the fishery is located (the corporeal fishery) or the fishing rights (the incorporeal fishery) (see Chapter 4). Either way he will own an exclusive fishery which means he has the right to prevent anyone from fishing in his fishery. Subject to any covenants or restrictions imposed by the vendor he can deal with the fishery as he wishes by selling it on himself, or letting it to a club. The most usual covenant imposed will limit the use of the fishery to recreational fishing by rod and line. Every subsequent purchaser, lessee or licensee will have to observe this covenant. Failure to do so may lead to an action by the seller, or someone who buys the property from him in the future, to enforce the covenant.

1.2 Lease

A lease is another means of transferring ownership, but only for a defined period. It may only be for a season, as long as ninety nine years or more. The landlord may lease either the corporeal or the incorporeal fishery. Both must be done by deed. This is especially important since a *profit à prendre* can only be created by deed. In *Fitzgerald v Firbank* (1897), Lord Elbury granted to the plaintiffs for a term of years 'the exclusive right of fishing' in a part of the River Colne. The document stated, 'The right of fishing hereby granted shall only extend to fair rod and line angling at proper seasons, and to netting for the sole purpose of procuring fish-baits.' The grant to the Plaintiffs was by way of a deed. The Judge held that it was what is known in property law as an incorporeal hereditament, 'It is more than an easement: it is what is commonly called a *profit à prendre* and it is of such a nature that a person who enjoys that right has such possessory rights that he can bring an action for trespass at common law for the infringement of those rights.'

This question also arose in *Whitby v Warrington Anglers* (1985). The dispute concerned the rateability of the club's fishing rights. The outcome depended upon whether the club owned the rights under a *profit à prendre*, or a mere licence. The club was granted the fishing rights by the Manchester Ship Canal Company under several deeds from 1905, but from lst January 1981 permission was granted by virtue of a letter dated 3rd February 1981 from the estate officer of the canal company to the secretary of the association. The letter provided for the payment of rent, imposed conditions on the exercise of the rights and allowed for an extension of the agreement. The Judge held that the letter did not grant a *profit à prendre*. It granted a licence. He stated, 'The purpose of this letter was no doubt partly that it should operate, under the byelaws, as a consent in writing to fishing and partly to make lawful that which would otherwise be unlawful.'

1.2.1 Meaning of deed

It is, therefore, important to distinguish a deed and other documents. Following Section 1 of Law of Property (Miscellaneous Provisions) Act 1989 (LP(MP)A), the requirement that a deed had to be executed under seal was abolished. Before the LP(MP)A, at the end of a document where it was signed, the words 'Signed, sealed and delivered by A. Trout in the presence of: ...' were necessary. Now, only the words, 'Signed as a deed by A. Trout in the presence of:' are used. These words are not actually required by the LP(MP)A, but solicitors use them as a matter of good practice.

As a further requirement, the document must make it clear on its face that it is intended to be a deed. Before the schedules, or at the end of the document the words 'In witness whereof the parties hereto have duly executed this deed' should also be written. Also, the document itself can start by saying 'This deed ...'. (In Appendix 1, there is a lease of a fishery which is a deed and can be used to grant a right to fish).

1.2.2 Advantages and disadvantages of leasing

The advantage to the landlord of leasing the fishery is that the ownership of the fishery will revert to him at the end of the term. He may also impose covenants upon the tenant to ensure proper use of the fishery and restrictions on the method to be used, the times of year that it may be fished, or reserve a rod to himself. In *Re Vicker's Lease* (1947), the owner leased a fishery on the River Test at Romsey, but reserved a rod for 'her own use'. When she died, the Court held that this right lapsed since it was only for her personal use.

For the tenant, the lease offers, as compared to a licence (see 1.3 below), a high degree of security. As long as the tenant observes all the covenants, he will enjoy the fishing rights for as long as the lease stipulates. Furthermore, to buy freehold fishing is expensive. Leasing offers a cheaper (although, some would argue, not cheap) way of enjoying fishing rights.

1.2.3 Landlord and Tenant Act 1954 and angling leases

If the landlord lets the fishery or the land to an individual, club or a company who runs it on a commercial basis by selling day tickets, the tenant may be entitled to the protection offered by Part II of the Landlord and Tenant Act 1954 (LTA).

However, the LTA only covers those premises which are occupied 'for the purposes of a business' (s.23 (1) LTA). Does an angling club's fishery or a commercial fishery fall within this definition? Section 23 (2) LTA does leave the door open since it states that the expression includes 'a trade, profession or employment and includes any activity carried on by a body of persons, whether corporate or incorporate'. An angling club is usually an unincorporated association, although it can form itself into a company. Furthermore, angling is an activity. There would, therefore, appear to be a persuasive argument that a fishery should fall under the protection of the LTA. There has been no decided case to answer this question, although there have been cases which have touched upon the issue.

The contrary argument runs along the lines that fishing rights do not form 'premises', since they do not include buildings. What is the position then of fishing rights that are let with a fishing hut? Many commercial fisheries have a building where tickets and refreshments may be sold. Would they fall within the protection of the LTA? The best that can be said is that probably a commercial fishery would fall within the definition of a 'business', but that a fishery without any buildings run by an angling club may not. Until a case is taken to court for a decision, no definite advice can be given.

1.2.3.1 Procedure

The operation of the LTA is beyond the scope of this book. However, in brief, the landlord has to serve a notice on the tenant, not more than twelve months but not less than six months before the end of the term of the lease, stating that he wants possession of the fishery at the end of the term (s.25 LTA). The tenant then has the option of either agreeing to vacate the premises or of applying to a court (usually the local County Court) for a new term. He must do this within six months of being served with the landlord's notice. The Court will decide what the terms of the new lease will be, including the length of the term and the rent. The tenant can also take the initiative by serving the first notice himself (s.26 LTA). Any landlord should be aware of this, since it could well affect his plans for his property. If neither the landlord nor the tenant serve the appropriate notice, the tenancy will continue until a notice is served. It is open to both the landlord and the tenant to apply to the Court to exclude the lease from the provisions of the LTA, before it is signed. This must nevertheless be done with the agreement of both parties.

1.2.4 Holding over

Lastly, angling leases are usually of a short duration. Leases of ten years or more are rare. It is often the case that clubs will sign a lease for three years, but continue in occupation of the fishery after the end of the term. They will usually continue paying rent annually. With secretaries and other club officials changing, matters such as renewal of leases are often forgotten. If the club continues to fish the water at the end of the lease, it is deemed to be holding over under the lease even though the term has expired. It must continue to observe the terms of the lease. However, the landlord may decide that he wants to give the club notice to quit whilst the tenant is holding over. The period that he is allowed to give the club is the equivalent of the usual interval between regular rental payments. If the rent is paid monthly, then a month's notice must be given. If it is paid annually, a year's notice must be given and so on.

1.3 Licence

A licence only makes what would otherwise be unlawful lawful. The quotation above from *Whitby v Warrington Anglers* distinguishes a lease and licence using these words. A licence is essentially permission to do something. If a landlord grants a licence to use his fishery, he is only giving permission to do so. A lease offers security in that the tenant can enjoy the fishing rights for the period set out in the lease. However, the security offered by a licence is considerably less. Notice to quit can be given at any time, as long as it is reasonable.

A licence can take many forms. It may be oral permission with no money changing hands. An example would be a farmer allowing a club to fish a lake on his farm, simply by telling its secretary that the club can do so. It may be more formal, such as an exchange of letters, or a one page document, headed 'Agreement', setting out the parties, the period and the rent which must be paid. It may even be under seal as a deed although, even if made by deed, it is still only a licence.

The case of *East Lothian Angling Association v Haddington Town Council* (1980) is a good example of how a licence is created. A letter was sent each year to the proprietors of the land from whom it rented fishing rights stating 'The Association would be very grateful if you could kindly renew your permission for the coming season under the same conditions.' The proprietors would then sign the part of the document which stated, 'Permission is granted to the E.L.A.A. to fish any waters during the season.' The heading to the letter described the document as a 'Fishing Privilege for River Tyne and Tributaries'. This was held by the Judge to be 'simply a personal licence or permission to fish for trout which is granted to the Pursuers [Plaintiffs] for a season'.

The most important aspect of a licence is that it does not confer any security upon the licensee. The landlord or licensor only needs to give reasonable notice to quit. This may be a matter of weeks even if the club has exercised the fishing rights for a number of years. If a club has adopted the practice of giving the landlord a bottle of whisky every Christmas by way of rent, then the landlord would be entitled to give only a very short notice period. With a lease, in constrast, notice to quit can, as long as the tenant has observed its terms, only be given at the end of the period.

The only protection a licence offers is derived from the granted contractual obligations created between the parties by the licence. For example, if the notice period is actually specified in the licence such as four weeks and the landlord forces the club off the fishery in two weeks then this a breach of the contract. However, the landlord is still within his rights to evict the licensee. The only action the licensee would have is the return of two weeks' rent because the licence was not terminated in accordance with its terms.

The distinction between a lease and a licence raises problems in suing for pollution. This is dealt with in Chapter 10.

1.4 Prescription

Prescription is the process whereby ownership of a fishery can be claimed, although no money has actually changed hands and there are no title documents. Essentially, ownership is claimed through long enjoyment of the fishing rights. However, only the fishery as a *profit à prendre* can be claimed in this way. Therefore, land cannot be claimed by prescription, only the right to fish the land.

Prescription is relevant to anglers where they have fished a fishery and do not know the identity of the owner. They have not bought any land or the fishing rights and have not paid rent, whether under a lease or licence. It may well be that an angling club has fished without interruption for a number of years and no one tries to stop the members from fishing. However, an event such as pollution, or a trespasser damaging or taking fish from the water, usually precipitates a dispute over the ownership of the fishery. If the polluter or trespasser can prove that the club does not own the fishery, then that will be a defence to any claim by the club for damages caused by the pollution or trespass respectively.

There are three ways to establish title by prescription: at common law; under the doctrine of lost modern grant and under the Prescription Act 1832.

1.4.1 At Common Law

Prescription at common law is based upon a presumed grant of the fishery assumed by the law to have been made before 1189, the date taken to be the commencement of legal memory. The law decides that since the fishing rights have been exercised for a certain period, then there must have been a grant of the fishery. It must be shown that the right has been exercised '*nec vi, nec clam, nec precario*'. This means neither as a result of force, secrecy or permission. Payment of rent (or even the permission of the owner) and a break in the enjoyment of the fishery would defeat a claim to a prescriptive right.

However, it is difficult to give specific rules as to when any claim may fail. Each case will depend on its facts, including how long the club has exercised those rights and how they were exercised. For example, the non payment of rent, signs erected stating the fishing was owned by the club and the expulsion of non members would all help in establishing the claim.

It will be impossible, in any case, to trace the ownership of the fishery through the various owners back to 1189. The law therefore, depending on each case, implies such a chain of ownership if a number of years' exclusive use can be shown. Periods of twenty and fifty years have been held sufficient to establish ownership. In *Neill v Duke of Devonshire* (1882), where an individual sued for trespassing tried to claim a public right to fish, the Court looked at documentary evidence going back as far as the reigns of Charles I and James I to establish the Plaintiff's title. It also accepted evidence of a judgment obtained by the Plaintiff in 1826 for trespass against an individual fishing in the same river because this was inconsistent with any public right of fishing. Overall, what must be shown is the use of fishery as of right and as a distinct and separate property.

1.4.2 Lost Modern Grant

The doctrine of lost modern grant is rarely used and, as the name suggests, this doctrine allows a claimant to show that a modern grant of the right has been lost. It was devised in order to avoid the problem that it is obviously easy to show a break in the ownership of the fishery since 1189.

1.4.3 Prescription Act 1832

The Prescription Act 1832 (PA) only applies to fisheries claimed as appurtenant to land. This means that the right must attach to a piece of land which the claimant already occupies. A fishery owned independently of any land is called a fishery in gross. An angler cannot claim a fishery under the PA if he does not occupy any land next to or near the water. In *Shuttleworth v Fleming* (1865), the Plaintiff failed in an action for trespass because he claimed ownership to fishing rights in gross and, as such, could not succeed in establishing a good title under the PA. It will, therefore, be very unusual for an angling club to use this Act because it usually does not actually own land in the way that a private individual does.

1.4.4 Proof and Prescription

Which of the above is used and in what circumstances? The answer is that all are used. When a claim to a fishery by prescription is made, the would-be owner can argue all three in the alternative. If he cannot show ownership by common law prescription, then he will try lost modern grant and if that does not succeed, then the PA. He only needs to prove one and he succeeds.

In many cases, there will not be evidence going back to Stuart times as in *Neill v Duke of Devonshire*. Anglers, in order to prove the ownership of fishing rights through prescription, will have to look for more mundane evidence. If a dispute over the ownership of fishing rights arises, what evidence will a court look for? How can one prove the necessary twenty or fifty years? There may be individuals who have fished the water for many years. They can be called as witnesses to verify that the rights have been enjoyed *'nec clam nec vi nec vicario'*. If a club is concerned that a dispute may arise, then formal sworn statements called statutory declarations can be taken from older members so that a record is preserved.

Often, ownership will not be challenged and such precautions may seem rather extreme. However, all that it takes is for someone to buy neighbouring land and start to claim title to the fishing rights for a dispute to arise. Similarly, a factory may be constructed and its discharge onto the river may adversely affect the fish. The factory owner may defend any claim for damages by arguing that the plaintiff does not own the fishing rights. Signs erected claiming the right to fish and a policy of evicting trespassers are other precautions which will help to demonstrate ownership.

It will be very difficult to claim a fishery by prescription in tidal waters. This stems from the concepts that the Crown owns the bed of tidal waters and that a public right of fishing exists over it. An exception is the case of *Carter v Murcot* (1768). The Plaintiff was able to show that he had an exclusive fishery at Arlingham on the River Severn. He was able to establish his right by prescription, although the usual rule is that the public has a right to fish tidal waters. Whilst this is an example of a successful claim, it is usually very difficult to establish a fishery by prescription in tidal waters. Even documentary evidence of title to such a fishery may not exclude the public right of fishing.

2. PROOF AND PROTECTION OF THE OWNERSHIP OF FISHING RIGHTS

Proof of ownership of a fishery is vital. If the fishing is ruined by pollution, any claim for damages cannot be sustained unless ownership can be proved. This is equally vital in a case of trespass, where the owner may wish to prevent unlawful fishing. It will be simple in the case of freehold and leasehold fishing rights because a document proving ownership should be available. The ownership of land in England and Wales is divided into two systems: registered and unregistered. The remainder of this chapter will look at these two systems, with an emphasis on how the ownership of fishing rights can be protected.

2.1 Land Registration

In 1925, the Land Registration Act (LRA) was passed and set up a system of land registration with the eventual goal that details of the ownership of all land should be kept on the register. This process is still ongoing and it will be many years before it is complete. The system is administered by the

Land Registry. The central office is located at Lincoln's Inn, London, but there are nineteen district land registeries.

If land next to a river is bought, the purchaser will receive a land certificate, a copy of which is kept at the local land registry. If the land has been bought with a loan from a building society or other source, then this loan will be registered and the lender will be issued with a charge certificate for security (s.63 LRA). Freehold land must be registered as must a lease of land granted for a period of twenty one years or more (s.8 LRA). However, leases of less than twenty one years cannot be registered. Neither a licence nor fishing rights claimed by prescription can be registered.

2.1.1 Registration of Fishing Rights

The distinction between incorporeal and corporeal fishing rights is especially important when it comes to registering land and it is vital in the registration of fishing rights. *Profits à prendre*, whether freehold or lease-hold, cannot be registered. This means that ownership of fishing rights cannot be registered.

How then can the owner of the fishing rights prove ownership? He could sell the rights to another club or individual. How is the angler protected? Under section 70(l)(j) LRA, fishing rights are classified as overriding interests. These are defined by section 3 (xvi) as 'all incumbrances, interests, rights, and powers not entered on the register but subject to which registered dispositions are by this Act to take effect ...'. Any purchaser of the land to which the fishing rights attach, does so subject to those fishing rights by virtue of section 70 LRA. A individual may, therefore, purchase land thinking he is buying the fishing rights, but he may find, after buying the land, that the fishing has been severed from the land and sold or leased to a club or individual. Thus, the angler is protected. Faced with this situation, the buyer will not have any remedy against the owner of the fishing rights who has the security of section 70(1)(j) LRA. His only course of action would be to sue the vendor.

How then is the purchaser of land protected? He should make all appropriate enquiries and also inspect the land. A specific question should be asked of the vendor's solicitors to establish ownership of the fishing rights.

The Land Registry, however, may allow a notice that the fishing rights have been sold to be registered against the title of the land to clarify the matter for future buyers of the land. It is, therefore, wise to try to register a notice by filing a copy of the conveyance (the document recording the sale of the fishing rights) at the Land Registry. The Land Registry will keep a copy of the conveyance and make a note on the Land or Charge Certificate stating that a copy has been filed at the Land Registry.

2.2 Unregistered land

Much land still remains to be registered. Most of this is located in rural areas and this, obviously, is where fishing is usually found. There is no central registry and the only evidence of ownership will be the title deeds. If a land certificate is lost, details will be kept by the Land Registry. If title deeds are lost, apart from individual memory, evidence of ownership is also lost. When land is sold, in order to check that the seller owns the property and can sell the rights, a copy or summary of the title documents showing the seller's ownership will be given to the purchaser's solicitor. This is called an epitome or abstract (respectively) of title and when the land is sold, the original documents will be handed over. The document which shows who owns the land is the conveyance. It performs the same function as the land or charge certificate in that it records the ownership of the land.

If the fishing rights are sold separately from the land, then a memorandum stating that they have been disposed of must be written on the conveyance of the land on which the fishing rights are located. This memorandum will state to whom they were sold and when. Obviously, any purchaser of the land will then be given notice of the sale of the fishing rights because the conveyance on which the memorandum is written will be shown to the purchaser's solicitor.

As a footnote to the above, all land in England and Wales is compulsorily registrable. This means that when unregistered land is sold, then the sale must be recorded at the Land Registry, thereby becoming registered land.

2.3 Conveyancing

The basic procedure for selling and buying fishing rights when located on unregistered and registered land is the same. Title to the land will be shown to the purchaser, questions known as preliminary enquiries will be asked; searches, such as a search at the local authority, will be made; contracts will be drawn up and exchanged and, finally, completion will take place transferring ownership. A detailed examination of this procedure is beyond the scope of this book. However, the vulnerability of fishing rights to outside threats, such as pollution and abstraction, means that detailed questions should be asked before contracts are exchanged. The following are suggested:

1) Have there been any pollution incidents in the last five years? If yes, what type, was there a fish kill and was the polluter prosecuted? Are there any factories or other sources of pollution located upstream?

2) Are there any fish farms upstream? If so, where are they? Have there been any escapes of fish?

3) Are there any licences to abstract water upstream? If yes, in favour of whom and how much can be abstracted? Has a drought order or permit been granted?

4) Have there been any convictions for poaching on the water in the last five years? If so, please supply details.

5) Does the owner exercise the fishing rights, or has he granted a lease and/or licence to an angling club or syndicate?

6) Has any person ever tried to claim title to the fishing rights?

7) Are there any catch returns for the last ten years?

Nos. 1-4 can be directed to both the vendor and the Environment Agency, but Nos 5 and 6 only the vendor. There may be a small charge for the provision of the information by the Agency.

3. ACCESS

Access to fishing rights is essential. Solicitors should always be careful to ensure that the purchase of any fishing rights also grants a right of access. This may seem self evident, but in *Rice v Dodds* (1970), the dispute arose from 'incompetent conveyancing' carried out by two firms of solicitors. When the plaintiff bought a farm next to the River Cothi, the conveyance failed to include any part of the river bed. The Plaintiff had bought the land thinking he had the right to fish the river. However, due to the omission of the river bed from the conveyance he found that he did not. The Defendant agreed to put this right by giving the Plaintiff the right to fish but denied that he was entitled to any easement or right of access to the river. The Plaintiff needed access to the land to exercise the rights but could not do so. Mr Justice Plowman found that it was necessary to imply in favour of the Plaintiffs a fishing path so that they could have access to their fishery, without which the rights were incapable of being exercised. It would appear, therefore, that the courts will be willing to imply a right of access. However, it would be foolish to rely on *Rice v Dodds* and attention to this aspect of conveyancing is essential.

QUESTIONS

Question 1

We have fished a lake, a good coarse fishery, for a number of years. The arrangement with the farmer has been very friendly. We usually give him something at Christmas. He has told us that he is going to change his land from dairy to arable and does not want us walking over his crops. Some members are saying he cannot do this. Are they right?

Answer

No. You only have a licence to fish the lake and the owner can terminate this when he likes. He only needs to give reasonable notice. In this instance, a month will be sufficient.

Question 2

Our club has owned the fishing rights to a river under a conveyance dated 1949. The downstream boundary of the fishery is about two hundred metres upstream from a weir. Over the years members began to fish the water to the weir quite innocently. It holds large shoals of roach and bream. Members could not resist the challenge. Finally, we put up signs saying that the fishing down to the weir was our property and for over thirty years now, we have been cutting weeds and branches and have even created a couple of pools. Now the local landowner has died and his son has come along saying that he has inherited this stretch from his father. What can we do?

Answer

The answer lies in relying on your right to this stretch by prescription. Initial indications are that you have exercised the rights '*nec vi, nec clam, nec precario*'. You have not paid rent and you have openly announced through signs that the property is yours. However, much will turn on the evidence, especially documentary, that he has to prove his claim. If he has got a conveyance which states that he owns the fishery, you may have problems.

Question 3

We have lost our title deeds. The Club Secretary's house was destroyed in a fire. How can we prove our ownership?

Answer

If the land is registered you will be able, for a fee, to obtain another land certificate. However, if the land was unregistered, then you will have to try and reconstruct the title in some way. You can do this by taking statutory declarations from existing members. This means they swear, as in an affidavit, to your club's ownership of the fishery, saying that it has fished the water for a number of years. Your club may even be able to register the fishery by making an application to the Land Registry. Title deeds should be kept with a solicitor, bank or other safe place.

Question 4

Our club has instructed a local firm of solicitors to buy fishing rights on a nearby river. The section we are buying is downstream of a small town. What are the problems we should be looking out for?

Answer

One of your major concerns will be pollution. Find out from the Agency if there is a sewage treatment works which discharges into the river. If yes, has the company operating been prosecuted for pollution; are there any plans to increase its capacity; do the storm sewer overflows operate during dry periods; do any local companies discharge into the sewerage system (ie. do they have a trade effluent consent)? Also, ask the seller if he has had any problems from pollution.

Consider abstraction: has the river ever dried up or the flow been reduced to such a level that fish have died? Direct this to both the Agency and the seller.

CHAPTER 6

RIPARIAN RIGHTS

The word 'riparian' is an adjective used to describe the owner of land bordering a river or lake. He enjoys riparian rights as a result of his owner-ship of such land. The concept of riparian rights is one which underpins the law of angling. It is the base upon which the protection of fisheries is built and it is a rule of law that was formulated in less regulated times than those in which we now live.

Whilst its significance is more than historical, statute law, to a large extent, governs everyday use of water. Thus, the quality of water is governed by discharge consents and the quantity of water taken from a river by abstraction licences. However, as was seen in Chapter 2, pollution legis-lation protecting fisheries has developed in a piecemeal fashion, changing with each re-organisation of the water industry from the fishery boards to the Environment Agency. Riparian ownership is still a fundamental tenet of English and Welsh law, granting rights and imposing duties and providing the starting point in a common law action for pollution. Most legal writers refer to the judgment of Lord Wensleydale in *Chasemore v Richards* (1859) when searching for a concise definition of riparian rights.

> It has been settled that the right of enjoyment of a natural stream or water on the surface *ex jure naturae* belongs to the proprietor of the adjoining land as a natural incident to the right of the soil itself; and that he is entitled to the benefit of it ... He has the right to have it come to him in its natural state in flow, quantity and quality, and to go from him without obstruction ...

The remainder of this chapter will focus on an analysis of how these rights affect fishery owners who have riparian rights. This chapter is only intended as an overview of riparian rights. If the reader is specifically inter-ested in such matters as obstructions, pollution, navigation, abstraction or land drainage, he should refer to those chapters.

1. HOW ARE RIPARIAN RIGHTS ACQUIRED?

Riparian rights not only attach to running waters, but also to lakes and ponds. The water must flow or be contained in a defined channel. Land must actually touch the water in the watercourse to acquire riparian rights. This can be either horizontally or vertically which means, respectively, either the bed of the water or the banks can be owned. This is qualified by the rule that the land itself must be in reasonable proximity to the water. A site too far from the water may be too distant to benefit from riparian rights - as expressed by Mr Justice Laurence in *Attwood v Llay Main Collieries* (1926) '... nobody in their senses would seriously suggest that the site of Paddington Station and Hotel is a riparian tenement, although it is connected with the River Thames by a strip of land many miles long.' Precise rules cannot be given on the definition of this rule of proximity and each case will depend on its facts.

However, the rights can only attach to the land itself. In *Tate and Lyle v GLC* (1983), the Plaintiff had constructed a jetty to enable it to land raw sugar. Lord Templeman stated that this jetty, erected on the foreshore in the River Thames at Woolwich, did not form part of the bank since it was not part of the land. As such, it was not capable of attracting riparian rights.

Other difficult cases arise where the river is tidal. Obviously, the land may not be in contact with the water twenty four hours a day. It has been decided that contact governed by the tides does not prevent the establishment of riparian rights (*North Shore Railway v Pion* (1889)).

The general position is different for artificial watercourses in that riparian rights do not arise automatically as a result of the ownership of riparian land (see 1 in Chapter 6). Riparian rights have to be established by presumption. Even then, the quotation above from Lord Wensleydale cannot be applied, since the precise nature of the rights will depend on the purpose and character of the watercourse. In *Whitmores (Edenbridge) Ltd v Stanford* (1909), the Plaintiffs owned a tannery on a mill stream artificially constructed centuries before the date of the case. There was no evidence of who owned the bed of the river. The Defendants owned an ancient corn mill upstream of the Plaintiffs' land. The stream ran through the land of several proprietors before reaching the Plaintiffs' land, who had installed pipes to take water from the stream for their tannery. The Defendants also operated sluice gates, which they closed in order to prevent the flow downstream, so that they could go onto the bed of the stream and remove the Plaintiffs' pipes. The Plaintiffs sued for damages and an injunction in trespass and succeeded. The Judge found that, in the absence of evidence to the contrary, each owner of the banks owned half the bed of the river. He decided that the stream had been constructed for the joint purposes of the tannery and mill. The pipes had to be put back.

Riparian rights cannot be bought and sold. Therefore, a riparian landowner cannot confer on anyone the benefit of his rights. The rights are acquired as a result of occupying the land. This means that any title deed, whether a conveyance or a lease, does not need to make any reference to the riparian rights being sold with the land. They automatically pass to any buyer.

Finally, it should be noted that riparian rights do not attach to water percolating underground. This means water which 'oozes through the soil in every direction in which the rain penetrates' (Lord Chelmsford in *Chasemore v Richards* (1859)). The key is that the water does not flow through a defined channel.

2. RIPARIAN RIGHTS AND THE ANGLER

In Chapters 4 and 5, the law regarding the ownership of fisheries is discussed and the various ways that a fishery can be owned are explained. Not every angling club will be a riparian owner. Much will depend on the manner in which it owns the fishing rights. The distinction lies in whether the club owns the land or the fishing rights. Riparian rights do not attach to the fishing rights, but to the land. If the club owns or leases the land in order to fish, it will be the riparian owner. As such, it will benefit from riparian rights.

However, if it owns, leases or licences the fishing rights, it will not be a riparian owner. Of course, it will be difficult to separate the riparian owner's interest from that of the angling club. If he is a farmer and uses the river to water his cattle, then he will be as concerned as the angling club over the quantity and quality of the water. Much will depend on the circumstances of the case. It could well be that a riparian owner has no interest whatsoever in the water flowing past his land. It will, therefore, be for the angling club to protect its rights without the help of the landowner. However, the club can negotiate a clause to be inserted in the lease or licence which places an obligation on the landlord to join in any litigation with the club to protect its fishing rights (see Paragraph 11 Second Schedule of the specimen lease in the Appendix).

Generally, however, the riparian owner must not spoil the angler's fishing. A conflict between the riparian owner and the fishery owners arose in *Bridges v Highton* (1865). The Defendant who owned the riparian rights proposed to carry out the works which would prevent the tide from flowing through channels which fed the fishery owned by the Plaintiff. The fishery produced vast quantities of seaweed and periwinkles and the breeding ground for these would have been destroyed. The Judge stated:

'It is immaterial in whom the ownership of the soil is vested, so long as it is clear that the piece of ooze or bed of sea-weed included in the Defendant's proposed wall is a material part of the Plaintiff's fishing ground, and will be destroyed if the enclosure is permitted to be made.'

The Defendant was not allowed to construct the works.

3. NATURE OF RIPARIAN RIGHTS AND DUTIES

To quote Lord MacNaghten from *Young v Bankier Distillery Co* (1893):

> Every riparian proprietor is thus entitled to the water of his stream
> in its natural flow, without sensible diminution or increase and
> without sensible alteration in its character or quality.

The riparian owner, therefore, is entitled to a good flow of quality water but, also, he must not do anything which may interfere with the quality or quantity of the water flowing past his fellow riparian owners' land. Any use of the water that is unreasonable may be the subject of an action in damages, a claim for an injunction or both (see Chapter 10). As the above quotation suggests, the nature of riparian rights can be broken down into its two separate arms, quality and quantity.

3.1 Quality

For the angler this means that his water should not be polluted. If the quality of the water kills or drives fish from his stretch of the river, or interferes with their breeding, then this interferes with his riparian rights. Lord Wensleydale stated that the right was to have the water in its natural state. The alteration may therefore be of any nature, for example, chemical or a change in temperature. In the *Pride of Derby Angling Association v British Celanese Ltd* (1953), the fishing was not only adversely affected by the sewage pollution but also the hot water discharged by British Celanese. Similarly, in the Bankier Distillery case, the change in the character of the water was the discharge of hard water into a river of naturally soft water.

However, the pollution must not be innocuous. If a discharge is polluting further upstream, but is no longer harmful by the time it reaches the riparian owner downstream, then there will be no cause of action. It could well be that a riparian owner discharges pollution which only harms his fishing on the river.

Nevertheless, if two polluters' effluent combines in one river, and one without the other would be innocuous, both will still be liable. In *Blair and Sumner v Deakin* (1887), when the polluters sought to deny liability by arguing that each of their discharges by itself was not sufficient to affect the Plaintiff's riparian rights, Mr Justice Kay stated:

> They might all laugh at him and say, 'You cannot sue any of us
> because you cannot prove that what each one of us does would
> of itself be enough to cause you damage': All I can observe is
> that, in my opinion, it would be a most unjust law if there was
> such a law.

Although the pollution has to be of a permanent nature, riparian rights will still be infringed even if no damage is caused. In *Crossley v Lightowler* (1867), the Judge summarised this point:

> ... the riparian proprietor has the right to the use of the water, whenever he may want to enjoy it. It is quite true that at this moment it is not made use of by the Plaintiffs for watering their cattle, or for any other purpose; but they have a right to the user, and a right to interfere with anything that injures that right of user in such a manner as that, if not interrupted for twenty years, the person so injuring the right would acquire a title.

As this quotation suggests, a right to pollute can be acquired by a riparian owner. This will override the riparian owner's right to receive water in its natural state. For example, the discharge of water from a copper mine impregnated with metals was upheld as a prescriptive right to pollute (*Wright v Williams* (1836) - see prescription at 1.4 in Chapter 5). However, the pollution must remain constant. If there is a change in the business of the polluter, even if this decreases the pollution, the claim to a prescriptive right will be defeated. It must be said that it is very unlikely that a Court will nowadays uphold a prescriptive right to pollute. In any event, the majority of discharges are regulated by consents granted by the Environment Agency (see Chapter 9).

3.2 Quantity

This second arm of riparian rights is closely linked with the abstraction of water (see Chapter 11). The riparian owner is entitled to the reasonable enjoyment of the water flowing past his land. If his use of the water is unreasonable and affects the rights of other riparian owners to the water, such that the quantity is diminished, then downstream owners will have grounds for an action against him. The essential question is how much water can the riparian owner use?

The case of *Embrey v Owen* (1851) is a good example of how the courts view the reasonable use of water. The Defendants, as upstream riparian owners, constructed 'divers sluices, trenches, channels, aqueducts and cuts to irrigate their meadows'. However, they diverted the surplus water back into the river and, at times, did not use any water at all. The Plaintiffs, operators of a water grist mill located downstream, took an action against the Defendants for interference with the flow. The Judge, after stating that there was no right to use water to the prejudice of other riparian owners, found that there was no sensible diminution of the flow in the stream or 'none cognizable by the senses' and dismissed the case.

The riparian owner is allowed to take all the water that he needs for ordinary or domestic purposes connected with his riparian land. These include water for drinking, cleaning, washing and cooking. If the whole of the flow in the watercourse is taken up by these uses then no complaint may be made by other riparian owners.

In addition to domestic purposes, the riparian owner is allowed to take the water for extraordinary purposes. This can only, somewhat unhelpfully, be defined as all purposes which are not ordinary. Whilst each case will depend on its facts, there are certain rules: the use must be reasonable, it must be connected with the riparian land and the water must be returned in the same quantity and character.

All of this must be read subject to the greater qualification that abstraction of water is governed by a licensing system. As will be seen in Chapter 11, this allows the angler certain rights, but also restricts them. The most important is the prohibition on any action for compensation in the civil courts for damage to fishing as a result of water abstraction carried out under a licence, the conditions of which have been observed.

3.3 Access

Together with quality and quantity, the riparian owner is also entitled to access to the water abutting his land, whether it is tidal or non-tidal, flowing or still. The rule remains good with tidal water in that although contact may only be intermittent, this does not take away the right of access. In *Lyon v Fishmonger's Company* (1876), the Fishmonger's obtained a licence from the Thames Conservators to build a wharf which would have put an end to the use of the Plaintiff's own wharf by depriving him of access to the River Thames. An injunction was granted preventing its construction. The Judge argued that not only would the construction of the wharf affect the Plaintiff's public right of navigation, but it would also injure him as a riparian owner in interfering with his right of access to the river.

This right of access is exclusive to the riparian owner. It is not a public right. If anyone without the permission of the riparian owner uses the land to reach the water, the owner will have the right to sue in trespass. It is similar to the right individuals have to walk out of the front door of their house and use the public highway.

3.4 Mooring

In addition, the owner will also have the right to moor boats adjacent to his land, to load and unload them. This applies even if the water is tidal, preventing the unloading of the boats at certain times of the day. In *Booth v Ratte* (1890), the Plaintiff, as the riparian owner, built a floating wharf in the river. The Defendant interfered with his use of the wharf by allowing waste from his saw mill to float downstream. This was so bad that gas built up in the river bed causing intermittent explosions. This prevented the Plaintiff from carrying on his business of hiring and housing pleasure boats. The Defendant argued that he had no right to construct the wharf. The Judge rejected this argument stating that 'as a riparian owner the plaintiff would be at liberty to construct such a wharf'. However, this right to moor can only be exercised if it does not interfere with any public right of navigation and the right of access of any neighbouring riparian owner.

QUESTIONS

Question 1

Our club leases the land next to a river where there is a public right of navigation. We find that pleasure boats moor against our bank and block off some of the best swims. It is very difficult to tell them to leave. What can we do?

Answer

If your club leases the land this is a private fishery and, subject to what the lease says, it will be the riparian owner. The public may have a right to navigate up and down the river, but this does not mean they have the right to moor against the bank you lease. The people using the bank to moor are trespassers. You can tell them to leave. A good idea is to put up 'No Mooring' signs to warn people against mooring and tell those mooring to leave. However, this must be qualified in the sense that much will depend on how you own the fishing rights. For example, the landowner may have reserved a right to moor and others may have obtained the right to moor by prescription.

Question 2

The flow in my river is very low and during hot summers it dries up. There are fissures in the river bed along a stretch of about half a mile. Up to 50% of the flow disappears down these holes. I want to fill these holes in to preserve the flow. However, the water that disappears down these holes flows into nearby springs which provide the flow for a fish farm. The fish farmer is concerned that if I block the holes this will reduce the flow through his farm.

Answer

When the water disappears through these holes, as long as it is no longer flowing in a defined channel, it is water percolating underground. As such, it does not attract riparian rights. The fish farmer is not a riparian owner and does not have the right to prevent you from blocking the holes. However, a land drainage consent will be needed from the Environment Agency to do such work.

CHAPTER 7

THE ANGLING CLUB

It is only the lucky few who actually own fishing rights. For the vast majority of anglers, participation in their sport is through angling clubs. Clubs vary in size and composition. The big city clubs like the Leeds and District Amalgamated Anglers and the London Anglers' Association count their members in the thousands. Other clubs restrict their membership to only a handful, preferring to retain a family atmosphere. However, the quality that they all ought to have in common is that they are run efficiently. Carefully drafted rules, fisheries owned on terms suitable for the club and effective accounting procedures all help to anticipate problems that may be expensive to put right. This chapter will focus on the different types of club and how their affairs can be conducted. At the end of the chapter, there is a model set of club rules. References in this chapter are to those rules.

1. TYPES OF CLUBS

There are two main kinds of clubs - the proprietary and the members' club. A proprietary club is owned by the proprietor who controls it. However, more relevant to anglers is the members' club, where the management of the affairs of the club is dealt with by the members. Generally, a members' club is seen as a society of people who pay some sort of subscription and, maybe, an entrance fee out of which the expenses of the club are paid. The bargain struck by the member is the payment of his/her subscription in return for the provision of the fishing owned by the club.

Unlike a company, which has a separate legal existence, a members' club is seen as an association of members. This means that while the club uses its name to the outside world, for example in correspondence, the law does not recognise it as being a separate entity. The law simply sees the members' club as a collection of individuals. In everyday terms this is something of an artificial distinction but, in law, the concept is very important, especially in the way that the club conducts itself in its relations with the public.

1.1 Club property

Club property is not held by the club. The argument runs that if the club does not have a separate legal existence then it cannot own property. The funds and property of the club belong to members jointly, in equal shares. It is only when the club is dissolved that the property is realised and divided between the members. The most obvious example of an angling club's property is its fishery. If the club is dissolved and its fishery sold, then the proceeds of the sale would be distributed to members in equal shares (unless the rules specified some other shares).

Whilst it is the members to whom the property belongs, the mechanism through which the club actually holds the property is the trustee. The reason behind this lies in the nature of the members' club. Since it has no legal identity and is seen by the law as a society of persons, it cannot hold property. A club will normally appoint trustees pursuant to its rules and the property, and assets are vested in them. It is the trustees who will own the property in trust for the members of the club. They should also be given the power to invest the funds of the club, at their own discretion or the direction of the committee, according to the club's rules (see rule 3.3). Investment includes the purchase of fisheries. Therefore, when buying a fishery, it is the trustees who must sign the document (conveyance or transfer - see Chapter 5) which transfers ownership to the club. It is, therefore, vital that a club appoints trustees and that the rules are explicit on how the trustees invest a club's property - whether it is on their own initiative or at the direction of the club committee. In the model rules at the end of this chapter, the trustees are given this power but at the direction of the committee.

1.1.1 Powers and duties of Trustees

As a trustee, a club member is subject to a number of duties. His overriding duty is one of good faith (*Head v Gould* (1898)). In the case of a trustee of an angling club, he must not use the club's property for his own purposes by, for example, using club money to purchase items for himself or sell club property and keep/take the proceeds. He is subject to other duties: he must strictly conform to and carry out the terms of the trust (*Booth v Booth* (1838)); he must execute the trust with reasonable diligence and conduct its affairs in the same manner as would an ordinary prudent man of business (*Re Waterman's Will Trusts* (1952)); he cannot make a gift from trust property (*Re Clore's Settlement Trusts (1966)*).

It is important when buying land to draw up a declaration of trust. This will set out the powers of the trustees. A provision should be included restricting the trustees from selling the land without the approval of the committee of the club. A trustee will be bound by this, although he also has the inherent power to do acts which are reasonable and proper for realising the trust property or to protect it.

Any act by a trustee in breach of, in neglect of or in excess of his duties, will be a breach of trust. If a club loses money as a result of a breach by one of its trustees, then that trustee will be liable to the club for the loss (*Re Franklyn* (1913)). Indeed, a trustee can be guilty of theft. However, this must be read subject to the qualification that a trustee is not liable for a simple error, nor if he dealt honestly and properly with the club's property (Re *Chapman* (1896)).

1.2 The external relations of clubs

The general rule is that a member is not liable to pay any sums to the club beyond the subscription which the rules require him to pay. This means that if the trustees enter into a business transaction (for example, a purchase of specimen fish), they cannot make the members pay any money to indemnify them over and above their subscriptions. By indemnify, it is meant that the members do not have to compensate the trustees for costs incurred by them on behalf of the club. It is upon this fundamental understanding that clubs are formed. People would be unwilling to expose themselves to a situation whereby the club could call upon their personal assets. If the committee finds the club's funds are insufficient to meet expenses, it must call a meeting to ask for further subscriptions.

Since a members' club is not seen as having a separate identity, what is the position of the member or members when contracts are entered into by him/them on behalf of the club? The question will depend upon the scope of the authority given to the officer of the club who entered into the contract. Generally, mere members will not have authority to contract on behalf of the club. If an officer acts beyond the authority given to him by the rules, either expressly or by implication, then he will be liable and not the members of the club. The members of a club will be liable on a contract only if the officer of the club acted within the authority given to him. If an officer acts within his authority then technically, all the members of a club will be liable in the sense that a creditor of the club can go against any or all the members to compensate him. Whilst this may cause members concern in that their own assets can be used to pay off their club's creditor, it is very rare for a club to expose its members in such a way. It is clearly very important for the authority of individual officers to be clearly defined.

An important qualification must be made in that the officer who enters into the contract must disclose the fact that he is acting on behalf of the club. The officer may be personally liable if he fails to disclose that he is acting on behalf of the club.

However, the liability of individual officers may go further. If an officer signs a contract in his own name, he is liable and can be sued for a breach of the contract without the other members being joined in the action. This is the case even if the officer was authorised to enter into the contract on behalf of the other members. Obviously, this imposes a heavy burden on someone acting in an unpaid role when he stands to lose his personal wealth.

Officers of the club can be protected from such an eventuality by the inclusion of an indemnity in the club rules. This will be a clause which states that an officer of the club will be indemnified against personal liability if he enters into a contract which is within the scope of his authority. Rule 15 of the model rules provides a precedent.

1.2.1 Law suits

A members' club cannot sue or be sued in its own name, nor can the secretary or other officer sue or be sued in the club's name. The trustees may sue or be sued in respect of any property owned by them on behalf of the club. However, if trustees have not been appointed, or a dispute arises over property not held by the trustees, the rules of court procedure allow the club to be represented by one member of the club. The rules state that all members must have a common interest in the subject matter, that they all have a common grievance and that the remedy sought from the court is beneficial to all the members (see Order 15 of the Rules of the Supreme Court). In *Bedford (Duke of) v Ellis* (1901), Lord MacNaghten stated: 'Given a common interest and a common grievance, a representative suit is in order if the relief sought is in its nature common to all whom the Plaintiff proposes to represent.' A classic example is pollution of a club's waters and it is self evident that all the members have a common interest in seeing that they are compensated for such damage. If a club wants to obtain compensation in the courts for pollution of its waters, it nominates a member who sues on his own behalf and on behalf of all members of the club. In general, the nominee should be one of the trustees who holds the land on behalf of the club. However, the club may want to join the landowner in the action (see Paragraph 11 of the Second Schedule of the specimen lease in the Appendix).

A club which is a party to a case can also receive financial support and encouragement from an outside body, formed to promote the interests of anglers. In the case of *Martell v Consett Iron Co Ltd* (1953), the River Derwent in Durham had been polluted. The Anglers' Conservation Association (ACA) had agreed to indemnify a riparian owner and angling club against any legal costs incurred as a result of the litigation. Financial support of litigation by paying a party's costs, known as maintenance, is unlawful. However, the Court found that in the case of pollution, there was a wider concept of common interest justifying the ACA in helping the club and riparian owner. Therefore, the ACA, as an association interested in the protection of rivers from pollution, could lawfully support actions brought by individual members to restrain the pollution of rivers.

2. CLUB RULES

Every club should be governed by rules. Rules specify how the club should be run: dealing with admission and expulsion of members, dissolution of the club and the formation of a committee, to name only a few matters. If they are well drafted, then the rules can anticipate any problems and quickly resolve any potential disputes. The model set of rules at the end of this chapter provides a starting point and can be amended according to any club's circumstances.

2.1 The objects

Obvious as it may seem, the rules should specify what are the objects of the club. They should be sufficiently wide to cover the activities which the members wish to pursue. This will avoid disputes over how the club's funds can be spent. For example, rule 2 defines the objects, but goes beyond the mere provision of angling facilities to the promotion of the interests of angling and anglers. This may extend to the encouragement of youth angling and the membership of outside angling bodies.

2.2 Membership

The rules should set out the categories of membership and the procedure to become members. The model rules set out three categories: ordinary, honorary and temporary. In the case of the first, a member must be proposed and seconded and then elected by the committee. Temporary membership is left to the discretion of the committee, but honorary membership has to be decided by the club at the annual general meeting, reflecting the importance of such membership.

2.3 Resignation and expulsion

The rules must provide for the resignation of a member. The model rules allow this to be done at any time, but do not permit a refund of any subscription. A member may also be deemed to have resigned by, for example, not paying his subscription. Once the honorary secretary receives the resignation, that is it. The member cannot withdraw it unless the rules provide to the contrary and he can only be re-admitted by re-election.

It is very important that a provision is included for the expulsion of a member whose conduct damages the club. There is no inherent power to expel and, if there is not, the rules must be amended to include such a power.

A member must be expelled in accordance with the rule. Any irregularity leaves the club open to an action in court that the power was improperly used and the withdrawal of the expulsion. Therefore, in accordance with the model rules, a member can only be expelled by a majority vote of the committee, after it has heard or received written representations from the member. The committee must make a fair enquiry into the truth of the alleged facts. This should be properly minuted to avoid any later misunderstandings. All of the above is subject to the overriding principle that the power of expulsion must be exercised in good faith for the benefit of the club and not for any improper motive. The club must observe the rules of natural justice in coming to a decision. This includes giving the offending member the chance to put his case.

2.4 Management of the club

The model rules provide that the management of the affairs of the club shall be in the hands of the committee. To that end, the rules must also lay down the powers and constitution of the committee. Rule 13.4 states how many times the committee should meet. A quorum should be specified, to avoid any claim by a committee member that a decision is not valid because he did not agree with it (see rule 13.5). The quorum should also be sufficiently large to avoid the possibility of an unpopular decision being taken by a handful of members.

Generally, the committee will run the club. As such, it should consist of the various officers of the club. The secretary's functions are to conduct correspondence, collect subscriptions and perform other work of a clerical nature. The treasurer keeps the accounts and reports to the committee and, if necessary, the club at its annual general meeting, on the state of the club's finances (see rule 17). These specific duties can be defined by the committee or set out in the club rules.

Most angling clubs will not be of such a size or nature to employ staff. Only some have premises, like a sports club, and only the larger clubs may employ staff, such as a river bailiff. The model rules do not give the committee power to employ staff. If the committee does decide to employ a bailiff, then it should empower an officer of the club to do so by a resolution of the committee. It is in such an instance that the indemnity in rule 14 becomes important. The committee member may become personally liable for the wages of the bailiff if he employed him on behalf of the club. The indemnity, together with the resolution, ensures that the officer is not liable. The resolution must define the scope of the officer's authority ensuring that he is aware of exactly what he can do on behalf of the club.

A provision has also been included in the model rules for the committee to borrow money (rule 14). This power enables the committee to do so as long as it is duly authorised by the club.

2.5 Byelaws

At the end of the model rules there is a set of byelaws. Angling clubs often rent fishing rights from landlords who want to ensure that their property is well looked after. Byelaws ensure any special requirements are observed, such as bag size or minimum size of fish to be taken. They are usually printed on the membership card so that a member cannot claim he has not received notice of them. Rule 10.1 allows the committee to expel a member who does not observe the byelaws.

2.6 Meetings

The model rules divide meetings into the annual general meeting and special general meetings. The former allows for an annual review of the club and the re-election of officers; the latter for meetings to be called to help the smooth running of the club. It is important that the manner of serving notices is strictly observed so that a member cannot claim he did not receive notice. The chairman of the meeting must preserve order and ensure that the proceedings are properly conducted. He does, however, have an inherent power to adjourn a meeting in the event of disorder.

2.7 Alteration of rules and dissolution of the club

A provision allowing the alteration of club rules is essential because, without it, the rules may only be amended with the consent of all the members. The legal basis for this lies in the contract between the members. The rules form this contract. If the rules do not allow for their alteration, any such alteration without the consent of the members would be a breach of contract. A member would, therefore, not be bound by any alteration if such a rule was not included.

Equally important, there must be a rule setting out what happens on the dissolution of the club. Without it, a club can only be dissolved by order of the court. The model rules state that the funds and property of the club will be distributed equally between members. Any debts and liabilities of the club must be met before the surplus is distributed to members.

3. TAXATION

A members' club is not usually carried on with a view to making a profit and is not liable to income tax as the result of mutual transactions with its members. The key word is mutual. An angling club is formed so that people can join together to achieve an object for their mutual benefit. This is the provision of angling facilities. If these facilities are extended to non-members, this mutuality is lacking and the resulting profits are liable to corporation tax. The most obvious example with angling clubs is the sale of day tickets for one of its waters to the public. Profits on sales of day tickets are liable to corporation tax.

It will be unusual for an angling club to charge value added tax (VAT). This tax is chargeable on any supply of goods and services made by a taxable person in the course of or furtherance of any business carried on by him. If a club does charge VAT, then it may register with Customs and Excise for VAT purposes. This will enable it to reclaim the VAT which it pays for any goods and services it purchases.

Finally, an angling club may hold fishing rights that are worth a great deal of money. If the club sells those rights, it may be liable to pay capital gains tax (CGT). This tax is charged on the gain made on the disposal of an asset. At present, either 25% or 40% (depending on whether you are a lower or higher rate tax payer, respectively) of any gain is subject to tax. However, there are provisions which enable a club to roll over any gain into the purchase of new fishing rights, which allows it to defer paying CGT. These rules are complicated and specialist legal or accountancy advice should be taken.

4. INSURANCE

We live in a litigious world. People, more than ever, are prepared to sue for compensation. Angling clubs should protect themselves against the consequences of liability for injury or damage arising out of their actions and this includes the actions of all its officers and members. As set out in paragraph 1.2 above, members may find themselves held personally responsible for damages and legal costs if an action is brought against members. Many insurance brokers offer insurance to cover such liabilities and have policies tailored to the needs of angling clubs. A club, according to its circumstances, should also consider the types of insurance available.

4.1 Public Liability insurance

Public liability, commonly known as third party insurance, includes liability to the public at large. This provides protection against the consequences of liability for injury or damage to third parties which arises from actions of the members. It can be extended to cover member to member liability, damage arising from pollution or trespass and even riparian owners of fisheries leased by the club.

4.2 Personal accident

An accident may result in the death or permanent total disablement of any member. A personal accident policy will ensure that compensation will be paid, without the need for dependants to take action through the courts, if the club is liable for the accident. Such a policy for all members may not be necessary, but consideration should be given to cover its officers, bailiffs and members of fishery working parties.

4.3 Employer's liability

If the club employs a bailiff, the club must provide employer's liability insurance. This will protect the bailiff if injured whilst working for the club.

4.4 Others

Cover is available to cover theft by officials. If a club travels to matches overseas, travel insurance should be taken out. Finally, insurance is available to cover the cost of legal expenses involved in legal disputes such as pollution or employment disputes.

5. RATING

5.1 New law

As from 19 March 1997, fishing rights are no longer subject to rates. Section 2 of the Local Government and Rating Act 1997 (LGRA) exempted fishing rights from non-domestic rating (council tax).

Chapter 4 makes the distinction between corporeal and incorporeal fishing rights. Section 2 LGRA states that where fishing rights attach to land, that land shall be assessed for rates disregarding the fishing rights. This means that the rateable value of riparian land (see Chapter 6) does not include the value of the fishing rights. This could mean a considerable saving for many angling clubs and fishery owners.

5.2 Old Law

Rates were formerly charged under s.42 and s.64 of the Local Government Finance Act 1988 (LGFA). This act saw the repeal of the General Rate Act

1967. The remainder of this section deals with the old system, since there may be outstanding disputes over the amount payable.

5.2.1 Valuation for rating

The rateable value of fishing rights was the rent at which it was estimated that they might reasonably be expected to be let from year to year if the tenant undertook to pay all usual tenant's rates and taxes and to bear the cost of repairs and insurance and the other expenses, if any, necessary to maintain them in a state to command the rent.

The actual rent paid for the fishing rights was not conclusive evidence of value. The valuation officer had to judge the open market rental value and take into consideration many factors: the quality of the fishing and the kinds of fish caught; the extent of the fishing rights; any special advantages and disadvantages of the water from an angling point of view; what demand there was for fishing in the area and whether the waters were reasonably accessible to prospective tenants; the extent of interference from navigation; whether the public had access to the banks, and, if so, the likely extent of interference; the estimated cost of maintenance including the cost of a water bailiff, weed-cutting, stocking, clearing unwanted fish and care of the banks, where any of these items of expense would arise. The valuation officer also used his knowledge of rents paid for any comparable fishing in the district and his experience of rating fishing rights.

In 1989, the local valuation courts were wound up and replaced by the valuation tribunals. Application can be made to these tribunals if the valuation is considered to be too high.

5.2.2 Rating relief

Under s.47 LGFA, if fishing rights were 'used for purposes of recreation, and all or part of it is occupied for the purposes of a club, society or other organisation not established or conducted for profit' then they might be eligible for relief on rates of up to 100%. An angling club, as a non profit making organisation, should fall into this category. Indeed, it does not matter that the club made a profit. What is important is that the club was not established with a view to making a profit. Application for rating relief must be made to the appropriate billing authority: district councils or London borough councils.

6. TO INCORPORATE OR NOT TO INCORPORATE?

All of the foregoing in this chapter has concentrated on an unincorporated members' club. However, it is open to an angling club to form itself into a company. Usually, a commercial company limits its liability by shares. Clubs tend to use the form of a company limited by guarantee. Instead of issuing shares, each member guarantees a certain amount of money to the club. This is usually a nominal amount, £1.

6.1 Advantages of incorporation

The most significant advantage of an unincorporated members' club is that the members are responsible for its management and administration. As the model rules show, this is usually delegated to committees but each member still plays an active role in running the club. Also, there is a certain informality about a members' club. It does have strict rules of procedure, such as the election of members, but it can retain a family atmosphere.

The main advantage of an incorporated association is that it limits its liability to the number of shares that it issues, or the amount guaranteed by its members. Each officer of the club could therefore conduct the club's business, if it was incorporated, knowing that he cannot incur personal liability. Earlier in the chapter, the danger of members incurring personal liability in a members' club was emphasised. Incorporation means that only the company is liable. The reason for this is that incorporation creates a separate legal identity for the club. It is no longer a society of persons, but a separate body. The contract to employ a river bailiff as referred to above would be with the club and not the members.

Moreover, the club could sue and be sued in its own name. Representative proceedings would not be necessary. Also, the property of the club is held in the club's name. There will no longer be any need to appoint trustees with the attendant administrative burden of appointing replacements. It is often a problem with members' clubs that, with trustees leaving or dying and officers changing, trustees are not replaced. This is a problem, since the club may want to sell its property but cannot do so because the trustees cannot be found or have died. In this instance, a club would have to go to court to appoint new trustees.

6.2 Disadvantages of incorporation

There are some disadvantages to incorporation. It costs money to incorporate. Directors and a Company Secretary must be appointed as with a club and accounts may have to be filed at Companies House. Depending on the turnover of a company it may need to employ an accountant or an auditor to prepare. However, if a company earns under £90,000 in any one year it does not need to have either. It has to be said that most angling clubs fall into this first category. If it earns between £90,000 and £350,000 then it has to file with its accounts an accountant's report. This means a report prepared by a professional accountant. Earnings over £350,000 mean the company must file an auditor's report. (See The Companies Act 1985 (Audit Exemption) Regulations 1994 (SI 1994/1935).

A short section such as this cannot give any definitive advice on whether a club should incorporate. Nevertheless, clubs should be aware of this option since it may suit their circumstances. Professional advice both from an accountant and a lawyer should be taken. Whilst this may involve expenditure, it will be money well spent in avoiding any future problems.

7. MEMBERSHIP OF OUTSIDE ORGANISATIONS

Angling is notorious for the fragmented nature of its administration. The nature of the sport, being individual and not team, does not perhaps lend itself to a single governing body in the same way that football or cricket does. Below are just a few organisations that a club may wish to join.

7.1 The Anglers' Conservation Association (ACA)

Set up in 1948 as a pollution fighting body, the ACA has done much over the years to protect the angler's fishing rights from pollution. It brought the landmark case of *Pride of Derby Angling Association v British Celanese*, which established that an angling club can be compensated and obtain an injunction against a polluter (see Chapter 10). It is still in the vanguard of the fight against pollution and did much to bring to the public's attention the damage that abandoned mines may cause to rivers. It has over 17,000 members and recovers thousands of pounds each year in compensation for damage to fishing rights. This money is paid direct to the members, often helping to ensure a club's continued existence.

It used to be known as the Anglers' Co-Operative Association and still retains its original ethos. Anglers, clubs, syndicates or individuals pay an annual subscription which is used to fund litigation against polluters. The club or fishery owner has its legal costs paid by the ACA. However, it is much more than a quasi-legal expenses insurance cover. By contributing, the angler is helping protect his fellow angler's fishing. It may be that one day he will call upon the ACA for help.

7.2 The Salmon and Trout Association (SATA)

The SATA is the only UK body which solely represents game anglers. Founded in 1903, it has some 115,000 individual and club members. The primary role of SATA is to represent the views of its members to Government departments and agencies, particularly the Environment Agency and the Sports Council.

SATA also monitors abstraction and discharge notices published in the *London Gazette* (see Chapter 11 for an explanation of the *London Gazette*), which are then circulated to a network of water resource officers throughout England and Wales.

During the past ten years, SATA has campaigned successfully against increased access for canoeists (Derwent Appeal 1991); reduced licence fees for trout anglers (NRA 1993); ended coastal netting by the Crown Estate Commissioners (1994); obtained increased funding for ladies, youth and disabled Fishing (1996) and has challenged the Government in many other areas.

Membership of SATA entitles anglers to free public liability insurance (£2M) when fishing, and a variety of discounts on fishing, holidays, tackle and clothing.

7.3 The National Federation of Anglers (NFA)

Set up in 1903, the NFA's mission statement is:

It is the mission of the National Federation of Anglers to promote and protect angling such that all anglers, following its codes of good angling practice, shall be at liberty to go fishing where and when they want with a reasonable expectation of good catches of fish.

Recognised by the Sports Council as the governing body for coarse angling, the NFA's primary role is as a pressure group that represents the interests of coarse fishermen. It has 500 affiliated organisations and, through them, nearly 300,000 fishermen and women. It operates through eight regional councils composed of club representatives, four policy-making committees, a National Committee and a National Executive Committee. It has two main areas of responsibility: protection of the aquatic environment and an overall role in the interface of angling with government bodies, water authorities and conservation groups. In this respect, it campaigns for a more environmentally responsible society.

It has a number of objectives to further its mission. These include, among others, the protection of riparian rights whether owned or controlled under a tenancy agreement; the availability of affordable and value-for-money licences; minimal interference from other recreational users of water and its environs; access for angling clubs to fisheries' management and other advisory services.

7.4 The National Federation of Sea Anglers (NFSA)

The National Federation of Sea Anglers was founded in 1904 to look after the interests of sea anglers. It is administered by a National Executive, with twelve Regional Divisions and has a membership of over 37,000, made up of 550 clubs, associate and individual members. The Head Office is at Newton Abbot, Devon, where the full time Development Officer and staff are based.

The NFSA is recognised by the Government and the Sports Council, which provide grant aid for its development programmes. It works directly with Government Departments and Agencies on matters of national and international importance, and with the sea angling groups in Scotland, Ireland and Wales, where efforts are united through the Sea Angling Liaison Committee of Great Britain and Ireland. It is a member of the World Governing Body, La Fédération Internationale de la Pêche Sportive en Mer, and, through the Angling Governing Bodies Liaison Group, is a member of the European Anglers Alliance, which assures a voice in the European Union.

It is responsible for processing claims for British records on behalf of the British Record (rod-caught) Fish Committee, for which it acts as secretariat.

7.5 Other organisations

There are many other organisations to which anglers may belong from the Grayling Society to the Catfish Conservation Group and the National Anguilla Club. They are too numerous to mention here individually. The Specialist Anglers Conservation Group (SACG) is worthy of note, however. The SACG consists of a number of these organisations. It produced a general code of conduct for specialist coarse anglers in April 1997.

8. THE FISHING SYNDICATE

The fishing syndicate is another form of association which anglers may set up to enjoy their sport. Essentially, it is a club. However, it conveys the impression of a small and rather exclusive club. The most common instance when it is used occurs when a group of anglers join together to buy fishing rights. It may be that they buy the freehold fishing rights, or rent them on a long lease. Whichever way they choose to buy the rights each has a financial stake in them. It is different from the club in that they do not pay an annual subscription. Each member of the syndicate has a quantifiable interest in the fishing rights, which he or she may, if permitted by the rules, sell to another angler.

This arrangement is formalised in a deed. The syndicate appoints trustees, like a club, to hold the fishing rights. However, each member of the syndicate records his contribution to the purchase in the deed. Provision can also be made in the deed for the appointment of the officers of the syndicate; alteration of the rules; insurance; the sharing of maintenance costs; the calling of meetings; an indemnity for the trustees and power to appoint new trustees and rules.

Due to the nature of a syndicate, the rules will usually stipulate to whom a member may sell his share. These may be very restrictive, allowing the member only to transfer his share during his lifetime, or by will, to a member of his immediate family. They may go further by imposing an obligation to offer any share to existing members of the syndicate. Finally, it is usual to provide, in the event that if none of the above can be done, that the syndicate shall approve a new member by vote.

The syndicate is a relatively uncommon form to hold fishing rights. It does not provide for the flexibility of an angling club. However, what it provides is an element of exclusivity. Rules regarding membership are likely to be very strict.

QUESTIONS

Question 1

The other night we had our A.G.M. It was a shambles. One member said it was invalid, another said he wanted the vice chairman to be expelled, one even accused the treasurer of stealing club funds. Nothing could be agreed. It became very heated and, as chairman, I had to call a halt. Our club's income is about £30,000 per year, but we do not employ accountants although the secretary is a solicitor. Our club rules are very sketchy - half a page of A4!

Answer

A new set of rules is required. It may well be that the vice chairman should be expelled or that the Treasurer has misappropriated funds. The rules will set out procedures that will allow grievances to be aired, members to be expelled and for meetings to be validly called - amongst a host of other matters. The rules in this chapter can be used as a starting point and tailored to your club's requirements. A notice to all members convening a meeting with a copy of the rules to be adopted should be sent to all members.

Question 2

A committee member has ordered £1,500 of fish from a local fish supplier. The meeting was properly minuted and it is clearly apparent that he was not given permission to do so. He is a bit impatient but he acted with the best possible motives. The trouble is that, while we need the fish, we only have £1,153 in our building society account. The supplier is demanding his money. Who is liable?

Answer

The basic rule is that members are not liable to pay any sums over and above their subscriptions. However, if an officer acts within the authority granted to him then all members of the club may be liable. In this instance, the committee member acted beyond the scope of his authority and, therefore, made himself personally liable. This will obviously require delicate handling, since the fish supplier may chose to sue him on the contract for the full amount. The matter depends on how the supplier will react. The best course is to negotiate a settlement with the supplier and try to find the funds from elsewhere.

Question 3

Recently, one of our members left us a considerable sum of money. We invested this in buying some fishing rights. Word has got around and membership has now increased to over 3,000 members. It even continued to increase last year when we doubled the membership fee. Income is now over £65,000 and looks set to increase. Members of the committee, especially, are concerned at the greater responsibility they are taking on. Should we employ full time staff? One member even suggested we become a company.

Answer

The decision on whether to incorporate is very important. It has advantages in that the members will not incur personal liability because they will be protected by the corporate veil. However, administrative burdens may increase although your club, with its level of income, is not obliged to file an accountant's report. It must be said that, with its present rate of expansion, this may change.

The best advice is to consult a solicitor and/or accountant to take specialist advice. Having done this, your club can take an informed decision.

MODEL ANGLING CLUB RULES
AND BYELAWS

(Note: Square brackets indicate gaps to be completed, instructions or numbers that may be changed as the club may require.)

1. NAME

The name of the Club shall be the [.......................].

2. OBJECTS

The general objects of the Club shall be to provide the facilities of an angling club for its members, including the organisation and provision of angling, and to promote the interests of angling and anglers.

3. TRUSTEES

3.1 There shall be not less than two nor more than three Trustees of the Club, save that a corporate body may be a sole Trustee. The first Trustees shall be [*name them*]. Subsequent appointment of Trustees shall be by the Committee.

3.2 Trustees shall hold office until death or resignation, or until removed from office by a resolution of the Committee.

3.3 All property of the Club (except cash, which shall be under the control of the Hon. Treasurer) including leases and fishing leases shall be vested in the Trustees to be dealt with by them as the Committee shall from time to time by resolution direct.

3.4 The Trustees shall be indemnified out of the assets of the Club against any risk and expense incurred by them in pursuance of their office.

4. MEMBERSHIP

4.1 The Club shall consist of the following classes of members, viz:
    i) Ordinary Members;
    ii) Temporary Members;
    iii) Honorary Members.

4.2 Membership in any class may be limited by the Committee subject to confirmation at the next General Meeting.

5. ORDINARY MEMBERSHIP

5.1 Every candidate for Ordinary Membership shall be proposed and seconded by two members of the Club in good standing who, as well as the candidate, shall sign the application form. Admission to Ordinary Membership shall be by election of the Committee who may refuse any application without stating a reason.

5.2 Every candidate elected to Ordinary Membership shall be notified of his election by the Hon. Secretary and upon paying [the entrance fee and] the first annual subscription (which shall be paid within [two] weeks of the said notification or the election shall be void) he shall be a member of the Club and shall be deemed to have agreed to be bound by the Rules and Byelaws of the Club.

6. TEMPORARY MEMBERSHIP

The Committee shall have power to elect Temporary Members on such terms as they may determine.

7. HONORARY MEMBERSHIP

Honorary Members may be elected at any General Meeting of the Club, for such period as the meeting shall determine, upon a two-thirds majority vote of members present and voting.

8. SUBSCRIPTION

8.1 The annual subscription payable by Ordinary Members shall be such sum as the members shall determine from time to time in General Meeting. It shall be payable on election to Ordinary Membership and thereafter, annually, on the [...] day of [...]. If the subscription has not been paid within one month after that date the defaulter shall, subject to a contrary decision of the Committee, immediately cease to be a member.

8.2 Any subscription unpaid by the above date shall be deemed to be a debt to the Treasurer of the Club.

9. RESIGNATIONS

A member may resign his membership at any time by notice in writing to the Hon. Secretary, but a member whose written resignation is received by the Hon. Secretary after his subscription for the current year has become due shall be liable for his subscription for that year.

10. EXPULSION

10.1 The Committee shall expel from the Club any member for conduct which, in its opinion, is injurious or tends to be injurious to the interests of the Club, or its objects, or its members, or angling, or which contravenes the Club's byelaws.

10.2 Before expelling a member the Committee shall inquire into his conduct and he shall be given a reasonable opportunity to defend and justify himself either in writing or by appearing (upon being given 14 days notice of the Committee meeting) before the Committee, and the Committee's power to expel shall be on a majority vote of those present at the meeting.

10.3 An expelled member shall forfeit all rights and privileges of membership, but shall remain liable for any dues or debts to the Club which became payable or were incurred before the date of expulsion.

11. MANAGEMENT

The management of the Club shall be vested in the Committee (except as otherwise provided by these Rules).

12. OFFICERS

A President, Vice-President, Secretary and Treasurer shall be elected annually at the Annual General Meeting of the Club, after being proposed and seconded and indicating their consent and shall be ex officio members of the Committee.

13. THE COMMITTEE

13.1 The Committee shall consist of the President, Vice-President, Secretary, Treasurer and not less that [5] or more than [10] Ordinary Members of the Club, elected at an Annual General Meeting and shall have power to co-opt up to two members and may, in their discretion, invite any persons, whether members of the Club or not, to attend any Committee meeting.

13.2 At the Annual General Meeting each year one-third of the Committee for the time being (or the number nearest to one-third) being those longest on the Committee since last elected shall retire from office, but shall be eligible for re-election, when every Ordinary and Honorary Member shall be entitled to vote for as many candidates as there are vacancies to be filled and, in the case of two or more candidates for a vacancy receiving an equal number of votes, the Chairman of the meeting shall have a second or casting vote.

13.3 The Committee shall have power to fill any casual vacancy on the Committee and any member so appointed shall retire at the next Annual General Meeting but shall be eligible for re-election.

13.4 The Committee shall meet in at least [8] months of each year to examine the accounts and to arrange the affairs of the Club and minutes shall be taken of every meeting.

13.5 The quorum at any committee meeting shall be [5].

13.6 The Committee may at any time appoint a sub-committee to consider any particular aspect of the affairs of the Club. Such sub-committee must report to the members of the Club at the Annual General Meeting.

14. BORROWING POWERS

14.1 If at any time the Club in general meeting passes a resolution authorising the Committee to borrow money:

14.1.1 the Committee may borrow for the purposes of the Club the amount of money (either at one time or from time to time) and at the rate of interest, in the form and manner and upon the security specified in the resolution and

14.1.2 the Trustees must at the discretion of the Committee make any disposition of the Club property or any part of it and enter into any agreement in relation to the Club property as the Committee thinks proper to give security for the loan and interest.

14.2 Every member of the Club, whether he votes on a resolution authorising borrowing or not, and everyone becoming a member of the Club after the passing of such a resolution, is deemed to have assented to the resolution as if he had voted in favour of it.

15. INDEMNITY

The officers of the Club, being the President, Vice-President, Secretary, Treasurer or any member of the Committee so authorised by the Committee shall not incur any personal liability for any duties properly carried out on behalf of the Club and any officer so acting shall be entitled to be indemnified from Club assets.

16. BYELAWS

16.1 The Byelaws set out in the Appendix to these Rules and any byelaws made under paragraph 16.2 of this Rule shall be binding upon the members until repealed by the Committee, or by a resolution of a General Meeting, subject to any amendment made under paragraph 16.2 of this Rule.

16.2 The Committee shall from time to time make, repeal or amend all such byelaws as they deem expedient (provided that they shall not be inconsistent with these Rules) to take effect unless set aside at a General Meeting.

17. ANNUAL GENERAL MEETINGS

The Annual General Meeting of the Club shall be held in the month of [....] in each year to receive and consider the audited accounts and annual balance sheet prepared by the Treasurer; to appoint officers and auditors; to fill vacancies on the Committee and to decide on any resolution submitted by the Committee or under Rule 19.

18. SPECIAL GENERAL MEETINGS

A Special General Meeting may be held at any time that the Committee shall determine and the Committee shall call a Special General Meeting upon the requisition in writing of any [20] members for a purpose stated in the requisition and, upon receipt of such a requisition, unless they shall determine the purpose to be frivolous, the Committee shall call the meeting within 40 days of the receipt of the requisition by the Secretary.

19. NOTICES OF GENERAL MEETINGS AND RESOLUTIONS

19.1 Notice of the date and time and place of every General Meeting, stating the last date for submitting resolutions, shall be sent to each member of the Club at his last known address at least 30 days before the date of the meeting.

19.2 Notice of any resolution to be moved at a General Meeting, unless recommended by the Committee, shall be submitted in writing to the Secretary at least 21 days before the meeting and signed by the proposer and seconder. Any such resolution, unless withdrawn, shall be included in the business of the meeting and notice of it shall be sent to each member of the Club at his last known address at least 10 days before the date of the meeting.

19.3 Accidental omission to give notice to, or non-receipt of notice by, any member under paragraphs 19.1 and 19.2 of this Rule shall not invalidate any of the proceedings of the meeting.

20. Proceedings at General Meetings

20.1 [6] members (not including temporary members) shall form a quorum at any General Meeting.

20.2 At every General Meeting, the President, or in his absence the Vice-President, or, in the absence of both, a member elected by the members present, shall take the Chair. The Chairman and all Ordinary and Honorary Members present shall be entitled to vote and, in the event of an equality of votes, the Chairman shall have a second or casting vote.

20.3 Except as otherwise provided by these Rules, a majority vote of the Ordinary and Honorary Members present and voting shall carry any motion or resolution, save that no Rule of the Club may be made, repealed or amended on a vote of less than two-thirds of the members present and voting.

21. Interpretation

21.1 The Committee shall be the sole authority for the interpretation of the Club Rules and Byelaws and the decision of the Committee upon any question of interpretation, or any matter affecting the Club not provided for by the Rules or Byelaws, shall be final and binding upon the members.

21.2 In the Club Rules and Byelaws, where the context permits, words importing the masculine shall include the feminine, and words importing the singular shall include the plural, and vice versa.

21.3 The headings to these rules are for ease of reference only and are not to be taken into account in their interpretation.

22. Dissolution of Club

If, at any general meeting a resolution for the dissolution of the Club is passed by a majority of the Members present and at a Special General Meeting held not less than six weeks later (of which not less than four weeks written notice has been given to each member) and at which not less than one-half of the members are present, that resolution is confirmed by a resolution passed by a majority of two-thirds of the members voting on it, the Committee must immediately, or at such future date as is specified in the resolution, proceed to realise the property of the Club and, after the discharge of all liabilities, must divide such property equally in proportion to the amount each Ordinary Member has paid in entrance fee and subscriptions among all the Ordinary Members and, on the completion of the division, the Club will be dissolved.

23. AMENDMENT OF RULES

These rules may be added to, repealed or amended by a resolution passed at any annual or special general meeting by a majority of at least two thirds of the Ordinary and Honorary Members voting on it.

APPENDIX

(NOTE: These can also be amended according to the Club's circumstances)

Club Byelaws

(a) Require compliance with the byelaws of the Environment Agency.
(b) Require fair and lawful fishing.
(c) Prohibit trespass, digging for bait and cutting or damaging trees, vegetation and other property.
(d) Prohibit leaving litter.
(e) Specify size limits and numbers of fish that may be retained from each Club water.
(f) Specify the number of rods that may be used and tackled up at any time.
(g) Specify means of access, parking places, etc., for each Club water, and require closing of gates.
(h) Regulate use of boats.

CHAPTER 8

SEA ANGLING

Written in 1787, *De Jure Maris* by Sir Matthew Hale recognises the public right of fishing in tidal waters as the legal pillar upon which the sea angler's sport is based:

> But though the king... as a consequence of his propriety hath the primary right of fishing in the sea and the creekes and armes thereof; yet the common people of England have regularly a liberty of fishing in the sea or creekes or armes thereof, as a publick of piscary, and may not without injury to their right be restrained of it.

This chapter has deliberately been entitled 'Sea Angling' and not 'Sea Fishing'. The latter encompasses the trawlerman fishing by net in the open sea. This book is only concerned with the angler who fishes for recreation. The commercial fishing industry is beyond its scope. The law governing sea angling is well established. What follows in this chapter will interest any sea angler by looking at the regulatory structure, ownership of the foreshore and specific problems such as bait digging.

1. REGULATORY STRUCTURE

1.1 The Minister of Agriculture, Fisheries and Food and Sea Fisheries Committees

The Minister of Agriculture, Fisheries and Food supervises and controls sea fisheries. This means, in general terms, that he regulates the landing of sea fish in the United Kingdom. The mechanism through which he delegates control is the sea fisheries committee (SFC). He has the power by making an order under s.1 of the Sea Fisheries Regulation Act 1966 (SFRA) to create sea fisheries districts and constitute local SFCs to regulate sea fisheries in those districts. The order may also lay down rules for the number of members of the committee and its constitution.

The application for the order is made by a county or metropolitan district council and the committee is a council committee. Members consist of those appointed by the council and additional members, including a representative of the Environment Agency, anyone appointed by the Minister as being acquainted with the needs and opinions of the fishing interests of that district and anyone with knowledge of or expertise in marine environmental matters.

1.2 SFCs and byelaws

The SFC, in turn, can make byelaws and this is the means by which it regulates sea fishing within its district. Under s.5 SFRA, it can make byelaws for the following purposes:

i) restricting or prohibiting the fishing for or taking of all or any specified kinds of sea fish during any period;

ii) restricting or prohibiting any method of fishing for sea fish or the use of any instrument of fishing for sea fish and determining the size of mesh, form, dimensions of any instrument of fishing for sea fish;

iii) prohibiting or regulating the deposit or discharge of any solid or liquid substance detrimental to sea fish or sea fishing.

The byelaws have to be confirmed by the Minister and he may revoke or modify them if he considers it necessary or desirable for the improvement or maintenance of sea fisheries (s.7 SFRA). Importantly, no byelaws can be made which prejudicially affect any right of private fishery or any right enjoyed by prescription (s.6 SFRA).

1.3 Other powers of SFCs

The SFCs have other miscellaneous powers, such as contributing to the cost of executing works for the improvement of any small harbour (s.13 (4) SFRA) or destroying fish predators (s.13 (1) SFRA). More generally, it may enforce any Act relating to sea fisheries (s.13 (5) SFRA).

It can adopt a pollution control function since, under s.19 (6) of the Prevention of Oil Pollution Act 1971, the committee may commence a prosecution for the illegal discharge of oil within its district. Under s.1 of the Sea Fisheries (Wildlife) Conservation Act 1992, it is under a duty to have regard to the conservation of marine flora and fauna and to try to achieve a reasonable balance between conservation considerations and any other considerations to which they are required to have regard. This is an environmental duty along the lines of those imposed on the Environment Agency (see Chapter 2). 'Fauna' will include sea fish and the committee therefore has a duty to ensure the conservation of sea fish. If it is felt that the SFC is neglecting this duty, then this section can be quoted to the SFC to ensure it observes this duty.

1.4 Fishery officers

Fishery officers are appointed by the SFC to enforce its byelaws. They are similar to water bailiffs (see Chapter 17) and are given various powers in order to enforce the byelaws. For example, they can stop and search any vehicle or vessel used in their district for carrying fish or a substance the deposit or discharge of which is prohibited or regulated by byelaw; they can examine any instrument used for fishing; they can search any container used to carry fish and seize any fish taken or instrument used in contravention of the byelaws (s.10 (2) SFRA).

Like water bailiffs, they are the equivalent of police constables (s.10 (3) SFRA), have powers of arrest and may obtain a warrant to search premises on which they suspect illegally caught fish or unlawful instruments are kept (s.12 SFRA). Finally, if anyone without reasonable excuse refuses to allow a fisheries officer to exercise his powers under the SFRA or resists or obstructs an officer in the performance of his duty, he is guilty of an offence and liable to a fine (s.11 SFRA).

There may be some overlap between the Environment Agency and the SFC. If the Minister creates a sea fisheries district, he must define its limits so that each knows its jurisdiction. He may give the Agency the same powers as a committee if a district has not been created. Therefore, the sea angler who wishes to consult with the Agency must enquire whether an SFC has been constituted. It could well be that their jurisdiction overlaps and this may involve a duplication of responsiblity.

2. The Sea Fish

The Salmon and Freshwater Fisheries Act 1975 (SAFFA) does not apply to sea fish. Its classification only applies to freshwater fish. The definition of sea fish is contained in many acts. Section 20 SFRA defines sea fish as 'fish of any description found in the sea including shellfish but does not include: (a) fish of the salmon species, or (b), trout which migrate to and from the sea'.

In contrast, section 8 of the Fishery Limits Act 1976 includes salmon and migratory trout in the definition of sea fish and section 22 of the Sea Fish (Conservation) Act 1967 defines them as 'fish ... of any kind found in the sea'.

Section 37 (1) of the Salmon Act 1986 (SA) goes further and specifically gives SFCs set up under the SFRA the power to make byelaws for the protection of salmon and to prevent any interference with their migration. This implicitly accepts that migratory fish are sea fish. The power is extended by sub-section (2) to the making of byelaws for the purposes of s.6

SFRA authorising the placing and use of fixed engines including their construction, design, material and dimensions. Such byelaws are, however, subject to the approval of the Environment Agency. Despite the original definition excluding migratory species in the SFRA, the SA overrides this, bringing such fish within the powers of sea fisheries committees at least whilst they are in tidal waters.

3. THE FORESHORE

3.1 Definition

In everyday parlance the foreshore or seashore is seen as that part of the beach on which the public can walk whilst the tide is out. However, there has been some judicial confusion in that judges have found it difficult to define the foreshore. Hale, in *De Jure Maris*, defines the shore as 'that ground that is between the ordinary high-water and low-water mark'. The common law reflects this and defines it as the portion of land which lies between the high and low water marks at ordinary tides: *Attorney General v Chambers* (1854). In *Lowe v Govett* (1832), the Court excluded from the foreshore those parts of the coast not covered by the high water of ordinary spring tides on the basis that they were not ordinarily overflowed by the sea. Referring to *Lowe v Govett*, Lord Chancellor Cranworth in *Attorney General v Chambers* (1854) felt that the best answer was that the foreshore was land not capable of 'ordinary cultivation or occupation'. Mr Justice Maule in the same case stated that 'the average of these medium tides in each quarter of a lunar revolution during the year gives the limit, in the absence of all usage, to the rights of the Crown on the seashore'. This average was to be determined over the course of one week.

The problem is that nature does not follow legal theory. The foreshore is moveable and high and low water marks will fluctuate. No matter how often the foreshore is surveyed, cartographers cannot keep up with nature. In addition, what of those areas of land periodically covered by the sea, but excluded from this definition? Section 41 (1) of SAFFA adopts a broader approach by defining foreshore as 'the shore and bed of the sea and of every channel, creek, bay, estuary and navigable river as far up it as the tide flows'. However, this only defines foreshore in the context of the SAFFA and does not apply to the ownership of the foreshore.

There is, therefore, some confusion in the law at present. The question of who owns the foreshore is very important for the sea angler. The extent of the foreshore, as will be shown later, affects his right of access to the sea and where he may dig for bait.

For the private owner of the foreshore, how far it extends is also crucial. When he sells his land, how does he define its boundaries?

3.2 Who owns the foreshore?

It is ancient law that the soil of the foreshore belongs to the Crown. However, this is a rebuttable presumption and the title of the Crown can be defeated by a stronger claim. The foreshore can be owned by an individual, company or local authority, among others. Whilst this was confirmed in *Malcomson v O'Dea* (1863) the Judge stated: 'That such a right may lawfully exist is clear ... and the right of fishery prima facie in the public', it must be said that the majority of the foreshore is owned by the Crown. If so, it will be managed by the Crown Estate Commissioners.

Whoever owns the foreshore has the rights which come with the ownership of land. He may restrain anyone who makes use of the foreshore without his permission and he may also sell or lease it or grant rights over it. Nevertheless, his ownership is subject to the public rights of navigation and fishing. The foreshore can pass by express grant, implied grant and prescription.

3.2.1 Express grant

The right of the Crown to sell the foreshore or rights over it was recognised in *Attorney General v Burridge* (1822):

> It is a doctrine of ancient establishment, that the shore between the high and low water marks belongs prima facie to the King ... but it is equally clear that the King may grant his private right therein to his subjects ... by grant, charter or prescription.

Disputes have arisen over the terms of a grant (which in this context means the legal document granting ownership). In *Attorney General v Parmeter* (1811), the Plaintiff relied on a grant by Charles I. However, he failed on two grounds. First, the grant did not contain a specific description of the land claimed. Secondly, the terms of the grant allowed the shore to be fenced in. This would have curtailed the public right of navigation. The Crown could not grant this 'because it would divest the subject of a public right which the King's grant could not affect'.

Each case will depend on its facts and the person trying to defeat the presumption in favour of the Crown will have to show that the foreshore was passed by the grant. Reliance would have to be placed on the terms of the grant and evidence would have to be called of acts of ownership such as anchorage, jetty construction and the taking of fish.

3.2.2 Implied grant

In the absence of an express grant, a plaintiff may show that rights granted over the foreshore imply ownership of the soil. In *Le Strange v Rowe* (1866), the defendant who had taken mussels from the foreshore claimed the plaintiff did not own the foreshore. The problem arose over the interpretation of the grant from the Crown which only referred to anchorage, groundage and wreck of the sea and not the soil. Erle C J affirmed that 'there is a strong presumption in law that by the grant of a manor with those terms annexed the soil of the seashore was intended to pass.'

3.2.3 Prescription

This is explained more fully in Chapter 5 but it provides a means of establishing ownership through long use. The right was recognised in *De Jure Maris*: 'If a subject hath by prescription the property of a certain tract ... even while it is covered with water ... the subject will have the propriety in the soil ...'

No general rules can be given. Each case will turn on its facts. In *Lord Advocate v Young* (1887) acts of the Plaintiff such as taking 'drift sea-ware', the construction some sixty years before of a retaining wall on the foreshore and the taking of sea and sand were seen as sufficient acts of ownership to establish a prescriptive right to the foreshore. The Crown argued that stones and sand had been taken from the foreshore to build a harbour. This was rejected by the Judge who, in addition, did not 'attach .. the slightest weight to the fact that some old women carried off sea-ware in creeks' to manure their gardens.

In the more recent case of *Fowley Marine (Emsworth) Ltd v Gafford* (1968), acts such as granting permission to lay moorings and letting a part of a tidal creek in Chichester were strong enough acts to establish prescriptive ownership of the foreshore.

Statute has intervened through the Limitation Act 1980 (LA). The Crown loses its right to recover the foreshore if it fails to bring an action to do so within sixty years of occupation by an individual (Paragraph 11 (1) of Schedule 1 LA). If any land has ceased to be part of the foreshore then an action to establish ownership must be brought within thirty years (Paragraph 11 (2) (b) of Schedule 1 LA).

4. RIGHTS OVER THE FORESHORE

There is a collection of rights available to the public which may be exercised on the foreshore. There are the long established rights of fishing and navigation. However, others, such as a general right of access, are not recognised by the law. The basis for this rests on the principle that the rights of the public attach to the water and not the soil. This was emphasised by Mr Justice Buckley in *Brinckman v Matley* (1904):

> But when the sea recedes and the foreshore becomes dry there is not, as I understand the law, any general common law right in the public to pass over the foreshore ...

This means that there is no general public right to bathe, gather seaweed or go beachcombing. These are tolerated by the Crown or the owner of the foreshore. This was aptly expressed in *Alfred F. Beckett v Lyons* (1966), 'it is notorious that many things are done on the foreshore by the public which they have no right to do'.

Furthermore, there is no public highway on the foreshore. In *Llandudno Urban Council v Woods* (1899), the Judge, in recognising this, maintained the council had 'a right to treat every bather, every nursemaid with a perambulator, every boy riding a donkey, and every preacher, on the shore at Llandudno as a trespasser.'

4.1 Right of fishing

The public right of fishing is the right to fish in tidal waters. This includes the sea, estuaries, tidal watercourses and from the foreshore. It is the cornerstone for the sea angler who fishes from the foreshore, or from a boat. The ownership of the foreshore, whether by the Crown or another, is subject to this right of fishing. For the angler who fishes from the foreshore, this means that he can only go on the foreshore if he actually intends to fish. The right to go on the foreshore is only ancillary to the right to fish and cannot be exercised as a right in itself. It may also be limited by custom. For example, in the case of *Fennings v Grenville* (1808), a whale was harpooned by the owner of the 'Caerwent', but it had already been attached to a buoy called a droug by the Plaintiff. It was the custom that the party who struck the fish with the droug should have one half of it. The Court applied this custom. The sea angler will not be fishing for whales, but there may be certain pecularities to be observed when fishing in a particular area.

4.1.1 The Sea Angler's rights

For the sea angler his rights over the foreshore allow him to cast from the beach, rocks or pier. In addition, and coupled with the right to navigate in s.4.2 below, he can fish from a boat. It must be remembered, however, that the right of access to the foreshore is not a general right, but only a right to go fishing.

4.2 Right of navigation

The right of the public to navigate in the sea is one that has been unchallenged from early history. It is a right which supercedes those of the Crown. It is not suspended when the tide is too low for ships to float. In *Mayor of Colchester v Brooke* (1845), the Court held the right includes all such rights as are necessary for convenient passage. This will include grounding when the tide is out. Therefore, if the Crown did make a grant of any part of the foreshore, estuary or tidal watercourse, it will be subject to the public right of navigation. The right does extend over the entire space over which the tide flows. It did not, however, help a claim by colliery owners for a right as members of the public to moor a coal hulk, in a public harbour, to supply coal to merchant ships in the harbour (*Denaby and Cadeby Main Collieries Ltd v Avon* (1910)).

4.3 Right of access

It may come as a surprise that there is no general public right of access to the foreshore. In *Alfred F. Beckett Ltd v Lyons* (1967), Lord Justice Win categorically stated:

> I have failed to find ... any support for the view that there has ever been a right in the inhabitants of the United Kingdom or any county town or district comprised in it, to have access to any foreshore, elsewhere than in Devon and Cornwall ... It seems clear that there has for long been a common - though it may be no less fallacious - belief entertained fairly generally by the public that there is a general right of access to the foreshore for the purpose of bathing.

In the modest Victorian era, bathing led to prosecution. Although men had bathed naked in the same place for fifty years, the Defendant was convicted in *R v Reed* (1871) for indecent exposure. He had to cross a path that 'as many as eighteen or twenty women passed along ... and that sometimes they had to turn back in order to avoid the bathers!'

The general rule is that the right of access is limited to facilitating the public rights of fishing and navigation. Mr Justice Cozens-Hardy, in *Llandudno Urban Council v Woods* (1899), confirmed that 'the public have no right at common law to enter upon the shore, when dry, except for the purposes of navigation or fishing'. In that case, the Defendant had claimed a right, as a clergyman of the Church of England, to hold services on the seashore. The Court did not uphold the right. This means that a boat may be navigated over the foreshore and the angler may walk upon the foreshore to fish, but this right of access can only be exercised to navigate and/or to fish.

4.3.1 Exceptions

However, there are exceptions to this general rule. First, access is permitted in cases of peril or necessity. Whilst the case does not rule on a general right of access for necessity, Lord Justice Romer in *Brinckman v Matley* (1904) states that, 'No doubt also the public have certain rights of necessity over the foreshore.' However, he does not elaborate on those rights of necessity.

Secondly, the owner of land next to the foreshore is allowed access in the same way as a riparian owner is to a watercourse. In *Coppinger v Sheehan* (1906), Mr Justice Barton likened this right to 'the owner of a house in a street or other highway to step backward and forward between this house and the highway.' He extended it to include access to the sea over the foreshore when the tide recedes, although only, in that case, for the purposes of navigation.

Thirdly, a right of access may be acquired by custom. In *Mercer v Denne* (1904), the inhabitants of a parish claimed a right over the foreshore to spread their nets to dry. The Defendant countered this by arguing that the beach had changed in that, in the 1840s, much of it was below the high water mark and unsuitable for drying nets. The Judge rejected this as a reason for denying access, despite finding that it was true, saying, 'the mere non-user during the period that the sea flowed over the spot is immaterial for it was no interruption of the right, but only of the possession ...'

Finally, local authorities have a wide range of powers to regulate the use of the foreshore. For example, s.231 of the Public Health Act 1936 allows a local authority to make byelaws regulating bathing in the sea and, under s.76 of the Public Health Act 1961, byelaws may be passed by a local authority regulating the speed and use of pleasure boats and hovercraft, to name only two.

4.3.2 The right of access and the sea angler

The right of access does not mean that the angler can march over private land to arrive at the foreshore. To do so is a trespass. He can only gain access to the foreshore by a public highway or footpath or in a boat.

4.4 Rights of common

A right of common is the right to take matter, such as seaweed and sand, from the foreshore. The basic position is that there is no such public right and that they belong to the owner of the foreshore. Whether a right of any kind exists may be the subject of a dispute and there have been several cases down the years. In the Irish case of *Stoney v Keane* (1903), the

Defendant, James Keane, maintained he had a right to cut seaweed from the foreshore of Innishmacross Island. He had exercised this right for thirty five years and had never paid rent for it. The Plaintiff then sold the land, but subsequently proved that Mr Keane was a trespasser on the basis that, when he had sold the land, he had reserved a right to take the seaweed. A claim to a right to collect driftwood also failed, on the basis that driftwood is not part of the natural produce of the soil (*Re Foreshore, Oreston* (Comm Reg Dec). However, a claim to take seaweed did succeed, on the basis that it 'was not the natural product of, in the sense of growing on, the beach', (*Re Porthallow Beach* (Comm Reg Dec).

Down the years there have been several cases of highway authorities attempting to take shingle and stones in order to repair roads. One such occurred in Devon when the Plaintiff applied for an injunction to stop the local highways board from collecting pebbles and stones from Lannacombe Cove (*Pitts v Kingsbridge Highways Board* (1871)). He claimed title to the land above the high water mark and argued that the removal of the stones increased the encroachment of the sea onto his land. The Defendant maintained that it had a customary right. Above the high water mark, Lord Romilly found that the Plaintiff was the Lord of the Manor, that his title superceded the Crown's, and that there was no custom to take shingle from another man's land. Hence, the highways board failed in its claim to a right to take shingle above the high water mark. He heard conflicting evidence on the effect on the beach of the removal of shingle. The Defendant argued that the shingle was replaced when there was an onshore wind. Below the high water mark the Judge held as a fact that the quantities of shingle taken did not accelerate the encroachment of the sea and, therefore, did not grant the injunction over that portion of the foreshore.

A similar claim also failed in *Padwick v Knight* (1852), when the surveyors of a local parish could not uphold a right to take shingle from the foreshore to repair local roads. In contrast, in *Lynn Regis v Taylor* (1684), a custom for the proprietors of ships to dig for gravel on the foreshore for ballast was upheld since it was for the maintenance of navigation.

4.5 Right of wreck

At law, the definition of 'wreck' extends beyond that of a ship that has been sunk to types of unclaimed property found at sea or on the foreshore, such as flotsam and jetsam. Interestingly, jetsam has been defined as items cast into the sea from a ship in danger of being sunk and afterwards the ship perishes and flotsam as items which float on the sea when a ship is sunk or otherwise perishes (*Constables Case* (1601)).

Wreck usually belongs to the owner of the foreshore. However, the right of wreck allowing an individual to take wreckage lying on the beach and the right to pass over the foreshore to do so may be granted separately or be acquired by prescription. In *Calmady v Rowe* (1844), the Defendant had entered the foreshore in Wembury, Devon, and taken seaweed. In an action for trespass, the Plaintiff succeeded by giving evidence of the grant of the right of wreck to his predecessors in 1564 by Queen Elizabeth I to show that he owned the soil of the foreshore.

Wreckage is further distinguished between that which has touched the ground and that which has not. In *R v Two Casks of Tallow* (1836), the Judge summarised the law that, whilst at sea, wreck belongs to the Crown; above high watermark it belongs to the 'Lord of the Manor as grantee of the Crown' but, if it becomes fixed to the land, it becomes wreck. However, if it becomes afloat again its status will depend on its state as the time it was seized. In that case, the Lord of the Manor claimed two casks of tallow that were taken by Customs. One had touched the ground, but one was floating. The Judge rejected the argument that as soon as they touched the ground they became the property of the Lord of the Manor and found in favour of Customs.

4.6 Bait digging

Strictly speaking, this subject should come under the heading of Rights of Common. However, due to its topicality and importance for the sea angler, it deserves a detailed analysis. The recent case of *Anderson v Alnwick DC* (1993) looked at this issue with Lord Justice Evans actually posing the question 'Is bait digging in fact ancillary to the right to fish?' He decided it in favour of the sea angler.

4.6.1 Bait digging as a right ancillary to sea angling

He looked at many of the cases referred to in this chapter, such as *Brinckman v Matley*. He did not doubt that the right to fish included ancillary rights such as crossing the foreshore to exercise the right. He observed that the right to dig bait had never been challenged: 'The most likely explanation is that no one doubted that the right to take fish from the sea included the right to dig worms from the foreshore as bait.' He also went further, asserting that the right to take fish from the sea was a vital source of food for coastal communities. Worms can only be found in the sand of the foreshore and, therefore, beneath the surface of the water when the foreshore was covered by tide. To restrict the use of worms for bait would, in itself, be a restriction on the right to fish.

In an important part of the judgment, he qualified the right by stating that the '... taking of worms must be directly related to an actual or intended exercise of the public right to fish. Taking for commercial purposes such as sale clearly is not justified in any way.' He said that there may be intermediate cases where worms are taken not by the digger, but for another who may be a companion or a paying customer on a sea angling trip. He did not rule on these examples saying that each case would have to be decided according to its facts.

For the sea angler who digs bait from the foreshore to enjoy his day's sport, this is clearly lawful. However, the tackle shop owner cannot dig bait to sell in his shop, since this is a commercial purpose. In between, there are grey areas. For example, is a club member allowed to dig bait to give to fellow members? A definite answer cannot be given, although it is certain that he must not sell the bait to fellow members.

4.6.2 Bait digging as a right of common

Finally, it could be that a right to dig for bait is registered as a right of common under the Commons Registration Act 1965 (CRA). The CRA created a system whereby rights of common, such as taking sea weed and shellfish from the foreshore, can be registered at a central registry in London controlled by the Commons Commissioners. Registration protects the right, such that it cannot be challenged as unlawful. The provisions of the CRA are too detailed for this book, but a right to dig bait can be protected as a right in common (see the *Foreshore and Saltings, Titchwell, Norfolk* (Comm Reg Dec) as an example). However, following *Anderson v Alnwick DC*, most sea anglers will rely on this case to protect their right to dig bait as ancillary to the public right, rather than by registering it as a right in common.

4.7 The High and Territorial Seas

The Territorial and High Seas are concepts which separate the seas over which, respectively, this country's law has jurisdiction and those that are international. Traditionally, territorial waters were subject to a three nautical mile limit. However, following the Territorial Sea Act 1987 (TSA), the breadth of the territorial sea is now twelve nautical miles. This is reflected in international law, under Article 3 of the United Nations Convention on the Law of the Sea 1982 (UNCLOS), which recognises that every coastal state can establish its territorial seas to a twelve mile limit. The baseline from which this is measured is the low water line around the coast, as set out in the Territorial Waters Order in Council 1964, which is still in force by virtue of the TSA. If there is any dispute over the location of this baseline, a certificate issued by the Secretary of State under s.1 (3) TSA will be conclusive. The high seas start at the limit of territorial waters. The basic understanding is that they are free and not subject to appropriation by any nation.

4.8 The ownership of the sea bed

As with the foreshore, the law of the ownership of the sea bed has caused some problems. By sea bed, it is meant that part of land extending from the low water mark of the foreshore to the limit of territorial waters. It is generally accepted that the sea bed is owned by the Crown. In *Trustees of the Port and Harbour of Lerwick v Crown Estate Commissioners* (1990), the Court held that a licence was required from the Crown Estate Commissioners before salmon farming operations affecting the sea bed could commence. It is, therefore, the Crown Estate Commissioners who manage the sea bed. In this capacity, they authorise dredging and grant licences for aggregate extraction.

It may be, however, that a subject may establish a title against the Crown, as happened in *Loose v Castleton* (1978). Mr Castleton removed mussels from the sea bed below the low water mark of the tide. The Plaintiff, Mr Loose, claimed a right of fishery from the Le Strange Estate. The Defendant tried to argue that when a several fishery exists in tidal waters, its seaward extent could not be further than the mean low water mark of ordinary tides. Relying on *Gann v Free Fishers of Whistable* (1865), the Court rejected this. The Plaintiff, remarkably, was able to show a chain of title to the eleventh century. The Court could not believe that the Crown granted a fishery all those years ago subject to an artificial line, the low water mark, and not granting a fishery where the right could be exploited - especially considering the best mussel beds lay below that point.

4.8.1 Rights over the sea bed

Whilst the Crown owns the sea bed, it only holds this, as with the foreshore, subject to public rights of fishing and navigation. In *Fitzhardinge v Purcell* (1908) Mr Justice Parker acknowledged the right of the Crown to grant rights of the sea bed to a subject, but qualified this in stating, '... no grant by the Crown of part of the bed of the sea or the bed of a tidal navigable river can or ever could operate to extinguish or curtail the public right of navigation and rights ancillary thereto ...'. This protects the rights of the sea angler. UNCLOS affirms this, since Article 19 preserves the right of passage through territorial seas of ships of all states, only provided it is not prejudicial to the peace, good order or security of the national state.

4.8.2 Navigation on the foreshore and sea bed

There has been some case law on what is lawful navigation or anchorage. In *The Swift* (1901), a vessel was grounded in an oyster bed, causing damage both to the bed and the oysters. The bed and the oysters were the property of the Plaintiff. The fishery was clearly marked by beacons and a warning had been given by a watch-boat. The vessel was not grounded in the exercise of an ordinary right of navigation. The owner had negligently navigated the ship and was, therefore, liable in damages to the owner of the fishery.

A contrast is the case of *Colchester Corporation v Brooke* (1846). The Plaintiffs owned oyster lays on the River Colne in Essex. They alleged that the Defendant had navigated his vessel so carelessly that it had sunk, causing damage to the oyster beds and the oysters themselves. The Judge found that the Defendant's conduct had not been wilful in that he had not deliberately damaged the oyster lays. The Plaintiff failed. The distinction between these two cases lies in the conduct of the Defendants. In the first, he could have avoided the damage but for his carelessness. In the second, he could not and he was justified in grounding his ship.

4.9 Pollution

Marine pollution is a large subject and is beyond the scope of this book. However, it is worth briefly looking at the position of the sea angler, since pollution may well affect his sport.

The sea angler is not in as strong a position as the freshwater angler. In Chapter 10, the law of private nuisance is seen as a major weapon in the armoury of the angler in his fight against pollution. However, to succeed in nuisance, the angler needs an interest in private property. The sea angler's report is based on the public right to fish. As such, he does not have a private interest in property and cannot use nuisance to claim compensation. It may be possible to convince the Attorney General to take an action in public nuisance. However, the Attorney General will only take such an action if a sufficiently large portion of the public has been affected. It could well be that sea anglers can fill this category.

4.9.1 Oil pollution

The most obvious source of marine pollution is oil tankers. Headline grabbing disasters have been many, from the Torrey Canyon to the Amoco Cadiz and, most recently, the Sea Empress. The regime to compensate victims of oil pollution is based on two international conventions: the 1969 Convention on Civil Liability for Oil Pollution Damage and the 1971 Convention on the Establishment of an International Fund for

Compensation for Oil Pollution Damage. These are administered through the International Oil Pollution Compensation Fund, based in London. It considers claims for compensation as a result of oil pollution. However, it does have its weaknesses in that only quantifiable claims for financial loss can be met. If a club or individual cannot enjoy his sport due to pollution then they can only claim for losses actually incurred, such as loss of income. A claim based on loss of sport cannot be made.

4.9.2 Pollution from land based sources

It is really polluting matter emanating from land that is the worst source of marine pollution. International Law does provide a measure of protection - for example, the Paris Convention for the Prevention of Marine Pollution from Land-Based Sources 1974, which covers the North East Atlantic and the North Sea. Signatories undertake to pursue measures to combat marine pollution from land-based sources. The Convention sets measures to control pollution and each party must adopt these. A Commission implements the convention, assesses its effectiveness and makes recommendations. Nevertheless, whether it has any real power, beyond applying pressure on a State, is debateable. In addition, on a more global scale, UNCLOS places a duty on States to protect and preserve the marine environment. This duty is interpreted as a duty to pass legislation to reduce pollution of the marine environment, but enforcement is left to the individual state.

4.9.3 The sea angler and pollution

However, it is really the individual country that regulates marine pollution. Up to 95 per cent of sea pollution comes from land based sources. The most obvious example is sewage outfalls. These are controlled by national legislation under the consent system (see Chapter 9). The sea angler will be looking to the Environment Agency and sea fisheries committees to ensure that pollution of the sea is effectively controlled. Section 104 Water Resources Act (WRA) includes 'coastal waters' and territorial waters in the definition of 'controlled waters'. Section 85 (1) WRA makes it an offence to pollute controlled waters. Therefore, the criminal law will protect the sea in which sea anglers enjoy their sport from not only from sewage, but, all types of pollution (see Chapter 9).

4.9.4 Civil actions and sea pollution

Actions in court for coastal pollution are rare although, in 1994, a Mr Saltmarsh, who was the owner of the foreshore at Croyde in North Devon, sought damages for the cost of cleaning up the beach and an injunction to prevent the continuation of sewage discharged against South West Water (Water Law November 1994/183). The main problem was sewage debris being washed up onto the beach. The source was a sewage outfall operated by the water company. The debris was so bad that a blue flag award was refused. The claim was made in nuisance and trespass (see Chapter 11). The trespass was the deposit of the debris on the beach and the nuisance was the interference which his property, the beach. The action was settled in favour of Mr Saltmarsh and did not go to trial. Therefore, no precedent was set. The case was unusual in that Mr Saltmarsh owned the beach and was able to sue in nuisance and trespass. The defences raised pleaded that the water company had kept within the terms of its consent and that it was under a statutory duty to provide sewerage services. It is disappointing that these were not considered by a judge. However, it serves to show that, in the right circumstances, pollution of the sea is not just a matter for the Environment Agency.

4.9.5 Litter and sea angling

Finally, an interesting comparison can be made between the sea angler and the freshwater angler regarding litter. The point was made in Chapter 16 that most of the legislation affects public places and, as such, the fresh water angler escapes the regime. However, the sea angler carries on his sport in a public place. He will, therefore, have to observe the law regarding litter.

QUESTIONS

Question 1

My club has dug for bait on the foreshore for many years. Older members of the club can remember doing this before the war. Now, a development company has bought a hotel which looks onto the beach. It has put up signs saying that digging for bait is not allowed from the foreshore. Members have ignored this, but matters came to a head when the manager told two of our members to stop digging bait in front of the hotel. They refused and were threatened with legal action. We only dig for bait either to fish from the foreshore or to go out in a boat. It is not sold, although if a member does not use all the worms he may give them to another.

Answer

Since the case of *Anderson v Alnwick DC*, it has been established that the right to dig for bait is ancillary to the public right of fishing. You are within your rights and the manager of the hotel is wrong. Providing there is lawful access to foreshore, he cannot prevent you from digging for bait. It is undecided that you can dig for bait to give to other members of the club, but it is unlikely that a Court would stop bait digging just for doing that.

Question 2

Members of my club have told me that a farmer whose land is next to the foreshore is telling them that they cannot fish from the foreshore. He has tried to prevent them using a public footpath which gives access to the foreshore. He has hinted that he owns the foreshore.

Answer

Without asking the farmer more about his claim to own the fishing rights, it is difficult to advise conclusively. However, you do have a right of access to the sea over the foreshore as long as you are fishing. He cannot stop you using the public footpath to go to the foreshore to fish.

CHAPTER 9

POLLUTION: PUBLIC REGULATION

The issue of pollution of fisheries is considered over the next two chapters. In Chapter 10, the use of private or common law remedies is dealt with, where an angler or fishing club may take a polluter to the civil courts to seek redress normally in the form of financial awards of compensation or court orders. This chapter, on the other hand, concerns itself with the public regulation of pollution and water quality, principally by the Environment Agency. The angler or angling club is often in a position to influence and assist the Agency in its pollution control functions and may find considerable benefits in relying on the Agency to use its extensive powers to control, regulate and clean up or prevent pollution. The system of public regulation of pollution is based on statutory law, mainly the Water Resources Act 1991 (WRA) and subsidiary legislation (regulations and orders) made under the WRA. Some of the law which has developed in relation to water and water quality is based on European law. The most significant single element to the system of public regulation of water pollution is the range of criminal offences which may be used to punish polluters who are successfully prosecuted. In addition to criminal law controls, the Agency has important powers to authorise pollution, prevent pollution and to monitor and plan for water quality. Finally, the Agency has wide powers allowing it to deal with pollution incidents by prevention, remediation and environmental restoration, with the polluter being responsible for the costs involved.

Given that there are over 30,000 reported pollution incidents each year affecting rivers, streams, lakes, ponds and estuaries, this is a very significant threat to fisheries.

1. POLLUTION SOURCES AND SIGNS

Some pollutants are directly toxic to fish, while others pollute by changing the characteristics of the water or aquatic environment, thus making fish life more difficult or survival impossible. Food sources for fish may be killed, for example, in turn causing damage to a fish stock. Alternatively, and commonly, pollution with organic substances often leads to oxygen depletion in water. Pollution arises from a myriad of sources. Some water pollution arises from a sudden incident, usually a spillage. Often, in these cases, the source is relatively easy to identify. Other pollution sources are diffuse and the contamination takes place over long periods of time. Examples of this are agricultural run-off of nitrates or phosphates from fertilisers, or pesticide contamination. In these cases, identifying particular sources of pollutants can be much more difficult, particularly as the pollution may well have taken several years to accumulate to levels which cause harm.

The effect of a pollution incident, or accumulative pollution over a period of time, it will depend on the sensitivity of the water. For rivers, the rate of flow is one factor that is often critical to pollution sensitivity. If a pollutant enters a river which is in full spate, it is very much less likely to do serious harm than if the flow is low. Sources of pollution of water range widely: from industrial spillages and run-off, to road transport incidents; from agricultural sources, to sewage treatment. Some of these sources are perfectly lawful and others involve a breach of environmental protection laws.

Anglers need to be vigilant for the signs of pollution: perhaps the most obvious is the presence of dead or distressed fish. However, other signs include serious water discolouration, the unusual presence of extensive scum or foam on the water's surface and, with some pollutants, (for example sewage and slurry) the water may smell. The Environment Agency operates on the slogan 'Don't ignore it, report it' and offers a freephone emergency 24 hour hotline (0800 807060) to report suspected pollution.

2. CONTROLLED WATERS

Throughout this section of the book there will be reference to 'controlled waters'. This is a legal definition of those waters which are under the regulation of the Environment Agency for water pollution control purposes. The definition is contained in s.104 WRA and consists of:

(a) Freshwater rivers and streams and canals, or any other artificial watercourses (for example leats) which are not sewers;

(b) Lakes or ponds, including reservoirs, which discharge into a river or stream, or into another lake or pond which itself is connected a river or stream;

(c) Estuaries;

(d) Coastal waters up to three nautical miles out into the sea from established tidal baselines; and

(e) Ground waters (ie. waters contained in underground strata).

Despite this comprehensive description of controlled waters in the legislation, there is always room for doubt and cases on the boundaries of the definition.

Two cases have been important in defining controlled waters. First, in *R v Dovermoss* (1995), the Court of Appeal had to consider whether controlled waters had been contaminated when water, which should have flowed down a blocked ditch, overflowed and crossed fields covered in slurry before entering a spring. The court held that controlled waters had been affected as the Act referred to inland freshwaters which were waters of any river or watercourse, not waters in any river or watercourse. Thus, pollution of the water even though outside its normal course of flow, was still covered by s.104. Secondly, in *National Rivers Authority v Biffa Waste Services* (1995), the High Court had to rule in the following circumstances. A tracked vehicle carried out some work in a river. In so doing, it disturbed the river bed and caused sediment to discolour the water. It was argued that no pollution had taken place because nothing had entered the river that was not already part of the river's waters. Perhaps surprisingly, the court upheld this argument, saying that the river bed formed part of the controlled waters.

3. POLLUTION PREVENTION

It is self-evident that the prevention of pollution is better than waiting for it to happen and then cleaning up (insofar as this is possible). Indeed, pollution prevention is one of the guiding principles for the European Union policy on the environment. Actually achieving prevention is not always particularly easy. However, there is a range of water pollution laws designed to promote it. In addition, the water pollution offences (described below) are seen by many as being a key part of prevention. If pollution is punished consistently and is taken seriously by the courts, then this should deter potential polluters, who will take steps to avoid pollution risks in order to avoid prosecution and punishment.

3.1 Pollution clean up powers s.161 WRA

These powers are considered in full at 6.1 below. They allow the Agency to carry out works to prevent pollution of controlled waters where such pollution is likely and to recover their costs from the person responsible for creating the risk.

3.2 Prevention regulations s.92 WRA

Section 92 WRA authorises the Secretary of State (for the Environment, Transport and the Regions and/or Wales) to make regulations requiring steps to be taken to carry out precautions against pollution. As it stands, only one set of regulations has been made: the Control of Pollution (Silage, Slurry and Agricultural Fuel Oil) Regulations 1991 (1991/324) which require precautions to be taken in the storage and use of silage, slurry and fuel oil on farms. Certainly, since the introduction of the pollution prevention requirements there has been a significant drop in the number of serious agricultural pollution incidents.

3.3 Water Protection Zones s.93 WRA

Water protection zones may be established by the Secretary of State (for the Environment, Transport and the Regions and/or Wales) under s.93 WRA, after following a complex procedure for consultation in Schedule 11 WRA. If a water protection zone is established, its precise effect depends on the terms of that zone. However, in general, within the area certain activities may be prohibited with a view to preventing or controlling water pollution, or may be permitted only with Agency consent. Although, in theory, this would seem to establish a good system for protecting particularly vulnerable watersheds from hazardous activities (for example chemical storage), in reality no zone has yet been established and the only proposed zone, in the Dee catchment in North Wales, has become bogged down in bureaucracy.

3.4 Code of good agricultural practice for the protection of water s.97 WRA

Under the WRA, a Code of Practice may be issued for the protection of water from agricultural activities. The current Code was issued in 1991 - although it is currently under review. Although in law the Code is of limited relevance - compliance with its terms does not protect the farmer from prosecution and nor does breach of its terms result in any legal liability - it is important in two ways. First, because it sets out guidance to assist in prevention of agricultural water pollution which, hopefully, the farming community will follow. Secondly, because breach of the Code may be good evidence of negligence which, if a pollution incident results, may assist in the bringing of a civil action (see Chapter 10), or in persuading the Agency to prosecute.

3.5 Nitrate pollution s.94 & s.95 WRA and the Nitrates Directive

The problem of nitrates in water has principally been concerned with ensuring that drinking water supplies from rivers and aquifers are in compliance with European Drinking Water Quality, set down in the Drinking Water Directive (80/778/EEC). However, nitrates can also damage the water environment generally. Action on nitrate pollution has been focused on preventive measures because the diffuse nature of such pollution (eg. nitrates washed off numerous fields which have been treated with artificial fertiliser or slurry makes identifying a particular pollution source and linking it to specific damage impossible.

Under the WRA, the Secretary of State (for the Environment, Transport and the Regions and/or Wales) may, by regulations, establish nitrate sensitive areas. These may take various forms, with different degrees of compulsion for farmers to take preventive measures. The Nitrate Sensitive Areas (Designation) Order 1990 (SI 1990/1013) establishes a number of areas in which farmers can voluntarily choose to enter into agreements with MAFF for payments of compensation in return for taking steps to protect water from nitrates.

This approach has been added to by the EC Nitrates Directive (91/676/EEC), which requires EC member states to establish nitrate vulnerable zones in which compulsory measures to reduce nitrates must be taken. This has been done in the UK by the Protection of Water Against Nitrate Pollution (England and Wales) Regulations 1996.

4. POLLUTION CONTROL

The control of pollution, rather than its prevention, lies at the heart of the system of water pollution regulation. Regrettable though it may be, water pollution from sewage and industry is a fact of life in a developed economy. Thus, the emphasis has to shift from prohibiting or preventing all pollution, to controlling it in an effective manner so that its harmful effects are understood and minimised.

This operates in two ways in terms of water pollution law. Firstly, through the system for monitoring and promoting water quality. Secondly, through the system of pollution consents.

4.1 Water quality

For many years there has been a classification system of water quality whereby rivers are graded as 1A, 1B, 2 or 3. This is an informal non-statutory system having no legal basis. Sections 82-84 WRA establish a new regime. The system is very simple. First, the Secretary of State (for the Environment, Transport and the Regions and/or Wales), by regulations, must set up classifications of water quality. Then, using this classification system, the Secretary of State (for the Environment, Transport and the Regions and/or Wales) may establish water quality objectives for particular controlled waters. There is a system for public consultation on any objectives that are proposed. Clearly, angling interests will want to be involved in this process. These objectives may be reviewed periodically. Once established, the Environment Agency and the relevant Secretary of State are under a duty to use the water pollution powers (which include the powers relating to discharge consents, prosecution and clean up) to ensure that the water quality objectives are achieved at all times (s.84 WRA).

The problem with this apparently sensible system for water quality management is that it is largely not yet implemented. Water quality objectives are being piloted in a few catchments at present, but the real, strength of the new system will depend on it being implemented nationally and on appropriate objectives being set.

4.1.1 Water quality and EC Freshwater Fish Directive

Water quality is one of few areas where European law is of significance to anglers. The Freshwater Fish Directive (78/659/EEC) aims to protect or to improve the quality of running and standing fresh waters which support, or, if pollution were reduced, would be capable of supporting fishlife. The Directive is based on designation of waters as being salmonid or cyprinid by Member States. Initially the designation was to be made by July 1980 although further designations could take place after this date. For designated waters, Member States had to set quality standards in accordance with Annex 1 to the Directive. Within five years of designation, the waters must comply with the European quality standards. The Directive sets down water quality standards for:

    (a) temperature
    (b) dissolved oxygen
    (c) pH
    (d) suspended solids
    (e) BoD
    (f) total phosphorus
    (g) nitrates
    (h) phenolic compounds
    (i) non-ionized ammonia and total ammonia
    (j) chlorine
    (k) zinc
    (l) copper

There are two problems with the Directive. First, the wording is not clear as to the extent and nature of the obligation of Member States to designate waters. It is not clear to what extent waters currently supporting, or able to support, fishlife must be included. This issue has not been clarified by the European Court of Justice. Secondly, despite a legal obligation to do so, the UK has not (until 1997 - see below) formally adopted the Directive into UK law. Instead it has dealt with it informally through the local decisions of the water authorities, NRA and Environment Agency.

4.1.2 Water quality classification - UK Regulations

Although objectives have not been widely set, a system of water quality classification has been set up through a series of regulations (primarily to implement European law obligations):

(a) Surface Waters (Dangerous Substances) (Classification) Regulations 1989, implementing the Dangerous Substances Directive (76/464/EEC) (SI 1989/2286) and further regulations made in 1997 (SI 1997/4560);

(b) Surface Waters (River Ecosystem) (Classification) Regulations 1994 (SI 1994/1057). These are by far the most important of the classification regulations introducing five classifications - RE1 (the best) to RE5 (the worst) - for freshwater rivers and watercourses. These will form the basis of the water quality objective system. The quality criteria adopted in the regulations relate quality to dissolved oxygen, biochemical oxygen demand, ammonia, hardness and concentrations of copper and zinc;

(c) Surface Waters (Fishlife) (Classification) Regulations 1997 (SI 1997/1331) provide two classifications for salmonid waters(SW) and cyprinid waters (CW), reflecting the standards in the Freshwater Fish Directive (78/659/EEC).

Further classification regulations concern shellfish water quality standards (Surface Waters (Shellfish) (Classification) Regulations 1997 (SI 1997/1332) implementing the Shellfish Directive (79/923/EEC) and bathing water and potable drinking water standards.

As a whole, these regulations set up a framework of legally binding quality criteria. They will allow legally binding standards to be set under the procedure under s.82-s.84 described above. However, until the framework leads to particular objectives being set for particular waters its potential to deal with pollution will not be realised.

4.1.3 Reform of water quality law and the European Union

The whole system of water quality may need to be reviewed in due course because the European Union is currently considering proposals to create a Framework Directive on the Aquatic Environment aimed at river basin management of both water quality and quantity.

4.1.4 Water quality and fishery interests

Anglers or angling clubs have important interests in the water quality standards being set for a particular stretch of water. They will want to be involved in any consultation process over quality standards which should be publicised through the press, the Environment Agency and the Regional

Fisheries Advisory committees. Once a water quality objective (see 4.1 above) is in place, this should be used as an argument or instrument of pressure against the Agency to ensure that discharge consents are not granted which would threaten attainment of the objective, and/or that existing consents are varied or enforced more rigorously.

Finally, the water quality objectives (and whether they have been attained) will be an important consideration in deciding whether and on what terms to acquire fishing rights.

4.2 Discharge consents s.88 and Schedule 10 WRA

The main system for controlling pollution is through discharge consents. These are permissions to pollute controlled waters granted by the Environment Agency or Secretary of State (for the Environment, Transport and the Regions and/or Wales), on appeal, which authorise pollution, but normally subject to conditions.

Anglers' interests can be protected in three ways. First, in ensuring that proper and reasoned objections are made to applications for discharge consents which may be harmful to their fishing; secondly, if a consent is to be granted, protecting the angling by arguing for the imposition of conditions; thirdly, by seeking the review of existing discharge consents where necessary and, finally, by trying to secure compliance with discharge consent conditions. There are estimated to be about 200,000 discharge consents nationally and these are a major source of lawful pollution. All that anglers can do is be involved in the processes to try to make sure that their interests are at least considered.

The law and procedure relating to discharge consents is contained in Schedule 10 WRA and the Control of Pollution (Applications, Appeals and Registers) Regulations 1996 ('the 1996 Regulations') (SI 1996/2971).

4.2.1 Applications for discharge consents

Applications for discharge consents are made to the Environment Agency. The Agency normally has four months in which to determine the application and may decide to refuse it, grant a consent conditionally or, in theory, grant a consent unconditionally. Exceptionally, the Secretary of State may take over an application under Paragraph 5 of Schedule 10 WRA. This process is known as 'calling in' an application. Applications to the Environment Agency are dealt with in writing with no hearing. Where an application is called in, the applicant or Agency can require there to be a hearing or public inquiry and, in any event, the Secretary of State can choose to have a hearing or inquiry of his own volition. In some cases involving discharges of major significance, it may be worthwhile for an angling club to try to persuade the

Secretary of State to call in an application, so that everyone gets a chance to be heard.

During the four-month period, a critical procedure for the advertisement of the application and consultation has to take place. It is during this time that angling interests need to be represented.

4.2.2 Advertisement of discharge consent applications

The 1996 Regulations require that applications for discharge consents are advertised in the *London Gazette* (see Chapter 12) and in a local newspaper circulating in the area likely to be affected. This is the main way that fishing interests will find out about applications. Applications are also logged on to a pollution control register held by the Agency. The advertisement will contain the bare minimum of details about the proposed discharge, but the full application details are available on the register. The advertisement will appear between 14 days and 28 days after it is received by the Agency and will give six weeks for representations to be made. Regrettably, there are some exceptions to the advertisement requirement. This means that some applications will not be advertised. Applications concerning national security may be exempted from advertisement. Much more importantly, those applications where the Agency considers that the discharge will have no appreciable effect on the controlled waters need not be advertised. The Agency applies certain criteria set out in its Discharge Consents Manual in determining 'appreciable effect'. These highlight any effects of environmental significance (for example, on a fish spawning area) as being significant and any change of more than 10% in its low river flow or the concentration of substances of importance to the quality of the water. In these cases, no advertisement is needed, although the application will still be entered on the register.

4.2.3 Consultation on discharge consent applications

Consultation follows on from the advertisement process. Consultation takes two forms under the 1996 Regulations. First, notification of certain interested bodies of the application and, secondly, receiving and considering any responses received from the public, angling clubs, etc. In all cases consultation has to take place with local authorities and the water company for the area in which the discharge is proposed in all cases. In special circumstances concerning coastal discharges, additional consultation with central government, harbour authorities or local fisheries committees may be needed.

The broader form of consultation is the gathering of responses from the wider interest groups. If an angling club is to respond to an application for a discharge consent, it is important that the response is well reasoned and, if need be, supported by expert evidence. Schedule 10, Paragraph 2 WRA places the Agency under a legal obligation to consider all of the results of consultation.

4.2.4 Determination of discharge consent applications and conditions

Once the period for consultation has passed, the Agency must then determine the application. If it has not done so after four months, the applicant is entitled to treat the application as refused and appeal. In practical terms, the Agency will either refuse the application or grant it conditionally. As a result of historical accident, there are some unconditional discharge consents in existence in respect of sewage discharges, but these are being reviewed by the Agency and conditions are being imposed.

Schedule 10, Paragraph 3 WRA sets out the sorts of matters which may be covered by conditions including:

(a) the places where any authorised discharge may be made;

(b) the design and construction of any outlets;

(c) the nature, origin, composition, temperature, volume and rate of flow of discharges and times when discharges may or may not be made;

(d) any requirements for prior treatment before discharge;

(e) the provision of facilities for taking samples of the discharge and for the installation, maintenance and testing of meters to measure the nature, composition, temperature, volume etc., of the discharge;

(f) the keeping of records of the discharges made and their nature etc., including details of any meter readings;

(g) the making of returns or surrender of other information to the Agency.

Conditions allow the Agency to control discharges very carefully both by control over what may and may not be discharged and verification of what has taken place.

Anglers can have a real influence on the discharge consent process provided that they make sensible, reasoned objections. It will often add considerable weight to any representations if an expert is employed. Obviously, this may be expensive. Chapter 12 paragraph 2.5.1 contains practical advice on the making of effective representations.

4.2.5 Appeals against discharge consent decisions

If a consent is refused, not determined within four months or is granted subject to conditions unacceptable to the applicant, they have a right of appeal within three months. The appeal is made to the Secretary of State (for the Environment, Transport and the Regions and/or Wales) who will appoint an Inspector to deal with the appeal on his behalf.

Details of the appeal will automatically be given to any person who made representations on the application and to the consultees. Appeals may be dealt with by way of written representations, an informal hearing or a formal inquiry (reg. 8 1996 Regulations). Further representations on the appeal may then be made (reg. 11 1996 Regulations) and if a hearing is held then any person who has made representations is entitled to be heard (reg. 12 1996 Regulations). Any person making representations will be entitled to notification of the outcome of the appeal or its withdrawal. There are no rights of appeal by any person other than the applicant for a discharge consent. This means that the only means of challenging a grant of consent which is acceptable to the applicant (by, for example, an angling club), is by means of an application for judicial review to the High Court. The limited nature of a judicial review challenge is considered in Chapter 1. Judicial review is also the only means of challenging the outcome of an appeal by the appellant or a third party.

4.2.6 Variation and revocation of existing consents

There is an important set of provisions in Schedule 10 WRA which allows the Agency to review existing consents and, if it wishes, subject to rights of appeal to the Secretary of State (for the Environment, Transport and the Regions and/or Wales), to vary or even revoke a discharge consent. Thus, conditions may be tightened, for example.

The power to vary or revoke consents (Schedule 10, Paragraph 7 WRA) is subject to important restrictions in Schedule 10, Paragraph 8 WRA. The position is that consents should contain a period during which they may not be varied or revoked. This period is normally four years from when the consent was granted or last reviewed. They may only be varied or revoked within that period on the direction of the Secretary of State and compensation may then be payable.

In practical terms, providing that a consent is reviewable under the above rules, it may be worthwhile for an angling club to write to the Agency to seek a review of a consent. Obviously, if such representations are supported by constructive suggestions for condition variation and an indication of the likely benefits, this will increase the likelihood of success.

4.2.7 Enforcing discharge consents

Where a discharge consent is in place, it is important to ensure that its conditions are being followed. Consent conditions can be enforced by the Agency either by serving an enforcement notice on the consent holder, requiring it to take steps to comply with the consent conditions (s.90 B WRA); or by criminal prosecution, as it is a criminal offence to breach consent conditions (see paragraph 5 below). Failure to comply with an enforcement notice is also a criminal offence.

4.2.8 Other water pollution authorisations

It is possible (but unusual) for other authorisations to permit pollution of water. These other consents are considered below at paragraph 5.2.1 in relation to s.88 WRA. In each case, there are similar systems for application for consent, making representations and appeals as to discharge consents.

5. POLLUTION OFFENCES

The criminal law is particularly important in relation to water pollution control. It is the prime instrument by which the discharge consent system can be controlled and enforced because it is, in general, an offence to pollute controlled waters. It is important to note that a discharge may be made under and in accordance with a discharge consent without committing any offence. Furthermore, each year there are several hundred water pollution prosecutions, usually brought by the Environment Agency, resulting normally in fines to the polluters which act as a deterrent to other potential polluters. Clearly, the exact breadth of the offences and defences and the penalties are of more than passing interest from an angler's point of view, as these offences form the basis of the protection of water from pollution.

Pollution offences may be directly relevant to anglers in a number of ways. First, when considering a purchase of fishing rights it may be important to discover whether any prosecutions for pollution offences have affected the river or lake in question (see Chapter 5 generally). Secondly, when a pollution incident occurs, anglers may be an important source of information to the Environment Agency. This may lead to a successful prosecution and clean up, at the polluter's expense. Indeed, anglers or clubs may wish to bring pressure to bear on the Agency to bring criminal proceedings because, although this is unlikely to lead directly to any recompense for harm to angling interests, it may act as a deterrent to future harm. Thirdly, a successful prosecution may be a useful part of the evidence for bringing a civil claim for compensation. Finally, in some cases anglers may wish to bring a private prosecution for one of the pollution offences (see below).

5.1 Section 85 WRA

The most important pollution offences are contained in s 85 WRA. In fact there are eleven separate offences in s.85 covering a range of different circumstances. angling Almost all of the offences prosecuted are for breaching s.85 (1) (which consists of two separate offences); s.85 (3), which also consists of two separate offences, and s.85 (6), which contains one offence.

5.1.1 Poisonous noxious or polluting matter s.85(1)

The offences in s.85(1) are based on the entry of poisonous, noxious or polluting matter to controlled waters. The two separate offences consist of either causing the entry or knowingly permitting it. These two phrases are considered below. In practice, most water pollution prosecutions are for causing poisonous, noxious or polluting matter to enter controlled waters. There are some notable features about these offences which offer some reassurance about the inability to protect the aquatic environment. First, there is no need in a prosecution to prove that anything was poisoned or harmed. The mere propensity of the material entering the waters to do harm is enough. Secondly, the courts have construed 'poisonous, noxious and polluting' in fairly broad terms. They have seen them as a hierarchy in which polluting is the least harmful. In *R v Dovermoss* (1995) the Court of Appeal held that polluting meant a tendency to taint or befoul and held that an unpleasant odour arising from drinking water but which did not render the water harmful in any way or in breach of any drinking water standards was nevertheless polluted. Often, in practice, there will be evidence of distressed fish or even a fish kill which will be very helpful in showing that poisonous (etc.) material was involved.

5.1.2 Trade or sewage effluent s.85 (3) WRA

In some cases, prosecutions may be brought for causing or knowingly permitting (see below) trade or sewage effluent to enter controlled waters (or even to the sea beyond controlled waters if via a land based pipeline, for example a long sewage outfall). The key aim of this offence is to bring all discharges of effluent from trade, industrial or sewage premises within the discharge consent system. However, they may be used to bring prosecutions where a s.85 (1) offence cannot be proved, perhaps because of lack of evidence about the harmful nature of the discharge. Trade effluent is any liquid discharge (other than surface water and domestic sewage) from premises used for any trade or business or industry, including agriculture and fish farming. Sewage effluent includes any effluent (except surface water) from sewage works.

5.1.3 Breach of discharge consent s.85(6) WRA

Section 85(6) makes it an offence to breach the terms of a discharge consent. It is not necessary to show that the person charged caused or knowingly permitted the offence merely that he held the consent and its terms were breached (*National Rivers Authority v Taylor Woodrow* (1995)). This is very important in ensuring that the exact conditions set down in a discharge consent are followed. In fact, in many cases where a discharge consent exists and has been breached there is a choice between prosecution under say s.85 (1) or (3) where the breach has resulted in a discharge of an unauthorised effluent or s.85 (6). In practice, the Agency tend to prosecute where possible under s.85 (1) reserving s.85 (6) for those cases where the condition broken does not relate to a discharge at all (for example, a condition that certain records are maintained by the polluter) or where they have problems establishing that the defendant caused or knowingly permitted the discharge.

5.1.4 Cause or knowingly permit

The prosecution in any case under s.85 (1)WRA must not only prove that the material was poisonous, etc., but that the accused was involved in that entry by causing or knowingly permitting it. Equally, in s.85 (3) WRA prosecutions, not only must the entry of effluent be shown, but also that the defendant caused or knowingly permitted the discharge.

What do these words 'cause' or 'knowingly permit' mean? In both cases the application of the words to any particular case is a question of fact for the magistrates or jury. However, the courts have laid down some important guidelines over the years as to what these words mean. Although many of the cases predate the 1991 legislation 'cause' and 'knowingly permit' have been the basis for criminal liability in water pollution statutes since 1951. The courts have determined that cause is an ordinary word of the English language meaning to bring about. Furthermore, they have decided that:

(a) Cause is unrelated to fault. So one can cause something to happen without being careless or at fault in any way. In the leading case of *Alphacell v Woodward* (1972), the paper factory had settling pools or tanks in which contaminated water was treated. A pump system ensured that the water did not reach a level where it went by an overflow into a nearby river. The court held that, without any fault on the part of the factory operators a pump became blocked with vegetation. The House of Lords upheld the conviction for causing water pollution;

(b) Causing something will involve the defendant in a positive act of some sort (for example, pouring a drum of chemicals down a drain or operating a factory, or maintaining a sewerage system), (*Attorney General's Reference No 1 of 1994* (1995)). As long as the defendant undertakes some positive activity, it does not matter if the immediate cause of the pollution results from a failure to do something (for example, failing to maintain a sewage pump system in *Attorney General's Reference No. 1 of 1994* (1995)).

(c) It is possible for there to be more than one cause and more than one causer in law. The House of Lords said in *Empress (Abertilley) Ltd v National Rivers Authority* (1998) that the correct issue for the court to address was not what is the cause of this pollution, but, did this defendant cause this pollution.

(d) It is not necessary to show that the accused knew about the cause or risk of pollution.

(e) In some cases, the unexpected intervention of a third party or natural event may break the causation. This issue has recently been reconsidered by the House of Lords in *Empress (Abertilley) Ltd v National Rivers Authority* (1998). In this case, the defendant stored diesel in a tank on their garage site. The site was open to the public although supervised by garage staff. The diesel tank had a tap on it. There was no lock on the tap. There was a bund around the tank, but a pipe lead from the tap to a drum outside the bund. Someone (it is assumed a vandal) opened the tap on the diesel tank and allowed the contents to empty. The diesel polluted a nearby river. The defendant was convicted of causing the pollution despite the fact that the immediate cause was the vandal. The House of Lords held that someone who carries on an activity (eg. storage of diesel) causes anything which arises in the ordinary or natural course of events. This includes vandalism. This new and stricter view of pollution liability has recently been applied to pollution arising from an unforeseeable failure of a pipe linkage (*Environment Agency v Brock* (1998)). It seems that the courts are expecting more and more care to be taken to avoid pollution risks.

5.1.5 Cause in practice – the Yorkshire Water case

It may be useful to see how these principles work in practice. The case of *National Rivers Authority v Yorkshire Water Services* (1994) arose out of an incident at the Brierley sewage treatment works. The works had a discharge consent which specifically prohibited the discharge of isooctonal. Someone (no one knows who) poured isooctonal (illegally) into a drain which lead to the sewage treatment works. The works operated on a gravity basis so that once material entered the works it inevitably would be discharged. The isooctonal passed through the works and into a nearby river. Isooctonal is very dangerous to fish life. Yorkshire Water was prosecuted for causing poisonous, noxious or polluting matter to enter controlled waters. The House of Lords upheld a finding that Yorkshire Water had caused the isooctonal to enter controlled waters despite the fact that someone else illegally placed the material in the sewer and there was nothing Yorkshire Water could have done to prevent the discharge. Yorkshire Water operated the sewage treatment works and that is enough to prove causation. In fact for reasons concerned with a special defence for water companies (see paragraph 5.2.5 below) Yorkshire Water was acquitted.

5.1.6 'Knowingly Permit'

The breadth of the meaning of the word 'cause' means that the majority of water pollution prosecutions are for this offence. However, it is also possible to commit the offences in s.85 by knowingly permitting the pollution. In broad terms 'knowingly permitting' will involve knowledge of the source of the pollution and failure to do any thing about it when having the power to do so. This offence concentrates on a culpable failure to act, whereas 'cause' generally focuses on carrying on an activity (and is not concerned with the polluters knowledge or foresight).

Until the House of Lords' judgement in *Empress (Abertilley) Ltd v National Rivers Authority* (1998), it was thought that *Price v Cromack* (1975) was a classic example of knowingly permitting.

In *Price v Cromack* (1975), the defendant owned land adjoining a river. He agreed that a nearby factory could build lagoons on his land for the storage of effluents prior to their disposal. The lagoons were built and effluent discharged by the factory into them. Breaches in the walls of the lagoons developed and effluent could be seen to be entering the river and caused a fish kill. The defendant was charged with causing the pollution and was acquitted as he had not brought it about (the factory had). However, the High Court noted that a charge of 'knowingly permitting' would have been likely to succeed as the defendant could see the discharge of effluent and failed to do anything about it, even though it was in his power to do so as the lagoons were on his land. Lord Hoffman in the *Empress* case said that the High Court had been wrong in *Price*. In fact, it is an example of causing pollution.

Knowingly permitting is likely in future to be limited to pure omission cases where the defendant has not in any way been involved in bringing about the pollution or risk of pollution. Often, it is difficult for the Environment Agency to acquire good evidence of knowledge of pollution and for this reason together, with the comparative ease of proving causation, few prosecutions rely on knowingly permitting.

5.2 Defences to s.85 offences

The WRA sets out a number of defences to the s.85 water pollution offences. If the accused can prove, on the balance of probabilities, that their circumstances fall within one of the defences (*R v Edwards* (1975)), then they will be acquitted.

5.2.1 Consents to pollute s.88 WRA

As has been noted, holding a discharge consent under Schedule 10 WRA entitles the holder to pollute in accordance with its terms. In addition, if a discharge to water is authorised by certain other types of environmental authorisation then this will be a defence under the WRA. These other types of authorisation, are listed in s.88 WRA but of most importance are integrated pollution control authorisations issued by the Environment Agency under Part I Environmental Protection Act 1990. These authorisations affect pollution emissions from the most polluting industries, such as chemical works, some printing processes and oil refining.

5.2.2 Emergency s.89 (1) WRA

There is a defence relating to discharges made in an emergency, in order to avoid a danger to life or health. The defence can only be relied upon where the extent of the pollution is minimised and the Agency is informed of the incident as soon as possible. For example if there was a road traffic accident leading to a spillage of petrol, the fire brigade may wash the petrol away (so that it pollutes a river) in order to avoid the risk of explosion or fire.

5.2.3 Discharges from vessels s.89(2) WRA

The WRA states that it is not an offence to discharge sewage or trade effluent from a vessel. This means that it is still an offence to discharge poisonous, noxious or polluting matter from a vessel. Furthermore, in many cases, discharges from boats are controlled under byelaws.

5.2.4 Abandoned mines and mine wastes s.89 (3) and (4) WRA

There are special defences relating to permitting water to escape from abandoned mines and the deposit of mine wastes with the consent of the Environment Agency.

However, the law is being tightened so that this defence will be removed in respect of mines abandoned after the end of 1999 and new rules requiring notification by mine operators of their intention to abandon are being drawn up (see s.58 and s.60 Environment Act 1995)

5.2.5 Sewage defences s.87 WRA

In broad terms, the sewage disposal system works on the basis that, once connected to the public sewers, there is a general entitlement to discharge domestic sewage (subject to paying rates) but if trade wastes are to be discharged, a trade effluent consent or agreement must be held by the industrial polluter under the Water Industry Act 1991. Trade effluent consents or agreements will specify exactly what may and may not be discharged into the sewerage system. If the sewerage undertaker (normally the water plc) receives a lawful discharge of domestic or trade effluent then s.87 WRA makes its disposal the sole responsibility of the sewerage undertaker. On the other hand, if an unlawful discharge takes place into the sewerage system (as for example happened in the *Yorkshire Water* case - see above), then, providing the water company does all that it can to prevent the unlawful discharge into the sewerage system, they have a defence to causing any resulting pollution. Although, if the source of the unauthorised discharge to the sewers was known, the person who caused or knowingly permitted that discharge could be prosecuted under s.85 WRA or under the Water Industry Act 1991.

5.3 The Salmon and Freshwater Fisheries Act offence s.4 SAFFA

Section 4 SAFFA creates a further criminal offence in respect of water pollution. This may be prosecuted as an alternative to or in addition to a charge being brought under the WRA.

Under s.4 SAFFA, it is an offence for anyone to cause or knowingly permit (see 5.1.4 above) the release of any solid or liquid matter which makes water containing fish poisonous or injurious to fish, to fish spawning grounds, or to the food of fish. The offence is rather different from those under WRA. It is concerned only with waters which do contain fish (and the prosecution will have to prove that fish were present). Furthermore, it is not concerned with the protection of water quality from any sort of pollution or effluent, but is limited to cases where fish may be poisoned or injured (or spawning grounds or fish food sources harmed). It seems that it is not necessary to show harm was actually caused (see *R v Bradford* (1860)) although in practice, in most cases, a fish kill will underpin a prosecution under s.4 SAFFA.

5.3.1 Defences to the SAFFA offence

There are a number of defences to the offence under s.4. Most importantly, it is a defence to pollute having a legal right to do so (s.4 (2) SAFFA). This will include discharges made under WRA discharge consents or other environmental authorisations. Furthermore, if the release of polluting matter has been in use from the same premises since before 1923 and the best practical means have been used to prevent harm to fish etc., then no offence will be committed under s.4 (but an offence may well be committed under the WRA). Radioactive substances are to be ignored under s.4 SAFFA (s.40 and Schedule 3 Radioactive Substances Act 1993), although action might be taken under the WRA or the radioactive substances legislation itself. There is a specific defence where the release of poisonous or injurious matter is for a scientific purpose or for the purpose of protecting, improving or replacing fish stocks, and its use for any of these purposes has been approved by the Environment Agency (s.4 (2) SAFFA).

5.4 Pollution by vegetation etc. s.90 WRA

There are specific offences relating to pollution by vegetation entering controlled waters. These are considered in Chapter 15.

5.5 Miscellaneous pollution offences

There are a number of fairly unimportant pollution offences which may be used. There is the common law criminal offence of creating a public nuisance which formed the basis of the prosecution following the Camelford water pollution incident. Furthermore, waters may become so polluted as to be a statutory nuisance under s.79 Environmental Protection Act 1990. In particular, under s.259 Public Health Act 1936, watercourses in a foul state are declared to be a statutory nuisance. Normally, action is taken by local authorities to abate statutory nuisances and this may result in prosecution. The framework of law relating to statutory nuisance is considered in Chapter 16.

5.6 Evidence and prosecutions

Any prosecution, whether brought by the Environment Agency or a private prosecution, must be based on sound evidence. The prosecution must prove each and every part of the offence beyond reasonable doubt. For this reason, swift action in contacting the Agency, retrieving dead fish (Byelaw 5 of Phase 2 of the National Byelaws, due in 1998, will prohibit the removal of trout or salmon even if dead, without Agency consent) and perhaps taking water samples (this is done carefully: noting exactly when and where they were taken and having them analysed as a matter of urgency) may be crucial to a successful prosecution.

The National Rivers Authority was subject to very strict rules relating to the admissibility of sampling evidence (formerly in s.209 WRA). These have now been abolished (s.111 Environment Act 1995), but it remains important that any sampling and its analysis is able to stand up to careful scrutiny. The abolition of these rules should allow reliance on some of the more sophisticated continuous water quality monitoring devices.

5.7 Penalties and sentencing

Under the WRA offences in s.85 the maximum penalties on conviction in the magistrates court is a fine of up to £20,000 and/or up to three months imprisonment and on conviction in the Crown Court an unlimited fine and/or up to two years in prison. Although the highest fine imposed was £1 million, against Shell for pollution of the Mersey the average fine is around £2,000. No one has yet been imprisoned for water pollution. The WRA contains provisions for directors and other officers of companies to be personally liable for the crimes committed by their companies in certain cases (s.217 WRA). The fine will reflect numerous factors which the court weighs up including the harm caused, the degree of fault on the part of the polluter, the response of the polluter to the incident (did they contact the Agency, undertake or cooperate and pay for clean up works, etc.) and so on. Under s.4 SAFFA, the maximum penalty in the magistrates court is £5,000, but in the Crown Court an unlimited fine or up to two years imprisonment may be imposed.

In addition to a fine, in most cases the convicted polluter can expect to be ordered to pay the legal and other costs of bringing the prosecution and, in some cases where the issue of compensation is straightforward, the criminal court may order a payment of compensation to the victim of the crime (for example an angling club) under the Powers of Criminal Courts Act 1973.

5.8 Prosecution by the Environment Agency and private prosecutions

The vast majority of prosecutions for water pollution will be brought by the Environment Agency. However, they are not obliged to prosecute in every case where they have evidence supporting the bringing of a case. The Environment Agency has developed an Enforcement Policy Statement which has as its starting point that there should be sufficient evidence to support the bringing of a prosecution. Any enforcement action should be proportionate, consistent, targeted on those matters which cause the most environmental harm and the decision making process in the Agency should be open and transparent. Specifically, with regard to prosecution, the Agency will need to consider whether any of three factors are established:

(a) is it appropriate to draw attention generally to the need for compliance with the law to establish a deterrent or fulfil a normal expectation of prosecution?

(b) where there was or was potential for considerable environmental harm; and

(c) where the gravity of the offence (taken with the record and approach of the offender) warrants prosecution.

From an angler's point of view, it is often worth co-operating and bringing some pressure to bear on the Agency (referring them, if necessary, to their own criteria on prosecution) to persuade them to prosecute.

In particular, decisions not to prosecute may be questioned at a policy level via the Regional Fisheries Advisory committees (see Chapter 1).

If the Agency decides not to prosecute one option, which is open to anglers or angling clubs, is to bring a private prosecution. Although this is an unusual course of action, there is a general right for any individual to bring a prosecution (s.4 Prosecution of Offences Act 1985), although any private prosecution may be taken over by the Director of Public Prosecutions at any time (s.6 Prosecution of Offences Act 1985). In the case of a private prosecution for the offence under s.4 SAFFA, the person bringing the prosecution must first obtain a certificate from MAFF that he has some material interest in the waters (eg., riparian rights).

Although private prosecutions are the exception rather than the norm they may be useful particularly in cases of ongoing pollution where the Environment Agency does not take action. There are examples of this where the Anglers' Conservation Association has brought private prosecutions, for example against Thames Water Authority in 1986, or following the Camelford incident (although that prosecution was taken over by the Director of Public Prosecutions). In general, the costs of bringing a private prosecution, even if it fails, will be paid out of public funds (s.17 Prosecution of Offences Act 1985).

6. POLLUTION CLEAN UP AND ENVIRONMENTAL RESTORATION s.161 WRA

The Environment Agency has important powers to enter onto land and carry out works to prevent pollution, clean up after an incident and, so far as is possible, restore the aquatic environment to its former state. These powers are currently contained in s.161 WRA. It is expected that they will be significantly reformed by the introduction of 'works notices', which are explained in paragraph 6.2 below.

6.1 The current powers

The first point to note is that there is *no duty* on the Agency to carry out clean up or prevention works. There is simply a power to do so. Thus, although an angling club which either fears or has suffered from a pollution incident can seek to put pressure on the Agency to make use of its powers under s.161 WRA, it cannot force the Agency to do so. Clearly, if the Agency uses its powers, this may save the angling club a great deal of trouble and effort in bringing its own civil proceedings. Although s.161 powers will never result in direct compensation to angling interests, it may, at best, operate indirectly by, for example, restocking. As the law stands, the onus is on the Agency to undertake the works of prevention, clean up and restoration and then to recover the costs of so doing from any person who caused or knowingly permitted the pollution or, in the case of prevention, any person who caused or knowingly permitted the material which is likely to enter controlled waters to be in the place where it is likely to do so. The costs which may be recovered include investigative costs in locating the source and nature of the pollution, as well as more direct costs such as works to prevent pollutants entering water, works to remove pollution from water and restoration such as restocking or planting weed.

Costs are not recoverable in respect of pollution arising from abandoned mines, although the position is being reformed at the end of the century. The powers also must not be used in a way which inhibits the use of a discharge consent or other lawful pollution (s.161 (2)).

Section 161 WRA provides the Agency with broad powers to prevent and clean up pollution. In 1996, the Agency recovered some £1.4 million using s.161 and in many other cases no doubt used the power to persuade polluters to undertake their own clean up works.

6.2 Works notices and the reform of s.161 WRA

The Environment Act 1995 has brought into effect important reforms to s.161 WRA which are likely to be brought into force in 1998. When in force, the effect will be that the Agency will retain its existing powers to carry out works itself and recover costs, but will only be able to rely on these powers in emergencies. If there is no emergency, then they will have to rely on s.161 A-D which will introduce works notices. The works notice will be served on any person who caused or knowingly permitted pollution to either enter or be likely to enter (in the case of prevention works) controlled waters. The notice will set out the works which are to be carried out by the polluter and a time period for their completion. Non compliance with a works notice will be a criminal offence carrying the same penalties as breach of s.85 WRA (see above). It will also be possible for a works notice to be enforced by High Court injunction or by the Agency carrying out the works itself and recovering the costs. There will be a system to appeal against notices to the Secretary of State. In essence, works notices will in many cases simply reserve the onus of carrying out the works to the polluter from the Agency. This may well encourage the Agency to use these powers even more, as they will not have to worry about spending large sums of money on clean up operations with uncertainties about their ability ultimately to recover the money.

The same qualifications as to the use of clean up powers in respect of abandoned mines and discharge consents apply as in the current s.161.

QUESTIONS

Question 1

I am Club Secretary of the River Dare Fly Fishers Club. We own a stretch of water on the River Dare. I have just been telephoned by one of our members who tells that the river is stinking of slurry, is discoloured and that there are a number of distressed and dead fish. The member has found the source of the slurry to be a ditch on Dare Hill Farm and has gone to speak to the farmer. We have recently stocked the river and I am extremely alarmed by this news. What should we be doing now and how might things develop over the next few weeks or months?

Answer

The first thing is to contact the Environment Agency as a matter of extreme urgency. (Stop reading this book and do it now!) Secondly, if you or another member of the club can get down to the water there are a number of positive steps you can take. First, tell the farmer so that he can do whatever is possible to stop the discharge. Secondly, take some samples of the water above and below the ditch and mark them carefully, stating exactly when and where they were taken, ideally with a witness present. Thirdly, take some photos if possible of the discharge and any dead or distressed fish. Fourthly, remove any dead fish and keep them. Fifthly, if you own water above the ditch, you may be able to remove distressed fish in landing nets and place them above the pollution source. In the immediate aftermath, you may be able to assist Agency officials or the farmer in preventing further pollution and cleaning up. Be guided by the experts.

On the same day, those club members involved should take the trouble to write statements of the events they witnessed with precise times, places and names, as experience tells us that memory fades very quickly. These statements may be very helpful in any later legal proceedings. Find out what the Agency is going to do about the incident. Will it prosecute? If not, why not? If the spillage arose from a failure of a slurry containment system on the farm it seems likely that a prosecution for causing pollution under s.85(1) WRA and s.4 SAFFA would succeed. Will it carry out works of clean up and restoration and help you to assess the damage or restock the river using its s.161 WRA powers?

Then it may be a case of consulting your lawyers (hopefully via the Anglers' Conservation Association membership, as this is free) and bringing a claim against the farmer, or in practice, his or her insurers.

Question 2.

We own some fishing rights on the River Smell and have been plagued for years by an outfall from a sewage treatment works which leaves the water scummy and smelly and our advice from a fishery consultant is that it is a significantly less productive stretch of water than that above the sewage works. We understand that the works only has primary treatment and screening and that the biochemical oxygen demand is increased by the discharged effluent. What can we do ?

Answer

First of all, you need to discover what the conditions of the discharge consent are. The consent is open to inspection at the Environment Agency offices. Secondly, you need to consider whether the conditions are being met. You can ask the Agency whether they are being met and what monitoring is taking place. If the conditions are being breached, it may be possible to persuade the Agency to take action to enforce the conditions by enforcement notice, prosecution or warning. If they refuse to take any action and you have clear evidence of breach of conditions, you might consider a private prosecution.

If the conditions are being complied with, it is a question of considering whether the conditions may be varied to improve the water quality. Are there any water quality objectives for the river ? How do these match with the actual performance ? In any event, can you use the evidence of your consultant to bring pressure on the Agency to vary the consent. Write to the Agency and/or have a meeting with them and perhaps your consultant.

In practical terms it may also be worthwhile developing a dialogue with the water company concerned. A number are now anxious to promote a greener image and may be willing to work constructively to improve water quality.

Finally, bear in mind that even if the discharge is perfectly lawful under the public regulation system, this may not preclude a civil action if fishery interests are being damaged (see Chapter 10).

CHAPTER 10

POLLUTION AND THE
COMMON LAW

Pollution is the greatest threat to an angler's enjoyment of his sport and the history of angling is littered with examples of fish kills caused by pollution. The previous chapter explained how the threat of pollution is combated by the Environment Agency. However, the fines imposed by the courts under criminal legislation do not compensate the angling club or riparian owner whose fishery has been damaged. Compensation is obtained through the civil law in either the county Courts or High Court. It is not the duty of the Environment Agency to seek compensation for the victim. The onus is on the angler to take the initiative. Paragraph 1.3 of Chapter 1 explained the difference between the criminal and civil law. Whilst Chapter 9 looked at the former, this chapter sets out the avenues available to gain redress for pollution.

1. *PRIDE OF DERBY V BRITISH CELANESE*

The persistent threat of pollution resulted in the formation of the Angler's Co-Operative Association (now the Anglers' Conservation Association) in 1948, a body specifically set up to fight pollution on behalf of anglers (see Chapter 7). The founder, John Eastwood QC, saw that the common law could be used to protect the angler's fishing. One of the first cases it supported on behalf of an angling club was *The Pride of Derby Angling Association Ltd v British Celanese* (1953). This serves as a good example of how anglers can use the courts to stop pollution of their fisheries.

1.1 The facts

The Pride of Derby and Derbyshire Angling Association Ltd was the owner or occupier of a fishery on the rivers Derwent and Trent. The second Plaintiff, the Earl of Harrington, was a riparian owner on both rivers. Below Derby, on the Derwent, the river supported game fish, but before reaching Borrowash Bridge it was so polluted that it contained little or no fish. The rivers were contaminated with various matter from a number of sources: with sewage by the Derby Corporation, the local authority, and with heated effluent combined with organic matter discharged by British Celanese. The effect of these discharges was aggravated by heated effluent discharged by the British Electricity Authority.

1.2 The issues

The Plaintiffs sought an injunction to prevent the river being polluted. The case was finally decided in the Court of Appeal. It had been heard first of all in the High Court where the Judge had decided in favour of the Plaintiffs and granted an injunction prohibiting any interference with their right of fishing. The Defendants had appealed on two points. First, that the sewage works, authorised by the Derby Corporation Act 1901, were completed satisfactorily in accordance with that Act and that if, with the increase in population over which the Defendants had no control, a nuisance was caused, the Derby Corporation was not responsible merely because it did not improve the works. Secondly, and quite simply, an injunction should not be granted against a local authority.

1.3 The decision

Lord Justice Denning found:

> When the increased sewage came into their [the Derby Corporation] sewage disposal works at Spendon, they took it under their charge, treated it in their works, and poured the effluent into the river Derwent, but their treatment of it was not successful in rendering it harmless. It was still noxious. Their act in pouring a polluted effluent into the river makes them guilty of nuisance.

This quotation captures the essence of the Court's decision. On the first point of appeal, the Court found that since local authorities built houses themselves or permitted others to build them they became responsible for any nuisance that results from the sewage system. The local authority tried to argue that it had statutory authority to commit the nuisance. Looking at the provisions of the Act, the Court found that the local authority was permitted to discharge a harmless effluent into the river, but not one that was polluting. On the second point of appeal, the Court found that an injunction should be granted against the local authority.

The Court did relent in one respect. The Derby Corporation had to apply to the Minister of Works for consent to extend the works. The Court, therefore, suspended the operation of the injunction to allow works to be carried out so that the discharge was made harmless.

1.4 The significance of the case

A court was prepared to impose an obligation on a polluter to carry out works to protect a fishery. This is the importance of the case. The Court of

Appeal acknowledged that anglers should be allowed to enjoy their sport without interference from pollution.

To put the case into its historical context, the planning system as we know it today had been implemented by the post-war Labour government. A local authority now had power to build houses and to object, under the planning system, to the construction of houses. The Court referred to the fact that the local authority had not objected to the construction of new houses and that it could have done so. In this new post-war era, an angling club, backed by the Anglers' Co-operative Association and supported by the Earl of Harrington, decided to take on the might of two industrial concerns and a local authority. They won and the Defendants were forced to spend time and money in taking steps to ensure the fishery was no longer polluted. The club did not know whether it would win. The right the Court upheld for anglers is summarised by Lord Justice Denning:

'The power of the courts to issue an injunction for nuisance has proved itself to be the best method so far devised of securing the cleanliness of our rivers.'

2. THE LEGAL TOOLS

In the Pride of Derby case, the anglers won since they were able to show that the pollution was a nuisance to their fishery. Private nuisance (or known more simply as nuisance) is one of the 'legal tools' which provide the basis for any claim for pollution. Together with nuisance there is also negligence, in which the angler claims that the pollution is caused by the negligence of the polluter, trespass and the Rule in *Rylands v Fletcher* - all explained in more detail later on. In strict legal terminology, each is known as a 'tort'. When suing a polluter, it is not necessary to choose between them. A plain-tiff can make a claim using only one, a combination or all of them, although this will depend on the facts of each case.

2.1 Private nuisance

Nuisance is the most often used legal tool in the protection of a private fishery. It formed the basis of the anglers' arguments in the *Pride of Derby* case. In its simplest terms, a nuisance is a condition or activity which unduly interferes with the use or enjoyment of land. As explained in Chapter 4, fishing rights, whether held by themselves or with land, are an interest in property. It is therefore a nuisance to interfere with fishing rights by polluting them.

2.1.1 The principles of liability in nuisance

Nuisance is known as a tort of strict liability. This means that, unlike negligence (see 2.2 below), fault does not have to be proved. However, the plaintiff still has to prove that:

    (a) damage was suffered as a result of the defendant's activity or condition of the defendant's land and

    (b) the damaged suffered was foreseeable and

    (c) that the use of the plaintiff's land was unreasonable.

    The recent case, *Cambridge Water v Eastern Counties Leather* (1994), helped to establish the present rules governing liability in nuisance. It is not an angling case, but involved the pollution of water and is the starting point to establish liability for nuisance.

2.1.1.1 The facts

Eastern Counties Leather, the Defendant, was a leather manufacturer which used a chemical solvent in its tanning process. Prior to 1971, when the process was changed, 1,000 gallons of this solvent were spilled in many small amounts. It seeped through the factory floor and found its way into groundwater. The Plaintiff took water from a borehole contaminated with this solvent and brought an action in nuisance to recover damages for the cost of finding an alternative safe drinking water supply. After losing in the High Court, the case was appealed to the Court of Appeal where the Plaintiff won. The Defendant appealed to the House of Lords.

2.1.1.2 The issues

When the case was appealed to the Court of Appeal, the defendant had abandoned its claim in nuisance. It appealed on questions involving liability under the Rule in *Rylands v Fletcher* (see 2.1.5 below). However, in the House of Lords, Lord Goff felt compelled to rule on questions concerning the law of nuisance. He had to decide whether foreseeability of harm is an essential element of the law of nuisance.

2.1.1.3 The decision

Lord Goff did not doubt that liability in nuisance has 'generally been regarded as strict' but he qualified this by saying that 'that liability has been kept under control by the principle of reasonable user.' This he defined as:

> The principle of give and take as between neighbouring occupiers of land, under which those acts necessary for the common and ordinary use and occupation of land and houses may be done, if conveniently done, without subjecting those who do them to an action.

He then went on to consider the question of foreseeability of the damage. After stating that the Defendant who has taken all reasonable care will not exonerate himself from liability (i.e. reasonable user) he added, 'But it by no means follows that the defendant should be held liable for damage of a type which he could not reasonably foresee.' He concluded by saying 'foreseeability of harm is indeed a prerequisite of the recovery of damages.'

In the end, the water company lost on the basis that the damage to the aquifer could not have been foreseen at the time of the spillages.

2.1.1.4 The significance of the case

For the angler who sues in nuisance he will have to show, first, that the use by the polluter of his land was unreasonable, and secondly, that the damage caused by the polluter was foreseeable. At present, application of this rule to the pollution of fishing rights can only be speculative. A case involving angling has not been decided since the decision. More importantly, each case will turn on its facts.

For example, if a club has suffered from sewage pollution continuously from a sewage works, it will have to show that the water company's use of the land was unreasonable. This will involve questions of how much money is available to the water company to improve the works, what improvements need to be done, how the population has increased in the locality and what works have been done in the past. As regards foreseeability, it must be foreseeable that such pollution will damage fishing rights. Of the two, reasonable user will, therefore, probably be the highest hurdle to overcome and the structure and regulation of the present water industry will be very relevant.

2.1.2 Nuisance and the fishery

There are degrees of pollution. Some rivers are subject to constant sewage discharges with its obvious effect on the fish. Others may be subject to a one-off incident. However, it is not strictly necessary to prove actual damage to the fish.

In *Nicholls v Ely Beet Sugar Factory* (1936), the Plaintiff owned a fishery which was polluted by the Defendant's factory. The Plaintiff claimed he suffered damage. This, however, only occurred during the period following the sugar beet harvest. Also, the financial loss was only minimal. The Judge put the damage at £50. Despite this Lord Justice Romer found:

'... if the Plaintiff can show that his rights of fishery have been invaded he is entitled to succeed in this action without having to prove that he himself has suffered any financial loss.'

On the facts, however, the Plaintiff failed because he could not show that the damage had been caused by the Defendant.

It is essential that the Defendant shows that his rights have been damaged. In *Elmhurst v Spencer* (1849), the Defendant diverted water in a stream and discharged it back polluted. By the time it reached the Plaintiff's land it was free from any noxious substances and did not cause any damage to the Plaintiff's land. Despite arguing that the water was not fit for irrigation, cattle, cooking and fish, the Defendant could not show any damage and the Court found there was no nuisance.

A more recent example of a successful action in nuisance is *Cook v South West Water PLC* (1992). The nuisance alleged was eutrophication caused by increased levels of phosphate discharged into the river and foaming caused by detergents in the effluent. In respect of the former, the Judge found that the effluent did not pollute the water but that the discharge of detergents 'results in such changes to the water quality as to damage existing and future uses of the waters.' The Plaintiff was awarded damages of £500.

The nuisance does not necessarily have to be noxious matter. In *Tipping v Eckersley* (1855), the Defendants owned a cotton mill and steam engine and discharged heated water into the stream, raising its temperature by 11° F. This was held to be a nuisance, since it interfered with the operation of the Plaintiff's own mill. The Judge found that the damage, although 'trifling', meant that the Plaintiff did not receive the water 'as is wanted for his works in its natural state.'

2.1.3 Defences

The angler may have a claim in nuisance against a polluter. However, many defences have been tried over the years. Some have succeeded and some have failed. The following is not a comprehensive list, but those most relevant to pollution of watercourses.

2.1.3.1 Multiple pollutions

Over the years, polluters have tried to argue that their pollution is only one of many into the same river. Judges have refused to accept such a defence. In *Crossley v Lightowler* (1867), the Plaintiff operated a print works on the bank of a stream. The Defendant owned a dyeing works upstream. He argued that because there were many other factories pouring polluted matter into the stream above the Plaintiff's works, he could never have the water in a fit state for use even if the Defendant ceased to foul it. The Judge acknowledged that there were many other nuisances and that it may be difficult to trace any particular one to its source. However, he rejected the argument. He saw that if such a defence was allowed to succeed, the Defendant would escape liability if all the other sources of pollution were cleaned up. Defendants would be allowed to say:

> ... "We began to foul the stream at a time when, as against you, it was lawful for us to do so, inasmuch as it was unfit for your use, and you cannot now, by getting rid of existing pollutions ... prevent our continuing to do what at the time when we began you had no right to object to"...

One polluter cannot, therefore, point the finger at another to deny liability in nuisance.

2.1.3.2 Infinitesimal pollution

In *Blair and Sumner v Deakin* (1887), the Eagley Brook, a tributary of the River Tonge in Lancashire, was polluted by several parties. The Defendant's works, being printing and dyeing processes, had increased capacity so adding to the pollution load and causing a nuisance to the Plaintiff's bleaching works, situated downstream on the Tonge. There were other works on the Eagley Brook also discharging into the river. The Defendant argued that its discharge was diluted sufficiently by the river to render it harmless by the time it reached the Plaintiff's factories.

The question, similar to that in *Crossley v Lightowler*, posed by Mr Justice Kay was, '... is it the law that, supposing it is impossible to say that any one of those persons pours into this stream foul matter enough by itself to create a nuisance but that what they all pour in together does create a nuisance, that the Plaintiffs cannot sue any of them?' He upheld the Plaintiff's right to sue relying on the right of the riparian owner to receive water of good quality: '... it does not lie in the mouth of one of the contributors to the nuisance who is sued to say the amount of his contribution is infinitesimal.'

Despite this, the law will not take account of minimal or insignificant changes to the water. This includes temporary changes as in *Taylor v Bennett* (1836). The Plaintiff owned a well which the Defendant filled up with rubbish making the water muddy. Mr Justice Coleridge directed that if this only made the water 'temporarily muddy, that would be too minute a damage to justify you in finding for the Plaintiff.'

2.1.3.3 A prescriptive right to pollute

To a large extent, this is a nineteenth century defence. Most of the cases relate to that time. In the same way that a fishery may be acquired by prescription, so can a right to pollute (see Chapter 5). It must be said, nevertheless, that it is difficult to see how this defence would succeed in the modern era.

In the early nineteenth century case, *Wright v Williams* (1836), the owner of a copper mine sunk pits on his land to fill with iron. He covered the pits with water from the mine to precipitate the copper and then discharged the polluted water into the river. He had done this continuously for forty years. The Defendant argued that he had a right to do so under the terms of the Prescription Act 1832 (see 1.4.3 of *Chapter 5*). The Judge found for the Defendant, essentially granting him a right to pollute.

Restrictions have been placed on this right to pollute, severely reducing its effectiveness as a defence. For example, in *Millington v Griffiths* (1874), the pollution had continued for twenty years before the case was heard. Mr Justice Keating found that as the pollution had continued to increase as the years went by this defeated the defence of a prescriptive right to pollute. To succeed, the pollution must continue at the same level. Moreover, if the business changes, then this defence will not be available, notwithstanding that the pollution may have decreased (*Clarke v Somerset Drainage Commissioners* (1888)).

Pollution of a watercourse is a criminal offence under s.85 of the Water Resources Act 1991 (WRA) (see Chapter 9). It is unlikely that the courts will find that a prescriptive right to pollute exists, especially if founded upon an unlawful activity. *Wright v Williams* was decided before anti-pollution laws existed (see Chapter 1).

2.1.3.4 Coming to a nuisance

Coming to a nuisance is not a defence to an action (*St Helens Smelting Co v Tipping* (1865)). Therefore, if an angling club bought fishing rights that had been polluted for some time by, for example, a sewage works, the polluter could not argue that the works had been in operation when the club acquired the rights.

2.1.3.5 Statutory authority

A polluter may escape liability if he has statutory authority. By this, it is meant that an Act of Parliament authorises a particular activity - for example, a water company as a sewerage undertaker having to supply sewerage services.

Importantly, this rule only applies in the absence of negligence. Nuisance is a tort of strict liability. Statutory authority absolves the polluter of liability in nuisance. If negligence can be proved, then the polluter will be liable (see 2.2 below).

In a case decided shortly after the *Pride of Derby* case, *Smeaton v Ilford Corporation* (1954), Mr Justice Upjohn had to interpret s.31 of the Public Health Act 1936 which stated, 'A local authority shall so discharge their functions under the foregoing provisions ... of this Act as not to create a nuisance.' The sewerage system, when overloaded, allowed sewage to escape through a manhole onto the Plaintiff's land. The Judge found that: '... the proper construction to be given to the section is to exclude liability for escapes in the absence of negligence ...'

Although polluted water flooded the Plaintiff's land, the local authority escaped liability because negligence could not be proved. Section 31 of the 1936 Act is now found in s.117(6) of the Water Industry Act 1991.

2.1.3.6 Discharge consents

Under s.100 (G) WRA, it is no defence to a civil action for a polluter to maintain that he holds a discharge consent and has kept within the consent conditions. Chapter 9 explained how each polluter is granted a consent which allows it to discharge effluent into a watercourse. A consent will have conditions. A breach of these conditions is necessary for a successful prosecution. However, damage to a fishery may still occur even if the conditions are met. Polluters frequently argue that, since they observe these conditions, they cannot be liable in a civil action. This is wrong. However, to make matters more complex, compliance with discharge consent conditions may be one of the factors in judging the reasonableness of the defendant's behaviour in testing whether a nuisance exists in the first place (see 2.1.1 above).

If this rule was reversed, then the angler's weapon of the common law would be severely curtailed. It contrasts with the rule that compliance with the terms of an abstraction licence is a defence to a civil action (see Chapter 11). Ironically, it may be that the abstraction reduces the flow to such an extent that pollution is not diluted effectively. An action will still be available against the polluter but not the abstractor.

2.1.4 Who can sue?

Nuisance is the interference with a property right. As stated in Chapter 5 fishing rights are a property right. Therefore, the basic rule is that interference with fishing rights is an actionable nuisance. This applies to riparian owners and the owners of incorporeal fishing rights (see Chapters 5 and 6). In *Mason v Clarke* (1950), the owner of a right to take rabbits from a plot of land was allowed to take an action for interference with those rights. By analogy, this also applies to incorporeal fishing rights.

Chapter 5 also referred to the loose arrangements that many angling clubs have with their landlords - the bottle of whisky at Christmas in exchange for fishing. In that chapter, the distinction is made between a lease and a licence (a licence merely makes what would otherwise be unlawful, lawful). This is very important for the success of an action in nuisance. If a club had a licence and its waters were polluted, then an action in nuisance by the club would probably not be successful, although the fishery owner (i.e. the landlord) might nevertheless bring an action.

Much depends on the nature of the agreement. It does not necessarily follow that because a document says it is a licence that it is, in fact, a licence. All the circumstances surrounding the agreement must be examined such as whether payment is made in the nature of rent and whether the supposed licensee took on obligations and rights more appropriate to a tenant. This is a complex subject and beyond the scope of this book. Suffice to say that it is the nature of the arrangement that has to be examined not just the wording of the document. However, a bottle of whisky at Christmas, with no written terms and no obligations or rights imposed on or granted to either party, will probably be a licence.

Recently, there have been cases to suggest that a licensee could sue in nuisance. For example, in *Khorasandijan v Bush* (1993), the Plaintiff was granted an injunction restraining the Defendant from harassing her. The Plaintiff did not have any interest in the property where she was living, but still succeeded in nuisance. The comments of the Judge who dissented from this judgement are interesting: 'Given that the purpose of an action in nuisance is to protect the right to use and enjoyment of land ... it seems to me wrong in principle if a mere licensee or someone without such right could sue in private nuisance.'

In another case, *Crown River Cruises Ltd v Kimbolton Fireworks Limited and London Fire and Civil Defence Authority* (1996), the Plaintiffs were licensees of a right to moor a boat in the River Thames (for anglers, read a licence to fish). The boat was damaged by a fireworks display. Mr Justice Potter rejected the argument that an action in nuisance should fail because the Plaintiffs were only licensees. They succeeded. This would seem to indicate that an angling club with only a licence to fish could sue in nuisance.

However, the recent House of Lords decision, *Hunter v Canary Wharf* (1997), appears to have swung matters back in favour the polluter. An action in nuisance was brought by residents of the Isle of Dogs for interference with television reception caused by the construction of the Canary Wharf Tower. Many of the residents had no legal interest in property. Recalling the words of the dissenting Judge in *Khorasandijan v Bush*, the House of Lords affirmed that people without an interest in property cannot sue in nuisance. The residents with no interest in property could not recover damages.

This appears to shut the door on anglers fishing under a licence. However, it must be said that the case concerned the interference with television reception and not water pollution. Also, those who claimed were members of a family household. The case can be distinguished, albeit tenuously, on these grounds. The message remains clear, nevertheless. The more formal the arrangement with the landlord, the better protection against pollution.

One way to solve the problem is to have a provision in the licence placing an obligation on the fishery owner to join in any litigation. Paragraph 11 of the Second Schedule of the specimen lease in the Appendix imposes just such an obligation on the landlord.

2.1.5 The rule in Rylands v Fletcher

In the *Cambridge Water* case, Lord Goff examined the relationship between nuisance and the Rule in *Rylands v Fletcher*. Formulated by Mr Justice Blackburn in *Rylands v Fletcher* (1868), the rule states that if matter that is likely to do mischief is brought by a person onto land and escapes from it to another's land and does foreseeable damage by polluting it, that person is under an absolute liability for the damage naturally consequent on the escape.

This particular tort sounds very similar to nuisance in that it involves the damage caused by an escape of matter from land. Indeed, liability is also strict. In *Cambridge Water*, Lord Goff stated:

> Seen in its context, there is no reason to suppose that Blackburn J intended to create a liability any more strict than that created by the law of nuisance, but even so he must have intended that, in the circumstances specified by him, there should be liability for damage resulting from an isolated escape.

Following these comments, this rule is now regarded as part of the law of nuisance to cover damage resulting from an isolated escape.

Whilst at first sight this rule may appear to help anglers, over the years its use has been heavily curtailed by the interpretation of the non-natural use of land doctrine. This dictates that the use of the land has to be non-natural to succeed in any action using the rule in *Rylands v Fletcher*. In *Rickards v Lothian* (1913), Lord Justice Moulton stated:

> It must be some special use bringing with it increased danger to others and must not be the ordinary use of land ..'

Courts have held that the storage of metal strips at an electrical component factory was a natural use of land (*British Celanese v A.H. Hunt (Capacitors) Ltd* (1969)). In the same way that the concept of reasonable user restricts liability in nuisance, so the non-natural use doctrine performs the same task in the Rule in *Rylands v Fletcher.*

Despite this restrictive interpretation, Lord Goff found in the *Cambridge Water* case that storage of chemicals is 'an almost classic case of non-natural use.' Lawyers have shown a reluctance to rely on *Rylands v Fletcher.* However, in the light of Lord Goff's comments and the fact that much pollution escapes from factories, it may be that it will be used more frequently in the future.

2.2 Negligence

A victim of pollution does not have to confine himself to arguing that the polluter is liable in nuisance. He can, alternatively or in addition, claim that the polluter was negligent. A choice does not have to be made between the two. Both can be used. Negligence is unlike nuisance in that fault has to be proved. Most importantly, a licensee can sue in negligence. This circumvents the problem of proving a sufficient interest in property.

The law on negligence could justify a book in itself. Of necessity, its treatment in this book can only be brief. There are two major elements in proving liability: first, the establishing of a duty of care owed by the defendant to the plaintiff and secondly, a breach of that duty of care by the defendant. Whilst these are the bare bones of any action in negligence, there are other matters which need to be proved. Thus, the defendant's behaviour must have been careless; there must be a connection between the defendant's conduct and the damage; it must have been foreseeable that the defendant's conduct would have caused the type of damage inflicted.

Beyond this, there are further considerations. It may be that others contributed to the damage and the extent of the responsibility will have to be apportioned between them. Finally, an assessment of the monetary loss has to be made.

A pollution case may not involve all these elements. For example, it is foreseeable that a factory discharging effluent into a river may cause damage to fishing rights located downstream and that the pollution contributed to the damage. However, what if the company owning the factory had not been careless, or if other works had contributed to the damage?

Negligence was successfully used in *Scott Whitehead v National Coal Board* (1987). During the drought in 1976, the Plaintiff irrigated his land from the Little Stour in Kent. However, on inspecting his crops one day, he saw that the foliage was going brown. The cause was the salinity of the irrigation water. The Defendants owned a colliery eight miles from the Plaintiff's farm. The water in the mine had a high chlorine content and it was pumped into the river. The water authority was also a defendant in the litigation. As against the water authority, the Judge found that it owed a duty of care to the Plaintiff:

> But all that was required here was that in a very dry year, such as 1973 and 1976, farmers downstream of the Wingham Main extracting water from the Little Stour for irrigating their crops should be told that salt concentrations might rise to dangerously high levels and they should check whether the water was suitable before use.

The water authority was negligent in failing to warn the farmers of the risk and breached the duty of care.

2.3 Trespass

At first glance, it may appear inappropriate to discuss trespass in a chapter on water pollution. However, it is a trespass to dump noxious material on another's land. This is exactly what the Plaintiffs argued in *Esso Petroleum v Southport Corporation* (1955). A tanker entering an estuary developed a steering fault and stranded on a revetment wall. It jettisoned four hundred tons of oil to save the crew from danger. The Plaintiffs, who owned a beach polluted by the oil, argued that the Defendants who operated the tanker were liable in trespass. In the Court of Appeal, Lord Justice Denning (1954) held that to succeed in trespass, the act done by the Defendant must be a physical act done by him directly on the Plaintiff's land. He found there was not a trespass in this case because '... the discharge of oil was not done directly onto their foreshore, but outside in the estuary. It was carried by the tide on to that land but that was only consequential, not direct.'

Most pollution cases involving anglers arise as a result of a discharge upstream, which flows down into their rights. The pollution is taken there by the flow of the river. It is not dumped on their land directly by the polluter. It is unlikely, therefore, that anglers would use trespass, unless the noxious substance was actually placed on their land or fishing rights.

Furthermore, the onus of proof in an action in trespass is on the plaintiff to prove that the trespass was intentional and negligent (*Fowler v Lanning* (1959)).

2.4 Public nuisance

Public nuisance is a criminal offence as well as a tort. It is a nuisance which materially affects the reasonable comfort and convenience of a section of the public. The classic example is an obstruction of the highway which prevents the public exercising its right of way. The former South West Water

Authority was prosecuted for public nuisance as a result of the Camelford water incident in 1988 (*AB v South West Water Services Ltd,*). The general rule is that the wrong must have a material effect on a large number of people - hence its use in the Camelford incident, where all the inhabitants of the town were affected.

It is the Attorney-General who initiates the prosecution on behalf of the public. However, a private individual can start a civil action for damages using public nuisance if he can show that he has sustained damage over and above that sustained by the general public. For example, in *Tate & Lyle v GLC* (1983), it was found that the interference with a public right of navigation on the River Thames was a public nuisance. The Plaintiff could not use his jetties and this was particular damage which the Plaintiff suffered. Therefore, it could sue in public nuisance.

This difficult hurdle makes the use of public nuisance in pollution actions rare. Nevertheless, a club would certainly suffer damage over and above that sustained by the general public if it could not enjoy its fishing rights as a result of pollution. It could, therefore, use public nuisance to recover damages. However, whether it would be successful is difficult to predict because the point is as yet untested by a court.

3. REMEDIES

Having established the liability of the polluter, the angler will want compensation and/or an injunction to restrain further pollution. Much will depend on the type of pollution. A one off incident, with little chance of a recurrence, will require monetary compensation (i.e. damages). A continuous pollution, for instance from a sewage works, will demand an injunction.

3.1 Damages

The general principle is that damages compensate the plaintiff. They put the plaintiff in the position he would have been had the injury not occurred. An angler's claim for damages will generally be twofold: loss of amenity and, assuming there has been a fish kill, restocking.

3.1.1 Restocking

In *Granby (Marquis) v Bakewell* (1923), a large number of fish were killed when the Defendant's gasworks discharged noxious waste into a river. The Court found that the death of the fish prejudicially affected the fishery. This is despite the fact that fish in a river are no one's property until caught (see Chapter 3).

3.1.1.1 How many fish?

In deciding what level of damages would replace the dead fish, the Court considered many factors. First, not all the dead fish were counted. Some will be taken by predators, some sunk to the bottom and others floated downstream. It was assumed that for every dead fish two more would not have been seen. Secondly, stocked fish have a lower survival rate. Thirdly, stocked fish have a lower value since, as stated by Mr Justice Lawrence, wild fish were '... well able to fend for themselves and therefore calculated not only to keep in better condition, but also to be more wary and to give better sport than the bought fish.'

Additional factors taken into account included the loss of the fish's food supply and the locality of where the fish kill had occurred. In this case, the fish kill area was flanked by trees providing food and shelter and the fish would have been of greater value to the fishery.

In contrast, there were factors which could not be taken into account. The Plaintiff argued that some fish would have migrated from the lower part of the fishery, so depleting stocks in that stretch and, therefore, extra stocking was needed for that stretch. The Court rejected this because it would amount to double compensation. The cost of replacing fish in the lower part could not, therefore, be added to the cost of restocking the upper part. Finally, no claim could be made for the loss of reputation of the lower part of the fishery because no angler knowing the locality would have been deterred from fishing there. All these factors were taken into account to reach an estimate of £150 to restock the fishery.

Restocking is an essential element in any claim for damages. Whilst the Granby case established the restocking can be claimed, it is impossible to replace the lost fish exactly. Not only are the above factors relevant, but also others, such as availability of fish on the market, the difficulty of finding large fish such as carp and the fact that fish cannot be stocked at once.

In general, fishery science is intricate. In order to estimate the population of a fishery it is electro-fished and then estimated using the *Seber Le Cren* method. This will give the weight of fish per unit area, or 'fish standing' crop. If this is 30 g/m2 and the area is 5,000 m2, the fishery can support a population of 150 kg. It is, however, wise in any restocking claim to employ a fishery expert to advise on the size, species and quantity of fish that should be restocked. He will also be able to compile a sensible restocking programme, to ensure the optimum survival rate of the fish.

3.1.2 Loss of amenity

If fish are killed or driven away from the fishery, the angler loses his sport.

He has nothing to fish for. This loss of angling enjoyment is known as loss of amenity. It is a recoverable (*Bone v Seale* (1975)).

In 1990, there was an escape of rainbow trout from a fish farm on the River Kennett. Downstream, the Savernake Fly Fishers leased fishing rights. This was a game fishery with brown trout as the main quarry. The rainbows interfered with their sport. As His Honour Judge Dyer observed, 'Among fly fishermen the brown trout is considered to be the aristocrat. Such fish are considered to be cunning and yet to be excellent fighters when hooked ... Fly fishing in trout streams when the brown is the only quarry carries a high premium. Flyfishing clubs go to great lengths to keep their water free of rainbows and grayling.'(*Broderick v Gale and Ainslie* (1992)).

The Judge found that the rainbows which escaped from the farm did create a nuisance and assessed damages at £10,500. The damages were calculated using the following calculation:

subscription income of the Savernake Flyfishers
x amenity factor of 1.5
x percentage of club's fishing rights affected
x percentage loss of fishing in the affected stretch.

An assessment of damages for loss of amenity is a subjective process but the Judge called this 'a sensible and practical method' to assess damages. The amenity factor is used on the premise that an angler's enjoyment of his sport is worth something more than he pays for it.

3.1.3 Other damage

An angling club may be involved in expenditure in cleaning up a pollution. For example, it may hire aerators to put oxygen in the water, or to employ waste contractors to take away dead fish. As long as such expenses are a direct result of the pollution and are foreseeable, they are also recoverable.

3.1.4 Duty to mitigate losses

All plaintiffs are under a duty to mitigate (i.e. reduce) their damage (*Moore v DER Ltd* (1971)). This means that they cannot claim damages for any loss they ought reasonably to have avoided. Mitigation will include restocking waters if fish have been killed. This will mitigate a claim for loss of amenity. However, the fish bought can be claimed from the polluter.

This duty is qualified in that the plaintiff does not have to put itself in an impecunious position (*Robbins of Putney v Meek* (1971)). The angling club does not, therefore, have to borrow to finance restocking, nor use up all its available resources.

3.2 Injunction

An injunction is a remedy granted by a court, by which a person is ordered to refrain from or to do a particular act or thing. These are known as prohibitory and mandatory, respectively. The former forbids an act, whilst the latter compels the defendant to do something. The injunction's use in fighting pollution is to stop that pollution. A mandatory injunction may force the defendant to carry out works so that the pollution ceases. However, the Courts are disinclined to grant this type of order. In any event, a prohibitory injunction ordering pollution to cease will force the polluter to carry out works to improve the quality of the discharge.

Mr Justice Parker granted a prohibitory injunction in *Jones v Llanrwst Urban Council* (1910) - this was another local authority sewage pollution:

> Under the circumstances possibly the best form of order will be an injunction restraining the Defendants from causing or permitting sewage from the town of Llanwrst to flow or pass into the River Conway by means of the existing outfalls ... unless or until the same shall have been sufficiently purified by the removal of excrementitious or other foul matter so as not to pollute the water ...

3.2.1 Perpetual and interlocutory injunctions

When court proceedings are issued claiming an injunction, the case will in the end be decided at trial. The judge, if he decides that the plaintiff has proved his case, will grant an injunction. This is known as a perpetual injunction.

However, it may take a case many years to come to trial. The pollution and the damage continues. What can the plaintiff do to protect the fishery in the meantime? He can apply for an interlocutory injunction before the trial. This means that the plaintiff applies for an injunction to stop the pollution, pending the outcome of the case at trial. Importantly, if the plaintiff does succeed in his application for an interlocutory injunction this does not mean that he will win at trial. It does not dispose of the dispute between the parties. It may be that, at trial, the injunction is made perpetual or, if the defendant wins, that it is lifted.

One important factor to consider when applying for an interlocutory injunction is the undertaking to pay damages that the plaintiff has to give if it turns out at the hearing that he is in the wrong. This means that the plaintiff must pay damages to the defendant to compensate him for any damage suffered whilst the injunction was in force.

3.2.2 Damages or injunction

The general principle is that an injunction will not be granted if damages is an appropriate remedy. No hard and fast rules can be given, but examples can offer guidance, although it appears that repeated pollution will require an injunction.

In *Pennington v Brissop Hall Coal Company* (1877), the Plaintiff's mill was damaged by pollution to such an extent that scale was deposited on the boilers and the ironwork in the mill corroded. The Defendant argued that damages, not an injunction, was the appropriate remedy. Mr Justice Fry found that the Plaintiff would be subject to repeated and successive actions for damages if an injunction was not granted. On that basis, he granted an injunction restraining the Defendant from discharging water so as to cause injury to the Plaintiff's engines.

A contrasting decision is *Chapman Morrison & Co v Guardians of Auckland Union* (1889). The nuisance was caused intermittently and the pollution only caused a nuisance in an extremely dry period. An injunction and damages were claimed by the Plaintiff. The question asked by Lord Justice Bowen was, 'whether the real object of the action (the injunction) is protection for the future or damages for the past?' He felt that, on the facts, the Plaintiff was adequately protected in the future without an injunction. In this case, damages afforded complete relief. He ruled that the object of an injunction is 'to prevent the continuance or repetition of acts which have been done and which the defendants are threatening to continue or repeat.'

An injunction may also be granted even if the pollution is intermittent. It is the threat of pollution that is the important factor. In *Bidder v Local Board of Health for Croydon* (1862), the Defendant built a sewer, which discharged sewage into the River Wandle killing many fish. The Judge found that, although the pollution varied in extent from time to time, there was a nuisance and that the Plaintiff was entitled to an injunction restraining the Defendants from polluting the river so as to cause injury to the Plaintiff.

3.2.2 Quia timet injunction

There is a third type of injunction, the quia timet injunction. This is granted if a plaintiff can show that there is a threat of damage. Essentially, the injunction prevents the damage occurring.

In *Fletcher v Bealey* (1885), the Plaintiff sued for an injunction because the Defendant, an alkali manufacturer, was depositing on a piece of land a large heap of refuse close to the river on which the Plaintiff's mill was located. The Plaintiff argued that polluting matter would seep from that refuse into the river. He had not sustained any injury as yet. The action failed because the danger of pollution was not imminent. It would take some years for the discharge to find its way into the river and, if it did, it would be discovered immediately and the Plaintiff could then apply for an injunction.

However, the decision was made, with the qualification that the Plaintiff could apply if a nuisance did occur.

3.3 Limitation of actions

For reasons of public policy, any court action for pollution must be commenced within six years of the date when the cause of action occurred (The Limitation Act 1980). This means that a writ or summons has to be issued in the county courts or the High Court respectively, within six years from the date of the pollution. The rationale behind this lies in the problems that could be caused if court proceedings were started years after the pollution had occurred. Whilst six years may sound like sufficient time, it is surprising how many potential plaintiffs miss this time limit and cannot, therefore, win any damages.

QUESTIONS

Question 1.

My club has decided to buy a fishery located just below a factory. Our solicitor enquired with the Environment Agency regarding previous pollution incidents. The factory, a chemical plant, was prosecuted six years ago for polluting the water and killing fish. By all accounts, it was serious, killing fish for three miles downstream. This would have destroyed nearly all the fish on our stretch. The lease allows us to fish for ten years. We will restock it and plan to carry out bank works. This will be expensive. The Agency has been reassuring about a chance of the pollution recurring. What can we do to protect ourselves?

Answer

There is nothing that you can do about the old fish kill but try to collect as much evidence as possible about the fishery. This will help to prove your case if the fishery is polluted again. Generally, build up a picture of the water and, more specifically:

i) Keep catch returns, or if it is a coarse fishery, match returns. This will, after a number of years, show how good the fishery is.

ii) If you carry out restocking, keep the receipts and the number, species and size of fish stocked. If there is any fish kill, then you should be able to claim the restocking costs. Receipts will be evidence of this.

iii) It is worth breaking down the fishery into stretches. Which are the best for chub, roach, trout, etc.? Where are the pools/swims? Which is the most prolific peg?

iv) Approach the factory owner. Inform him that you have bought the fishery. If there is a pollution, it is important that you contact the factory as soon as possible so that it can stop any noxious discharge.

v) Ensure that members have a telephone number to contact the Agency (normally this is a freephone number) so that any pollution is reported as quickly as possible. This will also enable the Agency to take samples which will link to the pollution to its source. Indeed, if there is a pollution, take samples yourselves and record when and where they were taken.

vi) If you have the finances, employ a fisheries expert to carry out a report on the fishery. He should also be able to suggest habitat improvements. Generally, it will serve as an authoritative statement of the quality of the fishery.

vii) Ask the Environment Agency to carry out a fisheries survey. This will establish a base line of the fish population against which the severity of any future fish kill can be assessed.

Question 2.

My club owns an excellent coarse fishery. Stretches have been acquired over the last forty years. We have different 'types of ownership' with the various riparian owners. We have been told that this may affect our success of recovering damages for pollution. Recently, we had a small kill on the top stretch and are worried that the next incident will be more serious. What is our position in the stretches we own freehold, under a lease, under a licence and have fished for a number of years without paying anything?

Answer

(It is important to note that this answer deals with a claim based on private nuisance. In all these situations a claim for damages in negligence is available.)

i) Freehold:
You can recover damages and/or obtain an injunction for those stretches you own freehold.
ii) Leasehold:
Similarly, you can recover damages and/or obtain an injunction for these stretches.
iii) Licence:
This is a little less clear cut. Recent cases have suggested that damages can be recovered. However, it is important that you try to obtain a lease or even buy the rights. Approach the landlord and see what he says.

iv) Stretch fished for a number of years:
You may own the fishing rights by prescription (see Chapter 5). Without further information, no definite advice can be given. If you do acquire ownership through prescription, damages can be recovered, but not otherwise. Only an actual court case will decide if you own the fishing rights by prescription. The trouble is, if you try to find the land owner, he may tell you to stop fishing and this may defeat any claim your club has to the fishing rights.

Question 3.

The valve on a farmer's slurry tank broke, allowing the slurry to leak into a tributary which feeds our best fishing lake. It was disastrous. I was telephoned by a member who went fishing there. There were dead fish littering the pond. Others were obviously in distress. We managed to hire an aerator and a pump to reoxygenate the water. Also, the Agency netted some of the fish and put them in a nearby lake not owned by us. Already, members are complaining and saying they will not renew their membership next season. How do we go about obtaining compensation and what do we claim for?

Answer

If your club is a member of the Anglers' Conservation Association, then it can ask the ACA to instruct its solicitors to act on your club's behalf to obtain compensation. Otherwise, it can instruct solicitors or make a claim itself.

In a one-off incident like this you will be looking for damages. First of all, you will have to prove that the farmer is liable. The Environment Agency may prosecute the farmer. Then it should not be difficult to pin the blame on him. Contact the Agency to ask if it will prosecute.

Turning to damages, the items for which you will claim are restocking, loss of amenity and the cost of hiring the aerator. You should also employ a fisheries expert to advise on the claim for restocking. He will be able to set out the size, number and species to restock and compile a programme of restocking. He will also be able to assess the length of time it will take the fishery to recover.

The fisheries expert can also advise on the claim for loss of amenity. A claim can be made for loss of amenity in future years. The expert can also estimate the loss until the fishery recovers. This is important if any long term damage has been caused to the fishery. It may take many years for the stock of fish, despite the restocking, to recover. The expert can therefore advise on any implications for the fishery in the long term. To calculate the loss of amenity, you can use the calculation set out in this chapter. This is a relatively subjective process. However, factors to take into account in assessing the percentage of your club's fisheries affected include: the polluted fishery's bank length, its productivity and popularity with members. Factors to assess the percentage loss of fishing are: the extent of the fish kill, the fishery's productivity, natural recruitment and how long it will take the fishery to recover.

Lastly, keep the invoice for the hire of the aerator and any other items of expenditure which were incurred as a direct result of the pollution.

CHAPTER 11

WATER ABSTRACTION

A good flow and quantity of water, obvious as it may seem, is essential to any fishery. This is not only necessary for the fish, but also for the invertebrates and vegetation that are the fish's food. It may well be that abstraction is not harmful to a fishery and some water may be returned to the river in as good quality as it was abstracted. However, an adequate flow will also ensure that any pollutants are washed through the watercourse quickly. The consequences of pollution can be dire for any fishery, but adequate flushing can lessen the impact upon the fish.

In addition, spawning success can be impaired, which may have a disastrous effect on the fish population. Trout spawn in gravels and a drop in the level of water could leave the eggs uncovered, leading to their destruction. Less water also means less space and greater competition between fish for the available food. Again, this leads to mortalities.

With an ever increasing population and the extra demands placed upon our water resources, this is an aspect of Angling Law that is growing in importance and, nowadays, shares as much public attention as pollution. The problem has been thrown into the media spotlight by the recent dry summers and the water companies' neglect of water pipes, with leakage being targeted as a major source of waste.

The forerunner to the present legislation dealing with the management of water resources, was the Water Resources Act 1963. Responsibility for administering the controls passed from the river authorities to the water authorities and, with the privatisation of the water industry, to the National Rivers Authority. After the passage of the Environment Act 1995, it is the Environment Agency which is now the controlling authority. The main statutory provisions dealing with water abstraction are found in Chapter II of the Water Resources Act 1991 (WRA) (s.19-s.72), although the common law still has a role to play.

1. COMMON LAW

Abstraction has no special meaning in common law. It is primarily a statutory term. The right to take water from a river or lake under common law is governed by riparian rights (see Chapter 6). A riparian owner can only make 'ordinary' use of the water flowing in his watercourse. This is not abstraction under the statutory licensing system. It is simply a riparian right.

160

1.2 Ordinary use

The riparian owner can make reasonable use of the water for domestic purposes. However, whilst domestic uses include drinking, cleaning and washing, it may also extend to, for example, watering livestock on a farm. As long as consumption is confined to these uses, water can be taken without regard to the effect this may have on downstream proprietors. Indeed, if the water in the river is so low that this ordinary use dries up the flow, the downstream riparian owner will not be able to sue for the disruption of his rights.

The law goes further in allowing a riparian owner to use the water for any other purpose, as long as he does not interfere with the water as used by upstream or downstream riparian owners. As explained in Chapter 6, riparian owners have rights which go with the land, but as long as the abstraction does not injure the rights of other owners, he can use the water as he wishes. This could even extend to such drastic uses as diverting water for irrigation, or damming a stream for use as a mill.

1.2 Extraordinary use

The logic of the ordinary use doctrine dictates that water cannot be abstracted for an extraordinary use which interferes with another's riparian rights. However, precise guidelines cannot be set for what is an extraordinary use. Each situation will depend on its facts. Irrigation on one river may fall within this category, such that no injury is caused. On another, irrigation of the same quantity may disturb the fishing downstream. The phrase used by legal writers to determine whether a use is extraordinary and, therefore, not permissible, is that it is an issue of fact which must be determined by reference to all the circumstances. For the angler this is not very helpful. Examples from case law do help and the following are some uses which have not been allowed: abstraction of water for a colliery without returning it to the river (*Attwood v Llay Main Collieries* (1926)); the abstraction of water by a railway company for use in the engines (*McCartney v Londonderry Railway Co.* (1904)); the collection of water in a reservoir to supply a nearby town (*Swindon Waterworks Co v Wiltshire and Berkshire Canal* (1875)).

Two particular uses of water, irrigation and diversion, have given rise to litigation on whether they are an extraordinary use of water. Regarding the former, the precise quantity that can be taken will depend upon the effect on the flow in the river. Essentially, the test will be whether the amount abstracted infringes the rights of downstream owners - for example, an angling club whose fishing enjoyment is reduced as a result of the loss of water. In *Rugby Joint Water Board v Walters* (1966), the Defendant was prevented from taking water for spray irrigation because he took nearly

10.8% of the monthly flow. This was found to be an extraordinary use of water.

With diversion, the test again is how much? If so much water is diverted as to leave insufficient for use by downstream owners, then this is not permissible. An obvious interference with the angler's sport is the prevention of the upstream progress of migratory fish (*Roberts v Gwyrfrai RDC.* (1899)). Diversion may prevent fish moving into the upper stretches of the river. Here, in a reversal of the usual situation it is the upper riparian owner who has an action, because the diversion prevents fish from reaching his stretch of the river.

2. STATUTE

As the law now stands, abstraction of water is governed by a complex licensing system whereby an individual or company, which wants to abstract water, must apply to the Environment Agency for a licence. There are provisions dealing with such matters as variations, revocations and appeals, which will be explained later in this chapter.

However, before embarking upon a discussion of the law, the essential question to ask is: What is abstraction for the purposes of the WRA? Section 222(1) WRA states that abstraction 'in relation to water contained in any source of supply means the doing of anything whereby any of that water is removed from that source of supply, whether temporarily or permanently ...' Strictly speaking, the example referred to above of a farmer allowing his cattle to drink from a river is abstraction under WRA. By drinking, the cattle are removing water from a source of supply. Similarly, a fish farmer who takes water from a river so that it runs through his farm is abstracting water. This is so, even if the water is returned to the river downstream, since the water has been removed from a source of supply, although only temporarily. However, the farmer who waters his cattle does not need a licence. It would be absurd to prohibit a farmer from watering his cattle, but a fish farmer in the situation above would have to be licensed.

2.1 Abstraction and the angler

In Chapter 10, the law regarding discharge consents was explained. Most importantly for anglers, compliance with a consent to discharge is not a defence to a civil action for compensation for damage to fishing rights caused by pollution. However, under s.48 (2) WRA, compliance with a licence to abstract is a defence to a civil action for damages. This means that, if an angling club saw its fishing deteriorate and was able to attribute this decline to over-abstraction, it could not sue the holders of the abstraction licence for damage to its fishery.

This must be qualified in that the abstractor must have complied with his licence. As explained below, a licence will have conditions imposed on it. If the licence holder breached these conditions and, for example, took more water than permitted under the terms of his licence, then, if this caused damage to its fishery, the angling club could sue the licensee for compensation. The Environment Agency will keep details of the amount of water abstracted and the club can find out if the conditions in the licence have been observed by inspecting these records. Nevertheless, the point remains that, if there is no breach of the licence, the club cannot sue. This is a strong defence available to abstractors.

2.1.1 Sections 55 and 56 Water Resources Act 1991

All is not lost. An important potential weapon in the armoury of the angler is s.55 and s.56 WRA. Section 55 allows any owner of fishing rights to apply to the Secretary of State for the Environment, Transport and the Regions to revoke or vary a licence. The owner of a licence to fish may apply, as well as the owner of freehold or leasehold fishing rights (s.55 (5) WRA; (see Chapter 5). The grounds for an application are that, as the owner of those fishing rights, the angler has sustained loss or damage which is directly attributable to the abstraction of water from a particular licence (s.55 (3) WRA). To succeed, those grounds must be established and the Secretary of State must be satisfied that the extent of the loss or damage is such as to justify the revocation or variation of the licence (s.56 (3) (b) WRA). The procedure is similar to that to apply for a licence, in that a notice is served by the owner of the fishing rights on the holder of the licence and the Agency and they both have twenty-eight days to make representations (s.55 (4) WRA).

2.1.1.1 Compensation

The applicant is entitled to compensation if he succeeds in establishing the grounds of the application (s.62 (1) WRA). However, if the Secretary of State decides that the licence should not be varied or revoked, but that the grounds of the application have been proved, the owner of the fishing rights is still entitled to compensation (s.62 (2) WRA). To avoid paying compensation, the Agency can offer to buy the fishing rights within six months of the decision (s.60 (3) WRA).

2.1.1.2 Drought

The draughtsman of the statute anticipated drought conditions because the Secretary of State shall not vary or revoke the licence if he is satisfied that the loss or damage was wholly or mainly attributable to exceptional shortage of rain or to an accident or other unforeseen act not caused by, or outside the control of, the Agency (s.56 (4) WRA). This is a difficult obstacle, since many problems do arise during a drought. Indeed in an application made under s.47 of the Water Resources Act 1963 (the forerunner of s.55 WRA), the Inspector specifically stated, '... I am of the opinion that the dry periods in those three years have been the major contributory factor in creating the need to remove more water from the stream.' He used the shortage of rain as one of the grounds to reject the application (*Weir and Nicholson v Yorkshire Water Services Limited* (1992)).

2.1.1.3 The Agency's duty to pay compensation

In addition, and probably more of a deterrent to granting such an application, the Agency has to pay compensation to the licence holder if his licence is varied or revoked (s.61 WRA). The holder of the licence has to show that he has incurred expenditure which is rendered abortive by the revocation or variation and has sustained loss or damage directly attributable to the variation or revocation (s.61(1) WRA). This means that if a club is successful in an application, the Agency will have to pay compensation to the licence holder by virtue of the modification or revocation. For example, if a fish farmer had constructed tanks to hold fish which became obsolete as a result of a successful action, the Agency would have to compensate him for this expenditure and, if he can prove it, any resulting loss of profit. With limited funding, the Agency will be loathe to place additional pressure on already hard pressed resources by supporting an application under s.53 WRA.

No compensation is payable, however, if no water has been abstracted in pursuance of the licence over the previous seven years (s.61(4) WRA). This takes into account the situation where a licence holder has not abstracted water for over seven years. Finally, any dispute regarding compensation can be referred to the Lands Tribunal (s.61(5) and s.62(5) WRA).

2.1.1.4 The Angler and s.55 and s.56 WRA

When making such an application, good evidence must be presented. Catch returns will go to show whether the fishing has declined. In addition to this, anecdotal evidence and expert evidence will be needed. An hydrologist may be needed to show how the licence has affected the flow in the river and a fisheries expert will give evidence on how the loss of water has damaged the fishing rights. Whilst this may be expensive, the costs should be recoverable from either the Agency or the abstractor.

This procedure has not often been tested and, to a certain extent, it is untried. It is difficult to know how the DETR would react to such an application having, as it does, to balance both fisheries and abstraction interests. Also, the Agency may not support an application if it means having to pay compensation to the licence holder.

2.2 Impounding

A chapter on water resources would not be complete without a short section on impounding. 'Impounding works' are defined in s.25(8) WRA as 'any dam, weir or works in any inland waters by which water may be impounded' or, 'any works for diverting the flow of any inland waters in connection with the construction or alteration of any dam, weir or other works.' A licence is required to carry out any impounding works (s.25 WRA). Thus, if a club or private individual wanted to construct a fishing lake, an application to the Agency is required to impound water in a stream to form the lake, or to take water from a source of supply to fill it.

As with abstraction, impounding is governed by both case law and statute. Similar common law rules apply to both in that upstream and downstream riparian owners' rights must not be infringed. The WRA does impose a condition not required in an abstraction licence, in that impounding works must not obstruct or impede the flow of an inland water, except as authorised by the licence (s.25(1) (b) WRA). As with abstraction, impounding without a licence is an offence punishable by a fine (s.25(2) WRA). Provision is made in the WRA for an application for a combined abstraction and impounding licence, where a licence is needed to abstract water to construct or alter impounding works (s.36 WRA).

2.3 The licence

The basic rule is that no one can abstract water without a licence granted by the Environment Agency (s.25(1) WRA). If water is abstracted without a licence, then the abstractor commits an offence and will be liable to either imprisonment and/or a fine (s.24(4) and (5) WRA). If someone wants to take water from a river or other source, then he must apply to the Environment Agency for a licence. The only people allowed to apply for a licence from inland waters are those who own land next to a river or lake, or have access to such land (s.35(2) WRA).

2.4 Exceptions

There are exceptions to the need to apply for an abstraction licence. It is not everyone you see taking water from a river that needs a licence. The first exception applies to small quantities. The taking of five cubic metres is permitted (s.27(1) WRA). Amounts of less than twenty but more than five cubic metres are permitted, as long as the consent of the Agency is obtained beforehand (s.27(2) WRA). These small amounts, called protected rights, must be one-off abstractions and not form part of a continuous series of abstractions. This, to a certain extent, reflects the common law which allows an individual to abstract water for ordinary purposes. Secondly, a licence is not required for water abstracted for land drainage purposes (s.29(1) WRA). Thirdly, no licence is required by a navigation, harbour or conservancy authority, if it transfers water from one inland area of water to another in the course of its functions (s.36(1) WRA). Finally, there are various miscellaneous rights to abstract (s.32 WRA). For example, water used for fire fighting is excluded. Also, the abstraction of water, construction of any well or borehole, or the installation or modification of machinery or other apparatus to test any underground water, or the effect of such works is permitted, following the consent of the Agency.

2.4.1 Licences as of right

The final category of exceptions is licences of right (s.65 and Schedule 7 WRA). The Water Resources Act 1963 introduced the present licensing regime. An abstraction was licensed under s.33 of that Act. This section entitled those abstracting under a statutory provision in force before 1st April 1965, or who had abstracted water at any time within the period of five years ending on 1st April 1965 (ie. under case law), to apply for a licence without the chance of being refused. Similarly, Schedule 26 of the Water Act 1989 (WA) allows those who own land contiguous to the water and who had abstracted water for either domestic or agricultural purposes (this category of abstraction having been an exception before 1990), other than spray irrigation, within the period of five years ending on 1st September 1989 to apply for a licence without the prospect of refusal. These are both known as licences as of right.

An interesting case of how case law interacts with statute, *Cargill v Gotts* (1981), involved licences as of right. The Plaintiff had been taking water from a pond on the Defendant's farm since 1927. Initially, this had been by horse and cart in quantities of 100 gallons at a time. Eventually, the Plaintiff was taking as much as 4,000 gallons a day. The Defendant objected to so much water and restrained the Plaintiff from taking any more water. The Plaintiff applied to the Court for a declaration that he had an easement and, thereby, a legal right to take water from the Defendant's pond. The Court found that, as he had been taking the water for over 20 years, he did have an easement. However, the Judge qualified this by saying that, since the introduction of the licensing system under the Water Resources Act 1963, every abstraction by the Defendant was illegal. The Defendant should have applied for a licence, since he was entitled to a licence as of right (i.e. he had been abstracting water for a period of five years ending on 30 June 1965). The Plaintiff, therefore, had to apply for a licence, despite being entitled to abstract water under case law. This case is a good example of how the licensing system has replaced case law.

2.5 Procedure to apply for a licence

Anglers view more abstraction from their river or lake with dismay. Lower flows can mean fewer fish. Anglers usually want more water. However, knowledge of the procedure will allow objections to be made to any application for a licence which may damage a fishery. The potential abstractor will apply to the Environment Agency and it is up to the angler to bring as much pressure to bear on the Agency to ensure that his interests are protected.

An eye must be kept on local papers, since the applicant has to publish a notice of his proposal in a newspaper circulating in the locality of the proposed abstraction and the *London Gazette* (s.37(2) WRA). This will state where a copy of the application and any map or other document may be inspected free of charge. Twenty-eight days is allowed from the date upon which the notice first appeared in the paper, or twenty-five days from the day on which it appeared in the *London Gazette*, in which to make written representations to the Agency (s.37(5) WRA). It is obviously quite a tall order to expect individuals to be so vigilant in looking at the local press. Often, a club or fisherman will hear of a proposed application by word of mouth - perhaps through a representative on the regional fisheries' advisory committee. It is, however, very important to act as quickly as possible to comply with the twenty-eight or twenty-five day period in which to make objections.

The *London Gazette* is a government publication which lists all matters such as insolvencies and bankruptcies. It is a daily paper published Monday to Friday. It costs £1.45 and can be obtained from Her Majesty's Stationery Office at 49 High Holborn, London. It can also be purchased on subscription. The Salmon and Trout Association (see Chapter 7) operates a very useful service whereby it actually monitors the *London Gazette*. It photocopies all notices of applications for abstraction licences and sends them to its county and regional officers. It also sends copies to those larger clubs that are members. The Association has a booklet which sets out guidelines on how to make representations.

The Agency must have regard to any representations made (s.38(3) WRA). It must also take into account the effect on any river flow (s.40 WRA) and the effect of the proposed abstraction on those already abstracting under a licence, or those abstracting small quantities (s.39(1) WRA). The new licence must not, therefore, interfere with those pre-existing rights. The Agency will grant or refuse the application (s.38(2) WRA). Often, it will impose conditions limiting the amount that can be abstracted or ensuring that the flow in the river is maintained. The Agency is not obliged to decide the application within the twenty-eight day period (s.38(1) WRA). It can agree with the applicant the time within which the decision should be made.

2.5.1 Making representations

It is no use, when submitting representations, simply to state baldly that the fishing will deteriorate. Good reasons will have to be given. The best way to object is to employ an expert who can give scientific reasons why the abstraction will affect the fish. A fisheries expert and/or hydrologist will be appropriate. The former will set out how the loss of water will affect the fish population. The latter will be able to assess what the effect of the abstraction will be on the flow in the river. It may well be that both may advise that there will be no adverse effect on the fish or the flow so as to disrupt angling.

There are two problems, however. The first is the time limit. For an expert to prepare a report within even twenty-eight days is asking a great deal. However, a club may object within the time limit and reach an agreement whereby the Environment Agency agrees to accept the expert's report after the twenty-eight days. The second and probably biggest problem is cost. Experts cost money. The cost of a report will not be funded by the Environment Agency and will not be recoverable if, as with a civil action for compensation, the licence is not granted or is granted with conditions.

It is very important to consider how best to use limited resources. The club can have access to any representations made by the Environment Agency. If the club disagrees with the recommendations made by the Agency, then it will have to decide whether to use expert evidence to substantiate its objections.

If such a report is beyond an objector's means, it is still worth making representations. Reference can be made to the already low flow in the river and a request made that a condition is included in the licence, if granted, that, if the flow falls below a certain level, then no water can be abstracted. As stated above, s.40 WRA obliges the Agency to take river flow into account. Even if a minimum acceptable flow (see below) has not been set, the Agency, when determining licence applications, must have regard to the following considerations by which a minimum acceptable flow for the waters is determined under s.21 (4) WRA: the flow of the water; the character of the water and its surroundings; any statutory water quality objectives. It is worth getting hold of a copy of this section as a useful framework for objections.

2.5.2 Call-in by the Secretary of State

The Secretary of State for the Environment has the power to 'call-in' the application (s.41 WRA). This means that it will be the Secretary of State who actually considers the application. He may order that a local inquiry is held before he makes his decision, or give the applicant a chance to appear before him to argue his case (s.42(2) WRA). It is open to individuals to ask the Secretary of State to call in the application, but he will only do so if the application raises exceptional questions and, it has to be said, this is rare. Anglers may ask for a 'call-in' by writing to the Secretary of State if they feel that the Environment Agency will not consider the club's objections or that special issues are raised by the application.

2.6 Appeals

The WRA provides that the applicant may appeal to the Secretary of State for the Environment against the determination of an application by the Agency or the conditions granted by the Agency within twenty-eight days of the date of the decision (s.43 WRA). Notice of the appeal must be served by the Agency on all those who made representations (s.43(5) WRA). The Secretary of State may uphold or dismiss the appeal (s.44 WRA). Representations may be made to the Secretary of State who may call for a local inquiry (s.44(2) WRA). The decision of the Secretary of State is final and no further appeals are allowed. He also has powers to vary or revoke the licence (s.44(6) WRA). Importantly, it is only the applicant who can appeal. The anglers who made representations to the Agency are not permitted to appeal to the Secretary of State, but will automatically be asked to make further representations if they did do so first time around.

2.7 Conditions

The licence will include many conditions when granted (s.46 WRA). It will deal with the quantity of water that can be abstracted; the period or periods in which it may be abstracted; the way in which the quantity is to be measured; the means whereby the water will be abstracted by referring to the works or apparatus necessary; the land on which the water abstracted is to be used; the time over which the licence remains in force; the points from which the water may be abstracted; the person to whom the licence is granted. For the angler, this means that even if his representations not to grant the licence do not succeed, he can still demand that conditions are imposed to protect his fishing. Representations could be made requesting that if the licence is granted, abstraction shall cease if the depth of water falls below a certain level.

2.8 Variations and revocations

The WRA also deals with applications to modify or revoke licences. Both the holder of the licence (s.51 WRA) and the Agency may apply (s.52 WRA). It is, therefore, open to anglers and riparian owners to write to the Agency requesting that it varies or revokes an existing abstraction licence. Powerful reasons have to be given. As with the licence application procedure, notice of the intended modification or revocation must appear in the *London Gazette* or a local newspaper on two successive weeks (s.51(3) and s.52 (4) WRA). This notice will state where the application can be inspected. Twenty-eight days is allowed for representations. If the holder of the licence raises objections to an application made by the Agency, it must refer the proposal to the Secretary of State (s.53(4) WRA). He may call for a local inquiry, or allow the licence holder to appear before him (s.54 WRA). Rights of appeal, as above, also apply to variations and revocations.

2.9 Register

The Agency must keep a register of all abstraction licences in force (s.189 (1) WRA). This will give the name of the holder, any variations together with a copy of the licence itself and any map. It will be a simple matter to obtain copies from the Agency's principal office for its area although there may be a charge for copies sent by post.

3. MINIMUM ACCEPTABLE FLOWS

The concept of minimum acceptable flows was first introduced by the forerunner of the WRA, the Water Resources Act 1963. There are complicated provisions in the WRA regarding the procedure (sections 21, 22 and 23 WRA). Until the Water Act 1989 there was a duty to set minimum acceptable flows. Since then, it has been discretionary. Briefly, it is the duty of the Agency to submit a statement to the Secretary of State, although he can actually direct the Agency to consider whether a minimum acceptable flow should be set for a river. There seems little point in going through the provisions in detail since, despite the legislation being in force for over thirty years, no minimum acceptable flow has been set for any river in the country. However, it is worthwhile if an abstraction problem arises asking the Agency whether it intends to set a minimum acceptable flow and, if not, if it intends to do so (see 2.5.1 above).

4. DROUGHT

Drought appears to be an increasingly frequent problem. Since the drought of 1976, dry summers have occurred with resulting problems for fisheries. The early nineties saw back-to-back dry summers. Whatever the causes for this, it brings anglers into conflict with other water users. The WRA gives the Secretary of State powers to make drought orders to alleviate the effect of dry weather on water resources.

4.1 Ordinary and emergency drought orders

There are two types of drought orders. Ordinary drought orders are made by the Secretary of State for the Environment if he is satisfied that, by reason of an exceptional shortage of rain, a serious deficiency of supplies of water in any area exists or is threatened (s.73(1) WRA). Emergency drought orders are made by the Secretary of State if he is satisfied that, as with an ordinary drought order, by reason of an exceptional shortage of rain, a serious deficiency of supplies of water exists or is threatened in an area and, over and above ordinary drought orders, that the deficiency is likely to impair the economic or social well-being of persons in the area (s.73(2) WRA).

Either the Agency or a water company can make an application for either type of drought order to the Secretary of State. Any abstraction carried out pursuant to the order does not need a licence. The Agency may be authorised by an ordinary drought order to take water from any specified source, to discharge water to specified sources, and to prohibit or limit the taking of water from specified sources even if the person has a statutory or common law right to take such water (s.74(1) WRA). The water undertaker has similar powers (s.74(2) WRA). Emergency drought orders may contain the same provisions, but water undertakers may be authorised to prohibit or limit the use of water for any purpose they think fit. Ordinary drought orders are limited to a six month period, unless specifically extended (s.74(3) and (4) WRA). With emergency drought orders this is reduced to three months, unless specifically extended (s.75(3) and (4) WRA).

4.2 Procedure

Schedule 8 WRA sets out the procedure for making the order. The application must be published in local newspapers and the *London Gazette*. Notice must be served, depending upon who is applying, on the Agency, water company and local authority, among others. Objectors must be given the opportunity to appear before the Secretary of State. A local inquiry can also be ordered by the Secretary of State. Anglers can therefore be heard. The same tactics and considerations apply when objecting as in 2.5.1 above.

4.3 Compensation

The significance for anglers of these powers is the effect that the extra abstraction will have on their fisheries. Schedule 9 WRA allows the owners or occupiers of land and all other persons interested in the land or injuriously affected by the orders to apply for compensation for loss and damage sustained as a result of water abstracted under an ordinary drought order. The claim is made by serving upon the applicant for the order a notice stating the grounds of the claim and the amount claimed, within six months after the end of the duration of the order. Angling clubs may, therefore, make a claim against the Agency or water company, whichever applied for the order, for loss or damage to their fishing rights.

If an agreement cannot be reached on the level of damages, then the club can make an application to the Lands Tribunal. To do this, as stated above, expert evidence on the damage to the fishing will have to be provided by a fisheries expert together, with an hydrologist. The cost of such an application using two experts will be considerable. Nevertheless, it provides protection for the angler whose fishing is disrupted by a drought order.

It should be noted that Schedule 9 only applies to compensation for damage caused by ordinary drought orders.

4.4 Drought permits

Under s.79A WRA, the Agency can issue a drought permit to a water company to allow it to take water from a specified source, or to suspend or modify any restrictions to which the company is subject. This new procedure, introduced by the Environment Act 1995, offers an alternative to the drought order procedure. The Agency can also authorise water to be taken from a source that the company has no right to use (s.79A(8) WRA).

Application is made by the water company to the Agency which has to be satisfied that, due to an exceptional shortage of water, there is a serious deficiency in supplies. The permit can only last for six months, but can be extended for up to a year (s.79A(4) and (5) WRA). The same procedures as a drought order apply (Schedule 8 WRA), except that the application is made to the Agency and no local inquiry may be called (s.79A(7) WRA).

For anglers, this is a potentially worrying development. Drought permits avoid the cumbersome procedures of a drought order. Publicity will also not be a major concern for the water companies, since they will operate at a local level.

In the case of both drought order and permit applications, the applicant has to show both a 'serious deficiency of supplies' and an 'exceptional shortage of rain'. Neither of these phrases is defined in the WRA, nor has any case law been established to assist.

QUESTIONS

Question 1.

A water company has advertised its application to vary its licence to abstract from our river. Can we object?

Answer

The first thing to notice about this question is that the angling club has actually spotted the notice of the application in its local paper or the *London Gazette*. Unless a member is constantly keeping an eagle eye on the local press it is probable that a club only hears about it 'on the grapevine'. The basic answer to the question is 'Yes, you can object.' After seeing the advertisement, obtain a copy. This must be available for inspection at the Agency's principal office in its area for at least 28 days from its advertisement in the local press, or 25 days from its appearance in the *London Gazette*. It is during this period that you must make representations. Twenty-eight days is not a long time, especially if you want to employ an expert. The Agency must make its decision within three months of receiving the application. If it does not, it is deemed to have refused it.

You can also write to the Secretary of State asking that he call in the application. This means that he and not the Agency will decide whether to grant, refuse or grant with conditions.

It needs a great deal of work to make effective representations. River flow is a complicated science and expert evidence will be expensive. Nevertheless, a notice objecting will alert the Agency to your interest and may lead to the inclusion of a condition in the licence protecting the fishery.

Question 2.

A fish farmer has applied to abstract water just above our stretch of river. It could mean that during the summer, when flows are already low, we will have no water. What about escapee trout and the threat of pollution? We already have a problem with eutrophication on our stretch and, with more nutrients going into the river, this could get worse. What can we do about this?

Answer

The comments in answer 1 apply. Object! This time, however, make specific reference to the pollution, escapee problems and the eutrophication. In your letter objecting make sure you make specific reference to each of these problems stating the base for each. What you will be looking for is not only conditions guarding against the chance of rainbows escaping, but also the steady trickle of effluent from the farm damaging your fishery.

Question 3.

We are certain that a factory which takes water upstream of our fishing rights and returns it in the middle of our stretch is damaging the fish. The water returned to the river is warm and contains pollutants. Your book says that, as the company has a licence, our club cannot go for an injunction and damages in the county court. There are certainly less fish below the discharge.

Answer

This is an example of how s.55 and s.56 WRA can be used. As explained, these give your club a right to apply to the Agency to vary or revoke the abstraction licence. Expert evidence will be needed to substantiate the damage to your fishery. In addition, oral evidence from members of the club stating that fishing is better above rather than below the outfall will add much weight to your application. In these circumstances, if successful, the most likely outcome will be the modification of the licence to the effect that the temperature of the water being discharged must be reduced - if that is the cause of the problem.

CHAPTER 12

ROD AND NET LICENSING

The licensing system is one of the few ways that all anglers are guaranteed to come into contact with angling law and regulation. It is well known, and this Chapter will explore the issues in some depth, that it is a criminal offence to fish without a licence (s.27 Salmon and Freshwater Fisheries Act 1975 - SAFFA). This is the case even if you are fishing on your own water. The licensing system covers fishing for salmon, trout, freshwater fish and eels, but not sea fish. The system of licensing has its origins in the late 19th century. The Commissioners' Inquiry into Salmon Fisheries recommended a system of raising money for use in the protection of fisheries by licence fees. In due course, as the licensing system has become more sophisticated, it has, in addition to its revenue raising purposes, also allowed conservation objectives to be promoted through the limiting of the number of net licences for salmon and trout. It has provided an additional sanction for anglers, or other fishermen, who break the law in the form of licence forfeiture or disqualification.

For many years, this was operated by the river boards and later the water authorities on a local and later regional basis. Anglers could not buy a licence which would cover fishing anywhere in England and Wales. With the creation of the National Rivers Authority in 1989, came the introduction of a national system of licensing in England and Wales. Different types of angling licence are available for salmon and migratory trout (which also covers fishing for non-migratory trout and freshwater fish and eels) and for non-migratory trout and coarse fish(see s.25(5) and (6) SAFFA). Some concessions are available for the disabled, the young (12-16 years) and the old (over 65 years). Anglers under 12 do not need a licence. Annual rod licences now run from 1 April each year. Other licences are also available for 24 hours or eight days. Annual rod licence fees for 1997/8 are £16 for non-migratory trout and coarse fish and £55 for salmon and sea trout. Licences also cover the use of nets or other non rod and line techniques.

The Environment Agency is now responsible for the licensing system. It aims for its fisheries functions to be largely funded from licence fees which, in 1996/97, aimed to raise over £11 million. It has undertaken a number of rod licence 'blitzes' over the last year to try and reduce evasion. It announced in April 1996 a 'no excuses' policy with regard to prosecution aiming to prosecute every angler caught fishing without a licence. The

Agency has promoted this policy on the basis (which harks back to the 19th-century origins of licensing) of providing fisheries services, such as in 1996: new stillwater fisheries, dace stocking of the River Tyne and providing equipment for angling clubs to clean trout spawning gravels.

Anglers' interest in licensing is two fold. First, the rules which affect rod licences and unlicensed fishing and, secondly, the rules relating to net licensing in so far as these may have an impact on fish stocks available for angling.

1. LICENCE FEE LEVELS

Licence fee levels are set by the Environment Agency in accordance with Schedule 2 SAFFA. If the Agency is to seek an increase in licence duties, then it must publish notice of its intention to do so and, if any objection is received, the changes must then be confirmed by the Minister of Agriculture, Fisheries and Food (MAFF).

2. EFFECT OF LICENCE

It is important to understand that an Environment Agency licence does not give the holder any right to fish at any particular time or place (Schedule 2, Paragraph 16 SAFFA). This has a number of important implications:

(a) the owner of the fishing rights must have given permission or there must be a general right to fish (as is often the case on the foreshore - see Chapter 8);

(b) the fishing must comply with any rules as to close seasons (see Chapter 14);

(c) the fishing must comply with applicable byelaws, which may cover a range of issues such as permitted techniques or baits and the making of returns to the Agency (see Chapter 1).

3. ROD LICENCES

A rod licences only allows the person to whom it was issued to fish in accordance with its terms - which allow the use of only one rod for angling for trout (including sea trout, rainbow and brown trout), char and salmon and up to two rods for coarse fish and eels. If fishing is to take place with multiple rods (in the few cases where this would be lawful under National Byelaws (see Chapter 13) and under the rules applicable to that fishery), then a separate rod licence will be needed for each rod (*Cambridge v Harrison* (1895)), if angling is to take place for trout, or a further licence will be needed if three rods are to be used for coarse fish or eels.

3.1 Byelaws and rod licences

It is important to note that the National Fishery byelaws made in 1996 regulate the use of multiple rods in angling (Byelaw 8). They provide that when fishing for salmon or trout in rivers, streams, drains and canals, only one rod may be used at the same time. If fishing for salmon or trout in reservoirs, lakes or ponds, no person shall fish with more than two rods (although commonly, where fly only is the rule, the fishery may have a one rod rule). When fishing for coarse fish or eels, the total number of rods in use at the same time must not exceed four. In any case, where multiple rods are used, they must not be spread over a distance of more than three metres.

3.2 Use of gaffs, tailers and landing nets

The licence entitles the angler to use a gaff, tailer or landing net ancillary to the use of the rod and line. It is important to note that the use of gaffs (previously banned on many waters by local byelaws) has now been outlawed altogether by the National Fishing Byelaws (Byelaw 4). The 1996 National Byelaws will also regulate the use of landing nets by requiring that they are knotless and of non-metallic material, when this part of the byelaws are confirmed (see Chapter 1).

3.3 Transfer of licences

Recreational fishing licences are non transferable. In addition, unless a person has been disqualified from holding a licence under Schedule 4 SAFFA (see below), then a licence must be issued to them on payment of the appropriate duty (Schedule 2 paragraph 15 SAFFA).

3.4 General licences

Most licences are individual angling licences. However, it is possible under SAFFA for the Environment Agency to grant a general licence to the owner or lessee (which might include an angling club or association) of a several fishery allowing any person authorised in writing (unless they are disqualified from holding a licence) by the owner or lessee to fish (s.25 (7) SAFFA). General licences are unusual and are on terms agreed between the fishery owner and the Agency. Unlike individual licences, the Agency may refuse to grant a licence but must have justifiable reasons for so doing. In *Mills v Avon and Dorset River Board* (1955), it was held that a fishery owner is entitled to a general licence unless there are good reasons for not so doing. On the facts of the case, the River Board refused a general licence because many fisheries on the river in question (the Hampshire Avon) had been commercialised. The applicants for the general licence had not commercialised their fishery which was restricted to the owner and his guests in each case. For this reason, the withholding of the general licence was unjustified. Had a commercial fishery sought a general licence, the result, of course, might have been different.

3.5 Returns

The final issue related to recreational licences is the question of fishing returns to the Environment Agency. This issue has to be distinguished from returns to fishery owners or clubs which will be governed by their own rules and may be essential to provide data for stocking.

The National Byelaws provide for the making of a return in respect of salmon and migratory trout by every holder of a rod licence which covers these species (Byelaw 3). Details of the dates, locations and time spent fishing, together with fish caught (including any returned alive) and the method of capture. The information is provided on a return form provided by the Agency. It provides important information on stocks to the Agency which may be used in a number of ways but may, for example, underpin conservation measures such as the making of a net limitation order (see below).

4. NET LICENSING

Although this section is entitled 'net licensing', it covers licensing of any lawful method of capture of fish, such as fixed engines or traps. For this reason, the Act refers to the use of an 'instrument' which in most cases will be a net but could cover the other types of capture methods used in commercial fishing. The applicable law is essentially the same as for recreational licensing, but with a few crucial differences.

First of all there is, unlike the position of individual recreational licences, a degree of transferability of net licences. This arises by means of the endorsement system which may allow a particular licensed net to be used by someone other than the licence holder.

Secondly, the number of net licences that may be issued may be restricted by the making of a net limitation order (NLO). The aim of NLOs is to protect fish stocks from over fishing. Where an NLO is in force, then licences may be refused on the basis that the limited number have already been issued.

Finally, Paragraph 17 of Schedule 2 SAFFA provides that no licence shall be issued in respect of an illegal method of fishing (see Chapter 13 but, for example, spears or crosslines). This paragraph was considered by the High Court in *R v National Rivers Authority ex p Haughey* (1996) (considered in greater detail in Chapter 19), where Dr Haughey had been refused licences for three fishing coops (types of traps attached to a weir) on the basis that he had made alterations to the weir which may have rendered the coops unlawful. The court reiterated the principle that, in the absence of disqualification, a net limitation order or a clear case of a licence being sought for an illegal fishing method, no refusal of licence was permissible (Schedule 2, Paragraph 15 SAFFA).

4.1 Net licensing - transferability

Licences other than for fishing by rod and line may be relied upon by persons other than the holders, if that person is named as an endorsee upon the licence (s.25 (3) SAFFA). Endorsees must be the employees or agents of the licence holder to be endorsed on the licence. The names endorsed may be changed on payment of a nominal fee to the Environment Agency (Schedule 2, Paragraph 12). At no time must the number of endorsees exceed twice the number of persons needed to operate the instrument (and, in any event, where the licensee plans to operate the instrument or net, one less than twice the number is the highest permissible number of endorsees).

The rules on transferability and endorsement were tightened following the Salmon Act 1986. There was concern that they ensured that nets were being used much more intensively than they would have been without the endorsement system, particularly where a net limitation order (limiting the number of net licences issued) was in place. A net which might have been used, say, once a week by the licence holder might have ended up being used daily by a series of endorsees (without the presence of the licence holder) on the other days. The conservation value of such orders was thereby being undermined.

The new rules (amending Schedule 2 SAFFA) require:
(a) That the names and addresses of endorsees are entered on the licence in accordance with Schedule 2 described above;
(b) The endorsee should be accompanied by the licensee at the time of the use of the instrument unless the consent of the Agency is obtained in the 'special circumstances of the case'.

If a net limitation order is in place, then the new rules are even stricter requiring that:
(a) That the names and addresses of endorsees are entered on the licence in accordance with Schedule 2 described above;
(b)The endorsee is not also the holder of a licence himself;
(c)That the licensee accompanies the endorsee except where independent use of the licence is permitted. Where an NLO is in place, this is limited to cases where the Agency has given its consent, but the Agency may only

consent to independent use where the licensee is unable to accompany the endorsee through sickness or injury.

These new rules are designed to ensure that nets are genuinely limited in their use (as well as their licensing) when a net limitation order is in place.

4.2 Commercial fishing and byelaws

The enforcement of the licensed use of nets, or other forms of commercial fishing, is often backed by byelaws which make the compliance with the rules easier to establish. Schedule 25 of the Water Resources Act 1991 allows byelaws to be made requiring that licensed nets and the boats or coracles which use them shall be marked. In addition, byelaws may prohibit the carrying of unlicensed nets, or licensed instruments out of season, in boats etc. The applicable byelaws vary from area to area, but it is apparent that these sorts of rules are likely to assist the Agency fishery officers.

The National Byelaws made in 1996 do provide for the making of fishing returns on a monthly basis by the holders of commercial licences for salmon or migratory trout. Phase 2 of the National Fisheries Byelaws (due in 1998) include proposals for eel catch returns and otter protection on commercial fishing.

4.3 Net limitation orders - s.26 SAFFA

The Agency has inherited powers previously operated by the National Rivers Authority (and before that, the water authorities) to propose orders to be made by MAFF limiting the number of licences to be issued for fishing, other than by rod and line, in any specified area in any year. In practice, this is used to limit the number of commercial net licences for the taking of salmon and sea trout. The order may provide a limit for a period of up to ten years (allowing planning for the conservation of stocks to take place over a realistic period of time).

4.3.1 Procedure

The procedure is that the Order is proposed by the Agency and then, if the Minister is proposing to confirm it, it must be publicised by the Agency. The publication of the notice is normally in a local newspaper appropriate to the area affected. There will be an opportunity for objections to be made to MAFF. In certain circumstances, where the order will have a significant effect (set out in detail in s.26 (3) SAFFA), a local inquiry must be established. Following this procedure, an NLO may be confirmed by the Minister either as drawn or with the consent of the Agency in an amended form.

NLOs may be revoked by an order of the Minister, or an order of the Agency confirmed by the Minister.

In deciding to make an NLO and, if so on what terms, the Agency and the Minster need to consider their duties in respect of conservation of flora and fauna under s.7 Environment Act 1995 and their duty to maintain and improve fisheries under s.6 (6) Environment Act 1995. A failure to do so may leave open the way to an application for a judicial review. Perhaps, more importantly, these duties may be compelling arguments in any discussions or correspondence with the Agency or MAFF or at any inquiry (see also Chapter 1).

Although the NLO powers may be used most readily where there is evidence of decline or threat to fish stocks, there is nothing in the Act which requires that the Agency or MAFF should find this is the case. In a recent public inquiry concerning a proposed NLO covering the net fishery off the Anglian coast, the National Rivers Authority put their case for the making of an NLO on the basis of the 'precautionary principle'. This is a developing principle in environmental protection generally. It has been adopted as one of the principles which the Agency will apply in the statutory guidance issued under s.4 Environment Act 1995 (see Chapter 1). It means that there is no need for compelling evidence of a link between an activity and environmental harm (say, in this case, net fishing and a decline in fish stocks) to be proved before action may be justified. Instead, action is permissible as a sensible precaution. This clearly is important for anglers who are seeking to argue that NLOs should be made. For more details on this particular case see (1996) Water Law 46.

Finally, when considering the making of NLOs in respect of salmon netting, the *NRA Strategy for the Management of Salmon in England and Wales* (1996) and any Environment Agency river based salmon management plans will be crucial documents to use in arguing for or against any proposed NLO.

4.3.2 Selection of licensees

Where the number of commercial netting licences is limited and demand exceeds this limit, there will need to be a selection system for granting such licences. The selection system has to be in the Order. One particular problem relating to NLOs and the selection of licensees is the protection conferred by s.26 (4) SAFFA. This states that a proposed order shall not be confirmed by the Minister unless he is satisfied that the selection system will ensure that any person who held a licence during the year preceding the NLO and who is dependent on fishing for his livelihood will be able to obtain a licence despite the NLO. If this protection of those dependent on fishing would prejudice the conservation of any fishery, then the qualifying period that a person must have held a licence may be extended from the previous year to a further year or (exceptionally) a further two years.

This may, however, limit the effect of the NLO by in practice requiring the issue of a greater number of licences than otherwise the Agency might wish.

The application of the dependency rules was considered in *R v South West Water Authority ex p Cox* (1982) where an NLO included the protection required by s.26 (4) SAFFA and required the issuing of licences to those dependent on fishing. A number of fishermen challenged the way in which the water authority interpreted the word 'depend' in the Order and how they applied it to their cases. The High Court, on a judicial review, held that it was wrong for the Authority to look for licence applicants to be 'wholly dependent'. The word of SAFFA and the Order was 'dependent' and this would allow persons who had another source of livelihood to fall within the category.

Although from an anglers point of view the main interest in NLOs is the ability to promote conservation of migratory fish stocks, this is not the only purpose for which NLOs may be used. In *R v Minister of Agriculture, Fisheries and Food ex p Graham* (1988), an Order was upheld by the courts where its clear purpose was to control the issuing of licences to poachers convicted in Scotland (or those not disqualified following conviction in the English courts).

5. UNLICENSED FISHING OFFENCES S.27 SAFFA

It is a criminal offence to:

(a) Fish for; or

(b) Take fish otherwise than by means of an instrument covered by the licence held (if any) or in accordance with the conditions of any licence held (eg. by fishing for salmon when holding a coarse fishing licence); or

(c) Possess with intent to use for fishing or taking fish any instrument not covered by a licence.

These offences cover fishing without a licence or other than in accordance with a licence held. There is a further offence in s.35 SAFFA of failing to produce a fishing licence when lawfully required to do so.

5.1 General Principles

Where a prosecution is brought under s.27 SAFFA, some basic principles will be applied. First, it is not permissible to purchase a licence retrospectively (*Wharton v Taylor* (1965)). These days, when a licence is purchased, the date and time it is bought should be entered on the licence providing any evidence of any attempt to obtain a licence retrospectively. Secondly, in any proceedings concerning whether a person held a fishing licence or not, it is for the accused to prove (on the balance of probabilities) that he did have a licence at the relevant time (s.101 Magistrates Courts Act 1980 and *R v Edwards* (1975)).

5.2 Unlicensed fishing offences - meaning of fishing

One of the problems with the offence of fishing without a licence is when fishing begins and ends. For example, are you fishing when tackling up or while looking for a good spot to start or for fish? Does fishing cease when you remove you line from the water temporarily to have a coffee or change flies?

There is no case law relating to this issue on fishing with rod and line. Some idea of the principles which apply may be gleaned from non angling cases. First, in *Moses v Raywood* (1911), a net was in a boat and was dry. One of two fishermen was walking the banks of a river looking for salmon and the other was in the boat with the net. It was held that they had started fishing. This would indicate that it is not necessary to have cast a line to be fishing - tackling up and finding a fishing pitch or looking for fish will probably be enough. Secondly, in *Alexander v Tonkin* (1979), the issues concerned the use of purse seine nets which encircle an area of water trapping any fish. Then the net is hauled in and the fish landed on the boat. It was held that fishing continued even after the net had been 'pursed', ie. after the fish had been trapped and were just being pumped onto the boat. This is an unsurprising result, but indicates that an angler continues to fish as he plays and lands a fish.

5.3 Unlicensed fishing offences - intention

One of the problems which arises in practice in relation to fishing other than in accordance with a licence is where the fisherman holds a licence but is believed to be fishing for a type of fish not covered. For example, an angler is fishing with rod and line in a migratory trout river and only has a trout and coarse fishing licence and alleges that he was fishing for coarse fish. This problem does not come into play where 'unlicensed' fish are taken (see below) or there is possession of an 'unlicensed' instrument with intent (see below).

5.3.1 Definition of intention

In order for an angler to be fishing for a particular type of fish, it is necessary to show that the angler had the *intention* to catch that type of fish.

'Intention' is a word that has caused a remarkable amount of problems in criminal law. Broadly, when applied to the angling situation, it does not require a wish or desire to catch fish of that type (although if such a desire can be shown intention will be proved) but, if there is no such desire, then it must be shown that the accused realised that capture of unlicensed fish was likely.

These principles emerge from the cases. In *Marshall v Richardson* (1889) the accused was fishing in a trout stream. He alleged that he had no intention of catching trout, but was fishing for coarse fish to use as bait. The magistrates convicted him on the basis that he must have known that he might have caught trout. On appeal, the court overturned the conviction, holding that intention to catch trout must be shown. In *Lyne v Leonard* (1868) putts (wicker fish traps) were being used in an area frequented by salmon. The accused said they were in use to try and catch shrimps and flat fish. The court convicted him (and on this occasion the appeal court upheld the conviction) on the basis if it could be shown that the actions of the accused were reasonably calculated to catch salmon, even if this was not the desired result.

5.3.2 Proof of intention

Proof of intention is always difficult because it involves attempting to look into someone's mind. However, in the absence of admissions by the accused made, for example, to a water keeper or in interview with an Environment Agency bailiff, intention may be inferred from the circumstances. The method and place of fishing are very important factors as will be the angling experience of the accused. An example of inference from the circumstances is the case of *Lee v Evans* (1980), considered in detail in Chapter 14. The accused was an experienced netsman who fished at night, he said for sea fish. He in fact caught ten sea trout in his net and placed the net in a bag and set off to walk home. When challenged by a water bailiff he said that he was intending to check the net at home and would then return any 'unlicensed' fish. The court inferred an intention to take sea trout from the circumstances. Mr Justice Watkins said:

> It is abundantly plain, so it seems to me, that the [defendant], before he was apprehended by the water bailiffs and went fishing with a net, knew that it was as likely as not that he would catch if anything, a variety of fish including salmon and sewin. And further that he intended when putting a net into the water, to take out of the estuary anything which became enmeshed in it.

5.4 Unlicensed fishing offences - meaning of take

It is also a criminal offence to take 'unlicensed' fish as well as to fish for them (s.27 SAFFA). This will cover a number of situations. First, taking may not involve a rod and line or indeed any instrument at all. For example, where fish are grabbed or 'tickled'. The effect of this is to render unlawful any method of taking fish for which no licence is obtained or available. Secondly, it is not possible to 'take' dead fish (*Gazard v Cook* (1890) and *Cain v Campbell* (1978)).

However, where, as in *Stead v Tillotson* (1900), fish are dying (in this case because of poisoning but it was not possible to prove that those accused had placed the poison in the river) then providing they are not dead when they are taken from the water the offence of taking is still committed. Byelaws sometimes prohibit the taking of dead fish from water without lawful authority.

One problematic issue (also considered in Chapter 14 in relation to close seasons) is where an 'unlicensed' fish is caught by genuine mistake. For example, where a trout fisherman (holding a non-migratory trout licence) hooks and lands and salmon. If the salmon is removed and killed clearly although not guilty of fishing for salmon (as the angler lacked the intention to catch salmon) the angler would be guilty of taking 'unlicensed' fish. What if the fish is landed and returned? The courts have considered this possibility describing it as the *de minimis* rule. This is where the 'taking' is so minimal as to not count at all. In *Lee v Evans* (1980), considered above, the court dealt with this possibility but made it clear that the return must really be at the same time and place as the fish is landed.

5.5 Unlicensed fishing offences - meaning of instrument

Not only are there offences of fishing and taking ,but also of possession of an instrument with intent to use it for an unlicensed purpose. Clearly, intent must be shown to use the instrument and to use it for some unlicensed purpose. For example, a net which might be used for catching sea fish or salmon would have to be shown to have been intended by the accused to be used for salmon in order for this offence to be proved.

The word 'instrument' has been considered by the courts. It is relevant not only to this offence, but also to the powers of forfeiture (considered below and in Chapter 1). It covers things which are directly concerned in the taking of fish, but not those only indirectly connected. For example, in *Gibson v Ryan* (1967) (a Scottish case and therefore only persuasively relevant) a rubber dinghy and fish basket were held not to be 'instruments'.

5.6 Unlicensed fishing offences - penalties

These are set out in Schedule 4 SAFFA. In the event of the unlicensed fishing being by rod and line, the maximum punishment is a fine of £2,500 and may only be dealt with by the magistrates court. The level of penalty allows the accused if he so desires to plead guilty by post rather than attending court (s.12 Magistrates Courts Act 1980). Where any other technique is used, the offence may be tried in either the magistrates court or the Crown Court. The maximum penalties are then £5,000 and/or three months imprisonment in the magistrates court, or an unlimited fine and/or up to two years imprisonment in the Crown Court.

On conviction, the court has the power to forfeit any licence currently held and to disqualify the accused from holding a licence in the future for up to five years (Schedule 4, Paragraph 17 SAFFA extended from one year by the Water Act 1989). In addition, there are powers to forfeit fish taken illegally, tackle, bait or any other instrument used in the offence. The Crown Court has additional powers to forfeit vessels or vehicles used in the offence. These powers are considered in more detail in Chapter 1.

6. PRODUCTION OF FISHING LICENCES

An Environment Agency water bailiff, police officer or any person who holds a fishing licence and produces it may require anyone who is fishing to produce his own licence and to state his name or address (s.35 (1) and (2) SAFFA). SAFFA in fact requires the production of the licence 'or other authority to fish'. The meaning of these words is not entirely clear. It seems likely that it refers to the written permission of the fishery owner or lessee where a general licence has been issued. The extension of the power to require production to other licensed fishermen does provide a strong basis for a club to have a policy of checking licences and for 'suspicious characters' to be approached.

If a person fails to comply with a request to produce a licence or state their name and address then, providing they produce the licence to an appropriate office of the Agency within seven days, they comply with the Act. The Agency suggests that a licence should always be carried by the angler when fishing.

Failure to produce a licence when it is lawfully requested is a criminal offence punishable by a fine of up to £2,500. As failure to produce a licence is a criminal offence, anglers need to keep their rod licences safely. If an annual rod licence is lost, a replacement can be obtained on production of a tear off slip (which is attached to the licence). The prudent or cautious angler should detach this on obtaining the licence and keep the slip separately in case of loss.

7. FIXED PENALTIES AND UNLICENSED FISHING

The fixed penalty system is considered in Chapter 1. It is likely that the offences described above under s.27 and s.35 SAFFA will be included in any fixed penalty system allowing a person to avoid prosecution by paying a fixed penalty within a specified time period.

QUESTIONS

Question 1.

Our syndicate own a stretch of salmon fishing in the middle reaches of a well known salmon fishery. Netsmen have for many years operated in the estuary fishing for salmon. We have discovered that there are more than 20 net licences issued on the estuary. In recent years, we have seen declining salmon catches and are concerned that this is due to over fishing by the netsmen. What can we do?

Answer

It is possible for the Environment Agency to make a net limitation order under s.26 SAFFA, subject to the confirmation of the MAFF. This will restrict the number of licences that may be issued for netting in a specified area (for example the estuary concerned). There are a number of things you can do to try and promote the making of a limitation order. First, contact other riparian owners, syndicates or clubs to see if they will support your efforts. Secondly, see what evidence there is of decline in salmon fishing. Bear in mind that the Environment Agency holds records of returns including those from netting licences. Can the decline of the fishery be linked to the netsmen? Thirdly, see what support may be available from organisations such as the Salmon and Trout Association or Anglers Conservation Association. Fourthly, try to develop a constructive dialogue with the Agency fishery officers. Finally, in any discussions with the Agency gently (and, if need be, firmly) remind them of their duty to maintain and improve salmon fisheries (s.6 (6) Environment Act 1995) and to have regard to conservation (s.7 Environment Act 1995). Finally, lobbying via the Regional Fisheries Advisory Committee of the Environment Agency may be effective.

Question 2.

I went trout fishing at a reservoir last Sunday with a friend. It was arranged at short notice and I did not have time to buy a rod licence and Post Offices were not open. When I was having my lunch, I was approached by a bailiff who asked me for my licence. I showed him my day ticket for the reservoir and he asked me for my rod licence. I said that I had left it at home and that I did not think any licence was needed for reservoir fishing: I thought it was all in the price. He took my details and warned that unless I produced the licence within seven day I will be prosecuted. Surely this is not a criminal offence like theft ?

Answer

It is a criminal offence to fish, etc. without a licence. It may not be as serious as theft but is (as for example with motoring offences) nonetheless criminal. You cannot buy a licence retrospectively. The offence is committed even if you did not know that what you were doing is against the law. The Environment Agency operates a 'no excuses' policy, but it may be worth trying to persuade them in the circumstances outlined above that you should just be warned rather than prosecuted. If you are prosecuted, check the summons carefully to see that it is correctly drawn up (the right date of offence and offence in this case either fishing or possession of the rod and line with intent to fish) and if it is you may plead guilty by post. If you are of previous good character, you may expect a small fine and to pay a small amount of costs.

See also Question 1 in Chapter 14 (Close Seasons) which covers the issue of showing intent to catch unseasonable fish, but is equally applicable to unlicensed fish.

CHAPTER 13

TYPES OF FISHING AND ILLEGAL METHODS

Traditionally, the owner of a fishery has had the right to take fish by whatever method they wanted. There was, prior to the Salmon Fishery Act 1861, a degree of regulation over methods of fishing (for example, statutes in 1389 and 1423 controlling the use of certain nets are noted in *Freshwater Fishery Law* by Howarth (1987) Financial Training Publications), but the 1861 Act first included a clear list of illegal methods and instruments for taking fish and for the protection of immature fish. This Act forms the basis of the current law and explains to some extent the arcane terminology still used.

This chapter concerns controls that exist over certain methods of fishing. In some cases there is an absolute prohibition against the use of a particular method (for example explosives). In others there is a ban but the method may be used with permission of the Environment Agency. All of the legal provisions are now in the Salmon and Freshwater Fisheries Act 1975 (SAFFA).

1. ILLEGAL IMPLEMENTS - GUNS, LIGHTS, LINES. ETC. s.1 SAFFA

A range of devices are prohibited for use in the taking of salmon, trout or freshwater fish (but slightly bizarrely, not eels - see below) by SAFFA. At the same time, the Act prohibits possession of any of the listed devices with intent to take or kill salmon, trout or freshwater fish. Possession will obviously cover physical custody of any of the banned items. But, it is a broader concept than that alone. Possession also includes, for example, having something in your control - perhaps someone else is holding it on your behalf. As to intention, this may often be inferred from the circumstances in which a person is found with an illegal implement. For example, in *Ryan v Ross* (1963), the defendant was found with an illegal type of net called a hang net which was set up and wet and placed in a wet sack in the defendant's car. The car was parked by a tributary of the River Tweed. The defendant said he had found it but, despite this, did not show it to the water bailiffs who challenged him until he was asked to open the sack. The court found that, from the circumstances, it was proper to infer the intention to use the net to take fish.

1.1 Banned implements

The illegal implements and devices banned under s.1 SAFFA include a range of fishing techniques.

1.1.1 Firearms

Firearms as defined in the Firearms Act 1968 are banned under s.1 SAFFA. This will include any lethal barrelled (this requirement will exclude spear guns and crossbows, but see below on spears and missiles) weapon. So, unsurprisingly, using a gun (including a powerful air gun) to shoot fish is illegal.

1.1.2 Otter laths, wires or snares

Otter laths, jacks or wires or snares are illegal implements. An otter lath or jack is further defined in the Act as a combination of *running out lures* (artificial or natural) by hand line, with rod and line or otherwise with any small boat or vessel, board, stick or other instrument. This might involve towing a line with a boat or attaching a line to a pole or piece of wood so as place it in places where otherwise it might not operate. In practice the application of the definition is tricky. It involves using something between the rod and lure or bait to help the fisherman to fish in places or ways that might not otherwise be possible. The ambiguity casts some theoretical doubts over practices such as 'long trotting' (running a floated bait a considerable distance down river with the current) or even dapping a fly from a moving boat. An extraordinary nineteenth century Irish case on 'otters' is *Alton v Parker* (1891). It was against Irish law to fish with an 'otter'. The defendant was seen fishing in a boat with a line extended to a piece of wood from which the line was fished. In his defence, the Irishman argued (with a straight face) that the definition 'otter' was limited to animate otters which could be trained to catch fish! Not unnaturally his defence failed!

1.1.3 Crosslines and setlines

Crosslines (a line from bank to bank with one or, more typically, several baited hooks or lures attached to it) or setlines (this is the same as a crossline only it need not be attached to both banks but is simply an unattended line with one or more baited hooks or lures) are both illegal methods. This raises the slightly difficult issue of when a line becomes unattended. It is not uncommon (although it may be unwise for fear of tackle theft or the 'big one' dragging off one's fishing rod !) for an angler to leave a rod with a cast line (especially when ledgering) to go and talk to a friend, have a drink or answer the call of nature!

1.1.3.1 The Lockhart case

These issues were considered in the Scottish case of *Lockhart v Cowan* (1980). Two experienced anglers went fishing on a loch in Ayrshire. They were fishing with worms for brown trout from the bank. On the same loch, three senior police officers and a water bailiff had gone fly fishing for trout from a boat. They noticed that the two on the bank were sitting some yards from three rods. The rods each had cast lines trailing into the water. The rods were lying on the rocky bank but were not fixed in any way. The boat party landed and confiscated the fishing tackle and six brown trout the two anglers had caught. The two anglers were accused of fishing not by rod and line but by set line. The court had to decide what fishing by 'set line' meant. There was no statutory definition in the applicable Scottish law. The court took account of the purpose of the legislation - to protect salmon and trout stocks - and the fact that fishing with worms was less sporting than with fly. The court also noted that fishing under the applicable Scottish law was only lawful if by single rod and line. Here, three rods were used and, therefore, there were several lines. This implied that if each angler had had only one rod and line they would not have been fishing with set lines. The Sheriff's Court concluded that:

> In my opinion where fishing rods are set down or arranged or put in a particular position, such as on the side or the bank of a loch and the lines are allowed to trail in the water, this constitutes fishing with set lines...

This case is Scottish and not decided under SAFFA and is therefore not binding in the English or Welsh courts, but is of persuasive value. It raises more questions than it answers for anglers.

1.1.3.2 Practical issues and set or cross lines

In practical terms, on waters where ledgering is an acceptable practice, it seems unlikely that a short absence from a line would leave it 'unattended' (in the sense meant by the law), but the best advice is to bring in all lines before leaving your pitch. If you discover a cross line or set line on your fishery then, if it belongs to a lawful angler and he does not appear, it may appropriate to bring in the line and have a word with him. If an unauthorised fixed line is discovered then - although it clearly does not belong to the fishery owner or angling club - it is recommended that it should be removed. In practical terms, as it is illegal and probably poaching, no one is likely to complain. It is arguable, in any event, if carried out by an owner, that they are merely using lawful self help to remove a trespass. This view is supported by an 1846 case (*Hughes v Buckland* (1846)) when gamekeepers of a private fishery were held to have lawfully seized the fishing equipment of a person who they reasonably believed to be poaching. The law on police and water bailiff powers has developed considerably since this case and caution is urged where the illegal tackle is still in the possession of the poacher. See also Chapter 17.

1.1.4 Spears, stroke hauls or snatches

Spears and stroke hauls or snatches (any device, whether used with a rod or line or in any other way, with the aim of foul hooking any fish) are banned under s.1 SAFFA. Thus, the use of, for example, a spear gun or sharpened pole is illegal. In addition, the not unknown practice of attempting to foul hook (where an angler seeks deliberately to get a hook into any part of the fish and does not seek or wait for a bait or lure to be taken by the fish) a distressed fish (which is much to be deplored) is also against the law. Some fishery byelaws require that accidentally foul hooked fish should be returned to the water immediately. In some areas other byelaws seek to minimise the risk of foul hooking by controlling the number or size of hooks which may be used on a single rod and line.

1.1.5 Gaffs

Gaffs are prohibited unless they are barbless and used in connection with a rod and line under s.1 SAFFA. In any event, national fishery byelaws have now prohibited the use of gaffs entirely - see below.

1.1.6 Lights

Lights are banned for the purpose of taking fish. This clearly does not and is not intended to prevent the night angler from having a torch or lamp but does prohibit using the torch or lamp to attract fish so that they may netted or caught.

There is some doubt about luminous lures but it seems likely that these would not be regarded as lights unless they had an independent source of illumination.

1.2 Penalties for use or possession of banned implements

If a person is found in possession of any of the above, or to have used them to take fish, then they are guilty of a criminal offence and may be prosecuted - normally by the police although in theory on a private prosecution basis - and the courts' powers to deal with an offender are as follows (Schedule 4 SAFFA). In the magistrates' court, a fine of up to £5,000 and/or three months imprisonment may be imposed. Up to two years imprisonment and an unlimited fine may be imposed by the Crown Court.

2. Stones and Missiles s.1 SAFFA

It is also a criminal offence to throw, or in some other way discharge, a stone or any other type of missile for the purpose of taking or killing or promoting or allowing the taking or killing of salmon, trout or freshwater fish. This would cover not only trying to drop a rock on a fish (a fairly hopeless way of trying to kill it !) but also, say, scaring fish into a net or trap by throwing stones. The penalties for the offence are the same as described above.

3. Eels and Illegal Methods

It is slightly strange that the law described (s.1 and s.2) above applies to salmon, sea trout and freshwater fish but not eels. This anomaly arises from the definition of freshwater fish in s.41 SAFFA. This gap may well be filled by byelaws imposing restrictions on particular methods. Byelaws on methods are considered below.

4. Fishery Development or Preservation Defence s.1 (2) SAFFA

The Act creates a defence to the use of illegal implements, or even stones or missiles, if the person accused can prove that what they did was for the preservation or development of a private fishery and was done with prior written permission of the Environment Agency. This will be a rare case for, in general, there are more humane and effective methods of capturing unwanted fish than by any of these methods.

5. Illegal Methods of Fishing s.5 SAFFA

The 1975 Act also includes a prohibition on the use of certain methods of fishing. This ban extends not only to salmon, trout and freshwater fish in inland waters, but also to coastal waters - to a distance of six nautical miles from the established baselines (basically, a mean tidal mark). Thus, estuaries and coastal fisheries and the sea fish species within them are protected under this part of the law.

SAFFA bans the use (or possession of with intent - see *Ryan v Ross* (1963) above on proving intent - to use for the purposes of taking or destroying fish which will include eels in this case) of:
(a) explosive substances with intent to take or destroy fish;
(b) poisonous or noxious substances with intent to take or destroy fish;
(c) any electrical device with intent to take or destroy fish.

The use of electro fishing apparatus is an accepted method of removing unwanted fish - eg. predator species or large numbers of stunted fish. Although s.5 (1) SAFFA prohibits the use of this method, it is lawful with the written consent of the Environment Agency, providing its use is for a scientific purpose or to protect, improve or replace fish stocks. In addition, of course, the consent of all the fishery owners will be needed. Technically, these consent provisions also apply to the use of explosives or poisonous or noxious substances. The control of the entry of substances which may pollute water and harm fish is much broader than under this part of SAFFA. In many cases, the entry of poisonous or noxious substances is not with intent to take or kill fish - that is merely an unfortunate side effect. For example, a spillage of oil from a factory. There are, therefore, a number of other pieces of law controlling the entry of such substances into water. If permission were given for the use of such substances under this part of SAFFA, it would authorise such use as against breaches of these other anti-pollution laws under s.4 of the 1975 Act (see Chapter 9) or s.85 Water Resources Act 1991 (see Chapter 9) or under any byelaw.

5.1 Penalties under s.5 SAFFA

The criminal offence under this section of SAFFA is punishable in the magistrates court with a maximum fine of £5,000. It may go to the Crown Court which may impose imprisonment of up to two years and an unlimited fine.

6. INTERFERENCE WITH DAMS, SLUICES OR FLOODGATES S.5 (3) SAFFA

It is an offence under SAFFA to damage or destroy a dam (which includes any weir or other fixed obstruction used to for damming water), floodgate or sluice with intent to take or destroy fish. These are separate from the controls over the use of or creation of weirs, which are considered in Chapter 19. These powers might be used where, for example, a fish ladder at a weir was interfered with so that the fish could not escape from the ladder.

The criminal offence under this section of the Act is punishable in the magistrates' court with a maximum fine of £5,000. It may go to the Crown Court, which may impose imprisonment of up to two years and an unlimited fine.

7. CONTROL OVER USE OF NETS S.3 SAFFA

SAFFA controls the use of nets for the capture of salmon or migratory trout (s.3). These controls are over and above the licensing controls (see Chapter 12). The size of nets and their use is regulated. None of the controls extend to anglers' landing or keep nets - although these might be controlled by byelaws (see below). The use of nets, generally, as either a means of fishing which may conflict with anglers' interests, or as a means of fishery management used by anglers is complex. This part of the book simply limits itself to s.3 SAFFA. Other relevant controls will be found in Chapter 12, Chapter *15* and Chapter 19.

7.1 Use of draft or seine nets

Seine or draft (these terms mean the same thing: basically a long net with weights on the bottom edge and floats on the top, stretched out into a river or estuary by a boat and then drawn in to the shore by the boat and hauled ashore having trapped the fish in the area enclosed) nets shall not be used in any waters (freshwater or estuarine) across more than three quarters of the width of such waters.

7.2 Mesh sizes

There is also control over mesh sizes in nets (s.3 (2) SAFFA). These provisions apply in relation again to the taking of salmon or migratory trout and do not apply to landing nets used in connection with angling with rod and line. The minimum dimensions are 2" in extension from knot to knot or 8" measured round each mesh when wet. There are additional provisions to prevent these rules being circumvented by putting a number of nets together or putting canvas behind the mesh. These rules establish a standard minimum mesh size. However, byelaws may further restrict mesh sizes or restrict what nets are made of (eg. banning the use of monofilament), or restrict may require the mesh size to be labelled or marked on the net.

7.3 Penalties for net offences under s.3

Breaching the law on the use of seine or draft nets or standard minimum mesh size is punishable by a maximum fine of £2,500.

8. CONTROL OVER FISHING BAITS S.2 SAFFA

It is illegal to fish for salmon, trout or freshwater fish using any fish roe. It is also an offence to buy or sell, or expose for sale, or even possess salmon or trout (but not any other freshwater fish) roe with a view to fishing.

9. PROTECTION OF UNCLEAN AND IMMATURE FISH AND SPAWNING GROUNDS AND FISH S.2 SAFFA

Anglers generally appreciate the importance of protecting spawning fish and young fish in order to promote a healthy fishery. Section 2 SAFFA offers protection in a number of important ways - protection of breeding fish and immature fish, spawn and spawning grounds from disturbance.

9.1 Protection of breeding fish

As to the protection of breeding fish, it is an offence to knowingly take, kill or injure any unclean or immature salmon, trout or freshwater fish, or attempt to do any of these things. For the purposes of the law, unclean means that the fish is either about to spawn or has recently spawned and has not yet recovered. In an unreported Crown Court case (*Pyle v Welsh Water Authority* (1986), the court held that a gravid fish, which, on expert evidence was thought to be about 10 days before spawning, was 'about to spawn' and was therefore unclean. It is important that anglers can recognise the signs of a fish being unclean and, in the case of fishing with a view to killing the fish for the table, that if in any doubt unclean fish are returned to the water when caught accidentally.

The Environment Agency advice on the identification of fish about to spawn and unclean fish which have recently spawned (or kelts as they are often called) is that fish about to spawn are easily identified by the ease with which eggs or milt can be extruded from the vent. As to kelts these are more difficult to identify but features to look for include: (a) gill maggots in salmon; (b) frayed fins; (c) belly normally black; (d) line of back and belly parallel; (e) distinct corner in profile of body at back of skull; (f) vent suffused or spread open.

9.2 Protection of immature fish

Immature fish are defined in relation to their size. The 1975 Act sets the size limit for salmon at 12" (30.5 cm), measured from the tip of the snout to the fork or cleft of the tail. In relation to other fish, immaturity is to be defined by byelaws and will vary from area to area. Once again, if an immature fish is taken it is important that it is returned to the water. The law reflects this good angling practice by providing a defence to offences where unclean or immature fish are caught accidentally. Provided that the fish is returned to the water with the least possible injury, the angler will not have broken the law. Care is needed not to confuse young salmon (parr) with brown trout. Tell-tale signs include distinct fork in tail of salmon parr and differences in fin colours.

9.3 Protection of spawning fish and beds

SAFFA also provides that it is an offence to wilfully disturb any spawn or spawning fish or any bed, bank or shallow where any spawn or spawning fish may be found. On the face of it, this presents a problem for the wading fisherman at a time when fish may be spawning. However, the inclusion of the word 'wilfully' requires that the act of disturbance should be deliberate and intentional. The intention does not have to relate to disturbing fish or spawn where the effect of disturbing shallows or the river bed or bank is to disturb spawn or fish (see *National Rivers Authority v Jones* below). Should an angler disturb an area of breeding fish or spawn, then clearly good sense and the law require him to minimise any disturbance and stop disturbing the area and fish (by, for example, getting out of the river if wading) as soon as possible.

9.3.1 The Jones case on spawning fish and beds

The protection in s.2 SAFFA for spawning fish was considered in the case of *National Rivers Authority v Jones* (1992), which illustrates the breadth of protection given by s.2. The defendant owned land on either side of a river (and presumably was also riparian owner of the stretch in question). He had used a shallow part of the river as a ford for many years for vehicles (though it was possible to use a bridge instead, but with a longer journey). To maintain the ford, gravel had been dug from the banks of the river at the crossing. The defendant was charged with wilfully disturbing a bed, bank or shallows by using the crossing and removing gravel from the bank. At the trial in the magistrates' court, the justices found, as a matter of fact, that spawning fish would be in the area in question. The magistrates acquitted the defendant and the NRA appealed to the High Court on the basis that the justices had misinterpreted the law. The High Court noted that two criminal offences were created in s.2 (4) SAFFA: that of wilful disturbance of spawn or spawning fish and wilful disturbance of any bed, bank or shallow in which any spawn or spawning fish may be found. The High Court directed that the defendant be found guilty of the second offence by the magistrates. He acted wilfully in the sense of having an intention to disturb the shallows or bank in question. Spawning fish were to be found in the area. The presence of a crossing place, however well established, affords no defence to this charge.

9.3.2 Disturbance of spawning fish or beds - defence and use of disturbance offences

The only specific defence to a charge in respect of disturbance of spawn or spawning fish is where there is an established legal right to take materials from waters (see Chapter 15). The disturbance offences may arise in a number of different situations and, for example, canoeists have been successfully prosecuted under s.2 for disturbing a spawning area.

9.4 Defences to disturbance of unclean and immature fish and spawning grounds and fish

SAFFA allows any of these protections to be overridden if the act is done for the preservation or development of a private fishery; or the artificial propagation of salmon, trout or freshwater fish; or for some scientific purpose. In all cases to override the Act, the prior written consent of the Agency is needed. This might be used to move or introduce (subject to the rules considered in Chapter 15) young fish at a fishery, for example.

9.5 Sale of unclean or immature fish

Finally, it is an offence to buy, sell or expose for sale or possess any unclean or immature salmon, trout or freshwater fish, or any part of such a fish.

9.6 Penalties under s.2 SAFFA

In all cases, the offence is punishable by a maximum fine of £2,500. If a prosecution is to be brought, key evidence in most cases will be the gravid or immature fish taken. This may be seized by a bailiff (see Chapter 17). It is obviously perishable and will quickly deteriorate and lose its evidential value. If it is to be disposed of, the prosecutor must, if it is reasonably practicable to do so, inform the accused and give him an opportunity to have the fish examined before disposal: *Anderson v Loverack* (1976). This case also decided that, where appropriate, secondary evidence (ie. not the fish itself but, for example, photographs of it or the water bailiff's description) might be allowed to be used by the prosecution.

10. BYELAWS AND FISHING METHODS AND PLACES

Byelaws clearly vary from area to area and, in many cases, from river to river. In that sense, any text is not very helpful as the only proper advice to the angler or angling club is to make enquiries at the Environment Agency about its local byelaws. However, the power of the Agency to make byelaws in relation to fishing methods and places is set out in Schedule 25 to the Water Resources Act 1991. This includes power to regulate:
  (a) the taking or removal of fish from a particular area;
  (b) the taking of fish by any means, within a specified distance above or below a natural or artificial obstruction, such as a dam or weir;
  (c) the nature of or use of nets for taking salmon, trout, freshwater fish or eels (over and above the requirements set out above). This might also include a ban on the carrying of nets in boats, unless there is a netting licence in place. In addition, it is not uncommon for keep or landing nets to be regulated - in particular their size and mesh;

(d) The use of any bait or lure type with rod and line - so byelaws might require that fishing should be fly only or with no live bait, etc. This may also typically prevent the use of certain baits or floats in fishing for salmon, or ban trolling a bait or lure behind a boat.

10.1 Sanctions for breach of byelaws

For the consequences of breaking byelaws, see Chapter 1. An example of byelaws on fishing methods being tested by the courts is *Brough v National Rivers Authority* (1993). A byelaw covering fishing in the Solway Estuary prohibited the use any net made wholly or partly of monofilament material. The defendant used a net for taking salmon made from a number of monofilament strands twisted together - multi monofilament. The defendant was convicted of breaking the byelaw. The High Court upheld the conviction stating the use of the word 'material' was critical as it encompassed nets made up of many strands of monofilament. The case was not only important for fishing on the Solway, but also shows how important it is for the exact wording of any byelaw to be examined very closely.

10.2 National byelaws Phase 1 and fishing methods and places

The first phase of national fisheries' byelaws, which came into force in 1997 (see Chapter 1), included some byelaws on fishing methods.

10.2.1 National byelaws Phase 1 and use of rods

The byelaws now govern the use of multiples rods (Byelaw 8). When fishing for salmon or trout on rivers, streams, drains or canals, no person shall fish with more than one rod or line. Where salmon or trout are sought in a lake, pond or reservoir, the limit is two rods and lines at the same time. Coarse fishing or eel fishing may allow the use of up to four rods at the same time. Where multiple rods are used, they must be placed such that the distance between the butt ends of the rods is under three metres. Clearly, any fishery owner may impose a more restrictive rule on that particular fishery (see below).

10.2.2 National byelaws Phase 1 and use of gaffs

The use of gaffs is now prohibited under the national byelaws (Byelaw 4).

10.2.3 National byelaws Phase 1 and keepnets, keepsacks and landing nets

Byelaw 5 is, at the time of writing, not yet confirmed but will regulate the use of keepnets, sacks and landing nets. It is proposed to introduce requirements as to their size and manufacture, with effect from 1 April 1998. If the byelaw is confirmed it will make it an offence to use:

(a) a landing net with any knotted meshes or metallic meshes;

(b) a keepnet with any knotted meshes or metallic meshes and having holes in the mesh larger than 25 mm (internal circumference), less than 2 m in length and with supporting rings or frames greater than 40cm apart, or less than 120 cm in circumference;

(c) a keepsack, unless constructed of a soft, dark-coloured, non abrasive, water permeable fabric and being at least 120cm by 90cm (if rectangular) or 150cm by 30cm by 40cm, with a frame or designed with the intention that a frame be used. It will also be an offence to keep more than one fish in a keepsack at any time.

The byelaw will not apply to retaining eels caught other than by angling (for example netted or trapped).

10.2.4 Fishing returns

Byelaw 5 governs the provision of catch return information to the Environment Agency. The Agency can make byelaws requiring the making of annual fishing returns by anglers holding rod licences. The byelaws extend only to those holding salmon and sea trout licences currently, but there is power to extend them to returns concerning freshwater fish and eels. The information required covers the fishing effort and the catch, including whether fish were returned or released.

10.3 National byelaws Phase 2 and fishing methods

Phase 2 of the National Byelaws for Fisheries which went out for consultation in 1997 and will come into force in 1998 include a number of byelaws concerning fishing methods.

10.3 1 Use of crayfish as bait

Byelaw 3 of Phase 2 introduces a ban on the use of live or dead crayfish as bait or parts of crayfish. The aim is to protect native crayfish from Signal Crayfish (see Chapter 16) and from a fungal disease called 'crayfish plague'.

10.3.2 Removal of fish

First, there is ban on the removal of salmon, migratory trout and non-migratory trout from rivers, streams, drains and canals other than by rod and line, unless Agency permission has been obtained (Byelaw 5). This is designed to assist the Agency in its fight against poaching by providing an additional charge which may be brought. It also means prior Agency consent will be needed before tickling trout! This ban applies to fish whether dead or alive. Technically, therefore, Agency consent is needed before removing dead fish which are suspected of being diseased or the victims of pollution.

Secondly, angling - rod and line fishing - is regulated. There is a ban on the removal of fish caught by rod and line on rivers, streams, drains and canals except salmon, trout, char, pike, zander, grayling, eels, minnows and non-native fish (Byelaw 6). Bag limits may apply locally either through fishery rules or through local byelaws. For example, in North Wessex no more than two migratory trout may be removed within 24 hours. Furthermore the new byelaw will not apply to still waters. Nor will the new byelaw prevent the removal of other species which are kept alive in a keepnet and then returned - for example, bream or tench caught during a match.

The removal of fish of less than 20cm by rod and line for use as bait (live or dead) is also permissible up to a maximum of 10 fish per day. Thus, small roach or dace may be removed for this purpose. This exception does not allow the removal of trout or salmon which are undersize. Where fish are to be used as live bait then the fish used in the same water from which they were taken and during the same period of fishing (Byelaw 8).

10.3.3 Return of foul hooked fish

Salmon, trout or sea trout which are foul hooked (other than those in still waters) must be returned immediately. This is designed primarily at assisting the Agency with its fight against poaching by dealing with the common excuse of the poacher that a fish had been foul hooked while lawfully angling (Byelaw 7).

10.3.4 Unattended rods

In addition to the rules contained in s.1 SAFFA concerning cross or set lines and the National Byelaws Phase 1 Byelaw 8 on multiple rods, Phase 2 (Byelaw 10) provides additional controls. It requires that where a bit or hook is in the water, the angler must at all times be able to 'take or exercise immediate physical control over the rod and line'. This clearly has implications for anglers. First, it will be an offence to wander off down the river bank leaving a line in the water. Secondly, it may be possible to be asleep or some distance from rod and line where a fishing alarm is being used.

10.4 Regional byelaws and fishing methods

There are already a range of byelaws affecting different regions in different ways concerning fishing methods. The local Environment Agency office can provide details. Some examples are set out here.

10.4.1 Removal of fish byelaws

Pending the introduction of Phase 2 National Byelaws there are a range of byelaws concerning fish removal. The Yorkshire region, for example, requires the return of foul hooked fish and the Anglian region has rules on the removal of fish for live or dead bait fishing on which the National Byelaws are based.

In addition to these rules many areas have rules on fish size and bag limits. For example, byelaws on size limits tend to set a minimum size of fish by length (from tip of the snout to cleft of the tail). The size limits do not apply generally to fish unintentionally caught and returned as soon as possible with minimum injury to the fish. Bag limits are now being imposed in a number of areas on salmon and migratory trout because of fears over stock levels. These may set limits for the number of fish to be taken in a 24 hour period, over a 7 day period or within a season.

10.4.2 Unattended rods

Not only do anglers risk breaching the rules on the use of cross or set lines in s.1 SAFFA (see above) by leaving a rod or rods unattended, but they may also commit a byelaw offence. These vary but, for example, in the Midlands Region state that

> No person shall leave a rod and line with its bait or hook in the water unattended or out of sight or so that that person shall be able at any time to take or exercise immediate physical control over the said rod and line.

A byelaw of this nature is designed to allow the use, for example, of audible bite alarms where the angler cannot see his rod. National Byelaws will extend this type of rule to all areas.

10.4.3 Fishing from boats

There are a wide range of byelaws governing trolling or trailing from moving boats. In many regions there are no applicable byelaws. In Anglian and Thames Regions, existing byelaws prohibit trolling or trailing except by rod and line where the boat is being rowed or drifting. In the Midlands, there is a total ban on rivers and streams of trailing or trolling from moving boats. These byelaws are to be revoked by the National Byelaws Phase 2. Trolling may well be illegal under s.1 SAFFA (see above 1.1.2).

10.4.4 Permitted baits

Different regions, rivers or even parts of rivers may have byelaws regulating the use of bait. These may also vary at different times of the season. For example, many salmon rivers will prohibit the use of maggot, worm, shrimp, prawn or even spinning. Alternatively, fishing byelaws sometimes say that fishing is to be by one method only - for example, artificial fly.

11. CONTROL OVER THE USE OF LEAD

Following great concern over the effect of lead on wild birds - in particular swan populations - the supply of lead weights weighing between 0.06 and 28.35 grams is banned by the Control of Pollution (Anglers' Lead Weights) Regulations 1986 (SI 1986/1992). Strictly, the use of lead shot or ledgers between those weights is not against the law but hopefully anglers have now used or disposed of their old lead weights.

12. FISH FARMING AND PROHIBITED METHODS

Fish farms require special rules on methods of fishing and use of apparatus which would otherwise fall foul of the many restrictions set out in this chapter. The Fisheries Act 1981 sets out the range of exemptions. In order to claim any of these special privileges as to method, etc., the fish farmer must hold an exemption granted by the Ministry of Agriculture Fisheries and Food. This might permit, for example, the taking of unclean fish for stripping, or allow the netting of a whole water, or the use of nets otherwise prohibited. This relaxation over the regulation of the fishery (together with other advantages) may make it worthwhile for a stillwater fishery to be registered as a fish farm. This issue is considered in Chapter 15.

13. CRIMINAL PROSECUTION FOR PROHIBITED METHODS, ETC. TACKLE FORFEITURE AND LICENCE DISQUALIFICATION AND FIXED PENALTIES. SCHEDULE 4 SAFFA AND S.37A SAFFA

All of the matters considered above in this chapter are criminal offences and the penalties vary from offence to offence, as has been seen. At extremes, a person may be imprisoned. At the very least, a fine may be imposed. In addition to these powers, if a prosecution is brought, the court may also order the forfeiture of any fish illegally taken (or in that person's possession), tackle or instrument used in committing the offence (Schedule 4 SAFFA). In some cases which are serious enough to go to the Crown Court, an order forfeiting a boat used in the offence (for example of illegal netting) may be made.

   In addition, the court may disqualify the offender from fishing or holding a licence (of any description specified, whether for rod and line or otherwise) for a period of up to five years (Schedule 4 SAFFA). If the offender held a licence, then they must surrender this to the court at the time of the disqualification. On conviction for any of these offences, the Agency will be sent a certificate of conviction and details of any disqualification. This will be particularly important where the Agency has not brought the case to court. For example, where it is a police matter, or a private prosecution.

Finally, the new provisions on issuing fixed penalty notices apply to prosecutions for many offences concerning illegal methods. The fixed penalty system is considered in Chapter 1.

14. METHODS AND THE PRIVATE FISHERY

It is very important to understand that this chapter has set out the public rules on fishing methods. These may vary from fishery to fishery, by virtue of byelaws. In addition to complying with these rules, any angler must also obey the conditions imposed by a private fishery owner, whether an individual or a club (often via the Club Rules). Fishery owners or clubs will often impose more strict limits on fishing method - for example dry fly only, or barbless hooks only, or catch limits. The consequences of breaking the public law rules are very serious: criminal prosecution, tackle forfeiture and being banned from holding a licence at worst.

Breaking the rules applied to an individual fishery by a fishery owner is not so serious in legal consequences. You may become a trespasser and be asked to leave the water immediately. You may be banned from obtaining a licence to fish that stretch of water again. You might be expelled from the club, in the case of club waters. There are, however, areas of uncertainty. If you exceed the number of fish allowed to be taken in a day: can that part of the catch be forfeited? If damage is caused to the fishery but breaking a rule about, for example, only fishing from established 'pegs': can compensation be sought for the necessary repairs? For certainty's sake, it is wise for the fishery owner or club to set out the consequences in their rule book so that everyone knows where they stand.

QUESTIONS

Question 1.

Our club owns the fishing rights to a stretch of water on a river. We have become plagued by small 'jack' pike which, not only interfere with the trout fishing, but also, we believe, are a cause of many of the fish being stunted. We wish to remove the pike and destroy them. We have found a local contractor who has agreed to electro-fish the water for us. What legal requirements do we have to consider ?

Answer

Two important legal issues arise. First, you will need to obtain the prior written consent of the Environment Agency for the electro-fishing. You will have to be in a position to convince the Agency of the need for the clearance of stock to protect or improve the fishery. You may need to consider what evidence you have to support your claim - this may just be anecdotal from club officers, or the club water keeper, or might be supported by fishing records (of fish size and numbers of pike seen or caught). Secondly, you need to be sure that you have, either from your ownership of the fishing rights or by specific consent, the permission of the riparian owner. Fishing rights may well be limited to rod and line requiring further consent for electro-fishing.

Question 2.

I recently caught a seatrout towards the end of the season. It put up little or no fight. When I landed it, I discovered it was in poor condition (ragged fins, etc.) and was very dark with no real sheen to the scales. I returned the fish. My friends down the pub told me that I should have taken the fish and it would have tasted all right. Did I do right ?

Answer

Yes. It sounds like the fish was unclean or gravid and probably had just spawned and was on its way back to sea. It is a criminal offence to take or kill an unclean fish. Try to catch it again on its way back up the river next year!

CHAPTER 14

CLOSE SEASONS

1.1 Sources of law on close seasons

The rules on close seasons are a complex mixture of law applicable to the whole of England and Wales under the Salmon and Freshwater Fisheries Act 1975 (SAFFA) and byelaws made by the Agency (or by, before them, the National Rivers Authority or regional water authority). These byelaws have to fit into the framework of rules imposed by the 1975 Act. This chapter will consider the rules applicable to angling with rod and line and, then, how these rules adapt to fishing by other methods, such as nets and traps. The 1975 Act required all water authorities (as they then were) to make byelaws determining close seasons and close times for their areas. The position has been simplified to a degree by the national byelaws which have standardised close seasons for coarse fishing (and in many cases removed the coarse fish closed season) and rainbow trout fishing.

Different rules are applicable for salmon, migratory or seatrout, other trout (primarily browns) and char, rainbow trout and freshwater fish, which excludes trout (of all kinds) and salmon and excludes eels. Within the definition of eels are included elvers and eel fry.

The purpose of the rules in all cases, of course, is to protect fish during spawning periods and prevent overfishing generally. In recent years, a gradual relaxation of the byelaws has taken place, especially on some coarse waters and many artificial fisheries holding rainbow trout. The Water Resources Act 1991 now states that byelaws may dispense with a close season entirely for freshwater fish or rainbow trout.

1.2 Anglers and close seasons

This chapter can only set out the general framework of rules and it is important that local byelaws are consulted for any fishery an angler is proposing to fish for salmon or trout. It is important to note that the close season for one type of fish may be different from the close season for another. For example, it is not uncommon for the seatrout season to close before the salmon season, or for brown trout fishing to end but fishing for grayling to be allowed to continue through the winter. It is common on coarse waters for eel fishing to be permitted during the closed season. This raises the issue of what anglers should do if they catch a species for which the season is closed and to what extent the angler needs to take steps (by choice of lure, bait or technique) to minimise the risk of catching a 'protected' fish.

Where a byelaw or the general law sets down a close season, then fishing is permitted on the dates stated in the byelaws or Schedule 1 SAFFA - for example, in the case of the standard salmon close season from 31st October to 1st February (dates are inclusive, ie. fishing is not permitted between midnight 31st October and midnight 31st January).

1.3 Close season law and fishery rules

Finally, all of these rules must be considered alongside the rules applicable to the particular fishery. A riparian owner (whether via a club's rules or directly in the terms of the day, week or season ticket) is entitled to set their own season - within the limits of the applicable law. So, for example, a particular river may have a byelaw season for brown trout closing on 31 October, but for whatever reasons, the riparian owner fixes the closed season for brown trout on his stretch of water for 30 September. In order to avoid the risk, at best of being thrown off the water and banned from the fishery or at worst being accused of poaching, anglers obviously have to comply with the earlier date. Anglers are not at risk of being prosecuted under the rules detailed in this chapter, but will be fishing without authorisation which has its own consequences considered in Chapter 15.

2. ANGLING CLOSE SEASONS - SALMON

Unless byelaws say otherwise, the annual close season for salmon angling is from 31 October to 1 February (Schedule 1 of the 1975 Act). Although the dates may vary from water to water - for example, byelaws in some late running West Country salmon rivers, such as the Camel or Fowey, start the close season in mid December.

It is an offence to fish for, take, kill or attempt to take or kill salmon with a rod and line during the annual close season (s.19 (1) SAFFA). However, there is an exception in respect of capture with the Agency's consent for scientific research or artificial breeding (although it seems unlikely that rod and line would ever be an appropriate method of capture in these circumstances) (s.19 (3) SAFFA).

More importantly, it is necessary to show an intention to catch salmon for the offence to be committed. Thus, in *Cain v Campbell* (1978), a fisherman set out nets to capture sea fish. Incidentally, he captured salmon. This was during the annual close season for salmon. However, the court held that he was not guilty of the offence because of the lack of intention. In relation to angling, clearly key factors are going to be the type of bait or lure being used and the fishing place and whether it was lawful to be fishing for other species. If an angler is, for example, fishing a mixed coarse and salmon fishery during the salmon close season and hooks a salmon whilst fishing for pike, it will be very difficult to establish the intention to attempt to take salmon. However, if the angler goes on to land and kill the salmon an offence of 'taking' will be committed. If the fish is gravid (a fish that is about to or has recently spawned) a further offence may be committed under s.2 SAFFA (see Chapter 13).

3. ANGLING CLOSE SEASONS - MIGRATORY AND BROWN TROUT

Subject to byelaws setting another season, the annual close season for trout but not including rainbows, is between 30 September and 1 March (Schedule 1 SAFFA). It is an offence for any person to fish for, take, kill, or attempt to take or kill trout (other than rainbows) during the close season. There are defences, as for salmon, in respect of taking for scientific purposes or breeding. The same considerations as to proving intention apply as for salmon.

4. ANGLING CLOSE SEASONS - OTHER FRESHWATER FISH AND RAINBOW TROUT

There is no standardised close season for rainbow trout set out in SAFFA. Schedule 1 to the Act merely says that byelaws may fix the annual close season. The national byelaws made in 1997 have removed the close season for rainbow trout where fishing takes place by rod and line in a reservoir, lake or pond. This is the case regardless of whether the fish can or cannot swim into other waters.

Byelaws may dispense with a close season for other freshwater fish altogether, but, where this is not done, the close season for freshwater fish is from 15 March to 15 June. However, the national byelaws have now gone some way to eliminating the coarse fishing close season. The statutory close season continues to apply to fishing in rivers, streams and drains and some canals (as listed in Byelaw 6) and in addition to waters in the Norfolk Broads and fisheries within listed sites of special scientific interest in (Schedule 3 to the National Byelaws). In all other waters - principally, any still waters - the coarse fishing close season has been abolished.

Even on those waters where the close season has not been lifted, it is permissible to fish by rod and line for eels between 15 March and 15 June.

It is a criminal offence to fish for, take, kill or attempt to take or kill freshwater fish or rainbow trout during a close season, where one applies. It is also an offence to fish for eels with rod and line during this period, despite their exclusion from the definition of freshwater fish (s.41 SAFFA).

4.1 Exceptions to out of season fishing offences for coarse fish or rainbow trout

There are, however, are a number of exceptions to these offences. These exceptions, in fact, allow freshwater fish and eels, in many cases, to be fished for out of season. In some cases, this may result in a risk of catching unclean or gravid fish. This is separately regulated and is considered in *Chapter 13*.

4.1.1 Eels and close seasons

First, it is common for byelaws to allow fishing for eels with rod and line (sometimes limited to ledgering with worm) during the close season and this exception is specifically mentioned in s.19 SAFFA. These rules will continue to apply to waters where there is a close season under the national byelaws.

4.1.2 Scientific purposes and removal for bait

Secondly, it is permissible to take freshwater fish or rainbow trout for scientific purposes. Thirdly, freshwater fish may be taken for bait if this is not prohibited by byelaw. For example, byelaws may govern the size of fish which it is permissible to take.

4.1.3 Special preservation of salmon or trout

In addition, there are a couple of further exceptions applicable to specific types of fishery. In respect of a several fishery (see Chapter 4, but basically a fishery where the fishing rights are held exclusively by one or more persons), in which salmon or trout are found and are being specially preserved the removal of any eels, freshwater fish or rainbow trout not being specially preserved, is permitted out-of-season. The removal of any such fish has to be by the owner or occupier or someone acting on their behalf (with the prior written permission of the owner or occupier). Thus, for example, if an exclusive wild brown trout fishery wishes to remove rainbows or grayling, then this may be possible by out-of-season fishing. It relies on establishing special preservation. This was considered in the 1981 case of *Thames Water Authority v Homewood*. The facts were that a 13-acre lake was operated as a commercial mixed fishery, offering both coarse and rainbow trout fishing. There was annual stocking with rainbow trout (approximately 200 each year). The owner of the fishery allowed fishing (on payment) during the freshwater fish close season for pike and perch. As a result, the owner was prosecuted for out-of-season fishing. The magistrates acquitted him, holding that the fishery was specially preserved and that the out-of-season fishing was aimed primarily at protecting the stocked trout from predation by pike and perch. On appeal, the High Court held that the key factors were to consider what had been done to preserve salmon or, as in this case, trout, and whether the out-of-season fishing was directed primarily at out-of-season fishing or at fishery preservation. As the magistrates had directed themselves at the correct questions, their decision was upheld, although the court expressed some surprise at the conclusion they reached, given the number of stocked fish and size of the lake.

4.1.4 Removal for bait in a several fishery

The final exception to out-of-season fishing is that freshwater fish may be taken for bait in a several fishery, with the permission in writing of its owner or occupier.

5. OUT-OF-SEASON ANGLING OFFENCES - s.19 SAFFA

Out-of-season fishing is punishable by a fine of up to £2,500 (Schedule 4 SAFFA). In addition, there are powers of tackle forfeiture, licence disqualification and the possibility of fixed penalty notices. These are considered separately in Chapter 1.

The close season offences are based on the words 'fishes for, takes, kills or attempts to take or kill.' These words are fairly straightforward but it is clear from *Cain v Campbell* above that some intention to take unseasonable fish must be shown. The meaning of the word 'take' was considered in *Lee v Evans* (1980). Although the charge was for unlicensed fishing, the same principles of interpretation apply. Mr Justice Watkins who dealt with the appeal in the High Court, when commenting on the defendant's version of events, said:

> I feel bound to say that the story told to the justices by the defendant was a tall one, measured even by the standards of fishing stories emanating from West Wales.

His story was that he had fished at night for sea fish with a net in an estuary. He hauled the net in and, although he says he did not know it at the time, he had caught ten sea trout. He then put the net with fish in it in a sack and walked home (his home was 300-400 yards away). On his way home he was challenged by a water bailiff. He said his intention was, once home, if he discovered any salmon or seatrout, to return them to the water. It was found that he knew it was likely as not that he would catch seatrout or salmon. He also knew that he would take out of the water all fish that he had caught. This was enough to show he had taken the fish. There might be an exceptional case where, as soon as possible - say, in this case, by torchlight at the estuary edge - fish were returned to the water. Anything less than such behaviour would justify a 'taking' conviction.

If no fish are taken and, therefore, the applicable law is fishing for unseasonable fish, it will be necessary to show an intention to catch unseasonable fish. This may be done by reference to the fishing methods, the types of fish likely to be in the waters in question and what the angler says he is doing. If fish are taken then, unless dead before they are taken, or returned as soon as they are seen to be unseasonable, it seems an offence will be committed. The meaning of 'kills' or 'attempts to kill' seem clear. Where fish are taken and form part of the evidence in the prosecution it seems likely the courts will require compliance with the rules in the *Anderson v Loverack* (1976) case, described in Chapter 13. See also Chapter 12 on rod and net licensing.

6. CLOSE SEASONS AND OTHER FISHING METHODS

For other fishing methods - for example, nets or traps - there are further fishing restrictions in many cases. The offences are again punishable by fine of up to £2,500 as described above (Schedule 4 SAFFA). Anglers will be interested in these rules to see that other fishermen (particularly in practice on the lower tidal and estuarine stretches of salmon and seatrout rivers) are not abusing the rules and, as a result, taking more fish from the water. First of all, there are weekly close times for salmon and trout. These are periods of 48 hours between 6am on Saturday and 6am on Monday. Byelaws again may vary these times. A distinction is drawn between fishing for salmon with putts and putchers (types of wicker baskets or traps) which may take place during the weekly close time and other types of non rod and line fishing which may not. Byelaws may set a separate close season for fishing with putts or putchers.

The scientific and breeding exceptions to the offences, mentioned above, also apply to fishing other than with rod and line. Fixed engines (see Chapter 19) have to be removed or made ineffective during the close season and weekly close time, except, once again, for putts and putchers which are exempted from the weekend close period rules.

Other than trout and salmon fishing, there are no special rules except for the position of eels and the protection of descending salmon and sea trout from traps, etc., considered below. It is therefore, a criminal offence to fish for freshwater fish and rainbow trout during the close season, unless one of the various exceptions outlined above in relation to rod and line fishing can be made out.

As to the special rules on eels, the basic proposition is that they can be sought with traps. etc., at any time. However, this presents the problem that other fish may be caught 'accidentally'. Therefore, it is an offence (s.21 SAFFA) to use any basket, net, trap or device for catching eels before 25 June in any waters with a salmon or sea trout run. It is also an offence to place on the apron of a weir any basket, trap or device for taking fish (except wheels or leaps for taking lampreys or, as they are sometimes called, lamperns) between 1 August and the following 1 March. However, this does not prevent the use of eel baskets (with a diameter of 10") provided it is constructed to be fished with bait and is not used in certain prohibited places. These include dams, obstructions, or artificial channels. The Environment Agency can also authorise the use of other devices for the taking of eels at any time.

Finally, there is protection for descending migratory fish on rivers containing salmon or seatrout. Before 25 June, anyone who places any device to catch or obstruct fish descending the river commits an offence (s.21 SAFFA).

7. INDIRECT SEASONAL CONTROLS - SALES ETC. OF SALMON AND TROUT

Indirect controls over dealing in salmon and trout during the close season and in suspicious circumstances attempt to reinforce the rules, both on close seasons and poaching.

There are various controls over salmon and trout sales to back the provisions relating to close seasons. There is a system of licensing of dealers in salmon under the Salmon Act 1986. In addition, s.22 SAFFA controls sales of salmon and trout (other than rainbow trout) during the close season. Sales are prohibited, unless the seller can show that the fish was lawfully received - for example, they were caught during open season or come from a fish farm (see s.33 Fisheries Act 1981).

There are also rules on the export of salmon during the close season. Finally, a person who receives salmon, or who assists in their retention or disposal in the belief or where they should suspect that the salmon was illegally taken, will commit a criminal offence under the Salmon Act 1986.

QUESTIONS

Question 1.

We operate a mixed fishery of stocked brown trout and salmon fishing but there are some rainbows in the water. We allow out of season fishing for rainbows. Recently, one of our club members was observed during the close season for salmon, casting a slow sinking fly line into one of the key holding pools for salmon on the fishery. When asked by another club member what he was fishing with, he showed the angler a Jock Scott - a large salmon fly. We have formally warned him that he is breaking the law. He denies this. Who is right ?

Answer

This is murky waters as far as the law is concerned. Certainly, it is an offence under s.19 SAFFA to fish for salmon out-of-season and the offence covers attempting to take fish as well as catching them. If it is unlikely that the fly in question would attract rainbow trout, or that rainbows would be found deep in that pool, then it might be possible to say that an offence had been committed. It would strengthen the case even more if there was evidence that salmon had been seen recently in the pool. However, the case would be an uncertain prosecution where the standard of proof is to show that he was attempting to take salmon beyond any reasonable doubt. If need be, consider whether your club rules allow any disciplinary action to be taken.

Question 2.

We operate a mixed coarse and rainbow trout fishery in a stretch of canal. There is a natural head of perch and pike in the water which we consider to be undesirable. Most of our coarse fishing is for carp. We wish to be able to stock the fishery with small rainbows which can grow on, but have been advised by a stocking firm that this is unwise, as given the head of predators, many would be eaten before maturity. In the light of this, we are considering out of season fishing for pike and perch. Will this be within the law.

Answer

This is a fairly unusual set of facts. However, they raise interesting legal issues, as the coarse fish and rainbow trout close seasons are assumed to be still applicable to this water. This concerns s.19 SAFFA and, in particular, the exemption from the criminal offence of fishing for freshwater fish or rainbow trout in a fishery where salmon or, as in this case, trout, are specially preserved. Assuming this is a several fishery (and that the club is the owner or occupier of the fishery) the real issue is whether it is 'specially preserving' trout. This was the issue in the *Thames Water Authority v Homewood* case. It is necessary to consider what has been done in the past to preserve the trout fishing, for the fishery must be specially preserved already. Has trout stocking already taken place? Is there a direction to remove pike or perch in the club rules, whether caught in or out of season? Given this is a stretch of canal, is the removal of predators pointless as others will simply move in from elsewhere? What other steps have been taken to promote the rainbow trout within the fishery? Is a charge to be levied for out-of-season fishing? Is there any way that it might be argued that this is merely a way of 'dodging' the close season? These are the sorts of issues that need to be weighed up before a final view can be reached. Even then, as the court noted in the *Thames Water Authority* case there is a considerable degree of ambiguity about the meaning of 'specially preserved'. It would seem sensible to discuss the matter with the local office of the Environment Agency. The Agency, nationally, is undertaking a review of the operation of close seasons on canals.

CHAPTER 15

FISHERY IMPROVEMENT

This chapter is concerned with fishery improvement by a fishery owner or club. It is based on the assumption that the fishing rights are owned together, with all riparian rights, by the persons seeking to improve or develop the fishery. This means that (see Chapter 5) the ownership of the bed and banks is vested in such a person. The chapter will consider a number of issues. In relation to rivers: what consents are needed to make bank improvements, alter the river course or remove weed and stock or remove fish. In addition, this chapter will briefly consider the issues involved in constructing a lake or pond.

1. PLANNING

There are a number of situations, considered below, where planning consent may be needed to improve or develop a fishery. The planning system is complex and all that can be included here is a fairly brief overview of the system and some indications of how it applies to angling issues. For further reference, see, for example, Telling & Duxbury *Planning Law & Procedure* (9th Ed. Butterworths), or Heap *An Outline of Planning Law* (10th Ed. Sweet & Maxwell). Planning permission is needed whenever 'development' is carried out. Development is defined, in s.55 Town and Country Planning Act 1990 (TCPA), as the carrying out of any building, engineering, mining or other operations in, on or under land or the making of any material change in the use of any land. Planning permission is generally sought from the local planning authority - basically the local authority and normally the district council of an area where there is two tier local government. In national parks, the planning application is made to the county council or, where established, the national park authority. In addition, there are one or two exceptional situations where local authorities do not deal with planning applications -for example, within the Norfolk Broads, the Broads Authority is the planning authority and, in areas of urban regeneration, urban development corporations may deal with planning matters.

1.1 Planning procedure

There are some general points to make about planning consent. First, any application requires the payment of a fee and completion of various forms that are available from the local planning authority. An application for planning permission can be made retrospectively (ie. after the building is built or change of use has taken place). This is not particularly desirable, but does mean that if it was not appreciated that planning consent was needed, an application can still be made to regularise the position. Secondly, the determination of the application is usually by councillors in committee, but may sometimes be delegated to a local authority officer - in the case of less important applications. Thirdly, in making any decision the local authority will have to weigh up all relevant considerations including, for example, any objections and the nature and impact of the proposal. Traffic implications are often important along with visual impact. Other relevant factors are the sensitivity of the area (for example, in open countryside, an Area of Outstanding Natural Beauty - designated by the Countryside Commission, under the Countryside Act 1968; or a National Park - designated by the Secretary of State for the Environment, Transport and the Regions in England, or the Secretary of State for Wales in Wales, under the National Parks and Access to the Countryside Act 1949; or a conservation area, under the Town and Country Planning Act 1990). However, this broad discretion is not exercised in a vacuum. There are sources of local and national policy which give broad guidelines on how an application may be dealt with.

1.2 Planning - policy guidance

National policy is laid down in planning policy guidance notes and Department of the Environment Circulars and, after May 1997, Department of the Environment, Transport and Regions (DETR) Circulars. Both types of documents are issued by the DETR and the Welsh Office. They are subjected to public consultation when in draft form but are *not* subject to any Parliamentary approval. Copies can be obtained from Her Majesty's Stationery Office. *Planning Policy Guidance Note 17 (PPG 17)* covers the issues of Sport and Recreation. It in fact only mentions fishing once in passing but some of the general policy statements clearly are relevant to angling. The policy is supportive of sport and recreation and encourages the planning system to make available sufficient land and water resources for recreation. For planning applications in the countryside (including National Parks, Areas of Outstanding Natural Beauty or nature reserves), the aim should be, where possible, to reconcile the interests of the sport with the locality.

1.3 Planning - development plans

Local policies are contained in any development plans for the area (and *PPG 17* encourages the inclusion of policies on sport and recreation). These are structure plans (for a county council), local plans (for a district council) and unitary development plans for an area where there is only one tier of local government. They are substantial documents, often with hundreds of policies covering a multitude of matters. In addition to the text, there will be a plan or series of plans colour coding different 'zones' in which different policies apply and where types of development would generally be acceptable. Plans take several years to create - going through detailed statutory procedures. Either a local authority office or reference library will hold copies of any development plans or drafts for the area. These plans will often have policies for dealing with planning applications to do with recreation which may provide useful arguments in favour of planning applications for fishing matters and in other circumstances when planning permission is needed. Local policies will obviously vary from area to area. Where a plan has been finally adopted, s.54A Town and Country Planning Act 1990 creates a presumption that the policies shall be followed. This is why these documents are now crucial. Section 54A TCPA says that, where a development plan policy applies, that policy shall be applied unless material considerations indicate otherwise. This means that for a development plan not to be followed there must clear identifiable planning related reasons. This presumption applies not only to planning applications but also to planning appeals determined by inspectors appointed by the Secretary of State for the Environment, Transport and the Regions, or for Wales.

It is possible for local policies to exist, but not in the formal development plan format. This may be because the plan is in a draft or, as it is often called, 'emerging form' which, unfortunately is not uncommon because of the complexity of finalising development plans. Alternatively, the policy may be of the sort that is not going to ever be included in a development plan - sometimes called 'bottom drawer policies'. In relation to angling, an example of a bottom drawer policy was considered in *Re Inverness, Loch Ness and Nairn Tourist Board* (1988). In this case, an application for planning permission for a trout farm was made to the Highland Regional Council. The structure and local plans had no policies on this type of development. An informal policy of encouraging fish farms in suitable locations was applied by the Council and upheld by the courts, even though it obviously had not been through the rigorous but lengthy process of being incorporated into a development plan.

1.4 The planning decision

Besides the applicable policies (local or national), the planning authority must take into account any representations which are made in support of or opposition to the proposal. These may come from members of the public or pressure groups. All planning applications are subject to some sort of publicity and most are advertised in the local press. The precise publicity requirements for different types of application are set out in the Town and Country Planning (General Development Procedure) Order 1995 (SI 1995/419). Finally, there are statutory requirements for consultation between the local planning authority and various other bodies. For example, the Environment Agency will be consulted on developments which may have an impact on water resources or a significant polluting effect. These consultation requirements are contained in the 1995 General Procedure Order and have recently been amended to ensure that British Waterways is consulted on developments which may affect various waterways.

The overall effect of the consideration of national and local policies, representations and the results of any consultation, is to give the planning authority all the information (or material considerations) on which to base their decision. Anglers and angling clubs are clearly entitled to be part of that process.

Planning permission may be granted, subject to conditions (for example, as to design or landscaping or access) or refused. In either case, an appeal may be lodged to the Secretary of State (for the Environment, Transport and Regions, or Wales) if the applicant is dissatisfied with the result (s.78 TCPA). Objectors do not have any rights of appeal against a grant of planning permission, although in some limited circumstances they may be able to challenge the decision of the planning authority by judicial review. There is a range of enforcement powers available to local planning authorities to ensure planning rules are followed (Part VII TCPA). These include the service of an enforcement notice requiring a particular building or structure to be removed or a use cease. Appeals can be made against such a notice to an inspector appointed by the Secretary of State for the Environment, Transport and the Regions or Wales. Grounds of appeal include that permission should be granted retrospectively.

Finally, it is important to note that planning permission can be granted automatically without the need for an application for planning permission by development order (s.59 TCPA). There is a general development order which automatically grants planning consent for a range of minor developments - the Town and Country Planning (General Permitted Development) Order 1995 (SI 1995/418). These automatic planning permissions are strictly called 'permitted development rights'. They may be withdrawn in a particular area by a local authority resolution (which normally has to be approved by the Secretary of State for the Environment, Transport and the Regions or Wales) called an Article 4 direction. It is important to check this has not been done before relying on permitted development rights.

In general, planning officers in local authorities are usually helpful and liaison with them often will assist in avoiding problems and overcoming planning objections.

1.5 Angling and planning

Anglers or clubs may come across the planning system in two ways. First, because an activity or project that they are undertaking may need planning consent. Secondly, because they wish to object to planning permission being granted for some development which may adversely affect angling interests. For example, planning consent may be sought for a sewage treatment works. In these cases, it is worth remembering that most planning applications have to be publicised in some way - normally by advertisement in the local newspapers. There is then an opportunity to send in written objections and lobby councillors.

The very act of using a pond or lake as a fishery when it previously has not been so used (leaving aside the need for planning consent for construction of a lake or pond which is considered below) will almost certainly amount to a material change of use. In addition, intensification of fishing on a lake or pond from, say, a few friends using a water to an organised club offering day and season tickets will probably need planning consent (as was the case in *Turner v Secretary of State for the Environment and Macclesfield Borough Council* (1992) where it was accepted that such an intensification of use of gravel pits for fishing was development). There are certain developments which do not require express planning permission and are deemed to have planning consent under the Town and Country Planning (General Permitted Development) Order 1995. These include, in Part 4 of Schedule 2, temporary uses or buildings allowing such uses for up to 28 days every calendar year. A farmer or landowner might use this, for example, to permit intensive fishing on a previously unused lake or pond.

2. BANK IMPROVEMENTS

Typically, this may involve removing trees or other vegetation (or planting new trees, etc.) and constructing better means of access to the water. Steps may have to be cut into the bank and, perhaps, small jetties or pegs constructed. In general, providing the owner of the banks is agreeable, there should be no legal problems. For a club it may be worth seeking the consent in advance in the form of lease or licence for fishing rights to carry out maintenance and improvements on the banks (see Chapter 5).

There are one or two possible small potential legal pitfalls. In unusual cases, trees may be protected by a tree preservation order under the TCPA, or by virtue of being in a conservation area under the Planning (Listed Buildings and Conservation Areas) Act 1990. Owners should be aware of any such restrictions or, if in doubt, contact the local planning authority. In due course, certain hedgerows may also be legally protected under s.97 Environment Act 1995. This section provides for local authorities to identify 'important' hedgerows which will then be legally protected. The criteria for 'importance' include the age of the hedge and whether it forms part of a traditional boundary. Owners will be notified should a hedge on their land be designated as 'important'.

Where vegetation is being cut back or removed in any quantity, care needs to be taken to comply with s.90 Water Resources Act 1991, which is considered later in this chapter.

Should bank improvements be on a major scale (for example by piling or placing rubble to protect banks from erosion), then it may constitute engineering operations requiring planning permission. If the works are being carried out for agricultural purposes, this may then remove the need to make any application for consent because the rights to develop may be conferred by the Town and Country Planning (General Permitted Development) Order 1995 (SI 1995/418). The use of major plant or machinery - JCBs or bulldozers - may be a rule of thumb test, but if in doubt, consult with the local planning authority

Where bank improvements are on a navigable river, it is important that they do not actually interfere with rights of navigation but, subject to that qualification, structures such as jetties, landing stages or fishing pegs are permissible, even if they protrude into the river (see for example *Tate & Lyle v Greater London Council* (1983)).

4. FISHING HUTS AND CAR PARKS

Strange though it may seem, fishing huts (even though they may be quite small), assuming that they are reasonably permanent in nature and therefore buildings within the TCPA, strictly need planning consent from the local planning authority. The planning authority will be concerned about the location and design of the hut (to ensure that it is not an eyesore) and that it is genuinely for use as a fishing hut. *PPG 17* says that even in areas of planning restriction (such as Green Belts) it may be possible to allow small unobtrusive buildings ancillary to sport.

As to car parks or hard standing areas (and roads or trackways linking them to the highway), these may be constructed by farmers (on larger farms) or foresters under the Town and Country Planning (General Permitted Development) Order 1995 (SI 1995/418) - see Schedule 2 Parts 6 and 7 for the details - without planning permission, if needed for agricultural or forestry purposes. These exemptions are considered in connection with the general issue of whether an angling club may find it advantageous to register as a fish farm below. If the hard standing or car park is needed for angling, then planning permission will be needed assuming that the works involved are building or engineering operations or even if there are minimal works involved where the creation of the car park will result in a change of use of the land (from, for example, agriculture to recreation). Where a trackway to a public highway is proposed, the traffic safety implications will be crucial.

It must be borne in mind that fairly major works such as these obviously will also need the consent of the landowner if the fishing club or angler does not own the land in question.

5. WEED

Rivers may become choked with weed particularly in summer months. Fishing can become impossible as a result. Weed cutting on many rivers has become a necessary event, once or several times a season. In addition, weed removal may be undertaken as part of a programme to improve or develop an existing fishery. It needs, first of all, to be established that the angler or club is entitled to cut the weed or bank vegetation. If the fishery owner also owns the land (ie. is a corporeal owner) and banks, no problems arise, except under statute (see below). If all that the fishing club or angler holds are mere fishing rights or a licence to fish, then the position is more complex. First of all, the document giving ownership of the fishing rights to the angler or club - such as the conveyance, Land or Charge Certificate, lease or licence - needs to be consulted. Secondly, certain rights may be implied into a grant or lease of fishing rights, where the lease or licence does not make the position clear (see *Caldwell v Kilkelly* (1905) - considered below).

A person who causes or permits weed or vegetation to be cut or uprooted in freshwater rivers, lakes, ponds or canals without Environment Agency consent is at risk of committing a criminal offence under s.90 Water Resources Act 1991. The underlying purpose of the s.90 offence is to prevent large amounts of vegetation getting into water and rotting, causing oxygen loss which may distress or kill fish. The offence may also be committed where bank vegetation is cut or uprooted so that it falls into such waters. However, there are a number of ways of avoiding committing the offence. First, if a consent has been obtained from the Environment Agency. Secondly, defences are available where all reasonable steps are taken to remove the vegetation from the waters. Thus, for example lakes or ponds can have weed cut without consent where the weed is then removed. This may be more tricky in flowing or fast flowing rivers. Even so, what is required to be shown is not that the weed was all removed, but that all *reasonable* steps were taken to remove it. Finally, weed cutting is permissible where a statutory power relating to drainage, flood prevention or navigation is being exercised.

Should the offence be committed the maximum fine is £2,500

The rather unpleasant habit of people dumping garden waste (grass clippings, etc.) into rivers may be a criminal offence under s.85 of the 1991 Act (see Chapter 9).

Where weed is cut and removed, legal issues may be encountered over its disposal. The weed is waste within Part II of the Environmental Protection Act 1990. This means that a *waste* management licence must be obtained from the Environment Agency for its lawful disposal. However, plant matter or dredgings may be deposited without the need for a waste management licence if there is compliance with the conditions in Paragraph 25 of Schedule 1 to Waste Management Licensing Regulations 1994 (SI 1994/1056). This states that the deposit of waste material must be along the bank or towpath where the dredging or clearing takes place (or elsewhere, so long as it is along a bank or towpath, and is of agricultural or ecological benefit) and must not exceed 50 tonnes per metre of bank on any day.

6. WATERCOURSE ALTERATIONS

6.1 Private fishing rights

In addition to bank improvements and access to the water, some fisheries may be improved by actually altering the watercourse. Particularly, in salmon and trout waters the creation of holding pools may improve the fishing. This may involve placing boulders in the river, creating small weirs or placing tree trunks across part of the river. Providing the consent of the riparian owner and landowner is forthcoming and there is no interference with upstream or downstream riparian owners, this should be possible without legal problems over ownership. This is, of course, presuming the water to be non-navigable.

If all that is owned are the incorporeal fishing rights (without ownership of the soil), the rights to carry out works on the river or banks are restricted - without the landowner's consent. For example in *Caldwell v Kilkelly* (1905), where the Plaintiff did not own the land and held only incorporeal fishing rights, it was said:

> The question in the present case is as to the extent of the Plaintiff's fishing right and as to what it includes as necessarily incidental and ancillary to it. I agree that it includes all things

222

necessary for the use of the thing granted, eg. in the present case, access to the river, the use of the bank and bed, and a right of cutting down these injurious and useless weeds. But these alleged rights of making artificial embankments and paths, and placing rocks in the bed of the river are not, in my opinion, necessary for the use of the right granted. They would constitute enlargements and extensions of that right, which, in the absence of express agreement, cannot be insisted upon by the Plaintiff.

Where mere incorporeal rights are owned, or worse still, fishing is merely by licence, the club, etc. may wish to expressly include rights to make certain fishery improvements in the title document. Otherwise, they may find themselves unable to do so without the consent of the landowner, which may be hard to obtain. See Chapters 5 and 6 generally on fishing rights.

6.2 Public regulation

However, the position with regard to public regulation is more complex. First, it is possible that planning consent may be needed as the works may be substantial enough to be engineering operations. The general rules are that the scale and nature of the works are the critical issues - is major plant or machinery involved? For example, in one case removal of earth banks was held to be an engineering operation (*Coleshill and District Investment Company v Minister of Housing and Local Government* (1969)). If in doubt, talk to the local planning authority.

Secondly, where these sorts of works are planned, it may result in poisonous, noxious or polluting matter or any other solid matter entering controlled waters (see Chapter 9) which, without a consent from the Environment Agency, is a criminal offence under s.85 Water Resources Act 1991 (see Chapter 9 generally on s.85 which is normally considered in relation to pollution). This may be the case where large quantities of silt or soil enter the waters or gravel or rocks are set loose. Whether and when an offence is committed is far from clear and is a question of fact and degree. For example, in *National Rivers Authority v Biffa Waste Services* (1995), the defendants operated a tracked vehicle on a river bed, disturbing a consider-able amount of silt which went into suspension in the waters of the river. The High Court held that no offence had been committed because the surface of the river bed, which had been disturbed was already part of the river. Therefore, nothing had entered controlled waters. However, the court made clear that this would not always be the case where the disturbance of the river bed was more substantial. In addition, where soil from the banks enters the waters as a result of these kinds of operations, clearly this 'it was already part of the river' argument will not work.

Thirdly, some care is needed to avoid breaching s.2 SAFFA on the protection of spawning fish and beds (see Chapter 11).

6.3 'In River' works

Finally, there are the important consent provisions from the Environment Agency or drainage board for 'in river' works under either s.109 Water Resources Act 1991 (WRA) or s.23 Land Drainage Act 1991 (LDA). Both sections are broadly similar and control works in watercourses - defined broadly in s.221 Water Resources Act 1991 as including rivers, streams, ditches, culverts and canals. A distinction is drawn between 'main rivers' and the remaining watercourses called 'ordinary watercourses'. The main rivers are defined in relation to a map made and subject to alteration by central government (under s.193 and s.194 WRA). The Agency keeps a definitive map of which rivers are 'main'. It is crucial that the correct powers are used (either under WRA or LDA) according to whether the watercourse is a main river. In *R v National Rivers Authority ex parte Haughey* (1996), (considered in detail in Chapter 17) the NRA served a notice on Dr Haughey under the LDA in respect of works to a weir on a main river - the River Eden. This notice was therefore fatally flawed and had to be withdrawn leading, ultimately, to the unlawful action being taken by the NRA in respect of Dr Haughey's licence.

6.3.1 Main rivers and works

In respect of a main river, no structure shall be erected in, over or under a main river, nor shall any works of alteration or repair be carried out if it is likely to affect the flow of water or impede drainage works, except with Environment Agency consent. If the section is breached, the Agency may alter or remove the work and recover their costs of doing this from the person who carried out the unlawful works. The consent procedures are governed by s.110 WRA. This requires payment of an application fee to the Agency. Furthermore, it provides that consent must not be unreasonably withheld by the Agency and may be granted subject to reasonable conditions. Applications for consent must be dealt with by the Agency within two months. If the Agency fails to determine the application within this period it will be deemed to have been granted. Disputes over consents can be referred, by agreement, to arbitration by an arbitrator appointed (unless otherwise agreed) by the President of the Institution of Civil Engineers. If arbitration is not agreed, disputes are resolved by the Secretary of State (for the Environment, Transport and the Regions or Wales).

6.3.2 *Non main river works*

For watercourses other than main rivers, the LDA applies. Section 23 LDA prohibits the erection or alteration of any mill, dam, weir or other like obstruction without the consent of the drainage board for the area. The consent of the drainage board is also needed to create a culvert or alter an existing culvert in a way which would be likely to affect the flow of the watercourse. The procedures for applications for consent are very similar to s.110 WRA. Disputes under s.23 are automatically referred to arbitration. The procedures which apply if unauthorised works are carried out are rather different from s.109 WRA. Section 24 LDA allows that the drainage board may serve a notice requiring the removal of alteration of the works to abate any nuisance created. The notice is served on the person having power to remove the obstruction. It is a criminal offence to fail to comply with a notice under s.24 LDA (maximum fine £5,000 with a daily fine of up to £40 per day for continued breach). In those circumstances, the drainage board may carry out the works in the notice itself and recover its expenses (s.24 LDA).

Clearly, there may well be ambiguities as to whether works on a fishery will affect the flow of water (under either section) or amount to a weir or like obstruction under s.23 LDA. These rules, obviously, have the potential to apply to 'in river' fishery works, such as creating pools or islands or altering existing weirs. Where there is doubt, consultation with the Agency or drainage board is wise.

The powers under s.23 and s.24 are exercisable concurrently between the Agency and any drainage board. This means that the Agency can take action in an area where no drainage board has been established and, in addition, may enforce the law on 'in river' works, even in respect of non main rivers (s.8 LDA).

6.3.3 *Disposal of Spoil and Dredgings*

Where the river alterations result in the removal of material from the river or banks (eg. dredgings), disposal of this material may require a waste management licence. This is considered above in relation to weed control. If in doubt the Environment Agency should be contacted to check whether a licence is needed or whether a waste contractor should be employed.

7. STOCKING - S.30 CONSENTS

Stocking may be a key part of a strategy to improve a fishery. This may involve the release of a few key specimen fish, or annual release of immature or mature fish for general sport.

The release of live fish or fish spawn into any inland waters (which includes artificial or natural lakes or ponds, rivers, streams or canals) is subject to licensing by the Environment Agency. It is a criminal offence under s.30 SAFFA to introduce any fish or spawn or to possess fish or spawn with the intention of introducing them. A fine of up to £2,500 may follow prosecution if the consent system is not obeyed. The consent must be sought in advance and must be obtained in writing before any stocking can take place. The offence is committed in respect of any fish or spawn. In 1996 the Environment Agency announced a new national guidelines on s.30 licensing. These require that health checks take place on all fish movements for stocking to rivers, canals and other 'open' waters. For stocking ponds and small lakes, the Agency will not require health checks but advises fishery owners to take care to avoid the spread of disease. The Agency has also published a guide to fish stocking - *Buyer Beware: Your Guide to Stocking Fish* (Environment Agency 1996) provides a range of sensible advice on stocking, including:

(a) only stock when it is necessary;

(b) check the s.30 paperwork - do not simply rely on the supplier of the fish stock to do this;

(c) bear in mind that, whatever they may say, no supplier is MAFF (Minister of Agriculture, Fisheries and Food) or Environment Agency recommended;

(d) if possible, attend the removal and certainly be present at the stocking and inspect the fish then;

(e) ask to see evidence that the fish have been health checked;

(f) take care over the terms and conditions of sale;

(g) call the Environment Agency for free advice.

See also Chapter 18.

8. STOCKING OF NON-INDIGENOUS SPECIES

The Wildlife and Countryside Act 1981 (WCA) may regulate fish stocking where it is proposed to stock with any animal (and, for the purposes of the WCA, animal includes fish) which is not normally resident (nor a regular visitor) in the wild or is listed in Schedule 9 to the 1981 Act. Section 14 WCA makes it a criminal offence to introduce into the wild such an animal (or to attempt to do so or have anything in your possession which may be used for such a purpose). The offence is punishable with a fine of up to £5,000 in the magistrates' court or an unlimited fine in the Crown Court. Fish species listed in Schedule 9 WCA (which are normally present in parts of UK waters, but which are covered by s.14 WCA) include:

(a) zander;

(b) large mouthed black bass;

(c) rock bass;

(d) pumpkinseed or pond-perch; and

(e) wels or European catfish.

The WCA creates defences of having a licence to introduce the fish from the Secretary of State (for the Environment, Transport and the Regions or Wales) and a general licence has been issued for rainbow trout (but this does not mean that a s.30 consent is not needed) and secondly, that all reasonable steps were taken to avoid committing the offence.

8.1 Practical problems of non-indigenous stocking

The issue of releasing *into the wild* creates some problems of interpretation in relation to fish. These might include the following. If fish are released into an enclosed lake, are they in the wild? Is wild to be contrasted with captivity ? Is the size of the lake and the ability to check on and, if need be, capture its contents relevant (eg. is there a fish trap in the lake or pond?)? There is no clear answer to this problem but, given the seriousness of the offence and the risk of the fish spreading (consider that zander originally were introduced to lakes), caution is urged. The Department of the Environment published guidance on the introduction of non-native species generally which focuses on s.14 of the 1981 Act - *Guidance to prevent the introduction of non-native species in Great Britain* (DoE 1997).

Further practical issues of concern when stocking is proposed is to ensure that the stock fish are disease free (see Chapter 18) and to be sure that if the club or anglers undertaking the stocking do not own the fishery, they are not likely to lose their stocking investment by loss of their fishing rights. This issue is considered separately in Chapter 5.

Finally, stocking with a species that causes harm to another person's fishery might give rise to civil liability (see *Broderick v Gale and Ainslie Ltd* (1993) considered in detail at Chapter 19).

9. FISH REMOVAL

This may be often combined with stocking and may involve removing selected predator species (such as pike or zander), or large numbers of stunted fish to increase the chances of the average fish size increasing or stock fish thriving.

The rules on fish removal have been considered in detail elsewhere in the book. This section is simply an *aide-mémoire* of important provisions on this subject. Rules which are applicable are those on otherwise illegal methods - such as the use of electro-fishing or certain nets (see Chapter 13) and the rules of fishing in close seasons and 'specially preserved' trout or salmon fisheries (see Chapter 14). In any event, if trout, sea trout or salmon are to be removed, Agency consent will be needed under Phase 2 National Byelaw 5 (see Chapter 13). Fish that are removed may be destroyed. If they are to be transferred to another fishery, stocking and transport requirements must be complied with.

10. TRANSPORT OF FISH

Fishery owners, anglers or clubs may be involved in transporting fish following removal (where fish are being transferred) or for stocking. In the case of stocking, the fish farm or supplier may well undertake the transportation. In the absence of specialist equipment and knowledge, it is probably desirable that fish transport should be undertaken by a professional.

The legal requirements on fish transport are contained in regulation 4 of the Fish Health Regulations 1992 (SI 1992/3300). This requires that the transport time should be as short as possible and that all steps should be taken to safeguard the health of the fish during the journey. This might necessitate the replacement of the water (at an approved water station and avoiding risks of disease being transferred), for example. Other requirements include proper disinfection and that the container for the fish should be secure. Where fish are despatched by a fish farm, they should be accompanied by a consignment note detailing matters such as the place of origin and a copy should be given to the receiving fishery.

11. SALE OF FISH

It is unlikely that anglers or clubs will be involved in the sale of fish. This is really the preserve of fish farmers. However, it is possible following, say, selective fish removal that fish may be sold. There are legal requirements concerning the marketing of live fish in the Fish Health Regulations 1992 (SI 1992/3300). These do not apply to retail sales.

12. CONSTRUCTING LAKES OR PONDS

There is no case law on whether or not planning permission is required. The legal position, therefore, has to be predicted from basic principles. Assuming that the lake or pond cannot be said to be reasonably necessary for agriculture, forestry and is not to be a fish farm on an existing agricultural unit, then planning permission is almost certainly needed. In any of those exceptional cases (ie. agricultural units, etc.), some development rights may exist without the need for planning permission under Part 6 or 7 of Schedule 2 of the Town and Country Planning (General Permitted Development) Order 1995(SI 1995/418). In all other cases, whether planning permission is required will depend on two matters: First, whether the works are so substantial (as is likely for anything greater than a garden pond) as to be engineering works; Secondly, whether the creation of a fishery is a material change of the use of the land from, for example, agricultural to recreational use.

If it is either a material change of use, or involves engineering operations, planning consent will be needed. In many cases, where a lake or pond is proposed near to a river, a condition will be included in the planning consent requiring consultation and approval of detailed designs by the Environment Agency, so as to protect the river.

13. STATUTORY FISHERY IMPROVEMENT SCHEMES

The Water Act 1989 introduced new powers (now contained in s.142 Water Resources Act 1991) for the making of a statutory scheme for owners and occupiers of fisheries to pay for the fisheries' functions of the Environment Agency. This might be used to fund fisheries' improvements, or simply to raise money for the general fisheries' functions. The power can be exercised by a statutory instrument being made by either the Minister for Agriculture Fisheries and Food, or the Secretary of State for the Environment, Transport and the Regions.

These powers are of interest and caused some controversy when passed by Parliament. However, they have not been used to date.

14. REGISTRATION AS A FISH FARM

A fishery may seek registration as a fish farm in order to obtain certain more favourable treatment under various pieces of legislation. For example, there may be some planning law advantages and exemptions from rules on close seasons, licensing and the use of certain fishing methods. On the other hand, the controls in respect of fish disease are much more stringent. This section considers the viability of this course of action and the potential advantages and pitfalls. Overall, on balance, the benefits seem to be fairly marginal. Of course this is only relevant where the fishery concerned is a lake or pond, or series of lakes or ponds, otherwise registration as a fish farm is not possible.

14.1 Definition of a fish farm
Fish farming is defined as: the keeping of live fish with a view to their sale or transfer to other waters (s.7 Diseases of Fish Act 1983). This definition

simply means that many fisheries cannot be regarded as fish farms whether it brings incidental legal advantages or not. However, where fish are periodically sold or transferred to other waters, or where the fishery consists of a stocking pond (which is separate from other fishing ponds) and other fishing ponds, then it may be possible to argue that this is a fish farm.

14.2 Procedure to register as a fish farm

If it is thought to be possible for the fishery to be regarded as a fish farm, then it will be necessary for it to be registered (within two months of the date on which the business of a fish farm is started) as such under the Diseases of Fish Act 1983 and Registration of Fish Farming and Shellfisheries Order 1985 (SI 1985/1391). The registration is with MAFF. A fee is charged for registration and various details have to be provided to MAFF. Annual returns of information also have to be provided and detailed records of, for example, fish movements have to be maintained. The full details are really beyond the scope of this work, but are specified in the 1985 Order (see also Chapter 6, Howarth, *Law of Aquaculture,* Fishing News Books). It has to be accepted that there is a bureaucratic burden concerned with registration and that, in addition, via these record keeping and information provisions it will soon become clear to MAFF if a fish farm is not being run and the registration is merely a sham. What will happen in these circumstances is unclear, but it is submitted that the registration would probably be lawfully terminated. In addition to the administrative burden, registration leads to much increased powers should disease break out (in particular under s.2A and s.2B Diseases of Fish Act 1937 allowing orders for the removal and disposal of fish).

14.3 Advantages of registration as a fish farm

What then are the possible advantages of fish farm status ? First, there may be some planning advantages. If fish farming can be said to amount to agriculture, then developing a fish farm will not require planning permission, as a change of use to an agricultural use is not 'development' under s.55(2)(e) TCPA. However, there are two major obstacles to taking advantage of this exemption. First, even if the use is outside the planning system, the actual works of creating ponds, etc. will probably amount to engineering works requiring planning consent in themselves. But it might be possible for a fishery to occupy existing ponds (eg. on abandoned gravel workings), thus avoiding the need for excavation works. Even if this is the case, the second obstacle will probably prevent reliance on s.5 (2)(e) TCPA. Although, the law is not particularly clear, it seems that fish farming may only constitute agriculture (defined in s.336 TCPA as including the breeding and keeping of livestock including any creature for the production of food) where the fish

230

farming is for the production of fish for food rather than sport. This follows from the case of *Belmont Farm Ltd v Minister of Housing and Local Government* (1962), where training and breeding horses for show jumping was held not to amount to agriculture. In addition, a decision of a planning inspector on appeal in 1980 supports the same view. In this appeal against a decision of South Kesteven District Council (reported in the *Journal of Planning and Environment Law* for 1980 at p. 480) disused gravel pits were to be used for fish farming. The fish farmer wished to retain the possibility of producing carp for sale to fishing clubs, as well as fish for food. The inspector held that this would place the whole operation outside the definition of agriculture. A decision of a planning inspector is only an indication of how the law may be applied and does not set a precedent for the future. Nevertheless, for the fish farm which is dominated by sport and has little or no food production objective, it is indicative that the agriculture exemption will not apply.

Besides the alleged (but, as has been shown, not real) advantage of not needing planning consent for setting up a fish farm, the other planning benefits are connected with the Town and Country Planning (General Permitted Development) Order 1995 (SI 1995/418). As has been seen above, this order grants planning permission automatically (unless the Order has been withdrawn in a specific area by an 'article 4 direction', which the local planning authority will know about). Part 6 of Schedule 2 to the Order has various items that relate to fish farming. These automatic grants of planning permission apply to existing agricultural units. This brings the issue of whether a fishery which operates as a fish farm is agriculture, which it seems it is not. However, these parts of the 1995 Order will also apply to farms (either conventional or proper fish farms producing fish for food). Thus, a farmer might rely on the Order to excavate ponds for fish farming. This will be the case, provided that the farm unit is 5 hectares or more and is not in a National Park, the Broads, or certain other listed parishes (see Schedule 1 to the Order). The farmer will have to show that the development of the fish farm is reasonably necessary for the purposes of agriculture. This may only arise where the land in question cannot be otherwise used for farming (see planning inspector's appeals in *Journal of Planning and Environment Law* 1981 274 and 1984 662). Where the true purpose of the fish farm is to provide sport fishing, the idea that this is reasonably necessary for *agriculture* on the farm becomes hard to sustain. Finally, if one can rely on the 1995 Order for pond construction, this must not involve removal of the minerals extracted from the farm. If a fish farm is properly developed, buildings within certain size limits to serve the fish farm can also be constructed without planning consent, under the Order.

For smaller farms, no planning permission is granted for pond construction. Thus, no new fish farm can be developed but incidental works of repair and improvement are permitted.

Having seen that, in practice, there are probably no planning benefits except for a 'real' fish farm, it remains to consider what other benefits exist under general fisheries legislation.

The need for a stocking licence under s.30 SAFFA is removed in respect of a fish farm which is 'enclosed' (s.34 Salmon Act 1986). Enclosed means that it either does not discharge into inland waters or, if it does, then it is through a conduit constructed or adapted for that purpose.

Other exemptions from the rules relating to fishing methods, licensing and close seasons are available from MAFF on a fish farm by fish farm basis (Fisheries Act 1981 s.33). There is a power to create general exemptions for fish farms from these provisions, but they have not been used.

Finally, setting a fishery up as a fish farm business may well have tax and rating consequences over and above the effects outlined above.

QUESTIONS

Question 1

Our club occupies part of a non-navigable river with brown trout and sea-trout fishing. We are planning to construct a small weir on the fishery to create a pool for sea-trout fishing. We also want to place a few large boulders in the river using a JCB to create some interest and 'holds' for fish on a dull, straight stretch. What legal issues should we be considering ?

Answer

Three broad issues arise. First, do you have the permission of the riparian owner (or is the club the riparian owner?) and do you have the consent of the necessary landowners for access for your JCB, etc. to carry out the works ? Lastly, you do not say whether you own, lease or have a licence over the fishery. Before investing considerable sums of money, consider how secure your future on the water is.

The second issue is whether planning consent is needed. Consultation with the local planning authority is advisable. An informal discussion with a planning officer is usually possible and helpful. It may be that the works are substantial enough to be 'engineering works' and therefore need planning permission.

Thirdly, there is the need for consent for 'in river' works under the Water Resources Act 1991 if it is a main river, or the Land Drainage Act

1991 if it is not. It may well be that if it is not a main river the boulders do not need such a consent, but the weir probably will. Last of all, bear in mind that creating a weir does trigger Environment Agency powers relating to fish passes (see Chapter 19).

Question 2

We are a small coarse fishing club and have recently been left a substantial legacy by a long standing member who died recently. The plan we have come up with is to purchase part of a field and dig a pond and stock it with large carp and tench. It will be called the Memorial Pool. What legal consents do we need ?

Answer

When you have located a possible site, it is suggested that before purchasing it you should see if planning permission is likely to be granted, as the works will almost certainly amount to engineering works. Discussions with the planning authority and checking any development plan policies will be needed. Various questions arise. Is a car park envisaged? Are any buildings planned? Is access to a highway to be built? Will the pond, car park or buildings be screened by trees? Are there environmental advantages in the proposals (eg. wildfowl habitat, etc.)? These are all relevant.

If planning consent is obtained, then once the pond is created still further legal matters need to be considered. First, for stocking, an Environment Agency stocking licence will be needed. If water is to be abstracted from groundwater or a river or stream, other regulations apply (see Chapter 11).

CHAPTER 16

CONFLICTS WITH OTHER WATER USERS

This chapter is concerned with a wide range of matters which anglers or angling clubs may come across where their interests come into conflict with the interests of others. It is not simply limited to the problem of conflicts with other persons (for eg. canoeists) but is also concerned with conflicts which may arise with wildlife (eg. cormorants).

Although this chapter sets out the applicable law, conflicts are very often best resolved *without* recourse to the law. Some tact and a little give-and-take, together with courtesy and politeness, will go a long way! An example of a statement of good conduct is the Specialist Anglers Conservation Group (SACG) *Code of Conduct for Specialist Anglers* (1997).

1. CONFLICTS WITH BOATS AND CANOES

These conflicts may arise broadly in two ways. Firstly, over whether the boats or canoes have rights of navigation. Secondly, where they do have such rights, over how they use the waterway.

In tidal waters, there are rights of navigation for the public. In inland waters, there are no such general rights. Instead, the position is more complex. A riparian owner has the right to navigate his own watercourse. A riparian owner may establish a private right of way over a watercourse by custom (*Bourke v Davis* (1889)). In addition, others or the general public may have rights of navigation over rivers. These rights may arise through statute (for example, the Thames Conservancy Act 1932); grant by one or more riparian owner; or immemorial user (long established user). Rights of navigation in tidal waters entitle anyone to use the whole of the channel at all times. The rights are in that sense unlimited. In non-tidal waters, where rights of navigation can be established, the rights are limited by the extent of the grant, statute or established user. Thus, this may limit the extent of the navigable part of a river. In addition, rights to moor or land do not normally exist, except where also established by grant, statute or use.

1.1 The Derwent case

Establishing that the public have rights of navigation over a river is a contentious issue. Where there is not a very long standing custom of navigation and canoeists or boaters are seeking to argue that there are public rights of way, the potential for conflict with anglers is substantial. An example of this sort of conflict arose in the case of *Attorney General ex rel Yorkshire Derwent Trust and Malton Town Council v Brotherton* (1992]. In this case, the Attorney General on behalf of the Yorkshire Derwent Trust (a charity established to try to restore the Derwent as a navigable river) and Malton Town Council (who supported the use of the river for recreational navigation) sought a declaration from the courts that a public right of navigation existed over the Derwent. Brotherton and others contested the declaration as riparian owners. The legal issue which concerned the courts and, ultimately, was decided by the House of Lords, was whether a right of navigation could be established in the same way as any other public right of way (eg. a footpath). This can be achieved under s.31 Highways Act 1980 (at the relevant time, the same law was contained in s.1 of the Rights of Way Act 1932) by proving over 20 years of continuous public user. The House of Lords held that a right of way did not extend to rights of *navigation* over water. Thus, the Highways Act method of establishing a public right of way by 20 years continuous use is not possible.

1.2 Canals

Canals are not subject to any special rules. Most are now owned by the British Waterways Board and are not subject to any public right of navigation. However, the Board allows the use of the canals for recreational and commercial boating, subject to observance of its byelaws and payment of its charges.

1.3 Anglers and navigation

Rights of navigation on non-tidal waters do not include any right to fish (*Smith v Andrews* (1891)).

In general terms, in a navigable water, the rights of navigation are said to take precedence over rights of fishery (Wisdom's *Law of Watercourses,* 5th Edn, Shaw & Sons). The case law underlying this proposition generally concerns damage to oyster beds by ships grounding. However, the same principles seem to underlie any significant conflicts between fishing and boating. Wisdom says that the rights of navigation must be exercised reasonably and must not be abused. Where these parameters are exceeded, there is likely to be a potential action available in the tort of nuisance.

1.4 Navigation and anglers in non-navigable waters

The position in non-navigable waters is obviously different. In *Ranson v Peters* 1972 canoeists were sued successfully in the tort of trespass for having disturbed a fishery in a non-navigable river, even though no one was actually fishing at the time the canoeists passed through. Nominal damages of 50p were awarded, but the fishery owner was permitted to return to court to seek an injunction if need be to restrain any future canoeing.

1.5 Reasonable use of navigable waters

As to the second problem of the reasonable use of navigable waters by boaters and canoeists, mutual respect is desirable but, regrettably, not always present. Deliberately casting a line to foul a boat's propeller or throwing ground bait at passing boaters is as anti-social as boats purposefully passing close to anglers or the river bank, or going too fast and creating a major wash. The Sports Council published *Angling and Canoeing - Statement of Intent* in co-operation with the National Anglers Council and British Canoe Union as a voluntary code of good conduct.

There is a myriad of problems which may be encountered. What role does the law have to play? First, byelaws may well set a speed limit (or indeed other rules concerning boating). Is that limit reasonable? Can anglers lobby for its reduction? Are boats consistently breaking the speed limit? Can you identify and prove that particular boats have broken the speed limit? The authority for the making and enforcement of byelaws on navigable waters is dependent on who owns or operates the waterway. The Environment Agency has power to make byelaws in Schedule 25 Water Resources Act 1991. These may regulate boating, sailing and fishing. Under the Transport Act 1968, the Secretary of State may authorise various bodies to make byelaws, including navigation authorities or local authorities. Where there is a navigation authority, or harbour authority in control of the inland waters, the Environment Agency may not make byelaws which cover boating (Schedule 25 WRA). Where there is such an additional authority any byelaws are left to them and the Agency cannot act. This division of responsibility has lead to major problems on the Rivers Wye and Lugg. Until the Water Act 1989, the mere existence of a navigation authority prevented the making of byelaws by the then water authorities. After the 1989 Act, the critical issue became whether such an authority was in control. In the early 19th century, a Company of Proprietors was established, by local Act of Parliament, to make the rivers Wye and Lugg navigable. Much of the Wye is navigable and there is a history of conflicts between anglers, canoeists and pleasure boats. The National Rivers Authority recently sought to make byelaws to govern navigation and felt able to do so because the Company of Proprietors has been dormant for well over a century. There have been recent, so far fruitless, efforts by the navigation lobby to reactivate the Company and, therefore, undermine the NRA's efforts (see *National Rivers Authority v Stockinger* (1996)).

Secondly, in the case of lakes, certain areas may be, by the rules applied to the lake by the owner or occupier, made 'no go' zones for boats to leave anglers in peace. Thirdly, in extreme cases, abuse of waters by boats may give rise to civil liability. In a 1980 case, *Kennaway v Thompson*, power boat racing on a lake, which caused considerable noise and upset a householder who built a house on the water sports lake, was held to be an actionable nuisance which could be restrained by injunction and could result in an award of damages. This might apply to fishery disturbance.

Finally, it is worth bearing in mind that certain parts of the Salmon and Freshwater Fisheries Act 1975 (SAFFA) may become an issue in these conflicts. For example, canoeists who have disturbed spawning grounds have been successfully prosecuted under s.2 SAFFA (see Chapter 13).

2. LITTER

One of the less desirable reputations anglers have acquired over the years is as a cause of litter on and around the river bank. In particular, abandoned monofilament line and discarded plastic bags and containers. Fishing line is particularly lethal to wild birds and is persistent because it is made of non-degradable materials. Anglers may also use temporary floats (eg., balloons) to take a bait to a particular area and then be jerked free. The SACG Code (see above) suggests that, unless the float is always recovered, this is an unacceptable method of fishing.

Clearly, any club will want to do what it can - through its rules and by putting up notices and, if need be, by taking disciplinary action - to ensure that anglers take away all of their litter. Fishery owners who licence others to use their fishery may also wish to include explicit conditions about litter. Clubs or fishery owners may wish to consider providing a litter bin at, for example, a car park.

As to the law, defacing certain places by litter is a criminal offence (s.87 Environmental Protection Act 1990 (EPA)). It is an offence to throw down, drop, deposit or leave any thing which may deface or contribute to the defacement of an area by litter. However, this is only the case where it is a public open place: one to which the public has access without payment (including land belonging to the Crown or a statutory undertaker such as a water company). This may include a few areas where fishing takes place: beaches and the foreshore, public parks or water company reservoirs to which the public has access. It may include a navigable river, but it is not clear from the EPA whether the definition of 'public open place' may include water. Byelaws for navigable rivers and canals may locally make it a byelaw offence to litter. However, in most cases, no one can be prosecuted for littering a private fishery.

There are one or two exceptional areas where it is an offence to litter *not* in a public place, but these are unlikely to affect anglers. For example, land belonging to schools, colleges or universities, or highways maintainable at public expense. The requirement that, to be an offence, littering must normally be in a public place creates a major loophole. It is possible for a local authority to designate an area of *land* as a litter control area under s.90 EPA. The power to do so extends to marinas and inland beaches, canal towpaths or the seashore which is frequently used by large numbers of people. If this is done, then it is an offence under s.87 EPA to litter. Where an area is covered by the EPA - probably in the case of fishing as an area to which the public have open access or, exceptionally, as a litter control area - not only is it an offence to litter the area but, in addition, the local authority is under a duty to keep the area clear of litter (s.89 EPA). Where this duty is not being discharged, a complaint can be made to the local magistrates court (s.91 EPA).

2.1 Litter and statutory nuisance

It can be seen that the law on litter is neither designed for, nor will it normally deal with, the problem of litter on the river or lake bank. It is possible, if the problem became critical, that a local authority or individual could bring proceedings for statutory nuisance under the EPA Part III. This includes any accumulation or deposit which is either prejudicial to health or a nuisance as being a statutory nuisance. In *R v Carrick District Council ex p Shelley* (1996), the High Court indicated that deposits of sewage debris (from an unscreened outfall) on a beach was capable of being a statutory nuisance. In general terms, for litter to constitute a statutory nuisance, a health risk to the public would have to be shown, or some degree of continuous interference with the use of the fishery or land associated with it. Part III EPA imposes duties on local authorities to investigate and deal with statutory nuisances in accordance with the 1990 Act procedures. If a local authority fails to do this, an individual may take the matter up themselves through the magistrates court. The person responsible for the nuisance is generally the person through whose act, default or sufferance it arises. But where - as may often be the case with littering - they cannot be found, the owner or occupier of the land is responsible.

Finally, even this avenue of statutory nuisance may soon be blocked off. The Government is proposing to introduce legislation which has passed through Parliament (the Environment Act 1995) but is not yet in force. This would amend the definition of statutory nuisance so as to exclude land contaminated with any substances, in or on it, which may cause harm.

3. ANGLERS AND WALKERS, CYCLISTS AND HORSE RIDERS

This type of conflict is really likely to arise in two sets of circumstances. First, where fishing takes place close to a footpath or bridleway and secondly, where angling is in a public place, such as a park or reservoir which is open to the public for recreation. The conflicts are fish disturbance by non-fishermen and avoiding risks to the general public from fishing. The latter is most likely to arise in connection with casting, particularly where fly fishing is used. In these cases, a line with one or more hooks may be airborne at speed some 15 or 20 metres from the angler.

The first point is that common sense will probably avoid legal problems. If fish are disturbed by passing walkers, riders, etc. then they probably will not take long to settle again. If an angler's concentration or pleasure is interfered with by having non-anglers around, they will probably soon pass and, if the area is very busy, perhaps the fisherman should consider fishing somewhere else! The law has no place with regard to these problems, except in two possible ways. First, it may be possible to seek the realignment of a footpath or bridleway under the Highways Act 1980 and Wildlife and Countryside Act 1981 Part III. Secondly, where anglers are being deliberately disturbed by passing walkers, etc. With regard to this issue, although it may not be animal rights related, it is considered under that heading below.

As to the problem of risks to the public from anglers - although there have been no reported cases in the law courts yet - it seems likely that eventually a passing walker will be injured by a fisherman and will sue. This is most likely through casting but might also occur in other ways, for example, if someone trips over tackle left lying around. Assuming that the injury is not inflicted deliberately or recklessly, it is likely simply to be a civil matter rather than a criminal matter involving the police. The law is likely to require that an angler and possibly an angling club or fishery owner takes reasonable steps to avoid risks of injury (see Occupiers Liability Acts 1957 and 1984 and *Slater v Clay Cross Co Ltd* (1956)). Although no fisherman or club has been the subject of any reported case, an example of how the law may impose liability on a sporting activity occurred when a person walking in a lane near to a golf course was hit by a golf ball and successfully sued the golf club for failing to take reasonable precautions to protect the public (*Lamond v Glasgow Corporation* (1968)). The steps which an angler, fishery owner or club may need to take are likely to vary according to the circumstances, but here are some suggestions:

(a) warning notices to warn passers by of the risks from fishermen;
(b) directions to the public to keep a distance back from the water, or to keep to a marked pathway which is safe from anglers;

(c warnings to fishermen - via notices, licences or club rules - to check for passers by before casting and to keep tackle visible and tidy;

(d) fencing off of angling areas where the public has general access, for example, in a public park or recreation area.

A failure to take reasonable steps may result in liability being imposed - either under the tort of negligence or the Occupiers Liability Acts - on individual anglers or fishery owners or clubs. Public liability insurance taken out by either a club on behalf of all members or by anglers individually may cover this (see Chapter 7).

4. ANGLERS AND ANIMAL RIGHTS ACTIVISTS

Animal rights activists have now turned their attention to angling. With an increasing likelihood that stag and, perhaps, fox hunting may be banned or restricted in the future, it seems that this trend is likely to continue. Demonstrations and even direct action are being taken against anglers by animal rights protesters. Sometimes this may be a noisy demonstration, or may involve deliberately disturbing the fish or anglers.

The law may become involved if matters get out of hand. A number of issues need to be considered. Are the demonstrators trespassing, or do have they have rights to enter the fishing area? If they are trespassers, the landowner or a person acting on his behalf may bring an action in the tort of trespass for damages and/or an injunction to restrain future behaviour. However, very often this will impracticable as the names and addresses of the demonstrators will not be known. Of greater importance is the right to use 'reasonable force' or steps to remove the trespassers if they refuse to leave. This right - although long established in law - may be unwise to attempt to use, for fear of provoking a public order problem. Where the demonstrators have rights of access, via a footpath or bridleway, they may nevertheless become trespassers where they stop using the path simply to pass and re-pass and start using it to try and disrupt fishing. A similar situation arose in the 1883 case of *Harrison v Duke of Rutland*, where a person used a footpath to try and interfere with a grouse shoot. He was lawfully evicted with reasonable force as he had become a trespasser.

Demonstrations may become a police matter. Indeed, if it seems likely that the situation may escalate, it may be sensible to call the police. If the demonstration turns nasty, various criminal offences may be committed: breach of the peace, public order offences or criminal damage to property (eg., tackle). For example, in *Nicol v Director of Public Prosecutions* (1996), two angling protesters took part in disruption of an angling competition by throwing sticks and twigs at lines and into the water, sounding air horns and arguing with anglers to the point where the police thought that the anglers would react violently. The protesters were imprisoned for what the court described as their unreasonable behaviour and their refusal to be bound over as to their future behaviour. The detail of these general criminal matters is really beyond the scope of this work. However, one criminal offence is worthy of consideration, as it was drafted partly with anti-angling protests in mind. This is the offence of aggravated trespass, under s.68 Criminal Justice and Public Order Act 1994. This is committed where a person - with the intention of intimidating, obstructing or disrupting persons who are involved in a lawful pursuit - trespasses on land. Not only do the police have powers of arrest, but trespassers may also be directed to leave the land by the police. The offence is punishable by up to three months in prison and/or a fine of up to £2,500.

Recently, the Protection from Harassment Act 1997 has provided another means by which the law may become involved in angling protests. This Act makes undertaking a course of conduct which amounts to harassment of another both a crime and civil wrong of (s.1). Although harassment is not defined in the Act, a course of conduct will require conduct on at least two occasions (s.7). If the Act is breached, the police may be called and offenders arrested and charged. Alternatively, of the application of an affected angling club or angler, the civil courts may issue a restraining order controlling future conduct, coupled with a power of arrest if the order is breached. It is early days to see how the Act will work. However, in *Huntingdon Life Sciences Ltd v Curtin* (1997), the High Court held (in relation to an anti-vivisection protest) that the Act could not be used to 'clamp down on the discussion of matters of public interest or upon the rights of political protest and public demonstration which is so much a part of our political tradition.' On this basis the court refused to allow a restraining order to be made against the protesters.

5. ANGLERS AND LIVESTOCK

Anglers inevitably come across livestock. Although there are restrictions on the types of bull which may be kept in fields containing footpaths or bridle-ways (under the Wildlife and Countryside Act 1981) these do not apply to fields used by anglers for access to fishing, or fields adjoining a fishery.

Two issues will be considered. Firstly, fencing of livestock and fishing and, secondly, liability in the event of livestock injuring a fisherman or damaging tackle or equipment.

As to fencing, it was held in one Irish case (*Boyle v Holcroft* (1905)), that a landowner is not entitled to erect fences or other obstructions which interfere with the exercise of fishing rights, where those obstructions are *not* necessary for farming the land properly.

The issue of liability is more involved and only some broad guidelines can be set out here. First, liability for injury or damage may arise following, for example, an angler or his equipment being trampled. This may occur under the Animals Act 1971, which applies to dangerous species (non-domesticated animals) and non-dangerous animals which have an abnormal character or dangerous tendency. Even if the Animals Act does not apply, liability may be imposed under the normal rules on negligence. Did the farmer take all reasonable steps to avoid damage or injury by warnings, fencing, stock location, etc. ?

6. PREDATOR CONTROL

Predator control has become a very topical issue in recent years as anglers have become increasingly frustrated by the voracious appetites of cormorants. In December 1996, it was reported in the national press that 'militant' anglers were taking the law into their own hands and killing large numbers of these birds (see, for example, *The Times* December 5 1996 including a leader urging anglers to stay within the law or risk losing public sympathy in the larger debate about fishing as a blood sport). The applicable law is contained in the Wildlife and Countryside Act 1981 Part I (WCA) which controls the methods which may be used to kill birds and animals and gives protection to certain species (including cormorants and goosanders - which are also a cause for concern by anglers). The Act also protects certain plants. The position with regard to cormorants is complicated by their inclusion in the lists of protected species under European Union law in the Birds Directive (79/409/EEC). It would be difficult for the UK to substantially change the law on cormorants without a change to European law. Certain other predator species of birds and animals are protected under either the Birds Directive or Habitats Directive (92/43/EC), although none are causing the same concern as cormorants or goosanders.

6.1 Species protection under WCA

Advice on what can be done by anglers and fishery managers to control predators depends, initially, on whether the predator species are protected or not. If they are not protected species, then there are two ways in which predator control is regulated. First, how the control is carried out and, secondly, in the case of birds, who is allowed to kill the predators. Even for species without protection it is a criminal offence to use certain illegal methods - such as, for example, traps, gins, snares, hooks and lines and live birds or animals as bait (see s.5 WCA, for birds, and s.11 WCA, for other animals). In the case of birds, the pest species listed in Part II of Schedule 2

WCA (including, for example, crows, some gulls and magpies) may be taken at any time but must be killed (or their nests destroyed) by an authorised person. Authorised persons include owners and occupiers of land or persons authorised by them, persons authorised by the local authority, English Nature, Countryside Council for Wales, the Environment Agency, a water plc or sea fisheries committee.

As to protected species - these are listed in the Schedules to WCA which may be regularly updated and varied. Anglers are currently lobbying for the removal of cormorants from the Schedules. Schedules include lists of birds and animals. In the case of animals (animals here means *other than* birds) the rules are fairly straightforward - animals which are listed (including, for example, otters) are protected. Those that are not listed are not protected except as to the methods used to take them. However, additionally, seals are protected under the Conservation of Seals Act 1970 and badgers under the Protection of Badgers Act 1992. Birds are subject to more complex rules. All wild birds are protected. Those in Schedule 1 are given the special protection of higher penalties for their destruction or disturbance and include rarer species (for example, kingfishers and divers). Those in Schedule 2 Part I may be taken by authorised persons, except during the close season (for example, many duck species) and those in Part II of that schedule may be taken or their nests destroyed at any time, provided that this is done by an authorised person. This leaves a range of species which are not listed and, as a result, are fully protected but not by special penalties. An example of this category are grey herons.

6.2 Enforcement of species protection

The police enforce the provisions of the Act with the assistance of various bodies such as the Royal Society for the Protection of Birds or Royal Society for the Prevention of Cruelty to Animals. The penalties for breaking the protection rules vary according to the species involved with maximum fines of £1,000 to £5,000.

6.3 Lawful killing of protected species

Regardless of this protection, there are two circumstances when it is lawful to take a protected species. First, when anglers or clubs can justify taking protected species to avoid serious damage to a fishery. Secondly, the availability of licences to take protected species.

It is possible for an authorised person to kill or injure a wild bird (but not one listed in Schedule 1) without committing an offence if he can show it was necessary for the prevention of serious damage to, amongst other things, fisheries (s.4 (3) WCA). An identical defence is available in respect of animals (s.10 (4) WCA), but in this case may not be relied upon unless there is a good reason for not having sought a licence.

The problem with these defences is the inevitable ambiguity of both establishing the necessity of the action and that 'serious' (whatever that may mean) damage would otherwise have been caused to the fishery. This may be relied on by anglers or clubs at their own peril.

The licensing exemption is more reliable. A licence may be sought under s.16 WCA for numerous reasons but amongst these is the prevention of serious damage to fisheries. Licences are granted in respect of fisheries by MAFF in consultation with English Nature and the Countryside Council for Wales. Licences are limited to specified areas, species (and may set out a maximum number to be taken), may set out the methods of destruction and are granted for a period not exceeding two years. In seeking a licence, anglers, clubs or fishery owners will need to be able to identify specific and reliable evidence of past or threatened damage to the fishery. This might include records of numbers of birds seen or catch records compared over a period of time. MAFF will consider what other alternatives there may be to the destruction of the bird or animal. To that extent, consideration of alternatives and attempting them (perhaps in consultation with MAFF or the Environment Agency) may be a sensible step before putting together a licence application.

6.4 Respect for wildlife

Besides the narrow issue of predator control, there is the broader issue of the potential harm and disturbance anglers can cause to wildlife. The SACG Code sets out what most anglers would regard as being good practice - that anglers should 'respect the environment and minimise disruption to waterside wildlife'.

The law intervenes in two ways to seek to protect wildlife. First, an area may be designated as a nature reserve or site of special scientific interest (SSSI). This is considered below. Secondly, in respect of species protected under WCA, there are criminal offences of intentional disturbance of nests and young (for birds s.1 WCA) and damaging or destroying any place which a protected wild animal uses for shelter or protection, or disturbing an animal while in such a place (s.9 WCA). Anglers need to be careful, for example, not to disturb nesting birds or otter holts.

7. FISHING IN NATURE RESERVES AND SITES OF SPECIAL SCIENTIFIC INTEREST (SSSIs)

Fishing may be permitted in designated nature reserves (under the National Parks and Access to the Countryside Act 1949) which may be local (local nature reserves or LNRs) or national (national nature reserves or NNRs). Fishing may also possible in SSSIs, notified by English Nature or the Countryside Council for Wales under the 1981 Wildlife and Countryside Act. However, where fishing licences are available for such an area, additional rules may apply restricting fishing methods, etc.

In LNRs and NNRs, the principal legal method of controlling activities within them is through byelaws. For SSSIs, the position is a little more complex. The notification of SSSI will include a list of potentially damaging operations which must not be carried out (or caused or allowed to be carried out by another) by the owner or occupier of the SSSI. Potentially damaging operations can only be undertaken with the consent of English Nature or the Countryside Council for Wales, or after either of those bodies has been given notice by an owner or occupier of the SSSI and four months has elapsed (s.28 (5) and (6) WCA). This four month period does create a major loophole in protection of habitats. Indeed, one judge described the protection of SSSIs as 'toothless' (see Lord Mustill in *Southern Water v Nature Conservancy Council* (1992)).

7.1 Effects on angling

Byelaws or potentially damaging operations might affect fishing in a number of ways. For example, they might restrict the hours when fishing may take place, prohibit the use of certain techniques or baits or ground-baits, ban any littering, forbid the use of fish traps and so on. The particular restrictions will be individual to each fishery. Byelaws will normally be posted in the area. The SSSI notification will not be posted but will be known to the owner and occupier of the fishery who will wish to see full compliance so as to protect themselves against any possible criminal liability. The byelaw restrictions or SSSI list of potentially damaging operations may also prohibit the development of a fishery - by, for example, controlling the removal of bank vegetation or weed.

In some cases, rivers or parts of rivers are designated as SSSIs. Such a designation is obviously desirable in many ways, since it seeks to protect the river as a whole from harmful activities. However, it is important that fishery owners are alert to protect their position since apparently innocent and otherwise lawful activities, such as bank clearance, may be illegal. Any club using a fishery restricted in this way must ensure that its club rules reflect the restrictions in place.

Finally, it is notable that although the coarse and rainbow trout close seasons have been abolished on still waters under the national byelaws, this relaxation does not apply to fishing in a number of listed (in Schedule 3 to the Byelaws) nature reserves and SSSIs.

8. NOISE ARISING FROM ANGLING

Fishing is generally seen as a silent, often solo pursuit. However, this is not always the case. Fishing competitions can often be quite noisy events as anglers, shout to one another, hooters mark the beginning or end of a match and the 'weigh in' and presentation of prizes brings enthusiastic competitors together. Noise can occasionally lead to conflicts between fishing interests and others. In practice, the problems arise where angling is taking place near to residential areas.

The law may seek to control noise if a dispute gets out of hand. The applicable law is either the statutory nuisance regime under EPA Part III, or common law nuisance (described in much more detail in relation to water pollution in Chapter 10). In the case of statutory nuisance, action is normally taken by a local authority serving an abatement notice requiring steps to be taken to reduce or remove the noise (s.80 EPA). Such a notice may be appealed to the magistrates court on various grounds, including whether the requirements and timing of the notice is reasonable or even whether the alleged noise is a legal nuisance at all (the Statutory Nuisance (Appeals) Regulations 1995 (SI 1995/2664)). In the event that an abatement notice is not complied with, criminal prosecution may result (s.80 EPA). There are powers for private individuals to bring statutory nuisance matters before the magistrates courts themselves, without the involvement of the local authority (s.82 EPA). Private law nuisance is a matter normally taken to the County Court or High Court (see Chapter 10).

In both cases, the definition of nuisance is an unreasonable interference with someone else's reasonable enjoyment of their property (*Read v Lyons* (1945) and *National Coal Board v Neath* (1976)). This is a flexible and unpredictable definition. However, in respect of noise, it means that the frequency, loudness, nature, persistence and timing of the noise and the character of the neighbourhood will be crucial factors in deciding whether the noise is a legal nuisance. For example, noise at night in a residential area is much more likely to be a nuisance than day time noise.

9. SIGNAL CRAYFISH

The conservation of the native crayfish has become a topical issue. It has suffered from the introduction of non-native species, especially the signal crayfish. Imported in the early 1970s for farming, this faster-growing species has inevitably found its way into native watercourses. The signal crayfish out-competes the smaller native species and it is a carrier of crayfish plague, a disease which has had a significant impact on the native species. It is interesting that crayfish farming makes only a very modest contribution to the output of the fish farming industry - around 10 tonnes out of a total of about 150,000 tonnes. It is likely that its environmental impact may considerably outweigh its economic benefit.

To counter this problem, the Prohibition of Keeping of Live Fish (Crayfish) Order 1996 (SI 1996/1104) came into force in 1996. Made under the Import of Live Fish (England and Wales) Act 1980, this order makes it an offence to keep non-native crayfish without a valid licence from the appropriate agriculture minister. An exception is made for signal crayfish where populations are already established in the wild. These licences will be subject to conditions which will probably include the effective containment of effluent from farms. It is an offence to keep crayfish without a licence. What this Order can do to control the spread of crayfish remains to be seen. A degree of cynicism is perhaps justified as it appears that 'the horse may have already bolted'. Phase 2 of the National Byelaws due to take effect in 1998 propose under Byelaw 3 that the use of crayfish or parts of crayfish (dead or alive) as bait is an offence.

QUESTIONS

Question 1.

Our club operates a brown trout fishery on a small chalk stream. We have become plagued by herons and mink. We stock the fishery with 6" and 10" brown trout each year and quite a number are eaten by herons we think. The stream in summer is shallow enough for herons to fish in most places. One of our members is a good shot and has offered to kill a couple of the herons and as many mink as he can find. Will this be legal ?

Answer

The law does regulate the control of predators. It is lawful, provided you have the permission of the landowner, for mink to be shot for they are not legally protected. However, herons are a different matter. They are legally protected under Part I of the Wildlife and Countryside Act 1981. There are a couple of possible ways by which it may be possible to lawfully kill herons. First, if there was very clear evidence that herons had seriously damaged the fishery then, providing again, that you have the consent of the landowner, you may shoot the birds. The problem is really in having any good evidence that the shooting was *necessary* to prevent serious damage. Given the risk of being prosecuted and the serious nature of the charge it would seem sensible not to take the chance. However, this is not the end of the story as far as the herons are concerned. You may seek a licence to shoot a limited number from MAFF. This, again, will be based on the need to prevent serious damage to fisheries. Instead of taking the chance of being prosecuted and trying to defend yourself, if a licence is sought, the arguments about the threat the herons pose will be made before any risk of prosecution arises. Again, some evidence of the damage caused would be helpful.

Question 2.

We operate a coarse fishery on a major navigable Midlands river. We suffer from disturbance caused by passing pleasure boats which create a substantial wash. We are concerned that they are speeding and have checked the byelaws which reveal a speed limit of 6 knots on one stretch of our water near a village and 10 knots elsewhere. Many boats are probably speeding and 10 knots seems very high to us in any event. What can we do?

Answer

First of all who made the byelaws and who operates the waterway? For the sake of the question, it will be assumed that these are Environment Agency byelaws. There are two separate issues here. First, the speeding boats. Contact the Agency to see if they will do something about the better enforcement of their byelaws. Ask when they last brought a prosecution and point out that one prosecution would probably be enough to bring most of the boating fraternity into line. If they seem uninterested, or no action follows, consider gathering evidence yourselves of speeding boats. All that is needed is a precisely measured distance and people to each end and someone with a stop watch to time the boat. Tell the Agency what you find out. Other practical steps might include investing in a loud hailer and liaising with any local boating or cruising clubs. The second issue is the 10 knot speed limit. Lobby the Agency with evidence of bank damage and fishery disturbance and of possible comparable speed limits on other waters. They have the power to change their byelaws under Schedule 25 Water Resources Act 1991.

CHAPTER 17

BAILIFFING AND POACHING

The image of the poacher is a romantic one - a likeable rogue going out in the dead of night to catch a brace of salmon for the table or to sell for a few shillings. The reality is usually different. With fisheries worth thousands of pounds and fishing tourists prepared to pay large sums of money, fish are a valuable resource to be safeguarded. Some of the methods used by poachers, such as poison, are indiscriminate and can ruin a river. There are many threats the fish have to overcome: netting in the estuary, pollution and drought, to name a few. Poaching is another.

The position of the water bailiff as protector of a fishery is an ancient one. *De Jure Maris* refers to 'the office of a water baillie... which the king doth or may appoint on those rivers or places that are in his franchise or interest.' Primarily then concerned with protecting the Monarch's fishing, their role has widened considerably in the twentieth century.

This chapter will focus on poaching and the powers of water bailiffs and keepers. Poaching is theft. The power of arrest available to both private and Environment Agency bailiffs will be explored, taking into account such matters as how much force may be used by the arresting bailiff.

1. THE THEFT ACT 1968

1.1 The poaching offences

There are three offences under this Act which can be used against the poacher:
Section 1 of the Theft Act 1968 states that:

A person is guilty of theft if he dishonestly appropriates property
belonging to another with the intention of permanently depriving
the other of it.

This must be read in the light of s.4(4) which qualifies the meaning of property in respect of wild animals:

... wild creatures, tamed or untamed shall be regarded as property;
but a person cannot steal a wild creature not tamed nor ordinarily
kept in captivity, or the carcass of any such creature, unless either
it had been reduced into possession by or on behalf of another
person and possession of it has not since been lost or abandoned,
or another person is in the course of reducing it into possession.

Paragraph 2 (1) of Schedule 1 creates the offence of taking or destroying fish. It applies where:

A person ... unlawfully takes or destroys, or attempts to take or destroy, any fish in water which is private property or in which there is any private right of fishing.

The third offence is taking or destroying fish by angling. Paragraph 2 (2) of Schedule 1 TA states Paragraph 2 (1)...

shall not apply to taking or destroying fish by angling in the daytime (that is to say the period beginning one hour before sunrise and ending one hour after sunset); but a person who by angling in the daytime unlawfully takes or destroys, or attempts to take or destroy, any fish in water which is private property or in which there is any private right of fishery shall on summary conviction be liable to a fine.

1.2 Meaning of angling

Both Paragraphs of Schedule 1 are similar except that the latter creates an offence of taking or destroying fish by angling. It is intended to differentiate the angler fishing without permission from the professional poacher. In *Barnard v Roberts* (1907), the definition of angling was discussed in relation to a statute since repealed, the Larceny Act 1861 (LA). Section 25 LA allowed the owner of the fishery to ask for and, if not surrendered, to seize fishing tackle. There was a similar qualification as contained in Paragraph 2(2) TA in that 'any person angling against the provisions of this Act ... be exempted from the payment of any damages or penalty for such angling'. This proviso meant that the offender was not liable to a penalty if he was only angling. Two individuals were caught using two small stakes driven into the bank of the stream with lines and hooks attached and with a stone weight attached to one of the lines to keep it floating with the stream. The Judge found that the two were not angling. Mr Justice Darling stated that 'there is a great difference between what may be called a sportsman who may poach and the more vulgar poacher, the person who poaches simply to get fish that do not belong to him in order to go and sell them.' Therefore, these two poachers could not avail themselves of the defence of angling and were duly prosecuted.

1.3 Relationship between Section 1 TA and Schedule 1 TA

However, when should section 1(1) and Schedule 1 be used? The difference is in the use of the words 'private property' and 'private right of fishing' in Schedule 1(1). Section 1 is used where the fish have been reduced into possession. Examples are: stealing fish caught by the angler from his bag or fish confined to a net or kept in a stock pond on a fish farm. In Chapter 3, the law regarding the ownership of fish was examined. Depending on the circumstances, fish contained in a pond can be owned. If such fish are stolen, then s.1(1) can be used. Schedule 1 is used where the fish which are wild and free to move between the waters owned by different individuals have been taken or destroyed.

However, this leads onto the question of what is meant by 'reduced into possession'? In *Young v Hitchens* (1864), Lord Chief Justice Denham stated that the test was whether custody or possession had been obtained and that this occurred only when a party had actual power over the fish. This test was taken a step further in *Wells v Hardy* (1964). The Defendant was fishing the River Thames and was prosecuted under s.24 LA 1861. The defendant had merely been catching fish and placing them in a net with a view to returning them to the water at the end of his day's fishing - i.e. classic coarse fishing. Lord Chief Justice Parker distinguished taking and carrying away. Taking does not include an element of 'asportation' (i.e. taking the fish away from the river). It means to lay hands upon, to grasp, to seize or to capture. Therefore, the fish were in an individual's possession, even if he had the intention to relinquish possession.

1.4 Penalties for poaching

The punishments available for each of these offences are:

i) s.1(1): a term of imprisonment not exceeding 10 years

ii) Paragraph 2 (1): a term of imprisonment not exceeding 3 months, or a fine not exceeding level 3 on the standard scale (at present up to £1,000)

iii) Paragraph 2 (2): a fine not exceeding level 1 on the standard scale (at present up to £200).

These reflect the relative seriousness of each offence.

A final point on these offences is their usefulness in helping angling clubs and fishery owners to enforce their fishery byelaws. A club may sell day tickets and impose a rule that fishing is by dry fly only. What if the visitor is caught spinning? This is outside the rules of the fishery and the visitor could be liable to prosecution under Paragraph 2(2). Theoretically, this provision could be used against club members who refuse to fish in accordance with the club's byelaws.

2. BAILIFFS

The term 'bailiff' is one used by the angling world to cover anyone who polices watercourses to ensure that fishery laws and byelaws are observed. The phrase, club bailiff, is applied to a member of an angling club who oversees his club's waters. Technically, however, he is a 'water keeper' rather than a bailiff. Water bailiffs can only be appointed by the Environment Agency under the Salmon and Freshwater Fisheries Act 1975 (SAFFA). The distinction is important. Water bailiffs have statutory powers under the SAFFA. Water keepers have no special powers beyond those exercisable by the ordinary citizen. It should be borne in mind that a club, when referring to its 'bailiff', is using the wrong terminology. The club 'bailiff' is the club water keeper. This terminology will be used throughout this chapter.

2.1 The water bailiff

Section 36 SAFFA deems water bailiffs to be constables for the purposes of the enforcement of the SAFFA. As such, they have the same powers and liabilities as a police constable. The production of evidence of his appointment shall be a sufficient warrant for him to exercise the powers conferred on him by the Act. Under s.36 (2) SAFFA, a bailiff must produce evidence of his appointment before exercising his powers under the Act. In *Edwards v Morgan* (1967) two bailiffs called out 'water bailiffs' when they saw two men behaving suspiciously. One man ran off, but a struggle then took place with the second. A bailiff is deemed to be a police constable when executing his duties and the accused was, therefore, convicted of assaulting a police officer. The Defendant appealed on the basis that evidence of the bailiff's appointment must be produced before exercising his powers. The Court decided that, when on patrol, he was deemed to be a constable on duty. This solved the problem that the bailiff had to act quickly when seeing the two men and had no time to produce any identification.

2.1.1. Power of search (s.31 SAFFA)

A bailiff has wide powers of search. These include the power to examine any dam, fixed fishing apparatus and artificial watercourse and he may enter land to do so; to examine any instrument or bait or container which he has reasonable cause to suspect of having been or being used or likely to be used to take fish; to stop and search any boat or vessel used for fishing or which he has reasonable cause to suspect of containing any fish caught unlawfully or instrument, bait or container; to seize any fish, instrument, vessel or vehicle liable to be forfeited under the Act. The definition of 'container' has caused problems. Does it include a person's pockets? In *Taylor v Pritchard* (1910), a water bailiff for the Usk Fishery District saw that the Defendant's pockets looked bulky. The bailiff produced his warrant of appointment and asked him to let him see what he had in his pockets. After a scuffle the bailiff searched the Defendant but did not find any fish. Lord Chief Justice Alverstone found that the bailiff did have a right to search the Defendant's pockets.

2.1.2 Power to enter land (s.32 SAFFA)

A bailiff may, under special order from the Environment Agency, enter land near to waters to prevent an offence being committed under the Act. This does not include a dwelling house or the curtilage (surroundings) of a dwelling house. This power can only be exercised under the order of the Agency and can only remain in force for twelve months.

2.1.3 Power to enter suspected premises (s.33 SAFFA)

This power complements s.32 SAFFA. However, unlike s.32, it is exercisable under the authority of a magistrate's order, as opposed to a special order of the Environment Agency. Under sub-section (1) the water bailiff must make a statement to the effect that he has good reason to suspect that any offence against the Act is or will be committed on land near to waters. Any order will permit him to enter and remain on land for not more than 24 hours to detect the persons committing the offence.

A further power is also provided by s.33(2) SAFFA for a water bailiff to apply to a Magistrate for a warrant to enter premises when there is probable cause to suspect that any offence against the Act has been committed on such premises; or that any salmon, trout, freshwater fish or eels which have been illegally taken, or any illegal nets or other instruments are likely to be found on such premises. The order will allow the bailiff to detect the offence, fish, nets or other instruments and to seize the illegal nets and instruments and fish. In contrast to the power under subsection (1), this power is given to any bailiff not just the one making the statement and it is wider because it gives the bailiff a power of seizure and may remain in force for one week. Sub section (2) is most likely to be used when the bailiff needs to seize fish or fishing instruments.

2.1.4 Power to apprehend persons fishing illegally at night (s.34 SAFFA)

This section actually gives the water bailiff a specific power of arrest without the necessity to apply for a warrant, although the person arrested must be put in the custody of a police officer as soon as possible. It allows the bailiff to arrest someone between the end of the first hour after sunset and the beginning of the last hour before sunrise. Designed, therefore, to catch the nocturnal poacher it covers the person who illegally takes or kills salmon, trout, freshwater fish or eels, or who is found near waters with intent to do so, or has in his possession an instrument prohibited by the Act (for a list of such instruments see *Chapter 13*).

2.1.5 Power to require production of fishing licences (s.35 SAFFA)

This allows a water bailiff to require any person who is fishing, whom he reasonably suspects of being about to fish or who has fished in the preceding half hour to produce his fishing licence and, finally, only if he is actually in the process of fishing, to state his name and address. Failure to do so will be an offence, but if the person produces the licence at the office of the Environment Agency within seven days he shall not be convicted. (See *Chapter 12* for a full explanation of the rod licensing system).

2.2 The water bailiff's power of arrest

Since he is deemed to be a constable the water bailiff's power of arrest is governed by the Police and Criminal Evidence Act 1984 (PACE). This particular Act rationalised the police constable's power of arrest. There are three additional powers outside PACE that are available to the water bailiff: first, the power referred to above under s.34 SAFFA to arrest persons fishing illegally at night; secondly, the common law power to arrest for breach of the peace (this is an ancient power, little used by water bailiffs and not explained in this book); third, the power to arrest under Paragraph 2 (3) of Schedule 1 TA.

Essential to the water bailiff is the distinction between an arrestable offence and a non-arrestable offence.

2.2.1 Arrestable offences

An arrestable offence is an offence for which a person of, or over the age of, 21 may be sentenced to imprisonment for a term of up to five years. None of the offences arising under the SAFFA listed above carry a maximum term of five years imprisonment and they are not, therefore, arrestable offences. However, water bailiffs may encounter arrestable offences if faced with the theft of fish under s.1 TA and assaults.

Section 24 (6) TA allows a water bailiff, where he has reasonable grounds for suspecting that an arrestable offence has been committed, to arrest without warrant anyone he has reasonable grounds for suspecting to be guilty of the offence. In addition, under s.24 (7) TA, a water bailiff may arrest without warrant anyone who is about to commit an arrestable offence and anyone whom he has reasonable grounds for suspecting to be about to commit an arrestable offence. An example is the water bailiff who comes across someone stealing fish from a fish pond in the ownership of one person.

The important aspect of these powers is that the water bailiff can arrest even if an arrestable offence has not been committed as long as he had reasonable grounds to suspect an offence had been committed or was about to be committed. In exercising these powers, the water bailiff, since he is exercising the powers open to a police constable, will be making the same judgments as a constable. Coming across someone carrying poaching equipment and a couple of salmon in a bag is an obvious example of reasonable grounds.

2.2.2 Non-arrestable offences

All the offences under SAFFA fall within this less serious category. The power to arrest for these offences is only permitted where 'general arrest conditions' are satisfied. Under s.25 (1) SAFFA, these exist where a water bailiff has reasonable grounds for suspecting that any offence which is not an arrestable offence has been committed or attempted. He may then arrest the relevant person if it appears to him that the service of a summons is impractical, or inappropriate because any of the 'general arrest conditions' is satisfied. The relevant person is the person who the bailiff has reasonable grounds to suspect of having committed or having attempted to commit the offence, or being in the course of committing or attempting to commit. The general arrest conditions in relation to fishery offences are:

   a) the name of the relevant person is unknown to, and cannot be readily ascertained, by the constable; or

   b) the constable has reasonable grounds for doubting whether a name furnished by the relevant person as his name is his real name; or

   c) i) the relevant person has failed to furnish a satisfactory address for service; or

   d) the constable has reasonable grounds for doubting whether an address furnished by the relevant person is a satisfactory address for service.

   This, obviously, solves the problem of an offender refusing to give his name.

   For example, if a water bailiff wanted under, s.31 SAFFA, to examine an instrument he had reasonable cause to suspect of having been used to take fish in contravention of SAFFA and if, upon request, he was refused and he doubted the address given was satisfactory, he could arrest the person who refused to allow him to examine the instrument.

2.2.3 Power of arrest under Paragraph 2 (4) of Schedule 1 TA

Paragraph 2 (4) of Schedule 1 TA gives anyone the power to arrest somebody committing an offence under Paragraph 2 (1) who is, or whom he with reasonable cause suspects to be, committing the offence. However, there is no power of arrest for the offence of unlawful angling during the daytime committed under Paragraph 2 (2) of Schedule 1 TA. The only avenue open to a water bailiff to arrest for the offence of unlawful angling would be if the general arrest conditions were satisfied.

2.3 The water keeper

A water keeper employed by an angling club or fishery owner is not a water bailiff. His powers are only those of an ordinary citizen and are much less than the water bailiff's. Therefore, what follows in this section applies not just to the water keeper but to any angler.

The law does not give a water keeper special status in the same way as it does to a water bailiff. He is empowered, under s.35 (2) SAFFA, to request any person fishing to produce his licence, but this is his only statutory power and it only arises if he holds a licence himself. In fact, this power is open to anyone holding a fishing licence. Any angler, holding a fishing licence, may ask another angler to show him his licence.

2.3.1 The water keeper's powers of arrest

The water keeper has the power to arrest for breach of the peace. Under statute, he has the power to arrest under Paragraph 2 of Schedule 1 TA for the offence of taking or destroying fish. He cannot arrest for the offence of taking or destroying fish by angling, unless the general arrest conditions are satisfied.

The water keeper has two powers under PACE. First, under s.24 (4) PACE, a water keeper may arrest, without a warrant, anyone who is in the act of committing an arrestable offence or whom he has reasonable grounds to suspect is committing such an offence. Secondly, under s.24 (5) PACE, if an arrestable offence has been committed, the water keeper may arrest - without a warrant - anyone who is guilty of the offence or whom he has reasonable grounds for suspecting to be guilty of it. This is different to the water bailiff's power of arrest. The important point to note is that the power only exists if an arrestable offence is being committed or has actually been committed. The water keeper, unlike the water bailiff, cannot make an arrest if an arrestable offence has not been committed. He must, therefore, be absolutely sure that an offence has been committed. If there is any doubt, the most sensible course of action is *not* to arrest but to inform a water bailiff or police constable. If an offence has not been committed, the water keeper may leave himself open to a charge of assault if he injured the person he supposedly arrested and/or a civil action for damages for personal injury and/or wrongful arrest and false imprisonment.

The point deserves emphasis that these powers are open to the general public. They are not exclusive to the water keeper.

2.3.2 *Trespass*

Trespass is the unjustifiable intrusion by one person upon land in another's possession (Clerk & Lindsell on Torts 17 Ed.). In the context of angling, it is one angler fishing on land without permission of the landowner. It is a feature of trespass that it is not necessary to show that there has been any actual damage (*Stoke-on-Trent Council v W&J Wass Ltd* (1983)). Therefore, it does not matter if the angler has not caught a fish. The mere fact that he is there is a trespass.

It does need special attention in this chapter because one of the principal duties of a water keeper is to ensure that the angler pays for his day ticket, or that he is a member of the club. If he does not pay for it or is not a member of the club he will be a trespasser and can, as such, asked to leave. There are not many trespass cases involving angling. One, however, is *Hughes v Buckland* (1846). The Defendants were the gamekeepers of the owners of a private fishery on a river in Carnarvon. They arrested Hughes on the grounds that he was fishing illegally in the fishery. However, the Court found that the place he had been arrested was outside the boundaries of the fishery but, despite this, that since the gamekeepers had reasonably believed Hughes to be fishing illegally, they were entitled to seize his fishing equipment.

If the person does not quit the property upon which he is trespassing when asked to do so, to what lengths can the keeper go to eject him? He may use reasonable force, if reasonably necessary, to remove a trespasser from his land.

Trespassers fall into two types: those who enter land unlawfully and without consent and those who have entered land with consent but remain in occupation after the consent has been withdrawn. A poacher will fall into the former category. An example of the latter is a day ticket holder who catches his quota of fish but continues to fish regardless.

At common law, the owner of a fishery can remove a trespasser and his tackle using as much force as is reasonably necessary, notwithstanding which category he falls under. The use of force is fraught with risks. Too much and the water keeper may be accused of assault and, if the alleged trespasser can subsequently prove he was on the land lawfully, of unlawful eviction or harassment. The best course of action is to seek the help of the police or a water bailiff. Courts have discouraged self help as Lawton CJ said in *R v Chief Constable of Devon and Cornwall ex parte Central Electricity Generating Board* (1982):

> In my judgment, based on my understanding of human nature and a long experience of the administration of criminal justice, the most important reason for not using self-help, if any other remedy can be used effectively, is that as soon as one person starts to, or makes to, lay hands on another there is likely to be a breach of the peace.

QUESTIONS

Question 1

My water keeper nearly got into a fight with a trespasser the other day. This person has been a thorn in my side for some time. He insists on fishing my stretch of the river without paying for a day ticket. He says he has a public right of fishing. This is nonsense. He also disturbs others who buy day tickets. I am afraid he is putting anglers off my fishery.

Answer

Your water keeper can only use reasonable force to evict him. However, in the nature of these things, if he grabs the man to evict him a full scale fight may start. The best advice is to give your water keeper a mobile 'phone so that he can telephone the police to come and evict him. If he tried to do it himself, he may open himself to an action for unlawful eviction or harassment. Also, since he is a trespasser, you can go to court to take an injunction out against him which forbids him from entering your land.

Question 2

Is it true that any angler can ask to see another's rod licence? The reason I ask is because my club is fed up with the public using its fishing rights and such a power might help us to ask them to leave by reporting them to the Agency.

Answer

Yes, under s.35 (2) SAFFA, any angler who holds a rod licence can ask another angler to see his. As a word of warning, if the trespasser refuses to answer, take the registration number of his car to verify his identity before reporting him to the Agency.

CHAPTER 18

FISH DISEASE

There are complex legal rules designed to prevent the introduction and spread of fish disease. The rules are concerned not only with disease within the fish population of rivers and lakes but also fish farms.

The critical sources of fish disease and the spread of disease are :

(a) stocking of diseased fish into disease free water.

(b) fish farms spreading disease via escapes of fish or discharge of effluent into rivers or lakes.

(c) disease simply emerging from no identifiable source in the general fish population.

The main thrusts of the law on fish disease are to set up systems for:

(a) the identification and monitoring of diseased fisheries.

(b) the isolation of those fisheries.

(c) the removal of diseased fish and eradication of sources of infection.

(d) the imposition of particularly stringent rules on fish farms (including rules for the registration of all freshwater and marine fish farms).

(e) prevention of the introduction of certain continental fish diseases by stringent controls over the movement and importation of fish.

1. LEGAL FRAMEWORK ON FISH DISEASE

Unlike many other areas of angling law, the law relating to fish disease is not located in one statute. There is, in fact, a complex web of rules. The first legislation on fish disease - which is still the most important single source of law on the subject - is the Diseases of Fish Act 1937 (DFA 1937). This has been developed and amended over the years, particularly to impose stringent controls on fish farming. The Act was supplemented by the Diseases of Fish Act 1983. These two main statutes have been added to by two sets of detailed regulations - the Fish Health Regulations 1992 (SI 1992/3300) and the Diseases of Fish (Control) Regulations 1994 (SI 1994/1447). These regulations implement European Union wide rules on fish disease.

Finally, relevant in practical terms to the issue of fish disease, are the laws concerning stocking in s.30 Salmon and Freshwater Fisheries Act 1975 (SAFFA) and s.14 Wildlife and Countryside Act 1981 (see Chapter 15).

In addition to all of this, the Ministry of Agriculture, Fisheries and Food (MAFF) has published two relevant guides to the rules *Combating Fish Disease* (1995 MAFF) and *A Guide to Importing Fish* (1995 MAFF).

2. RELEVANCE OF FISH DISEASE LAW TO ANGLERS

In many ways, the rules on fish disease are of much more relevance to fish farmers than anglers. However, sadly, anglers do periodically have to be concerned with fish disease issues.

2.1 Discovery of diseased fish

First, anglers may come across diseased fish in a river or lake. They may catch a diseased fish or see dead or distressed fish. Furthermore, an angling club may discover evidence of diseased fish in its water. In this event, what should the angler or club do? Any responsible angler or club should notify the local office of the Environment Agency and the Fishery Department of MAFF if a notifiable disease is suspected. The notifiable diseases are described below.

Even if the disease is not thought to be notifiable, clearly it may well be worthwhile to contact the Environment Agency. Not only is this common sense, but also, in respect of listed notifiable diseases, there is a legal duty to report suspected cases(s.4 (5) DFA 1937). This legal duty applies to anyone having the right to fish or anyone employed to look after a fishery (for example, a bailiff). These duties also apply to fish farms - thus, their owners and managers are under these duties to inform the authorities.

2.2 Formal Action taken under DFA 1937

Secondly, where disease is either suspected or known, because formal action has been taken by MAFF, anglers and clubs need to ensure that care is taken to disinfect fishing tackle, waders and other footwear, nets and, if need be, boats and any equipment used on the infected waters for works such as bank repairs. In respect of infected waters, MAFF guidance also suggests that the use of keep nets or carp sacks is to be discouraged. This is not only because they may become a source of infection (and they should, of course, be disinfected if used) but, in addition, may bring infected fish into close contact with other fish.

2.3 Protection against disease spreading

Thirdly, anglers may be concerned that the laws on fish disease are being properly applied, so as to protect their waters or deal with a potential threat of infection. This may be particularly relevant in connection with fish farms which are abstracting water from a fishery and/or discharging water into a fishery. What are the applicable rules and what can the angler or club do to ensure that they are fully applied?

2.4 Steps to be considered when buying fish

Fourthly, anglers or clubs may be involved with fish disease where stocking goes wrong and, as a result, disease is introduced into a fishery with stocked fish. MAFF has issued guidance (*Combating Fish Disease*) on the practical steps that should be taken when buying fish. These include making the following enquiries of any fish supplier:

(a) what examinations (including their nature and regularity) are made of fish stocks and who makes the examinations;

(b) whether examinations are limited to sick fish or include random checking of apparently healthy fish;

(c) whether samples of bacteria, viruses or parasites are subject to laboratory analysis and, if so, which laboratory carries out the work;

(d) will the supplier provide a list of tests which are carried out and the results;

(e) will the supplier provide a list of the steps taken to ensure the health status of the fish supplied;

(f) are ova disinfected before supply.

The Environment Agency has also issued guidance on fish disease and stocking - *Buyer Beware: Your Guide to Stocking Fish* (see Chapter 15 for further details).

3. TYPES OF NOTIFIABLE FISH DISEASE

This section includes a basic description of the diseases with which the law is concerned - notifiable diseases - which may result in steps being taken to isolate and ultimately eradicate the disease.

Notifiable diseases are defined under DFA 1937 (s.13) and the list may be added to or reduced by the Minister making an order. There are currently eight notifiable diseases. For the purposes of the law, they are split into Lists I, II and III diseases. ISA, IHN and VHS (see below for full names) are the most serious but are almost completely unknown in this country. The remaining diseases are List III diseases.

The descriptions of the diseases here are based on information published by MAFF.

3.1 Infectious Salmon Anaemia (ISA)

ISA is contagious and is currently limited to Norway. It occurs in Atlantic salmon. Symptoms include swollen bloodshot eyes, bleeding from the bowels, severe anaemia, darkened liver and high rates of death.

3.2 Infectious Haematopoietic Necrosis (IHN)

IHN has never been found in British waters and, although common in the USA and Canada, has been recorded in some mainland European countries. It can affect all salmonids, especially juveniles. Symptoms include bleeding fins and anus (and may have long faecal casts), swelling of the stomach, protruding eyes and darkening of the body. Fish are generally lethargic, but may be hyperactive at times.

3.3 Viral Haemorrhagic Septicaemia (VHS)

This disease principally affects farmed rainbow trout but may also be transmitted to brown trout, grayling, pike and turbot. There has only ever been one recorded outbreak of the disease in Great Britain - at a fish farm in Scotland.

The disease is typified by a large increase in mortality. It can attack fish of all ages, although it is particularly common in fingerling and yearling fish.

Symptoms include bleeding fins and gills, swelling of the stomach, protruding eyes and darkening of the body. Fish may often collect around outlets or pond sides and show peculiar swimming habits.

3.4 Spring Viraemia of Carp (SVC)

SVC may affect common carp, mirror carp, koi carp, leather carp, grass carp, bighead carp, silver carp, crucian carp, goldfish, orfe, pike, roach, rudd, tench and Wels catfish. It is contagious and can result in significant deaths among both wild or farmed fish.

Symptoms include abdominal swelling, pale gills, trailed faecal casts and protruding anus, as well as a darkened skin and lethargy. There may be bleeding in skin and gills.

The disease is common on the continent and, since 1976, there have been a number of significant outbreaks in this country.

3.5 Gyrodactylosis

This is caused by a parasite and can cause considerable mortality in farmed and wild salmon. Skin irritation and increased mucous production are the typical symptoms, developing into fin loss and fungal growths. This disease has never been found in British waters, but is found in Scandinavia and is thought also to affect rainbow trout.

3.6 Bacterial Kidney Disease (BKD)

BKD may affect any salmonid and has been recorded in wild and, occasionally, farmed salmon populations in the UK. Symptoms of this bacterial disease include swollen abdomen, bleeding fins, pale gills and protruding eyes.

3.7 Furunculosis in salmon

This is another bacterial disease of salmonids. It is regrettably widespread in the UK. Diseased fish do not always show symptoms. However, the symptoms are large swellings or furuncles on the sides of the fish. Bleeding gills and fins are also common. It is treatable in farmed populations.

3.8 Infectious Pancreatic Necrosis in salmon (IPN)

IPN is a disease which affects fry, parr and smolts. In farmed fish, the main sign is fish going off their food. The disease develops in the gut and pancreas. Fish become thin and may well die. The disease does affect other fish, but is only notifiable among salmon. It is widespread in the UK, especially in salmon farms.

4. Fish Disease Regulation by MAFF

Unlike most fisheries regulation, fish disease is dealt with by MAFF rather than the Environment Agency. As the Agency has water bailiffs (who may well discover signs of disease) and overall responsibility for fisheries they, of course, are far from uninterested, but most statutory responsibilities lie with MAFF or the Welsh Office in Wales (see below for details).

4.1 Location of infected waters and notifiable diseases

The first step in the system of regulation of fish disease is to put in place structures to ensure that the presence of notifiable disease is brought to the authorities attention, so that the measures for isolation and eradication can take place.

The law assists this process by providing for the appointment of MAFF inspectors with powers of investigation and imposing an obligation on certain persons or bodies involved with fisheries to inform MAFF of any suspicions they have about the presence of disease (s.6 DFA 1937).

The law is based, ultimately, on the identification of infected waters. These are defined as those waters containing fish with any of the eight notifiable diseases or the causative organisms of them.

MAFF fishery inspectors are appointed under DFA 1937. Their powers are found in s.6 and in the Diseases of Fish (Control) Regulations 1994 (SI 1994/1447). They have the power to inspect inland waters, fish farms and fish cages in marine waters. They may take samples of fish or of mud or vegetation or fish foodstuff. If they take away fish which later transpire to be uninfected, compensation must be paid. It is a criminal offence to obstruct a MAFF inspector who is properly exercising these powers (s.6 (2) and (4) DFA 1937). There is also an obligation to provide the inspector with any information or assistance which 'they may reasonably require'. These powers reinforce a policy of regular inspections of fish farms, in accordance with MAFF policy. For example, according to its 1995 policy document, MAFF will inspect all fish farms holding salmon for IPN at least once every two years.

If the Environment Agency is concerned that waters may be infected, then it must report its suspicions to MAFF. The Agency has the power to remove dead or dying fish and dispose of them (s.3 DFA 1937). As mentioned above, these duties also extend to fishery owners and persons employed to look after fisheries who, in the case of inland waters (rather than a fish farm), should inform the Agency rather than MAFF (s.4 (5) DFA 1937). Failure to carry out this duty is a criminal offence, punishable with a fine of up to £2,500.

Where the Agency or the occupier of a fishery requests that MAFF carry out an inspection, then MAFF must respond (s.5 1937 DFA 1937) unless the request is too soon after a previous examination.

The results of any MAFF examination, carried out following such a request, are available free of charge on request by the fishery occupier or Agency (s.5 DFA 1937).

4.2 IHN ISA and VHS - Notification and other provisions

The notification duties are supplemented in respect of fish farms for the diseases IHN, ISA and VHS, under the 1992 Fish Health Regulations. As there has so far been only one isolated case of VHS within the UK, - and the whole of the UK (with the exception of the Island of Gigha in Scotland) is within the EU an approved zone - this indicates that it is clear of these diseases. Therefore, it is not proposed to consider the special provisions concerning those diseases in any greater detail.

4.3 Isolation of diseased fish farms - 30-Day Notices

The powers to serve a 30-day preliminary notice are available under s.4 and 4A DFA 1937 and the 1984 Diseases of Fish Regulations (SI 1992/3300). 30-day notices are served on the occupier of a marine or inland fish farm. They allow MAFF to take swift isolation action whilst avoiding the need for the more dramatic move of making a designated area order (see below). The notice may be served by MAFF where it suspects that the waters of the farm are infected. In fact, this is broadly defined so as to include not only the ponds and fish but also facilities holding foodstuffs, eggs, etc. This will allow control to be exercised over all possible sources of infection on a farm.

The service of a 30-day notice prevents the movement of live fish or eggs in or out of the farm. In addition, fish foodstuff may not be removed. Movements are permitted with the written consent of MAFF. The MAFF guidance document *Combating Fish Disease* contains some indications as to when consent may be granted, depending on the type of disease.

If need be, a second 30-day notice can be served to allow any tests to be completed (where the presence of disease is uncertain) or to allow the clearance and disinfection of the premises.

If, following the service of a 30 day notice, tests prove the suspicion of a notifiable disease to be unfounded, then the notice will be lifted immediately.

After service of a 30-day notice, Schedule 2 of the Diseases of Fish (Control) Regulations (SI 1994/1447) requires a census to be carried out on the fish farm and for the census to be updated with details of deaths or new cases of disease.

The notice may be lifted if the fish farm voluntarily undertakes a clearance and disinfection programme, under the supervision of MAFF, to eliminate the disease. In themselves, however, notices cannot force a fish farmer to carry out any measures to eradicate the disease.

It is a criminal offence to breach the terms of a 30-day notice. The making of 30-day notices is not normally publicised by MAFF.

4.4 Designated Area Orders (DAOs)

The principal long term legal instrument for dealing with fish disease and the only legal instrument for combating fish disease outside fish farms (ie. in lakes, rivers or ponds) is the designated area order (DAO).

DAOs are made by ministerial order under s.2 DFA 1937. Following MAFF policy set out in *Combating Fish Disease* (1995 MAFF), they are usually made in one of the following circumstances:

(a) when ISA, IHN or VHS is suspected on fish farm or in inland waters or coastal waters (thankfully, an unlikely prospect at present);

(b) when a List III notifiable disease has been confirmed on a fish farm but the fish farmer has chosen not to clear and disinfect the site voluntarily under MAFF's supervision - normally following the service of a 30-day notice;

(c) when a List III infection is strongly suspected on a fish farm but has yet to be confirmed - normally following the service of one or two 30-day notices. MAFF guidance indicates this situation might arise where the disease is difficult to identify at that time of year;

(d) when a notifiable disease is either reasonably suspected or has been confirmed on a river, lake, pond, estuary or in coastal waters and MAFF considers, it sensible to make a DAO to control movements.

4.4.1 DAO procedure

The DAO will cover specified waters which are or are suspected to be infected - together with land adjacent to them. Any designation is publicised by MAFF in the *London Gazette* and a local newspaper and is available for public inspection. The DAO will be based on a MAFF report into the fishery, which is available free of charge to the occupier of any inland waters or a fish farm.

4.4.2 Effects of DAO

The effects of the DAO depend on its particular terms. However, it may prohibit or control movements of live fish, eggs or foodstuffs *into, from or within* the infected area. Consent may be sought from MAFF for prohibited movements (s.2 DFA 1937). There are some additional effects of designation. In the case of a fish farm MAFF may serve a notice (s.2A and s.2B DFA 1937) requiring the farmer to remove dead or dying fish from the farm or marine fish cage and dispose of them, as directed. Failure to comply with such a notice is an offence and MAFF may execute the notice and recover its costs. In the case of ISA, IHN or VHS, the DAO may go further and require steps to be taken for the eradication of the disease.

4.4.3 Lifting DAO

A DAO is therefore principally an instrument of isolation. Nevertheless, anglers affected will be keen to see such a designation lifted as soon as possible. MAFF will lift a DAO where the infection is no longer thought to be likely to exist at the designated site. That is what the law says. MAFF guidance gives some clearer indications as to what may happen in practice. A DAO lifting may occur where all fish have been removed from the site and a comprehensive cleaning and disinfection programme has been completed under MAFF supervision. Alternatively, if only diseased fish have been removed, then lifting a DAO is only likely where there has been disinfection of any holding facilities or equipment (relevant to fish farms primarily) and tests for a period of usually up to two years have proved negative. Finally, where fish stocks remain - as will often inevitably be the case for rivers and many lakes - tests over a period of usually three years have proved to be negative.

4.4.4 DAOs and angling

Where an angler's fishery is subject to a DAO, it is interesting that angling is not unlawful, although it may be unwise. In most cases, providing disinfection precautions are taken angling can continue without a serious risk of infection being spread. MAFF offers guidance in *Combating Fish Disease* on how disinfection may be undertaken effectively.

5. PROTECTION AGAINST FISH DISEASE - IMPORTATION RESTRICTIONS

When the 1937 Act was passed by Parliament, this was principally in response to an outbreak of furunculosis. It was thought that this had been imported from the continent. One of the key provisions of the original act, therefore, was to prevent the importation of live fish under s.1 DFA 1937. This provision prohibits the introduction of salmon and imposes licensing requirements (from MAFF) for the introduction of live freshwater fish or eggs. These rules still apply to imports from non EU countries. However, within the EU the rules have become more complex, following the creation of the Single Market.

The new rules follow EC Directives 91/67 and 93/53 and are contained in the Diseases of Fish (Control) Regulations 1994 (SI 1994/1447). The new system is based on areas of the EC known as 'approved zones', a network of fish farms ('approved farms'), pre-notification of fish movements and movement documents. Approved zones are those free from IHN and VHS. The idea is that they will be strictly protected by controlling fish movements to ensure that disease free areas only receive imports from disease free zones or farms. The whole of Great Britain (except the island of Gigha) is approved for IHN and VHS. Parts of France and Denmark are also approved for IHN or VHS or both - MAFF has details.

Approved farms are defined as being IHN and/or VHS free (depending on their approval status) and are subject to regular testing for these diseases. In addition, they must be supplied by well or borehole water and have barriers between the farm and any other migratory fish. Lists of approved farms are held by MAFF.

There are detailed movement documentation requirements and restrictions on the import of fish from approved zones or farms which are set out in *A Guide to Importing Fish* (MAFF 1995).

6. FISH STOCKING

Fish stocking is often a cause of problems of fish disease because a key source of infection outside fish farms are stock fish, whether imported or home bred. Stocking is subject to legal requirements, which are considered in Chapter 15.

7. LIABILITY FOR FISH DISEASE

Where fish disease gets into a productive fishery, the consequences can be very serious. There may be substantial losses of fish through the effects of the disease. An angling club may lose the ability to fish the water. There may be lost revenue in day or season tickets. The fishery may have to undertake expensive disinfection measures: providing washing points and disinfectant, as well as notices requiring anglers to carry out such steps. There may be expensive clearance and disinfection works in extreme cases (including stock destruction) to try to eradicate the disease entirely. What can the law do where a fishery owner or angling club has become involved in this unpleasant scenario?

A great deal will depend on what the source of infection is and whether there is convincing evidence to show that it originates from particular farm or fish stock, etc. Proof of the source of the infection and that this has caused particular losses to the fishery can be difficult to find. This section will consider the legal issues arising from three scenarios.

7.1 Liability for disease introduced by stocking

This will discuss the situation where the source of the disease is from a particular identifiable source of fish stock, which was purchased by the fishery owner or angling club (and presumably lawfully introduced to the river or lake). This, in itself, may be difficult to show. Fish disease may lie dormant in waters during an incubation period or until the conditions (particularly water temperature) trigger its manifestation. The need for prompt expert advice, which may later form the expert evidence on which legal action will be based, cannot be underestimated.

7.1.1 Contractual liability - general principles and implied terms

Assuming evidence showing an identifiable source of the disease can be found, the club or owner will want to consider what redress is due to them from the person who sold them the live fish for stocking. This will be determined primarily by reference to the law of contract. What were the contractual terms concerning the fish purchased? A contract may be in writing or it may be oral. Written contracts are generally preferable, because the terms are easier to establish at a later date when a dispute arises. If the person offering to sell fish has his own standard form contract there are a number of important matters to consider before it is signed:

(a) What provisions are in the contract about the quality and health of the fish?

(b) Is there anything in the contract which limits the liability of the seller to a particular sum (in some cases this is the purchase price of the fish) or removes any liability whatsoever for particular problems with the fish? These are called limitation or exclusion clauses and are subject to very careful scrutiny by the courts under, in particular, the Unfair Contract Terms Act 1977 and Unfair Contract Terms Regulations 1994. The courts may limit or even overturn such terms if they consider them to be unreasonable. Matters such as the relative bargaining strengths of the contracting parties, knowledge of the term and its effects and the extent of the exclusion or limitation of liability will be weighed up by the courts.

In the absence of clear express terms, the Sale of Goods Act 1979 (s.14) will require that the fish supplied are of satisfactory quality and are fit for the purpose for which they were supplied. If they are diseased, then it seems unlikely that they could be either.

7.1.2 Contractual liability - express terms

In addition to these implied terms, there may be express terms agreed concerning the quality of the fish and the absence of disease. For example, the contract may specify that the fish or fish farm has been subject to particular health checks (for example by MAFF). Where fish are bought from an overseas source, this raises additional importation requirements (see above) and also contractual concerns. Ideally, the contract should specify in what jurisdiction any dispute is to be resolved. England and Wales is probably the most sensible for the sake of ease of use and access. Furthermore, a warranty on health checks or regulatory approval may not be worth very much if the country of origin does not have a very thorough or rigorous system of regulation.

It is open to those purchasing fish to negotiate for the contract to include better guarantees. The Environment Agency and MAFF guidelines, referred to above, should be consulted when purchasing fish and, if in doubt, it is worth speaking to the Agency or MAFF. It is also worth enquiring whether the seller has insurance to cover any losses arising from the supply of fish.

7.1.3 Contractual liability - damages

In the absence of any exclusion or limitation clause (or even if there is one but it is unenforceable because of the rules mentioned above), then damages may be awarded to put the angling club or fishery owner in the position they would have been in had the contract had been properly fulfilled (ie. if uninfected fish had been supplied), provided any losses claimed were foreseeable by the parties when the contract was made. If a fishery is likely to suffer a major loss because of some unusual feature it is, therefore, necessary that the supplier is made aware of this risk *before* the contract is made. For example, if a carp fishery had a number of large specimens which were very valuable, this information would probably have to be made known to the supplier to stand a reasonable chance of recovering their value

Evidence of losses will be crucial. Thus, numbers of dead fish (with samples being retained for expert examination) and other losses incurred (for example, in lost season or day ticket revenue, disinfection, restocking, etc.) This is the theory, but remember to bear in mind that any rights you may have are only as good as the solvency and assets of the supplier.

Finally, it may be possible to insure fish stocks against losses through fish disease (see Chapter 7).

7.2 Disease from fish farms

The second situation to be considered is where the disease has spread from a fish farm into a river via escaped fish, or the effluent discharged from the farm. In this situation, the law of contract is irrelevant as no contract will exist between the fishery owner or club and the offending fish farm. Instead, it is the law of tort which may offer redress to the harmed fishery against the fish farm. Although there is no reported case on the particular issue of disease, it seems likely that courts would treat it in a similar way to pollution getting into a fishery (see Chapter 10), or the escape of rainbow trout from a fish farm harming a fishery (see *Broderick v Gale & Ainslie Ltd*, considered in Chapter 19). This means that liability is likely to be imposed on the basis of the tort of nuisance or negligence. The main problem in a case of this nature will probably be showing convincingly that the disease came from the particular fish farm.

7.3 Passing disease from fishery to fishery

The third scenario is where a fishery becomes infected and that disease escapes to another fishery. Will the owner of the first fishery or angling club occupying that fishery be liable for its escape? It seems likely that they may be on the basis of the second scenario, considered above. Much will depend on the facts. For example, was it foreseeable (as will have to be shown under the law of tort(see Chapter 10) that the disease would get into the fishery affected? How close is that fishery? Is it an adjoining lake, or a river many miles away infected by an angler's fishing tackle? Is there evidence (as opposed to mere suspicion) showing that the disease came from the first fishery?

All that can be done is to ensure that all steps are taken to minimise the risk of spread. These include closing the fishery, or the provision of proper warnings and disinfection facilities. In addition, ensuring that any DAO is fully complied with and that the authorities are kept properly informed. This will not guarantee that legal liability will be avoided, but it should minimise the risks. Should a fishery owner or club be faced with this unpleasant scenario it may be that their public liability insurance will assist (see Chapter 7).

QUESTION

I am the owner of a day ticket specimen carp fishing water covering four lakes, totalling about 10 acres. Merlin Pool is the most expensive to fish as it boasts several 30lb plus fish. It has been stocked at various times over the last few years. Last year, I purchased five 25lb specimen fish for a total of £10,000 and put them in Merlin. They were supplied by a fish farm from near London. No written contract was entered into - everything was agreed on the phone. I had had no trouble with disease previously and asked no questions about the quality of the fish other than asking if they were healthy and I was assured that they were. Now it seems that I have spring viraemia of carp (SVC). My vet has informed MAFF who says that it is going to make a designated area order (DAO). What can I do?

Answer

There are three separate issues to consider. First, the making of the DAO and dealing with MAFF. If your fishery has SVC, a DAO is likely to follow. So, you may wish to see the MAFF report and/or commission your own research to verify that the fishery has SVC. If the DAO is made, it is important to see whether it covers the whole fishery or just Merlin Pool. Assuming SVC is not present in any other parts of the fishery, a DAO may still be made over them if MAFF considers that they are, or may be, infected. Do the water supplies connect? If a DAO is made, then this requires isolation of the fishery (or perhaps just Merlin pool). You will need to discuss with MAFF and perhaps your own experts what you should do next (pool clearance and disinfection, or waiting for the disease to run its course, etc.).

That leads into the second issue. Should the fishery be closed? Part of the answer depends on whether the whole fishery is subject to a DAO or not. A DAO does not close a fishery and, in theory at least, fishing could continue with strict health and disinfection procedures. However, if Merlin Pool is the only infected part of the fishery, it seems wise to close it to minimise the risk of spreading the disease.

Thirdly, there is the issue of compensation. You seem to assume that the disease has come from the newly stocked fish. That may be so but can you find much evidence to prove this? A number of questions arise. Could the infection have lain dormant? What other fish have been stocked recently? Could it have come from another fishery in the area (or possibly anywhere) via a fisherman's tackle? Are the newly stocked fish amongst the casualties? Have the dead fish been retained for examination? Has SVC been recorded at the supplier's farm? Where did the supplier get the fish from? Even if an expert is convinced that the latest stocking is the source of supply, your failure to have clear contract may cause some problems. It should be possible to argue that the fish (if you can show they were diseased when supplied) were of unsatisfactory quality in breach of the implied term under s.14 Sale of Goods Act 1979. Damages might be sought to recover sums such as lost revenue, clean up and disinfection works, veterinary fees, etc. Did you insure against any of the losses? Compensation is a complex issue and legal advice will need to be sought. Finally, there is the side issue of whether the stocking was in accordance with a licence from the Environment Agency (see Chapter 15). Bear in mind that the authorities will now be fully aware of the situation.

CHAPTER 19

OBSTRUCTIONS TO THE PASSAGE OF FISH

1. INTRODUCTION AND BRIEF HISTORY

A particularly effective way of capturing fish - especially migratory fish - is the construction of barriers (whether permanent or temporary) across a river which trap the fish in a part of the river from which they may be extracted by whatever means. As a result of the threat to fisheries caused by obstructions, they have long been regulated by statute. For example, Magna Carta in 1225 made specific reference to preventing obstructions to the free passage of fish. The Salmon Act 1861 marked an important turning point in the law on obstructions. This Act prohibited any new fishing weirs, mill dams and other means of obstructions called, collectively, 'fixed engines'. This sounds like some kind of machine but, in fact, is an outdated term for a range of non-angling methods of extracting fish. For example, nets fixed to the soil or made stationary in some way.

The legislation permitted the continued use of fixed engines used lawfully (by virtue of ancient right or very long established use or, as it is called, 'immemorial' user) for taking salmon or migratory trout in the fishing season. The Salmon Fishery Act 1865 then established commissioners to enquire into the legality of all fixed engines in use in England and Wales. The Commissioners were abolished in 1873 and it seems unlikely that there are very many privileged or exempted fixed engines (ie. fixed engines found to be lawful by the Commissioners) in use now - although the *Haughey* case, considered below, does concern 1861 authorised fixed engines still in existence today.

The legislation on obstructions is almost exclusively concerned with protection of salmon and migratory trout. Besides the controls over the use of obstructions for the taking of salmon and migratory trout, various pieces of law are concerned with the creation and maintenance of fish passes, such as salmon ladders. The law is concerned often with the use of nets or traps of various types, sometimes in conjunction with obstructions such as weirs or dams, which make it more likely that passing fish will be trapped. The legislation is not directly concerned with the use of rod and line. In addition, the law regulates points of abstraction of water to protect migratory fish from swimming into an abstraction pipe or drain.

The legislation is largely concerned with techniques of taking fish which are not likely to affect anglers directly. However, the protection of fisheries - especially salmon and seatrout waters - is a major concern of anglers and angling clubs. This section is likely to be of most importance therefore in establishing the lawfulness of activities which represent a threat to the health of the anglers' fishing.

2. FIXED ENGINES S.6 SAFFA

As mentioned above, this term covers a range of devices for capturing fish which are fixed in place, either permanently or temporarily. According to the definition contained in the current applicable law - the Salmon and Freshwater Fisheries Act 1975 (SAFFA) - a fixed engine (s.41) includes:

(a) a stake net, bag net, putt or putcher (these latter two are wicker baskets or traps);

(b) a net secured by anchors and net fixed to the soil or made stationary in any other way;

(c) any unattended net left suspended or placed in inland or tidal waters. *Ingram v Percival* (1969) is an interesting case on the extent of tidal waters. The court held that tidal waters extended some distance into the sea. In that case, a net was fixed in the sea about 100 yards from the shore. It was a fixed engine if within tidal waters. The High Court upheld a conviction under previous legislation on fixed engines on the basis that if the justices concluded that there was a perceptible ebb and flow, irrespective of whether this was above or below the low water mark, waters were properly to be considered tidal;

(d) any fixed implement or engine for taking or assisting in the taking of fish.

2.1 Fixed engine offences

The placing or use of any such apparatus in tidal or inland waters is a criminal offence (punishable by a fine of up to £2,500)- s.6 SAFFA. The offence was amended in 1986 by the 1986 Salmon Act s.33. This removed the previous problem that for the offence of using a fixed engine, it was necessary to prove a specific intent to take salmon or seatrout. Whereas, for the offence of placing a fixed engine in waters, it was not necessary to show any intent to obstruct or take salmon or seatrout. For example, in *Champion v Maughan* (1984) there was an intent to take cod by netting but in waters where salmon were known to run. The court held that placing a net in waters was all that need be proved. This anomaly has now been removed so that in no case is it necessary to prove more than the placing or use of the fixed engine. In *Gray v Blamey* (1990), the effect of the new law was shown. A large net was set in tidal waters in order to catch herring. The defendants were charged under the amended s.6 SAFFA with placing a fixed engine in tidal waters. They argued that although the 1986 Act removed the need to show an intention to obstruct salmon the definition of fixed engine in s.41 SAFFA stated (and still says) 'any net placed or suspended in inland or tidal waters unattended by the owner or a person duly authorised by the owner to use it for taking salmon or trout'. Thus, there was a need, the defendants argued, to show that the net was for taking salmon or trout. This was rejected on appeal stating that the words relating to taking salmon. etc. in s 41 only concerned the authorisation by the owner, although the court did comment that perhaps s.41 should have been reconsidered by Parliament when it amended s.6. In any event, s.6, as amended, does clearly now cover any use of an unauthorised fixed engine, regardless of intent.

2.2 Fixed engine exceptions

There are some exceptions, besides the rights established historically under the nineteenth century fishing law, when the use of fixed engines may be permitted. Both the Agency (under the Water Resources Act 1991) and local sea fisheries' committees (under the Salmon Act 1986) have the power to make byelaws authorising the use of specified fixed engines. If the Agency is seeking to make byelaws affecting waters covered by a local sea fisheries' committee then the committee must consent to the making of the byelaws. Equally, if a local fisheries' committee is proposing to authorise a fixed engine, the Agency must consent. If the fixed engine is to be below the high water mark of ordinary spring tides (marked on navigation charts) then the Secretary of State for the Environment, Transport and the Regions also needs to consent.

2.2.1 The Haughey case and ancient fixed engines

The case of *R v National Rivers Authority ex p Haughey* (1996) (also considered in Chapter 12 in relation to licensing and in Chapter 15 in relation to alterations to rivers) is an interesting illustration of ancient lawful fixed engines. The engines were salmon coops (wooden frames with a 9" entrance angled at 45° into which the salmon can swim but from which they cannot escape, with internal traps from which they can then be hand netted) and which date back to the twelfth century. They were certified as privileged fixed engines by the Commissioners under the Salmon Fishery Act 1861, provided certain alterations were made to the weir by which they are located. These alterations were made. In recent years, another adjacent weir had fallen into disrepair and had been subject to works of repair by the current owner, Dr Haughey. The extent and effect of those works on the water flows was in dispute between the NRA and Dr Haughey. Having failed to take effective action concerning the lack of consent for weir alterations, the NRA chose to deal with the issue in another way. They alleged that the water flow to the coops had been so changed so as to make the coops unlawful (ie. they lost, the NRA argued, their ancient privileged status). On that basis, they refused to licence Dr Haughey's use of the coops (even if a fixed engine is lawful, a licence is needed to operate it - see below).

This decision was overturned by the High Court as being unlawful. Not only was it far from clear that the NRA were right that the coops had *lost* their privileged status, but it was entirely wrong of the Authority to rely on this to refuse a licence.

2.3 Anglers and Obstructions

Clearly it is likely that anglers' interests will not be served by the creation of fixed engines. For this reason, those involved with angling on major salmon and seatrout rivers may wish to keep an eye on the local press or even have a dialogue with the Environment Agency so that should any byelaws be proposed, anglers can have their say under the byelaw making procedures (see Chapter 1).

In addition to byelaws allowing the lawful use of fixed engines, the 1975 Act was amended in 1989 (by the Water Act) to permit (by specific consent or general authorisation made by MAFF or Secretary of State for the Environment, Transport and the Regions) for the placing of, and use of, fixed engines by the Agency. This might be used, for example, to deliberately stop fish entering a particular stretch of water whilst works were being carried out. The Agency has powers to acquire the necessary rights to create obstructions, including a fixed engine authorised by central government under s.115 Water Resources Act 1991 (see Chapter 1).

Where anglers or an angling club encounter an unauthorised fixed engine then, besides the general considerations set out at Chapter 17 on dealing with illegal activities, s.6 (2) SAFFA allows the removal of such apparatus under the direction of the Agency. Thus, if the Agency is informed and asked if it will direct the removal of the engine then, it may be removed. In some case, the Agency may be anxious to remove the obstruction itself so as to maximise the opportunities for prosecution.

3. FISHING WEIRS S.7 SAFFA

A fishing weir is a structure or obstruction fixed to the soil or river bed across the whole or part of a river and used *exclusively* for the purpose of taking or helping to take fish (s.41 SAFFA). A weir may be permanent or temporary. The 1975 Act prohibits the use of a fishing weir (which is not authorised) for the taking of salmon and migratory trout or to promote the taking of such fish. The meaning of the word 'weir' has caused some concern for the courts. In *Maw v Holloway* (1914) a row of six hatches extended across the entire width of a river. When the hatches were closed, the river passed down a mill stream. When open, the water passed through the hatches which were located on a sloping masonry slope and down to an eel trap. The court held that this construction was a weir as it banked up the water partly. It did not matter that it was on a slope because of a natural fall in the river bed. The other issue which arose was whether the hatches were for the taking of salmon or migratory trout. There was evidence of salmon being caught in the trap, but not for some years. The court held that as it was a device whereby salmon may be caught it was for the taking of salmon (see also s.16 SAFFA below and licensing).

An unauthorised fishing weir means a weir not lawfully in use on 6 August 1861 by virtue of a grant by the riparian owner or charter or long established or 'immemorial' user.

For authorised fishing weirs, the 1975 Act includes requirements that, if the weir extends over half the width of the river (at its lowest tidal state), then it is not to be used to take salmon or seatrout unless it has an opening which complies with detailed requirements (in s.7 (2)). In addition, the gap must be between 40 feet and 3 feet wide. To ensure that the gap is not then made ineffective through being blocked, etc., the Act makes it a criminal offence to alter a river to reduce the flow of water through the gap (s.7 (4) SAFFA).

4. FISHING MILL DAMS S.8 SAFFA

A fishing mill dam is a dam used, or intended to be used, partly to take fish and assist in the taking of fish and partly to supply water to power a mill, or for some other purpose. However, it is, in fact, a very restricted definition. It has been held that a dam built to provide water for a mill is not a fishing mill dam, even though it makes it easier to catch fish (*Garnett v Backhouse* (1867)).

Once again, the 1975 legislation is a little arcane. It draws the distinction between pre 6 August 1861 lawful dams (those lawfully in use on that date by virtue of grant by the riparian owner or a charter or long established use) and unauthorised dams. The use of unauthorised fishing mill dams for the taking of, or to help the taking of, salmon or migratory trout is a crime punishable by a fine of up to £2,500

Furthermore, for those authorised dams to be used to fish for salmon or seatrout, there is a requirement that an approved fish pass is in place and in use. Following its creation, the Environment Agency has responsibility for the approval of fish passes, which has passed to it from central government. Not only is it an offence to contravene the requirements as to fish passes, it also results in the right to use the dam being forfeited for ever. If this happens, the Agency may remove from the dam any apparatus for catching fish or obstructing their passage such as cages, cribs (a frame of logs or sticks forming a dam or trap), traps, boxes or cruives (a wicker work coop).

5. Boxes and Cribs in Dams and Weirs s.16 SAFFA

If a fishing weir or fishing mill dam is authorised and used to take salmon or migratory trout, then, if the means of capture is by box or crib, they must comply with s.16 SAFFA. The rules are too detailed to be worth reproducing here, but relate to both the construction and placing of boxes or cribs. Breach of the rules is a criminal offence.

6. Obstructions and Fishing Licences

It is important to understand that not only are obstructions which are methods of taking fish such as fixed engines, traps and nets subject to the rules outlined in this chapter, but they are also subject to the general licensing rules considered in Chapter 12. When anglers are trying to take action against the taking of fish by one of these methods, they may consider not only the lawfulness of the method but also whether control can be exercised through the licensing system and, in particular, net limitation orders considered in Chapter 12.

7. Fish Passes and Dams s.9 - s.12 SAFFA

SAFFA is concerned not only with 'fishing' weirs and 'mill fishing dams' - the key feature of which is that they are constructed partly or wholly with the *intention* of using them to catch fish - but also with the protection of migratory fish from the impact of dams or weirs built for any other reason. For example, a dam may be created to provide a water supply for abstraction purposes or to water animals or to supply a mill or hydro-electric plant. Sections 9-12 SAFFA are concerned with the creation and maintenance of fish passes at any dam or weir, on waters which may carry salmon or migratory trout. In general terms, the Act creates duties on owners or occupiers of dams or weirs to build fish passes in certain cases; empowers the Agency to create fish passes and imposes a range of obligations not to interfere with the working of fish passes. These parts of SAFFA together with s.13 (considered below on water flows in passes) are of practical importance to anglers seeking to maintain a run of migratory fish. If fish passes are not created, maintained, or operated properly, fish runs may be impaired particularly at times of low water.

7.1 Angling interests and fish passes and dams

Where a new dam is being constructed or an existing dam altered (so as to increase or cause obstruction to salmon or seatrout), or an existing dam is being rebuilt over half of its length, then s.9 SAFFA is triggered. This allows the Agency to serve a notice requiring the making of a fish pass for migratory fish. The notice will set out the form and dimensions of the pass and set a time limit for it to be built. Those involved with angling on salmon and seatrout rivers might bear this in mind and inform the Agency of any known proposal or works to build or rebuild dams or weirs, so that the Agency can consider whether to use its powers. Failure to comply with a notice, or to maintain the pass in an efficient state, is a criminal offence punishable by a fine of up to £2,500. In addition to prosecution, the Agency has the power to carry out works to create or maintain a pass in accordance with s.9 SAFFA and to recover the costs from the owner or occupier of the dam in question.

Section 9 SAFFA is only brought into operation by the building of a new dam or significant works of alteration. On the other hand, s.10 SAFFA allows the Agency to create, alter, improve or maintain fish passes. This section may be important where a dam or weir exists but has no effective means of allowing the passage of migratory fish, or where salmon or seatrout are being reintroduced to a river where migratory fish have not been present for some time (perhaps centuries). There are some limitations in SAFFA to prevent the powers interfering with navigation or milling power. If anyone damages a fish pass created under these powers they may be liable for the costs of repair.

Any angler wishing to see a fish pass installed will need to demonstrate that the existing weir does inhibit the passage of migratory fish. This might be done by, for example, compiling catch returns above and below the obstruction.

8. ENVIRONMENT AGENCY CONSENTS FOR FISH PASSES S.11 SAFFA

The Environment Agency may have to approve fish passes under s.8 SAFFA (fishing mill dams) or s.9 SAFFA (dams or other obstructions). Where any approval for a fish pass is given by the Agency, s.11 SAFFA (as substantially amended by the 1995 Environment Act) allows for the approval to be provisional until the Agency is satisfied that the pass is working properly. The applicant for approval is responsible for the Agency's costs of checking the fish pass. Consents for fish passes may be revoked if they are provisional and then an extended period for the construction of a satisfactory fish pass may be substituted. Where approval is finally given, the pass is then deemed to conform with the approval and SAFFA.

9. PROTECTION OF FISH PASSES S.12 SAFFA

Fish passes, whether created under the provisions of SAFFA or not, are protected from interference under s.12 SAFFA. Interference may be by physical alteration or by doing something to discourage fish from passing. In addition, unintentional interference may arise from a failure to repair or keep clear a fish pass.

It is a criminal offence to wilfully alter or damage a fish pass, or to obstruct the passage of salmon or trout through a pass, or to alter the dam or river bed or bank to make it more difficult for fish to pass or, finally, to use anything or act in any way which will put fish off passing through. In addition, any costs of reinstating the pass incurred by the Agency may be recovered from the person responsible for the interference.

These rules are given added strength by the imposition of duties on the owners and occupiers of dams and weirs. The position is that the owner or occupier is deemed to have altered a fish pass if it is damaged, destroyed or *allowed to fall into disrepair* and they are served with a notice under s.12 SAFFA (by the Agency) and fail to repair or rebuild the pass within a reasonable time. The words relating to disrepair effectively put owners and occupiers under a duty to repair fish passes. This might, for example, extend to making sure that a fish pass does not become blocked with weed or flood debris. This needs to be borne in mind by angling clubs and riparian owners having weirs and fish passes and may be of use where it becomes known that fish passes elsewhere on the river are not operating properly.

The Act also creates separate offences of taking or attempting to take salmon or trout from a fish pass (more than tempting to poachers and children, but clearly against the law) and acting in a way to put fish off or prevent them from using a fish pass or free gap in a weir or dam (s.12 (3) SAFFA). The only exception is that it is permissible to place a temporary bridge or board over a free gap to allow the gap to be crossed, provided that this is removed immediately after the person has crossed over.

10. SLUICES AND WATER FLOWS S.13 SAFFA

A fairly minor provision in the 1975 Act is aimed at making sure the maximum volume of water is flowing through a fish pass if there is one in place, or over the weir or dam, in any event so as to give migratory fish the best possible chance of being able to run. This works by requiring that any sluice for drawing water from the pool behind the weir or dam is only used when needed. SAFFA specifically prohibits opening any sluices on Sunday or at any time when water is not required for milling. It is permissible to use sluices at these times with the consent of the Agency. The Act also allows sluices to be used in a few additional circumstances, including times of flood; for navigation; or for cleaning or repairing the dam but, in this case, only with prior notice to the Agency. It is a criminal offence (maximum fine £2,500) to breach these rules. The rules only apply to waters having a run of salmon or trout.

The effect of this law appears to be that unless water is needed for milling (and even then not on a Sunday, which may conflict with the fact that many mills are now tourist attractions) then consent will be needed to operate the sluices unless it is for one of the exceptional reasons given above, or at time of flood.

11. PROTECTION OF FISH FROM ASTRACTION PIPES AND CHANNELS S.14 SAFFA

There is a risk that any fish will be threatened by abstraction pipes or channels. The risks are obviously particularly serious for migratory fish. The channels may lead to canals or leats or into mill workings or fish farms. Abstractions may also be used for water supply purposes by the water undertakers, or for agricultural irrigation or private domestic supply purposes. Some factories or even power stations use significant quantities of water which may be abstracted from rivers used by migratory fish. The threat to migratory fish is particularly severe at abstraction points (where they may, at worst, be diverted into machinery) but outfalls also pose problems for migratory fish. Finally, the problem of fish escaping from fish farms into the rivers which supply water to them has developed as a problem in recent years.

It is this context that s.14 SAFFA must be viewed. This description of the legislation will fall into two parts - the law as it stands and the new s.14 established by the Environment Act 1995 which will come into force on 1 January 1999, but for which riparian owners and those involved in abstraction need to prepare.

The introduction of the more effective fish protection rules in s.14 by the Environment Act 1995 is interesting in itself. This came about following lobbying by the Anglers' Conservation Association, which had become very concerned by escapes of rainbow trout from fish farms and entrapment of salmon and seatrout in abstraction channels.

11.1 Current law on screens and gratings

The current law applies where water is diverted from a salmon or seatrout river by a conduit or artificial channel and is to be used for:

    (a) a water undertaking;

    (b) a canal undertaking; or

    (c) a mill.

SAFFA requires the placing of a grating or gratings across the abstraction channel or conduit. In the case of a mill, the obligation to install gratings also applies to outfalls. The construction and placing of the gratings is subject to central government approval (by the MAFF). There are a few exceptions to these rules. First, the obligation does not apply if the Agency grants an exemption (or an exemption has been granted by the National Rivers Authority, or water authority before it). Secondly, byelaws may be made prescribing that the gratings need not be in place at certain times of the year - presumably when migratory fish are not running. Thirdly, gratings must not interfere with the passage of boats on a canal. Finally, in respect of mills, the obligation only arises where the abstraction or outfall channel was constructed after 18 July 1923.

11.2 The new law on screens and gratings

The new rules coming into effect in 1999 are broadly similar but refer to the rather broader term 'screens'. This will be defined so as to include gratings or any other device which will prevent salmon or migratory trout or farmed fish from passing through. The new law will similarly apply only where waters are *frequently* used by salmon or migratory trout. This does weaken the provisions in respect of fish farm escapes, as they will not apply to, for example, brown trout waters threatened by an escape of rainbows from a farm. The obligations to fit screens arise in respect of outfalls and abstraction channels where the water is used for any of the purposes in the current legislation, plus fish farms.

    Screens must be placed so as to prevent the descent of salmon and migratory trout into an abstraction channel or conduit and or their entry into an outfall. In respect of abstraction channels, where a screen is fitted, the legislation will require the provision of a continuous 'by wash' immediately upstream of the screen. The by wash is a passage by which any migratory fish can return to the river. In the case of fish farms, screens must also serve the additional purpose of preventing the escape of farmed fish. The construction and siting of screens and by washes must ensure, so far as is possible, that salmon and seatrout are not harmed by them. As with the existing law exemptions may be sought from the Environment Agency: no screens must interfere with canal navigation and the rules do not apply to mill channels created before 18 July 1923. Byelaws may remove the need to keep screens in place at certain times of year, but no byelaws can exempt a fish farm from the duty to use screens to prevent escapes.

11.3 Enforcement of the rules on screens and gratings

Both the existing law and new provisions are enforced by means of criminal sanctions being imposed on the owner of any water or canal undertaking, the occupier of any mill and the owner or occupier of any fish farm (after the 1999 law). The maximum fine is currently £2,500.

11.4 Environment Agency powers to install gratings, etc.

These duties to install and maintain gratings (and, in due course, screens) are supplemented by additional powers for the Agency to install gratings or widen or deepen channels, mill races, leats, etc. in which gratings have been installed, so as to preserve water flows (s.15 SAFFA). This power is extended to take steps (which might include gratings) to keep salmon or trout from entering waters in which they or their spawning or ova would be at risk of being destroyed. This might be the case, for example, if a channel was subject to periodic sudden high flows as a mill or factory releases a discharge. These powers may not be used if they would interfere with manufacturing processes, milling, drainage or navigation.

It is a criminal offence to damage, remove, open or interfere with a grating fitted under these powers by the Agency or the National Rivers Authority or relevant water authority before it.

12. FISH FARM ESCAPES

The provisions in the section above on gratings are, from 1999, to be directed not only at the direct protection of salmon and seatrout, but also for the protection of waters against fish farm escapes. However, the rules in SAFFA (as amended) are not the end of the story. The new rules will not come into effect until 1999. When they do, they will merely require screens to be fitted to prevent escapes, with a prosecution by the Environment Agency the likely result if the rules are broken. There is also the separate but related question of liability between the fish farm operator and the owners of any fishing rights in the river to which the fish escape. Rainbow trout, in particular, may have an adverse effect on the natural wild brown trout population.

These liability issues are already significant for fisheries and will remain so even after 1999. This is because of past escapes, the possibility of the new rules being broken, or screens (even if fitted) failing and the fact that the new rules will only apply to migratory fish waters.

12.1 Liability for fish farm escapes - the Broderick case

A number of claims have been brought against fish farms seeking compensation, but only one has actually been decided by the courts - *Broderick v Gale and Ainslie Ltd* (1993) (unreported decision of Swindon County Court). In this case, there had been a series of escapes of rainbow trout into the River Kennet, caused by ineffective screens. Despite escapes taking place and some electro-fishing to seek to recover escaped fish, the fish farm continued to use a pond suffering from ineffective screening. Then a further major escape took place and the fishing club and a riparian owner brought a civil action in common law nuisance and negligence (see Chapter 10). The court held that there was ample evidence that the escape of rainbows was both foreseeable and known to be harmful to a high quality brown trout water. There was also evidence of a lack of care on behalf of the fish farm in its failure to properly investigate the cause of the escapes and in its continued use of the pond. The court was satisfied that the presence of rainbows was a material interference with the fishing rights. Rainbows tend to drive out the wild brown population and may result in a loss of available food. Even if this does not happen, they may lead to a loss of sport (and fishery value) as they are regarded as a lesser fish than wild brown trout and, because of their voracious feeding, may well be caught easily and to the exclusion of brown trout. The fishing club had done its best to remove the escaped fish and, fortunately, had very detailed catch returns to refer to, showing the decline in the numbers and quality of brown trout caught and the growth in the number of rainbows taken. On that basis, the court awarded damages for loss of amenity, inconvenience and lost enjoyment. The total sum was £10,500 (see Chapter 10 on methods of calculating damages).

12.2 Practical points for liability for fish farm escapes

This case represents an interesting case study on the effects of escaped fish and seeking compensation. For angling clubs facing such a situation, critical features included:

(a) the maintenance of angling records and very clear and detailed records from the river keeper (which covered the period before and after the escapes);

(b) detailed expert evidence explaining where and how the fish had escaped;

(c) the fact that several escapes had occurred which certainly assisted in showing negligence. It would be a more difficult but not necessarily impossible case if the escape had been a 'one off' occurrence.

(d) the taking of steps to try to eradicate the escaped fish.

See also Chapter 10 on the practicalities of bringing claims generally.

13. POWERS OF THE AGENCY TO DEAL WITH OBSTRUCTIONS OR CREATE FISH PASSES S.154-S.156 WATER RESOURCES ACT 1991

The Agency has powers to purchase or take a lease of property - if need be compulsorily (with compensation) - for a wide range of purposes. These powers are in s.154-s.156 Water Resources Act 1991. They are only powers and therefore the Agency cannot be forced to exercise them. However, pressure may be brought to bear by anglers to see them used to deal with an obstruction which cannot be dealt with in any other way. That pressure may be reinforced by evidence of the effect of the obstruction on upstream fishing and reference to the Agency's duties, particularly concerning flora, fauna and recreation (see Chapter 1).

In this chapter it is important to note that these powers of acquisition extend beyond just buying land to acquiring any dam, fishing weir, fishing mill dam, fixed engine or other artificial obstruction and any fishery being worked with the obstruction. The powers, then, specifically authorise the Agency to alter or remove the obstruction (or indeed, although this seems unlikely, itself or via its own lessees, to work the obstruction as a fishery). Thus, an obstruction which is for some reason lawful, despite the provisions described in this chapter, may be dealt with by the Agency. For example, if it could be shown that serious harm was being caused to migratory fish, then the Agency might be persuaded to use these powers. The powers also extend to acquiring land, rights of access and fishery rights in order to erect and work a fixed engine.

Finally, the powers may be used to assist in the making or mainte-nance of a fish pass adjoining a dam.

14. COMMON LAW AND OBSTRUCTIONS

As has been seen above in relation to fish escapes, the common law has a role to play in the protection of angling and this is true in relation to fish escapes, pollution (see Chapter 10) and obstructions. This section will briefly detail the ancient and arcane laws on weirs under the common law and then consider how the common law may operate with reference to obstructions.

The policy of the law since Magna Carta in 1225 has been against the creation of weirs. At that time, of course, and for many centuries after, rivers were a crucial transport network and weirs a major impediment to navigation. The law was prepared to countenance weirs on the coast but not on navigable rivers (*Leconfield v Lonsdale* (1870)). Weirs granted by the Crown before the reign of Edward I, are lawful, even on navigable rivers. On non-navigable rivers, weirs may be or have been constructed lawfully by grant by the riparian owner, or have become lawful by long established user.

Disturbance of fisheries is actionable at common law as a private nuisance (see Chapter 10). Thus, although this is most likely to be used these days following pollution, it could be used where the free passage of fish up a river is prevented by building a temporary or permanent dam or weir, or blocking a crucial fish pass or gap (*Pirie & Sons v Earl of Kintore* (1906)).

QUESTIONS

Question 1

Our club owns a stretch of salmon and seatrout fishing on the tributary of a major river. We have noticed in recent years a very substantial fall in our fishing returns, when the overall catch in the main river has been stable. After some investigations, we now consider that the problems are at a weir near the point where the tributary joins the main river. The weir is not part of our fishery. It appears that some repair work was carried out on the weir a few years ago and, as a result, fish now have trouble getting past it. There is no fish ladder. What can we do ?

Answer

If the works to the weir amounted to substantial alterations then two important matters arise. First, the Environment Agency may be able to serve notice under s.9 SAFFA requiring the making of a fish pass by the owner of the weir at his or her expense. In addition, the works to the weir may have been unauthorised and in breach of either s.23 Land Drainage Act 1991 or s.109 Water Resources Act 1991 (see Chapter 15). This depends on whether the Agency or its predecessor authorised the works. If they did not, they have powers to remove or alter the earlier works. On the other hand, if this is not possible because the works to the weir were too trivial, the Environment Agency has powers, in any event, to create a fish pass under s.10 SAFFA.

Question 2

On a stretch of water owned by our club , there is a fish farm on the opposite bank. It abstracts water from one point above the farm via a fast flowing culvert (which enters the farm via a grated drain) and discharges water about 100 yards further downstream. We have been at loggerheads with the fish farm owner for some years about various matters. Recently, a member saw salmon struggling to swim free of the abstraction culvert. Another member reported seeing a dead salmon washing around in the culvert. We have heard of 'by washes'. What can we do ?

Answer

At the moment, the law does not really offer any solutions. In 1999, when the new s.14 SAFFA is brought into force, a screen and by wash will have to be fitted. In the meantime, can the fish farmer be persuaded to place a grating across the end of the culvert by the river, or can a by wash be built now? Perhaps the club could share some of the costs?

CHAPTER 20

LAND DRAINAGE

Land drainage and flood defence is of considerable significance to anglers. It is clear, since s.100 Environment Act 1995 (EA) came into force, that land drainage includes management of water levels. In addition, flood defence schemes may often have a serious impact on fishing interests. A river may be straightened or dredged. Sluices may be fitted to control flows, or concrete walls raised to contain flood waters. Spoil from dredging may be deposited on the river bank. All of these matters can have a serious impact on the fish holding capacity of a fishery and the amount of interest and pleasure which may be derived from angling on it.

The law is now contained in the Water Resources Act 1991 Part IV (WRA) and the Land Drainage Act 1991 (LDA). Land drainage and flood defence is defined in s.113 WRA and s.72 LDA as defence against coastal and inland floods and irrigation and, as noted above, includes management of water levels.

This chapter considers the organisation of land drainage before considering the powers that the various regulatory bodies have and the safeguards that are in place to protect angling interests.

1. ORGANISATION OF FLOOD DEFENCE AND LAND DRAINAGE FUNCTIONS

1.1 Outline of system

The organisation of land drainage and flood defence functions is regrettably complex. The Environment Agency is the key regulatory body. It is responsible for flood defence and land drainage with respect to 'main rivers' (defined below) and any coastal or territorial waters, but exercises these responsibilities through Regional and Local Flood Defence Committees (RFDCs and LFDCs). Main river matters are governed by WRA. In respect of non main rivers, land drainage and flood defence is dealt with normally by internal drainage boards and, in certain cases, by local authorities under LDA. There are, however, overlaps and circumstances in which the powers or responsibilities may pass from one body to another. In addition, the Agency exercises general supervision over all matters relating to flood defence (s.6 (4) EA).

1.2 Main rivers and non main rivers

It is already clear that the distinction between main rivers and non main rivers or 'ordinary watercourses' (s.72 LDA) is critical to establishing which body is in charge of any land drainage or flood defence system or proposal. Main rivers are defined by reference to a main river map which is approved by MAFF and is kept at each of the Agency offices (s.113, s.193 and s.194 WRA). Each main river map is based on the area of a RFDC. Any main river includes, for the purposes of administrative responsibility, the river banks (s.107 WRA). The map should be clear as to what is and is not a main river. However, MAFF will determine any dispute (s.73 LDA). As the name suggests, main rivers comprise all major rivers and their tributaries.

1.3 Main river functions and RFDCs

The Environment Agency's flood defence and land drainage functions are carried out by RFDCs. These are established under s.14 EA and cover the whole of England and Wales. The Agency may give general or specific directions to the RFDC as to the carrying out of its works (s.106 WRA) if the carrying out of flood defence or land drainage functions is likely to materially affect the Agency's general duties with regard to managing water. The Agency maintains an office for each RFDC.

The RFDC consists of somewhere between 11 and 17 members (s.16 EA) and they are appointed by MAFF or the Welsh Office and by local authorities within the area of the RFDC.

1.4 Local flood defence schemes and LFDCs

Local committees need not be established, but arise where a local flood defence scheme is established (s.17 and s.18 EA). A draft scheme is prepared by the RFDC and submitted to the Environment Agency or prepared by the Agency itself. After a consultation process, the scheme may be approved by MAFF or the Welsh Office. If this is the case, a LFDC will be established. The committee will be made up of persons appointed from the RFDC and local authorities in the area of the scheme.

1.5 Environment Agency powers and main rivers

As noted above, the Agency is responsible for flood defence and land drainage with regard to main rivers and coastal and territorial waters. Although these functions operate through either RFDCs or, if a local scheme is in place, a LFDC, the powers with regard to land drainage and flood defence are vested in the Agency. These powers are found in WRA.

1.5.1 Control over structures in and alterations to main rivers

These powers are contained in s.109 WRA. They are very important where in-river works are contemplated, either to improve angling or for other reasons, but which may adversely affect fishing. They are considered in Chapter 15.

1.5.2 Flood defence and drainage works

The Agency has powers in s.165 WRA to undertake flood defence and drainage works. These include powers to cleanse, repair or maintain existing works. Existing works may also be improved by widening or deepening watercourses, or removing or altering weirs or dams or other obstructions. Finally, there is a specific power to undertake new works, which includes the power to create a new watercourse, undertake drainage work and erect any machinery (eg. sluice gates).

Where the Agency exercises its powers to dredge or deepen a watercourse it has the power to dispose of any spoil which arises (s.167 WRA). This may be done by its removal or by depositing it on the banks of the river. This includes an area which allows removal and deposition in one mechanical operation. If spoil is deposited on the river banks, then this must not be done in way which constitutes a statutory nuisance under Part III of the Environmental Protection Act 1990 (EPA). This means that if the deposit is prejudicial to health, or an unreasonable interference with the use or enjoyment of the land or river bank, then it is not to be permitted under s.167 WRA. In many cases, the proposed works will be publicised either as part of the planning process (considered below) or under the Land Drainage Improvement Works (Assessment of Environmental Effects) Regulations 1988 (SI 1988/1217) (considered below).

Under s.107(4) WRA, the Agency is given identical powers to those of an internal drainage board in respect of works to ensure that a proper flow is maintained in a main river. These powers are considered below in relation to internal drainage boards.

The Agency has a power in s.166 WRA to provide and operate a flood warning system.

The Agency has broad powers of entry and purchase of land (if need be, compulsorily).

These are broad powers which may have a significant adverse effect on a river from a fishing point of view. The applicable law on compensation, and the conservation matters which must be taken into account by the Agency before using these powers, is considered below.

1.6 Internal drainage boards and ordinary watercourses

The organisation of regulation for ordinary watercourses is very flexible, allowing powers and duties under the LDA to be transferred or moved. The starting point is that non main rivers are to be regulated by means of internal drainage districts (which fall within the RFDCs) and through local internal drainage boards (IDBs). These are independent bodies having elected members (s.1 and Schedule LDA). The electors for membership of an IDB are those who occupy land on which a drainage rate (which funds the operations of the IDB) is levied. The nature and scope of drainage rating is beyond the scope of this work (see Part IV LDA). Not all areas will have established IDBs.

An IDB shall exercise a general supervision over all matters relating to the drainage of land within its internal drainage district and operates within the powers and duties of the LDA (s.1 (2) LDA). The area of an internal drainage district may be reviewed and altered - normally on review of the Environment Agency who send a scheme to MAFF who then decide whether to make any changes (s.2 and s.3 LDA).

It is possible that the Environment Agency may be granted the powers and duties of an IDB under the LDA (s.4 LDA). In any event, any IDB is subject to supervision by the Agency by its issuing general or specific directions to the IDB. An IDB may not carry out works which would affect another IDB (without the Agency's consent) or carry out works which involves the discharge of water into a main river, except on agreed terms with the Agency (s.7 LDA). Finally, the Agency retains important powers to take over the functions of an IDB if land is likely to be harmed by inadequate drainage or flood protection (s.9 LDA). The Agency may then exercise those powers itself, or transfer them to a local authority (s.10 LDA).

It is permissible for the functions of an IDB to be transferred by agreement to another IDB or to the Agency or, indeed, the Agency may pass some of its land drainage and flood defence matters concerning main rivers to an IDB (s.11 LDA).

1.6.1 Control over structures in and alterations to ordinary watercourses

An IDB has control over the placing of structures in ordinary watercourses - for example, a small dam to create a new pool. In addition its powers extend to altering the watercourse itself (s.23 and s.24 LDA). These powers are exercised concurrently with the Environment Agency and are considered in detail in Chapter 15.

1.6.2 Flood defence and drainage works

IDBs have identical powers to maintain, improve or construct flood defence or land drainage works (s.14 LDA). These powers are combined with similar rights to dispose of spoil from dredging or deepening (s.15 LDA). For details, see above. Thus, they may also undertake very major works by, for example, dredging and straightening a river. These may have disastrous effect, on fishing. The issues of the duties to consider fishing and environmental concerns before exercising their powers and compensation are considered below. In many cases, the proposed works will be publicised either as part of the planning process (considered below) or under the Land Drainage Improvement Works (Assessment of Environmental Effects) Regulations 1988 (SI 1988/1217) (considered below).

1.6.3 Additional powers of internal drainage boards

IDBs have a range of other powers concerned with land drainage. Broadly, from an angling point of view these are not going to be as important as s.14 and s.15 LDA.

1.6.3.1 Works for maintenance of flow

Under s.25-s.27 LDA an IDB may take action to ensure that the 'proper' flow of any ordinary watercourse is maintained. Proper flow may be impeded in any number of ways, for example, by an obstruction or vegetation in the river. Action can be taken, whatever the cause of the loss of flow, except where this is due to mining operations. The IDB may serve a notice on any person having control over that part of the watercourse where the flow is impeded, or on any person who owns or occupies land adjoining that part of the watercourse, or on any person to whose act or default the condition of the watercourse is due. Clearly, a person holding angling rights may fall within any of these three categories. There are rights of appeal against a notice served under s.25 LDA. It is possible, on appeal, for the court to vary the works to be done or the time period, or who is to do or pay for the works (s. 27 LDA).

In the event that a s.25 notice is not complied with, a criminal offence is committed by the person served with the notice (s.27 (6) LDA).

The powers under s.25-s.27 LDA concerning maintenance of flow may be exercised by the Environment Agency (rather than an IDB) where the watercourse does not fall within an internal drainage district. In these cases, however, the power is still limited to ordinary watercourses. As noted above, the Agency may use s.25-s.27 in connection with main rivers or, in any event s.107(4) WRA.

These are important powers for the Agency or IDBs which may result in significant changes to the nature of a river. An angling club may face service with such a notice or, alternatively, may find that a river is changed because someone else has had to comply with a notice. There are no rights of appeal against a notice served under s.25, except by the recipient. There are no rights for compensation under the LDA for anyone adversely affected by the works carried out.

1.6.3.2 Other powers

Other miscellaneous powers of IDBs include requiring works to be carried out to restore or improve ditches (s.28 and s.29 LDA) and powers to acquire and dispose of land - if need be compulsorily with central government authorisation (s.62-s.63 LDA). New powers were introduced by the EA for IDBs or local authorities (acting with the consent of the Environment Agency) to facilitate spray irrigation by the control of water levels (s.61F LDA).

1.7 Local authority powers

To make the regulation arrangements for land drainage even more complex, in some cases local authorities have an important role to play. This may arise in a number of ways:

(a) where the IDB powers are transferred under s.9 LDA because they are not being exercised and the Environment Agency directs that they shall be exercised by a local authority (s.10 LDA);

(b) where an internal drainage district has not been established (and therefore there is no IDB) then, if the Agency or a local authority believe that the land may be improved by land drainage, a small area scheme may be set up under s.18 and Schedule 4 LDA. The local authority will then have power to enter land and carry out drainage works under s.14 and s.15 LDA (see above);

(c) where a local authority, for flood prevention reasons, wishes to exercise the powers of an IDB under s.14 and s.15 LDA (see above).

This will mean that in many cases local authorities have concurrent powers in respect of non main rivers with an IDB or, if there is no IDB, for flood prevention in any case and for general land drainage works if a small area scheme is in place.

1.8 Private land drainage works

There are two aspects to the issue of private landowners and land drainage works which need to be considered. First, there are powers under s.22 LDA for MAFF or the Welsh Office to make an order allowing a private landowner to carry out land drainage works which need the consent of another private landowner who will not agree to take part in the proposed scheme. Thus, subject to complex procedures for consultation and compensation (s.22 (7) LDA), a private land drainage scheme can be put into effect.

Secondly, it is possible historically for private landowners to be responsible for the maintenance of a watercourse, bridge or drainage works. This may arise under a customary arrangement, a lease or other property law obligation, prescription (see Chapter 5 generally), or otherwise (perhaps for example under a local Act of Parliament). The LDA and WRA include powers for either the enforcement of those obligations or their transfer to the relevant land drainage authority. In any case, where a person is under such an obligation to maintain, s.21 LDA (in respect of non main rivers) and s.107 (2) WRA for main rivers, allow an IDB or the Environment Agency to serve a notice requiring that person to fulfil their obligations. Under s.33 LDA (or s.107 (4) WRA for main rivers), where a person is under such an obligation, the Agency or an IDB may (with the consent of MAFF or the Welsh Office) have that obligation 'commuted' or transferred to them.

1.9 Byelaws and land drainage

The Environment Agency (under s.210 and Schedule 25 WRA), IDBs and local authorities (under s.66 LDA) all have the power to make byelaws in connection with land drainage and flood defence. In all cases, the byelaws have to be confirmed by central government (MAFF or the Welsh Office). Byelaws made under these powers might restrict access or use of flood defence or drainage works vested in the responsible body. This might, for example, prevent fishing from a sluice or weir. Byelaws may also require those in control of a watercourse to cut bank vegetation or weed and remove the material.

2. ENVIRONMENTAL AND OTHER DUTIES IN RESPECT OF FLOOD DEFENCE AND LAND DRAINAGE

So far as anglers are concerned, very often land drainage and particularly flood prevention works will be damaging to fishing interests. This maybe because the fishing deteriorates, or the amenity of the area is spoiled by removing trees and vegetation or straightening a river. In trying to oppose a proposed scheme it will be important to ensure that the regulatory authority has evidence supporting the need for the works and that they will actually achieve their object.

All of the regulatory bodies concerned with land drainage and flood prevention are under important duties to take into account environmental and, to some extent, fishery interests. These duties will be critical in any discussions or consultation which takes place between the regulatory body promoting the scheme and those likely to be affected, including anglers. They may be referred to in correspondence. The regulatory body may be asked to offer its reasoning as to how it has fulfilled its duties and, in the last resort, judicial review might be sought if there was evidence that the duties have been carried out (see Chapter 1 on judicial review). In practice, this may be very difficult to establish as the duties are limited to 'having regard to...' and apply 'so far as is consistent...' with the land drainage and flood prevention functions. Indeed, in one case on the fisheries duty imposed on the then River Boards under the Land Drainage Act 1930, Mr Justice Harman described a duty to have due regard to fisheries as: '...a pious ejaculation which was put into the Act when the drainage enthusiasts were met by the fishery interests. It was difficult to say what "due regard" meant. It was impossible to say that the Board had overstepped the mark...' (see *Proctor v Avon and Dorset River Board* (1953))

In that case it was argued that, because of the fisheries duty and s.4 Salmon and Freshwater Fisheries Act 1923 on the protection of spawning fish and spawning beds (now protected by s.2 Salmon and Freshwater Fisheries Act 1975), major land drainage works were unlawful. An injunction was sought to stop the drainage works. The court refused to grant an injunction, holding that the Board was able to carry out the works under the 1930 Land Drainage Act.

The duties are principally contained in s.61 A-E LDA (inserted by the Land Drainage Act 1994). However, the Environment Agency is under some important additional duties in the Environment Act 1995 and WRA.

2.1 Who is subject to the environmental and recreational duties?

Since the amendments of the Land Drainage Act 1994, the Environment Agency, central government ministers, internal drainage boards and local authorities are all subject to the duties.

2.2 Conservation and enhancement of the environment

A duty is imposed under s.61 A and s.61 B LDA in formulating or considering proposals to, so far as is consistent with the purposes of the LDA, exercise any power so as to further the conservation or enhancement of natural beauty and the conservation of any flora, fauna and geological and physiographical features of special interest. Furthermore, regard must be had to any effects any proposal would have on the beauty or amenity of any rural or urban area, or on any flora, fauna, geological or physiographical features or buildings or sites of interest (see below). Strictly, this duty is concerned with the exercise of powers under the LDA, but the Agency is under its own separate and virtually identical duties in the EA (see below).

Fauna would clearly include fish life. The duties are, however, much broader and might cover landscape impacts and amenity, which could include recreational use for angling.

A further duty is imposed in s.61C LDA concerning sites identified as being of special interest by English Nature or the Countryside Council for Wales. In these cases, such sites are to be notified to any IDB or local authority (the Agency is already notified under s.8 EA) and duties are imposed to consult with the notifying body about any damaging works.

2.3 Protection and conservation of buildings, etc.

Duties are also imposed under s.61A and s.61B LDA in respect of buildings, sites and objects of archaeological, architectural or historic interest. Where a proposal may affect any of these, due regard is to be had to conserving or protecting such sites, etc. The duty also extends to having regard to the desirability of maintaining public access to such a site, etc. and to take into account any loss of access which would follow from the proposal.

2.4 Recreation

There is a range of duties in respect of recreation. First, there is a general duty to have regard to the desirability of maintaining free public access to open spaces of various kinds including moors, cliffs and foreshore and woodlands and other places of natural beauty. Secondly, IDBs are under a duty to take reasonable steps to secure that, so long as the IDB has rights to use water or land connected with water, those rights ensure that the land or water is made available in the best way possible for recreation - which might include angling, of course.

2.5 Codes of practice and ministerial directions

Section 61E allows a Code of Practice on these duties to be issued to offer guidance on their implementation. Section 61D allows the Minister to issue directions concerning impacts on flora or fauna or sites of national or international importance.

2.6 Additional duties on Environment Agency

The Environment Agency is also under duties in respect of the environmental and recreational matters under s.7 and s.8 EA. It has to take into account costs and benefits in exercising any powers (s.39 EA). It is under a general duty to promote fisheries (s.6 (6) EA). These duties will apply to its land drainage and flood defence functions. They are considered in detail in Chapter 1.

Finally, s.105(3) WRA specifically requires due regard to be had to the interests of fisheries in exercising the flood defence powers under WRA. This is the modern day re-enactment of what Mr Justice Harman described as the 'pious ejaculation' (see *Proctor v Avon and Dorset River Board* (1953) above).

3. COMPENSATION FOR LAND DRAINAGE OR FLOOD DEFENCE WORKS

If it cannot be successfully argued, either that a proposed land drainage or flood prevention scheme should be abandoned or altered to safeguard angling interests, then the issue unfortunately may turn to compensation for the harm caused.

There are two key provisions providing for statutory compensation.

3.1 Statutory compensation for land drainage or flood prevention works

Local authorities, IDBs and the Environment Agency have identical powers under s.165 WRA and s.14 LDA to carry out new land drainage or flood prevention works or, indeed to improve or maintain existing works. Any of these activities may cause damage for which compensation is payable. Compensation for the exercise of LDA powers is governed by s.14 (5) and (6) LDA and the equivalent and identical provision for main river works is s.177 WRA and Schedule 21, Paragraph 5 WRA.

In either case, the legislation provides that:

Where injury is sustained by any person by reason of the exercise by [the Environment Agency, local authority or IDB] of any of their powers under this section [they] shall be liable to make full compensation to the injured person.

Statutory compensation, if it is *not* agreed, is to be determined by the Lands Tribunal. The normal basis for compensation will be the difference in value of the land affected before and after the works have been done (*Giles v Wessex Water Authority* (1990)). Compensation is available for the interference with fishery rights. Compensation is available even where the works are not on the land, or directly impact on the fishery rights of the claimant. Thus, for example, upstream works might affect angling some distance downstream but this, it seems, will not prevent compensation being claimed.

These matters and the whole issue of compensation for interference with angling was considered in detail in the case of *Burgess v Gwynedd River Authority* (1972).

3.2 Burgess v Gwynedd River Authority

This case arose out of flood prevention works undertaken on the River Dovey in 1967. Very serious flooding had taken place in 1964 and 1965.

Statutory compensation was sought under s.34 Land Drainage Act 1930 which was in virtually identical terms to the current legislation. As the amount and, indeed, the right to compensation could not be agreed between the claimant, Mr Burgess, and the drainage board Gwynedd River Authority, the matter was referred to the Lands Tribunal.

3.2.1 The facts

The Claimant did not own any land on either bank of the river. He held a *profit à prendre* (see Chapter 4) to fish and take away his catch along about two miles of the right hand bank only. The left hand bank fishing rights were vested in an angling club. The River Dovey was particularly well known for its seatrout fishing. The works which were undertaken in 1967 were to 're-train' the river. This involved the removal of gravel obstructions by pushing them to the banks of the river by means of a bulldozer and a pushing machine. The works were on a large scale. It is reported that 1,200 tons a day were moved, five days a week for some months. The disputed issues before the Lands Tribunal ranged over fact and law. The factual disputes were whether the fishery had changed significantly and for the worse and, if it had, whether this was due to the floods of 1964 and 1965 or the 1967 works. Evidence was called from various anglers who had known and fished the river for many years, as well as from expert engineers, fishery scientists and valuers. Details of catch returns - pool by pool - proved invaluable in making out the case that the fishing had really gone badly wrong after 1967, when a series of the key holding pools had been very badly damaged. The Tribunal concluded that, on the balance of probabilities, the works were responsible for seriously damaging the fishery.

3.2.2 Legal issues

The legal disputes in the case concerned two matters. In what circumstances there was an 'injury' for the purposes of the legislation and whether it made any difference that the claimant held single bank fishing rights.

As to the first issue, the Tribunal held that:

...a river authority has a duty to the owners of fishing rights to carry out any necessary protective works in a way as to do no unnecessary damage to those rights and if they do not, their action is unreasonable and is an actionable wrong and an 'injury' within the meaning of the Act for which they must pay full compensation.

This view of the law was not novel and applied a previous case (*Marriage v East Norfolk Rivers Catchment Board* (1949)). It requires that a degree of unreasonable behaviour be shown. That said, on the facts of *Burgess*, the Tribunal found that the flood works justified compensation because of the harm caused even though there was no evidence that the works were entirely unnecessary. This is a difficult issue which the courts may have to cons:der further

The second issue of single bank rights was also determined in the claimant's favour. The Tribunal held that the fact that parts of the fishery affected were beyond the *medium filum* was irrelevant from the point of view of claiming compensation. Even if the works were some distance from the harmed fishing rights, compensation could be sought.

3.2.3 The amount of compensation

On the issue of damages, the Tribunal assessed these on the basis of a capitalised rental figure produced by an expert valuer with experience of buying and selling fishing rights. This was calculated by assuming five rods on the beat at £100 per rod, less £50 for maintenance. This was capitalised over a 20 year period (£9,000 in total). The same method was applied to the post works river by halving the rod price and reducing the number of rods on the water to three (because of the loss of pools). The total loss on this basis was £7,000. Bear in mind that all of these figures are from 1972.

3.3 Statutory compensation for spoil deposits

The powers to deposit spoil from dredgings and deepening watercourses have been noted above (s.167 WRA and s.15 LDA). The provisions for compensation are identical between the two powers. In each case, the regulatory authority has a discretion to pay compensation unless the injury caused by the spoil deposits could have been avoided by reasonable care being taken. In those cases, compensation must be paid and, if it cannot be agreed, will be determined by the Lands Tribunal (s.177 and Schedule 21, Paragraph 5 WRA and s.15 (4) LDA). Presumably, the duty to pay compensation will only arise where it can be shown that the nature of the depositing operation lacked care, rather than that the deposit itself was not the most careful method of disposal.

These compensation provisions will only arise where the power to deposit was exercised lawfully. It may be possible, in many cases, where substantial harm is likely to be caused by the deposit, that this will make the operation a statutory nuisance and, therefore, outside the scope of s.15 LDA or s.167 WRA.

4. PLANNING CONTROLS AND LAND DRAINAGE WORKS

In many cases, flood defence or land drainage works will amount to 'development', within the Town and Country Planning Act 1990 (see Chapter 15 on planning generally). This is probably because they are substantial enough to be building or engineering works but also, in some cases, where a new permanent installation (for example a sluice) is proposed because there is a material change in the use of the land. If the works amount to development, planning permission is needed. This may be granted expressly on application to the planning authority, or automatically under the Town and Country Planning (General Permitted Development) Order 1995 (SI 1995/418).

4.1 Permitted development and land drainage

Drainage bodies (which will include the Environment Agency, any IDB or a local authority having power under the LDA) are granted permitted development rights under Parts 14 and 15 of Schedule 2 to the 1995 Order. This means that, in many cases, no application for planning permission will be needed. The permitted development rights cover any development connected with the improvement, maintenance or repair of any watercourse, or any land drainage works (which will include flood defence and controlling water levels - see above). Notably, this excludes construction of new works, which consequently will need express planning permission. Quite where the line will be drawn between improvement and maintenance and construction of *new* works is not very clear. Certainly, if there is an ongoing programme of, for example, dredging, this may well qualify as maintenance rather then new construction.

If planning consent is not needed, because the development is covered by the 1995 Order, then, from the planning point of view, all that can be done by those opposed to the proposals is to try and persuade the local planning authority to make a direction under Article 4 of the 1995 Order. This removes permitted development rights and requires an application for express planning permission to be made.

4.2 Express planning permission and land drainage

If express planning permission is needed, this will give an opportunity to anglers to object to the local planning authority and lobby their local councillors. Any application for planning permission will be subject to publicity, normally by means of a notice in a local newspaper which should give anglers fair warning of the proposals. The local planning authority will be particularly concerned in making their decision about planning matters - the impact of the development on landscape and on the environment.

4.3 Environmental impact assessment

In extreme cases, an 'environmental impact assessment' (EIA) may be needed because the impact of the works on the environment is so serious.

The obligation to go through the process of EIA arises from the 1985 EC Directive (85/337/EEC) on assessing the environmental impact of certain major public and private developments. This Directive has been implemented into UK law by various regulations - most importantly the Town and Country Planning (Assessment of Environmental Effects) Regulations 1988 (SI 1988/1199), where the development is subject to express planning permission and the Land Drainage Improvement Works (Assessment of Environmental Effects) Regulations 1988 (SI 1988/1217), where no express planning permission is needed. The Directive and regulations operate on the basis that there is a list of developments which may require the close scrutiny of an EIA.

Canalisation, flood relief and land reclamation (from the sea) works may be subject to the impact assessment requirements, if there is likely to be a significant environmental impact. This will be determined in respect of a matter requiring planning permission by the local planning authority (or, if there is a dispute or a planning appeal, by the Secretary of State for the Environment, Transport and the Regions or Wales).

Whether an impact is 'significant' or not will be decided in the light of a range of environmental factors, set out in *Department of the Environment Circular 15/88*. If it is found to have a significant effect then, in broad terms, the planning process is slowed down and an large amount of information on the environmental effects of the works has to be submitted to the local planning authority who then carry out the assessment of the impact. This will be an important factor in deciding whether to grant planning permission.

4.4 Environmental impact assessment outside the planning system

If the development benefits from permitted development rights, the Land Drainage Improvement Works (Assessment of Environmental Effects) Regulations 1988 (SI 1988/1217) apply. These apply to works to deepen, widen, straighten or other improve any existing watercourse, or to remove or alter dams or weirs or other obstructions, or raise, widen or otherwise alter any existing drainage works.

If a drainage body proposes to carry out any of the above, then they must first advertise its intention to do so and state whether it proposes to undertake an EIA. If it says that it does not intend to go through this process then, unless objection is received from anyone, the drainage works may progress. If any objection is received, either the impact assessment process must be adopted, or the drainage body must refer the issue to MAFF or the Welsh Office to decide whether an EIA is needed.

If the works have to go through the impact assessment process (either because the drainage body has so decided, or MAFF or the Welsh Office have so indicated), then regulation 8 applies. This requires that a full statement of the likely environmental effects has to be prepared and publicised. Only if all objections on environmental grounds are withdrawn may the drainage body itself approve the works. If this does not happen, the final decision on whether and how the works are to be allowed is left to MAFF or the Welsh Office.

QUESTIONS

Question 1

We have heard that the local drainage board is planning to undertake some works on a stretch of river where our club owns the fishing rights. The river was straightened and flow improvements were made a few years ago, but these proposals seem more radical. The river is a coarse fishery with a range of species including, notably, good stocks of roach, tench and bream. The proposals include removing a number of trees to allow the channel to be dredged by an excavator to improve water flows. The reason, we have been told, is to reduce flooding, which affects a local village about one winter in every five or six years. We are concerned that our fishing will be adversely affected. What can we do?

Answer

At this stage you need to be putting together your case against the works that are being proposed. You can attack the proposals in a number of ways.

First, are the works needed? If they are, will they achieve the solution which is desired? In looking at these issues, ideally you might have a civil engineer look over the drainage board's plans. Alternatively, if this is not possible, set up a meeting with the drainage board and press them to justify each and every part of their proposals.

Secondly, what harm will be caused to fishery interests? A fishery scientist may offer guidance, but may be expensive to employ. Why not ask the Environment Agency fishery officer for the river to meet you and discuss what he thinks of the plans and their likely effect?

Thirdly, see if any other opposition to the works exists. This may lie in the local community concerned about the state of the environment, or the shifting of flood waters further downstream. Alternatively, it might lie with a local nature conservation society, or even English Nature or the Countryside Council for Wales if a nature reserve or SSSI is likely to be affected. What are the views of the local authority or Parish Council? See if you can create a coalition of objectors.

Fourthly, when you have tried to negotiate and have put together your evidence to show why the scheme will not work or will be harmful, formally object in correspondence drawing attention to the duties which the drainage board must follow. Ask them to explain and justify what they are doing in the light of your objections. Copy your correspondence to the Environment Agency. Consider lobbying members of the local drainage board.

There are no rights to have a public inquiry or formal independent review of this sort of decision by the drainage board, so putting together your case as best you can is all you can do. If the works require planning permission, you can lobby the local planning authority (via the planning officers or elected councillors) on the same basis. If the environmental impacts are significant, the Land Drainage Improvement Works (Assessment of Environmental Effects) Regulations 1988 (SI 1988/1217) may apply.

If it looks likely that the works may proceed and there is a real fear that they will cause serious harm to the fishery, consider preparing for making a compensation claim. Have the fishery surveyed. The Environment Agency may be able to help. This may involve netting or electro-fishing to establish the current fish stock and range of species and size. If you have maintained match records over a period of years, so much the better.

Question 2

Following on from our question above, we took your advice, but all was in vain and the works were carried out two years ago. We have noticed a significant decline in the quality of the fishery. What can we do about compensation?

Answer

First of all, you are entitled to compensation under s.14 LDA. If this cannot be agreed, you can take the matter to the Lands Tribunal. It is a question of proving that:

    (a) the fishery has been harmed;

    (b) the harm is due to the works; and

    (c) establishing the extent of that harm and placing a value on it.

This may be done by reference to fishing records, fishery surveys before and after the works and the individual impressions of anglers who have fished the water for many years. If there is a dispute about any of these issues, you may need expert evidence from a civil engineer, fishery scientist and valuer.

303

The basis of the valuation should be the lost value of the fishery to the club. In *Burgess*, this was calculated on the basis of capitalising a per rod rental. Other bases of establishing damage may be more suitable to a coarse fishery and a claim may be included for lost enjoyment (see Chapter 10 and *Broderick v Gale and Ainslie Limited* (1993).

Appendix

There follows a draft lease and licence for use by an angling club or fishery owner. The terms of each are not set in stone. Each water is different: it may be a lake or river; perhaps a game, coarse or mixed fishery; the geography of any fishery may need special terms. They can, therefore, be altered according to the fishery's circumstances. For instance, Paragraph 13 of the First Schedule of the lease highlights restrictions that may be required if a lock or weir is located on the fishery; stocking arrangements may vary (see Paragraph 4 of the Second Schedule of the lease); the landlord may wish to cut trees himself (see Paragraph 4.2 of the First Schedule of the lease). Separate tenant's covenants have been suggested for a coarse and a game fishery.

The main purpose of these drafts is to raise issues so that the owner and the tenant/licensee can consider them. Careful drafting can anticipate problems and prevent disputes. The 'red pen' adding or deleting to these documents, therefore, rests with you.

Note:

1. Square brackets have been used to show words and numbers that will have to be changed according to the circumstances.
2. Words in italics form no part of the lease or licence and are just instructions as to what to include.

Sample Lease

THIS LEASE is made the .... day of .... BETWEEN (1) (*name of owner*) of (*address*) ('the Owner') and (2) (*names and addresses of the trustees of the angling club*) ('the Trustees') the present trustees of the (*insert the name of angling club*) ('the Tenant')
 NOW THIS DEED WITNESSES as follows:

1. DEFINITIONS

In this deed:
1.1 'the Plan' means the plan enclosed with this deed
1.2 'the River' means so much of the ...... (*insert name of river*) at .... (*describe place*) in the County of .... as flows between the points marked A and B and is shown coloured blue on the Plan

  OR

1.2 'the Lake' means the (*insert name of the lake or pond*) at .... (*describe place*) in the County of .... as is shown coloured blue on the Plan (*insert 'the Lake' instead of 'the River' in the remainder of the lease*)
1.3 'the Fishing Rights' means the exclusive right to fish in and take and carry away fish from the River [(*or in the case of coarse fishing*) the right to fish in and catch and retain in [knotless] keep nets before returning to the River] by means of rod and line only

2. GRANT

In consideration of the Tenant's covenants the Owner grants to the Tenant the Fishing Rights TOGETHER with the right of access from and to the public highway as shown marked red on the Plan and of passing along the banks of the River between the points marked A and B on the Plan for the purposes of the Fishing Rights but not for any other purpose [(*to be used if the Owner keeps a rod*) RESERVING for the use of the Owner or of such person as he may from time to time appoint a rod in the River] TO HOLD the same to the Tenant for the term of ...... (*insert number*) years from ..... (*insert date term to commence*) ('the Term') paying during the tenancy the annual rent of £[ ] (.....(*in words*) pounds) in advance on ..... (*insert date for payment*) the first payment to be made on the date of this deed

306

3. TENANT'S COVENANTS

The Tenant covenants with the Owner to comply with the conditions specified in the first schedule

4. OWNER'S COVENANT

The Owner covenants with the Tenant to comply with the conditions specified in the second schedule

5. GENERAL

The provisions specified in the third schedule apply to the arrangements agreed between the parties

6. SUCCESSORS

The expressions Owner and Tenant where the context so admits include the respective successors in title of the parties to this document

[7. STAMP DUTY

We certify that there is no agreement for lease to which this gives effect]

IN WITNESS whereof the parties have executed this deed the day above written

FIRST SCHEDULE
Tenant's Obligations

1. RENT

To pay the rent on the days and in the manner specified

2. RATES

To pay all rates taxes and outgoings in respect of Fishing Rights

3. FISH STOCKS

To protect and preserve the fish in the River including spawn and young fish and subject to the written consent of the Environment Agency to establish and maintain a sufficient hatchery approved by the Owner and until the same is in working order to restock the River in each year at such places and times as the Owner directs with not less than .....(*insert number and weight*)

4. DAMAGE

4.1 To exercise the Fishing Rights so as not to cause damage to the banks of the River and to pay full compensation for any damage caused by such exercise
4.2 Not to cut or break any trees, bushes, hedges or fences on any land of the Owner except with the prior permission of the Owner

5. EXERCISE OF RIGHTS

5.1 To exercise the Fishing Rights properly and in a sportsmanlike manner by rod and line angling and only during proper seasons and not to permit the Fishing Rights to be exercised by any persons other than members of the Tenant
5.2 To keep any dogs brought onto the Owner's land under control
5.3 To keep all gates used by the Tenant closed

6. NETS

Not without the Owner's written consent to capture or attempt to capture fish by netting or electro fishing or other similar device

7. UNAUTHORISED APPARATUS

To remove from the River all unauthorised nets and apparatus for taking fish and to pay all costs relating to the prosecution of poachers and other trespassers killing or attempting to capture fish in the River

8. CLAIM BY THIRD PARTY

To give immediate notice to the Owner if any third party under a claim of right or otherwise attempts to take fish from the River and to permit the Owner at his own expense to use the name of the Tenant in any proceedings against any unauthorised person attempting to capture fish in the River

9. ASSIGNMENT

Not to assign underlet or transfer the Fishing Rights or any part of them without the written consent of the Owner

10. BYELAWS

To comply with the fishery byelaws for the time being in force of the Environment Agency

11. INDEMNITY

To indemnify the Owner against all claims proceedings costs and expenses arising from or in connection with the grant of the Fishing Rights (EXCEPT to the extent that the same is shown to have been caused by the negligence of the Owner or his employee or agent) PROVIDED that the Owner may not settle or compromise any such claims or proceedings without the written consent of the Tenant (such consent not to be unreasonably withheld)

12. YIELD UP

At the end or sooner determination of the Term peaceably to yield up the Fishing Rights to the Owner

13. RESTRICTIONS (*There may be some parts of the river or lake that must not be fished by the tenant and these paragraphs can be used if part of the bank is not to be used for fishing*)

13.1 Not to fish from the lock to a point 30m upstream from the constructed layby which comprises a concrete wall with tying points shown by the points marked X and Y on the Plan
13.2 Not to fish opposite the weir shown on the Plan in high flow conditions in such a manner as to obstruct the free passage of craft on the towpath side

14. REMOVAL OF TACKLE

To remove tackle in the stretch between the lock bridge and the lock shown on the Plan if a craft requires to moor

15. OBSTRUCTION

Not to cause obstruction to the access steps or surrounding area used by canoes nor fish opposite moored plant so as to cause an undue obstruction to navigation

16. RUBBISH

To ensure that the banks of the River are kept free from rubbish at all times and the grass thereon regularly cut to the reasonable satisfaction of the Owner

17. STRUCTURES

Not to erect or permit to be erected any structure of any kind (whether permanent or temporary in character) on the Owner's land save for the erection of [four] notice boards bearing the name of the Tenant of a type and size to be approved in writing by the Owner

18. NUISANCE

Not to permit anything to be done which in the opinion of the Owner is likely to become a nuisance or annoyance to any person or property adjacent to the lock and in particular not to burn rubbish refuse or any other matter on the Owner's land

19. INSURANCE

19.1 To effect in some reputable insurance office in England a public liability policy which indemnifies the Tenant in respect of its liability at law for accidents causing death of or bodily injury to any person or loss of or damage to property other than property belonging to the parties hereto up to a limit of (*insert amount*) .... for any one accident and for an unlimited number of accidents in any one year arising from the exercise of the rights hereby granted to the Tenant including all costs and expenses and to pay all annual premiums necessary for effecting and maintaining such insurance as aforesaid and whenever so requested to produce to the Owner the policy of insurance and the receipt for the premiums payable in respect thereof within 7 days of the request

19.2 If the Tenant shall at any time fail to effect and maintain such insurance as aforesaid or to produce to the Owner upon request as stated in Paragraph 19.1 any receipts the Owner may do all things necessary to effect or maintain such insurance and all monies paid or expenses incurred by the Owner for such a purpose shall be repayable by the Tenant on demand.

(Covenants for salmon and trout waters)

20. RECORDS

To keep an accurate record of all fish taken and to permit the Owner or his water bailiff (or gamekeeper) to inspect the record at any reasonable time.

21. TAKING OF FISH

21.1 Not to kill or take away from the River any trout measuring less than [15] cm from the snout to the fork of the tail, but to return immediately to the water any such fish taken from the River.

21.2 Not to kill or take from the river more than [2] salmon or trout per person per day

22 PROHIBITED METHODS

Not to angle by means of worming, spinning, float fishing, minnowing or wet fly fishing except that between the .... day of .... (Specify what kind of fishing may be carried out and when)

23. BAILIFFS

(*If not undertaken by owner*) To employ at the Tenant's expense at least [2] [full-time] competent bailiffs to supervise the River and protect the fish in it and to expel all persons poaching or trespassing on the River for the purpose of fishing

(*Covenants for coarse fishing waters*)

24. TAKING OF FISH

24.1 Not to kill or take away from the River but to return immediately to the water any fish of the following species measuring less than [20] centimetres (from the snout to the tip of the tail): (*insert details, i.e. species of fish and length*)
24.2 Not to permit or carry out fishing for pike before the ..... day of ..... (*insert details*) in any season
24.3 Not to kill or take from the River more than [2] fish in total per person per day of the species of fish referred to in paragraph 24.1 above

25. PROHIBITED METHODS

Not to use any hemp seed, live bait or gorge bait in the river except that between the .... day of .... (*Specify what may be done and when*)

26. MATCH FISHING

Not to permit or carry out match fishing in the river

SECOND SCHEDULE
Owner's Obligations

1. BANKS

To keep the banks of the River in good condition and on receiving written notice from the Tenant immediately to make good any damage to the banks (unless caused by the Tenant) and to cut and trim the trees and bushes growing on the banks

2. POLLUTION

To use his best endeavours to prevent the River from being polluted so as to materially affect the proper exercise of the Fishing Rights

3. FISH-EATING BIRDS

To use its best endeavours not to allow swans or ducks or *(specify other fish-eating birds)* upon the River and to pay the Tenant the sum of £.... (.... pounds) for every pike caught and killed

4. PROTECT FISH

To protect and preserve the fish in the River and for that purpose to employ at the Owner's expense at least [2] full-time competent bailiffs to supervise and protect the fish in the River and to expel all persons poaching or trespassing on the River for the purpose of fishing [(*if the Owner is going to restock*) and to keep the River properly stocked with fish and to restock the same as when considered reasonably necessary by the Tenant]

5. NO INTERFERENCE

To permit the Tenant if he complies with the conditions specified in the first schedule peaceably to enjoy the Fishing Rights without any interference by the Owner or any person rightfully claiming under or in trust for him

6. PEGS

To allow the Tenant to install pegs along the banks of the River and to allow the Tenant to make such pegs suitable for the use of disabled anglers

7. REMOVAL OF FISH

(This paragraph to be inserted in the lease of a lake only)

7.1 At the end of the Term to permit the Tenant on giving not less than [one] month's notice to remove fish it stocks in the River
7.2 No fish may be removed of less than [15] cm in length the measurements to be made from the snout to the tip of the tail
7.3 The Tenant shall provide the Owner with reasonable evidence that the fish it proposes to remove were originally stocked by the Tenant

8. STORAGE OF MATERIAL

Not to store or deposit or permit to be stored or deposited any waste matter mineral or chemical substances or refuse of any kind including agricultural upon or in the vicinity of the banks of the River or any channel or ditch connected to it so that it may be liable to flow into the River

9. NOT TO INTERFERE WITH FLOW OR PURITY OF WATER

Not by himself his employees or agents to do anything which may cause the River to be raised lowered drawn off or result in the Owner being rendered liable to any action or proceedings by a riparian owner or occupier above or below the Owner's property

10. CUTTING OF WEEDS

Whenever the Owner cuts the weeds in the River to cut or cause the same to be cut in such a manner as not to affect injuriously the fish or fishing in it

11. LITIGATION

To join in any action commenced by the club for the recovery of compensation for damage to the Fishing Rights or injunction to prevent damage to the Fishing Rights provided that the Tenant shall indemnify the Owner in respect of all legal costs.

THIRD SCHEDULE
Provisos

1. ACCIDENTS

The Owner will be liable for any injury to the Tenant (whether to persons or property) due to giving way of the banks of the River but only if he has received written notice from the Tenant that the same were unsafe and for [90] days after the date of that notice has failed to repair them

2. DETERMINATION BY OWNER

The Owner may by [6] months notice in writing to the Tenant determine the grant of the Fishing Rights (but without prejudice to any subsiding right of action of either party under this deed) in any one of the following events:
2.1 if the rent is [30] days in arrears
2.2 if there is any breach of the conditions specified in the first schedule

3. DETERMINATION BY EITHER PARTY

Either party may determine the grant of the Fishing Rights at the end of the [third or sixth] year upon giving [6] months previous notice in writing to the other (but without prejudice to any subsisting right of action of either partly under this deed)

4. NOTICES

Section 196 of the Law of Property Act 1925 as amended by the Recorded Delivery Service Act 1962 applies to any subsisting right of action of either party under this deed

5. ARBITRATION

5.1 If any dispute arises between the parties in relation to this deed the same is to be referred for determination by a single arbitrator under the Arbitration Acts 1950 to 1979 or any statutory modification or re-enactment for the time being in force
5.2 The arbitrator is to be agreed to in writing by the parties or failing such agreement within [one] month is to be nominated by the President for the first time being of the Salmon and Trout Association

6. LIABILITY

It is agreed that so long as the Fishing Rights shall be held in trust for the Tenant by the Trustees the Tenant shall be liable under this deed only to the extent of the assets vested in the Trustees or in any other person or persons in trust for and for the benefit of the Tenant and not further or otherwise

7. OPTION TO RENEW

If the Tenant wishes to take a further lease of the Fishing Rights from the expiry of the Term and shall not less than six months before the end of the Term give to the Owner notice in writing provided the Tenant shall on expiry of the Term have paid the rent reserved and performed and observed the conditions in the first schedule the Owner shall grant to the Tenant a further lease of the Fishing Rights for a term of (*insert number of years*) commencing on the day following the last day of the Term upon the same terms as this lease save for the rent

    SIGNED as a deed by (*insert name of Owner*)   }
    in the presence of: }
    SIGNED as a deed by (*insert name of trustee of Tenant*)   }
    in the presence of: }
    (*Repeat this clause for each trustee*)

Sample Licence

NOTE: Licences are generally used for shorter periods than leases. This licence envisages a term of one season. However, a shorter term does not mean that the licence needs to be shorter. Clauses can be lifted from the lease and put in the licence and vice versa, but care should be taken to amend the terms 'lease' and 'licence', as appropriate.

THIS LICENCE is made the .... day of .... BETWEEN (1) (*name of owner*) of (*address*) ('the Owner') and (2) (*names and addresses of the Trustees of the angling club*) ('the Trustees') the present trustees of the (*insert name of angling club*) ('the Licensee')

IT IS AGREED as follows:
1. Definitions
    In this document:
1.1 'the Plan' means the plan enclosed with this document
1.2 'the River' means so much of the .... (*name of river*) at .... (*describe place*) in the County of .... as flows between the points marked A and B and is shown coloured blue on the Plan
    OR
1.2 'the Lake' means the (*insert name of the lake or pond*) at .... (*describe place*) in the County of ...... as is shown coloured blue on the Plan (*insert 'the Lake' instead of 'the River' in the remainder of the licence*).
1.3 'the Fishing Rights' mean the exclusive right to fish in and take and carry away fish from the River [(*or in the case of coarse fishing*) the right to fish in and catch and retain in [knotless] keep nets before returning to the River] by means of rod and line only

2. LICENCE

The Owner permits the Licensee [(*to be used if the Owner can allow others to fish the river with the Licensee*) and any other persons duly authorised by him not exceeding [one] person at any one time] to exercise the Fishing Rights in the River between the points marked A and B on the Plan TOGETHER with the right to use the banks of the River for the purpose of exercising the Fishing Rights but for no other purpose and TOGETHER with a right for the Licensee and other persons authorised by him as previously specified to cross on foot over the land of the Owner to the River from the nearest public highway by the path coloured red on the Plan ..... (*insert date licence to commence*) to .... (*insert date licence to terminate*) ('the

315

Term') (both inclusive) paying the sum of £...... (............. pounds) in advance on the signing of this document

3. LICENSEE'S OBLIGATIONS

The Licensee agrees with the Owner to comply with the conditions specified in the first schedule

4. OWNER'S OBLIGATIONS

The Owner agrees with the Licensee to comply with the conditions specified in the second schedule

5. GENERAL

The provisions specified in the third schedule apply to the arrangements agreed between the parties

AS WITNESS the parties have executed this Licence the date above written

FIRST SCHEDULE
Licensee's Obligations

1. PAYMENTS

To make the payments on the days and in the manner specified

2. EXERCISE OF FISHING RIGHTS

To exercise the Fishing Rights with a rod and line only such rod and line to be used in a fair and sportsmanlike manner and only during proper seasons and not to use any nets or other apparatus for the capture of fish except rod and line and landing or keep nets as auxiliary to angling with rod and line

3. SIZE OF FISH

Not to take from the River any salmon measuring less than [50] cm in length or any trout measuring less than [30] cm in length the measurements to be made from the snout to the fork of the tail but immediately on catching such salmon or trout measuring less than the specified length to return the same to the River with the least possible injury

4. QUANTITY

Not to take from the River more than [4] trout or [2] salmon on any one day in respect of any one rod

5. DIRECTIONS OF OWNER

In the exercise of the Fishing Rights to obey all reasonable directions of the Owner or his authorised representative and to give immediate notice to him (or them) if any person not authorised by the Owner to the knowledge of the Licensee attempts to fish in the River

6. DAMAGE

To exercise the Fishing Rights in such a manner as not to cause damage to the banks of the River and to pay full compensation for any damage caused by such exercise

7. ASSIGNMENT

Not to assign or sub-license the Fishing Rights or any part of them

8. BYELAWS

To comply with the fishery byelaws for the time being in force of the Environment Agency

9. INDEMNITY

To indemnify the Owner against all claims proceedings costs and expenses arising from or in connection with the licensing of the Fishing Rights (EXCEPT to the extent that the same is shown to have been caused by the negligence of the Owner or his employee or agent) PROVIDED that the Owner may not settle or compromise any such claims or proceedings without the written consent of the Licensee (such consent not to be unreasonably withheld)

10. INSURANCE

10.1 To effect in some reputable insurance office in England a public liability policy which indemnifies the Licensee in respect of its liability at law for accidents causing death of or bodily injury to any person or loss of or damage to property other than property belonging to the parties hereto up to a limit of (*insert amount*) .... for any one accident and for an unlimited number of accidents in any one year arising from the exercise of the rights hereby granted to the Licensee including all costs and expenses and to pay all annual premiums necessary for effecting and maintaining such insurance as aforesaid and whenever so requested to produce to the Owner the policy of insurance and the receipt for the premiums payable in respect thereof within 7 days of the request

10.2 If the Licensee shall at any time fail to effect and maintain such insurance as aforesaid or to produce to the Owner upon request as stated in Paragraph 10.1 any receipts the Owner may do all things necessary to effect or maintain such insurance and all monies paid or expenses incurred by the Owner for such a purpose shall be repayable by the Licensee on demand.

SECOND SCHEDULE
Owner's Obligations

1. BAILIFFS

To use his best endeavours to preserve the fishing and to prevent unauthorised persons from fishing or poaching in the River and for these purposes to employ an adequate number of bailiffs and to take all reasonable precautions to prevent the River from being polluted lowered raised or drawn off so as to materially affect the exercise of the Fishing Rights

2. METHODS OF FISHING BY OWNER

Not by himself his employees or agents to fish or authorise any person to fish in the River by any means other than by rod and line

THIRD SCHEDULE
Provisos

1. NOT A TENANCY

This licence is personal to the Licensee only and nothing in this document entitles the Licensee to exclusive possession or use of any property of the Owner nor amounts to a lease or tenancy nor to an agreement to grant any such lease or tenancy

2. DETERMINATION

If there is any breach by the Licensee of the conditions specified in the first schedule the Owner may immediately determine the Fishing Rights by written notice sent by post to the Licensee (but without prejudice to any subsisting right of action of either party under this document)

3. LIABILITY

It is agreed that so long as the Fishing Rights shall be held in trust for the Licensee by the trustees of the Licensee ('the Trustees') the Licensee shall be liable under this licence only to the extent of the assets vested in the Trustees or in any other person or persons in trust for and for the benefit of the Tenant and not further or otherwise

4. OPTION TO RENEW

If the Licensee wishes to take a further licence of the Fishing Rights from the expiry of the Term and shall not less than [three] months before the end of the Term give to the Owner notice in writing provided the Licensee shall on expiry of the Term have paid the rent reserved by and performed and observed the conditions in the first schedule the Owner shall grant to the Licensee a further licence of the Fishing Rights for a term of .... (*insert number of years*) commencing on the day following the last day of the Term upon the same terms as this licence save for the licence fee

SIGNED by (*insert name of Owner*) }
in the presence of: }
SIGNED by (*insert name of trustee*) }
in the presence of: }
(*Repeat this clause for each trustee*)

Bibliography

Anglers and the Agency Environment Agency (1997)
Ball S. and Bell S. *Environmental Law* Blackstone Press Ltd, 4th Edition (1997)
Bates J. *Water and Drainage Law* (1990)
Blackstone's Criminal Practice Blackstone Press Ltd (1997)
Blackstone's Criminal Practice Blackstone Press Ltd (1997)
Blackstone's Guide to the Environment Act 1995 Lane and Peto, Blackstone Press Ltd (1995)
Carty P. *Taking the Waters* (1995) Solicitors' Journal, September, 946
Carty P. *The Ownership of Fish* (1995) Water Law, July-August, 105
Code of Good Agricultural Practice for the Protection of Water (MAFF/DoE 1991)
Department of the Environment Circular 15/88 (Department of the Environment)
Dept of the Environment *Freedom of Access to Information on the Environment* (1992)
Department of the Environment Planning Policy Guidance Note 17 *Sport and Recreation*
Discharge Consents Manual (Environment Agency)
Freedom of Access to Information on the Environment (DoE 1992)
Garner and Jones *Countryside Law* Shaw & Sons (1991)
Gibson J. *Foreshore: A Concept Built on Sand* (1977) J.P.L. 762
Green Rights & Responsibilities: a Citizen's Guide to the Environment (DoE 1992)
Gregory M. *Angling and the Law* (1974)
Grayson *Sport and the Law* (1993)
Howarth W *The Law of Aquaculture* (1990)
Howarth W. *Freshwater Fishery Law* (1987)
Howarth W. *Wisdom's Law of Watercourses* 5th Edition (1992)
Hull H. *Oke's Fishery Laws* 4th Edition (1924)
Jackson S.R.B. *Joe Public and Dried Up Rivers* (1992) Water Law, September, 153
Law Enforcement and the Environment Agency (1996) Water Law 95
Loveland R.L. *Hall's Essay on the Rights of the Crown and the Privileges of the Subject in the Sea Shores of the Realm* (1875)
Macrory R. *Water Act 1989* Sweet & Maxwell (1989)
MAFF *A Guide to Importing Fish* (1995)
MAFF *Combating Notifiable Disease* (1995)
Moore S.A and Moore H.S. *The History and Law of Fisheries* (1903)
Moore S.A. and Moore H.S *A History of the Foreshore* (1888)
Payne S. *The issues arising out of the Croyde Bay Case* (1994) Water Law, November, 83
Phase out of net fishery for sea trout off Anglian Coast (1996) Water Law, 46
Polden and Jackson *Law and the Environment* (1994)
Sentencing Guidelines Magistrates Association (1997)
Strategy for the Management of Salmon in England and Wales National Rivers Authority (1996)
Woolrych H.W. *Law of Waters and of Sewers* (1830)

Index

ALSO PUBLISHED BY MERLIN UNWIN BOOKS
PALMERS HOUSE, 7 CORVE STREET, LUDLOW
SHROPSHIRE SY8 1DB, U.K.

Direct mail orderline: 01584 877456

Trout & Salmon Flies of Scotland
Stan Headley £20 Hb

Trout & Salmon Flies of Ireland
Peter O'Reilly £20 Hb

Trout & Salmon Flies of Wales
Moc Morgan £20 Hb

Confessions of a Shooting, Fishing Man
Lawrence Catlow £17.99 Hb

The Far From Compleat Angler
Tom Fort £16.99 Hb

Trout & Salmon Rivers and Lochs of Scotland
Bruce Sandison £20 Hb

The Dry Fly - Progress since Halford
Conrad Voss Bark £20 Hb

The Pursuit of Wild Trout
Mike Weaver £16.95 Hb

A History of Flyfishing
Conrad Voss Bark £25 Hb/£12.95 Pb

Oliver Edwards' Flytyers Masterclass
a step-by-step guide to tying 20 essential fly patterns
Oliver Edwards £19.99 Hb

The One That Got Away
tales of days when fish triumphed over anglers
Jeremy Paxman, George Melly, David Steel, et al £16.95 Hb

Chalkstream Chronicle
Neil Patterson £17.99 Hb

Rivers of Ireland - an angler's guide
Peter O'Reilly (4th edition)

Loughs of Ireland - an angler's guide
Peter O'Reilly (3rd edition)

330